The Tarnished Door

The Tarnished Door

The New Immigrants
and the Transformation
of America

John Crewdson
Winner of the Pulitzer Prize

Times
BOOKS

Published by TIMES BOOKS, a division of
The New York Times Book Co., Inc.
Three Park Avenue, New York, N.Y. 10016

Published simultaneously in Canada by
Fitzhenry & Whiteside, Ltd., Toronto

Library of Congress Cataloging in Publication Data

Crewdson, John, 1945 -
  The tarnished door.

  1. Aliens, Illegal—United States. I. Title.
JV6507.C73   1983   323.6'31'0973   82-40367
ISBN 0-8129-1042-7

Book design by Doris Borowsky

Manufactured in the United States of America

83 84 85 86 87 5 4 3 2 1

For my father

CONTENTS

PREFACE

This book is not intended to be a scholarly or definitive study. It is, rather, an account of what I saw and heard and thought during my journeys around the United States. For that reason, I have avoided the use of footnotes and citations. Whenever a particular fact or number is included without attribution, the reader may assume that it either is generally accepted or else represents a consensus; in most cases where facts are in dispute, conflicting views have been noted.

Although I have throughout the book referred to those foreigners who are living in this country without official permission as "illegal aliens," I am aware that there are objections to this term among many in the Hispanic community, who prefer the term "undocumented workers" or something similar. I have used "illegal aliens" for purposes of consistency and also because those who enter this country without permission are, in fact, breaking the law (26 USC 1325), even if most of them are never prosecuted.

It is impossible to thank adequately everyone who contributed in some way to this book, but among those at *The New York Times* who put their indelible mark on the more than forty articles that formed the basis for it were Dave Jones, Nick Horrock, Martha Miles, and Maryann Bird. Special thanks are due to Wanda Holder of *The Times*'s Houston bureau, without whose dedicated and skillful research this book could not have taken shape, and to Bill Stevens, my *Times* colleague in Houston, for his forbearance during my extended reporting trips. Thanks also to Robert Pear of *The Times*'s Washington bureau, for his unstinting advice and counsel, and to Prudence Crewdson, whose careful reading of the manuscript improved it immeasurably.

Too many people contributed to my understanding of immigration policy and practice in America for me to name them all here. Those who freely shared their knowledge of the workings of the Immigration and Naturalization Service include Alan Murray, Ed Begley, and Nick Estiverne, as well as others still in the service whose names are better left unmentioned but to whom I am no less grateful.

I am particularly indebted to Lupe Sanchez and Jesus Romo of the Arizona Farmworkers Union and Herman Baca of the Committee on Chicano Rights for the time and effort they devoted to assisting me in my research. Verne Jervis, the knowledgeable public affairs officer at INS, was unfailingly polite and frequently more helpful than he had to be.

Finally, I owe a special debt to Denny Walsh, but for whose unending compulsion to seek the truth this book would never have been written.

The Tarnished Door

CHAPTER ONE

"This Is the Only Way
I Can Make Money"

It is the sweetest and gentlest of desert evenings, pitch-black except for the faint light from a sliver of new moon and 100,000 stars. Presently the stillness is broken by a brief two-toned whistle from beyond a rise, followed by the blink of a flashlight—the signal that the way is clear. Within seconds shadowy figures, smiling and talking softly, materialize from the darkness of the desert and gather in a circle near a little-used Arizona highway. After a moment one of the men steps forward. A cheerful, dignified fellow with a fondness for battered hats, ''Don Bernabe'' Garay has led the others here over 1,000 difficult miles: by bus from their cloud-high stone-poor village of Ahuacatlán in the Sierra Madre north of Mexico City, then by pickup truck from the Mexican border town of Sonoyta to the gap in the barbed-wire fence where a few hours earlier they became illegal aliens, and now on foot, pressing hard, wary of rattlesnakes and border patrols, to the prearranged pickup point here in the Arizona desert.

Despite his fifty-five years, Bernabe set the others a rapid pace. They have covered the twenty miles from the border in less than four hours, but they are, after all, mountain men, and for them the walk was just a brisk stroll. Like the uncounted millions before them and the millions yet to follow their well-worn path, the men of Ahuacatlán are fleeing the astounding

3

poverty of rural Mexico, where life is reduced to the simplest of equations: work or starve. Since there is no work for them in Mexico, they are here. As it is, they were among the last men to leave their tiny village for America. The only ones still there, Bernabe says, "are those that are older than me."

The first leg of their journey was remarkable only for its monotony. As in years past, the men traveled for two days and nights by third-class bus to Sonoyta, a favorite jumping-off place for those seeking to enter the United States illegally. They had no reason to expect problems there, but this year their crossing proved more nettlesome than usual. It was very near here that thirteen other border crossers, Salvadorans fleeing their country's murderous civil war, had died a few months before, abandoned without water by their Mexican guides to the unforgiving ways of the desert. The discovery of thirteen dehydrated bodies caused some embarrassment to the immigration authorities in Mexico, who began one of their periodic half-hearted "crackdowns" on the migrants moving north—nothing serious, but enough to cause Bernabe Garay and his friends some unneeded annoyance.

The men of Ahuacatlán are old hands at such crossings—Don Berna, as he is known to the others, has been coming to the United States to work for nearly three decades now—and they know enough to walk through the desert in the cool of the evening. Their problem came in finding someone to ferry them to the crossing point. Two days earlier Don Berna, two of his sons, and four of the other men, all wearing the straw cowboy hats favored by workers from Mexico, gathered by the side of a sluggish creek in Sonoyta to plan their route. In a dusty gully littered with red and silver Tecate beer cans, the men huddled over maps showing the spot thirty miles east of town to which José, a man who owns a truck, had promised to ferry them for $7 apiece. The matter settled, or so he thought, Bernabe scrambled up the creek bank, walked to a nearby gas station, and placed a call to a number in Phoenix. The voice on the other end assured him that a ride would be waiting for his group at the pickup point on the Papago Indian Reservation. But when Bernabe returned, José, the driver, announced that he was now reluctant to make the trip. Considering the attitude of the police, José said, anyone caught ferrying workers into the desert at the moment was sure to get into trouble. For $600, however, he might consider taking such a risk. A second conference was held, but the answer was no. "The workers feel that it is too much money," said Bernabe diplomatically. "*Ladrón*," he muttered under his breath. "Robber."

As it grew dark, half the group, more eager than the others to reach the citrus groves around Phoenix where the work was waiting, set off along the border on foot, while Bernabe and the others, possibly sensing some kind of danger, elected to stay the night in Sonoyta. José, ever accommodating, sold them tacos filled with beans and chorizo, the spicy Mexican sausage his wife had prepared that same morning. After dinner the men scoured the area for cardboard boxes to use for mattresses and carried them into the arroyo above the creek. The next morning Bernabe and his friends learned how fortunate they had been. A U.S. Border Patrol agent from the tiny station at Why, Arizona, riding his horse through the desert at dusk, spotted the dusty tracks left by the splinter group as it filed across the border. For six hours the Mexicans walked, with the Border Patrolman hard on their trail. At midnight, when they finally reached the ranch of a Papago Indian named David, whose business it was to arrange transportation for border crossers, they were met by a surprise: a squad of Border Patrol agents.

While their fellow villagers spent the night in an Arizona jail, Bernabe and the others slept soundly on the ground in Sonoyta, and when they awoke, they went to tell José that they had decided to meet his price. Through the day the group languished in town, telling stories and waiting for dusk. At noon they bought some chicken from a restaurant for $4 a plateful, an exorbitant price. The chicken, Bernabe said, was terrible, but the merchants in Sonoyta know that those who come there to walk across the border are a long way from home, and they press their advantage accordingly. At 4:30 P.M. José arrived with his truck, collected his money, and drove the men to a desolate spot east of Sonoyta where crossing the border is about as easy as crossing the street, where the only evidence of the international frontier is a barbed-wire fence slung between red metal poles, its twisted strands filled with gaps large enough for a man to climb through. An hour later the group was in the United States and walking north, alert for signs of danger.

The real menace was not the Border Patrol, which has only five officers to watch over this 3,300-square-mile stretch of desert—arrests like the one at David's ranch are not an every-day occurrence—but the rattlesnakes that come out to bask in the cool of the desert night. To step on one means to be bitten and die, and those who pass through this country tell of the skeletons of snakebite victims they see along the way. The men of Ahuacatlán are traveling light. Bernabe carries with him only a single gallon jug of water and a sack containing two spare shirts and two pairs of trousers. "We walked very, very fast," he says after arriving at the pickup point, a large sand dune just off Arizona Highway 1, which leads directly to the border. "We pushed it very hard." It was an easy journey. They saw no sign of the Border Patrol and only three snakes, which they killed with sticks. As he stood with the others waiting for a ride, Ber-nabe spoke about the village he would not see again until the citrus harvest ended six months later and about Pilar, his wife, and the five children he had left behind. He was very sorry not to be with them, he said, but "this is the only way I can make money."

Like Bernabe Garay and the men of Ahuacatlán, more than half of this country's illegal immigrants come here from Mexico. Some, the younger men, do it for the pure adventure of cross-ing the border, others for reunions with long-lost relatives, a few pregnant women so that their children will be born Ameri-can citizens. But the vast majority comes for the simple reason that while Mexico is among the most efficient nations in the world at producing people, it is among the least efficient at meeting their needs. Mexico's efficiency as a people producer is improving. At the end of World War II the country's population was less than 20 million. Today it is 72 million, and by the mid-dle of the next century it may be twice that number. As Mex-ico's population grows, so does the number of Mexicans who are unemployed.

At the moment half of Mexico's work force is either out of work or what economists term underemployed, selling lot-tery tickets or cigarettes on street corners, shining shoes, or doing other make-work jobs that would not exist if there were no one to do them. Every year another three-quarters of a million Mexicans enter that country's job market, which for the majority of them means joining the ranks of the unemployed. Much has been made of the promise that Mexico's recently discovered oil reserves holds for the future of its economy, but even with the "oil boom," fewer than half the necessary number of jobs has been created each year. And now, with a worldwide petroleum glut that threatens to last through this decade, Mexico's oil-based economy has turned soft. The country's economic crisis, however, is almost beside the point. Even if its impressive real growth rate could somehow have been sustained, by the end of this century Mexico would have been short 10 million jobs.

Where does one go to escape from a crippled economy, from a country where a third of the people suffer the malnutrition of an unvarying diet of tortillas and beans, where half the population never drinks milk, where 1 person in 6 lacks clean drinking water, where 100,000 children die each year before reaching adolescence, where 60 percent of all adults are functionally illiterate, where more people perish from dysentery than heart disease, where more than half the homes have neither electricity nor water? Mexico City is not the answer. Already the largest city in the world, 10 million strong and growing, the capital is swollen with millions from rural villages like Ahuacatlán who went there in search of a better life and ended up living in cardboard boxes on the edge of town.

To the east and west of Mexico there are only the oceans, and to the south lies Central America, convulsed by politics and violence and poorer still. Then there is the United States, and for Bernabe Garay and millions like him, the decision to go north is a matter of simple arithmetic. The minimum wage in Mexico City is 400 pesos a day—about $4—if one is lucky enough to find a job. A foundry worker in a suburb of Chicago can make twice that in a single hour. In rural Mexico a subsistence farmer might earn $40 a month. On an American farm he can earn $40 a day. In an assembly plant in Juárez young Mexican women are paid $7 a day to sew blouses or solder electronic circuits. Keeping house for an American family will bring twice that much, with room and board thrown in.

Nor, for Mexicans, is the country to the north entirely an alien land. Much of the Southwest was, after all, once a part of

7

the Hispanic empire. The names of the cities, towns, mountains, and rivers are familiar, and many Mexicans tend to regard the United States as their extended neighborhood, especially now that there are sizable Hispanic communities in nearly every big American city. For millions of Mexicans, going north is not an act of surrender but a tradition handed down from father to son, a rite of passage, a calling, a goal to be aspired to, a part of life.

Since its founding sometime in the late sixteenth century, Ahuacatlán has endured its 400 years of solitude without complaint. Hidden away in the impossibly blue-green Sierra Madre, Bernabe Garay's village is reached only by a narrow, twisting roller coaster of a road, high enough in some places that travelers can look down upon the clouds. So isolated, so inconsequential a place is it that many residents of San Juan del Rio, 100 miles to the south, cannot tell a stranger how to find it. But perhaps that is understandable. In recent years Ahuacatlán has been a place for leaving, a village known more for its departures than its arrivals. Seen from a distance, its pastel houses dripping color against the lush mountainside, it might be mistaken for Shangri-la. Up close, no such mistake is possible. Few of the houses have electric lights. None has indoor plumbing, and some seem barely able to stand beneath their thatched roofs. A handful of ill-stocked shops faces the town plaza, where women, their faces hidden behind bright shawls, pass by with baskets tottering on top of their heads. Like everyone else in Ahuacatlán, they walk slowly; what is there to hurry for?

Ahuacatlán means "land of avocados," and its residents agree that avocado trees must have once covered these steep hillsides. But avocados grow here no longer, and neither does much of anything else. Like many of the men of Ahuacatlán, Bernabe Garay owns a few acres of the mountainside, and in the summertime, when he is home, he tries to grow some corn and beans. But somehow there is never enough to harvest. It is, he says, "a lot of work for no money." For a man with a family to feed, the money is to be found in the United States, so, like hundreds of Mexican villages, Ahuacatlán these days is a place without fathers, brothers, or husbands. "I call my parish a widow's parish," Padre Tomás Canó says with a sigh as he sits in the rectory of his crumbling church. "Most of the wives are alone here with their children. This is a very big problem for them, the family disintegration. The men don't want to work in the fields here. The harvest is very bad, and people are so poor that they need the money quickly, in order to eat."

Each autumn the men go north, and each summer they return with the money they have earned in the United States. Summers are the happiest of times in Ahuacatlán. "But when the money is finished," says the young priest, "the men say, 'Let's go again,' and then the women are not so happy. They come to me and say, 'I have no money, no food, my husband is not here, I don't know what to do.'" Shopkeepers extend credit, and money may be sent home from the United States; but the mails are not reliable, and eventually the credit runs out. The winters in Ahuacatlán are long and cold. When the men return, they bring with them not just money but wonderful presents—transistor radios and tape recorders, cameras, toys, dresses in the latest styles—and they speak of their time in the north as a great adventure. To the young boys who long to follow in their footsteps, the men are returning heroes. But Padre Tomás, who hears their confessions, knows more of the truth. "Up there," he says, "the problems are very terrible for them." Each summer fewer men return to Ahuacatlán than left the autumn before, and it is always to the padre that their wives bring the telegrams for translation. "They have an accident in the fields or by the knife or by the gun," he says. Or else there is no word at all. "They go, and we know nothing about them. Their wives go to the authorities, nothing. Some of these women want to marry again, but they cannot," for there is no divorce in Ahuacatlán.

The village is a patriarchy without patriarchs, and it has not yet learned to cope with the stresses that result. The children grow up without fathers, and each year they seem a little more restless. "Now they want to go to *dances*," says Padre Tomás, arching his eyebrows, and there are no fathers to tell them no. Ahuacatlán has a school, but the children do not want to study hard, and what would it get them if they did? The young boys, the padre says, "dream only to go to the United States, to have a good adventure and have money." At twilight a man appears

9

in the plaza with a bass drum and beats it loudly to announce that the cantina is open. The priest pulls on his white cassock and hurries off to counterattack with a peal of church bells for evening mass. "My people drink too much beer," he says.

The cock crows early in Ahuacatlán, and though it is not yet dawn, Bernabe's wife, Pilar, has been up for some time, tending the fire beneath the grate in her spare kitchen, its fragrant pine smoke mingling with that of a hundred others, as all across the village water begins to boil for porridge and coffee. The Garays' adobe house, which Bernabe built himself a quarter century ago, is one of the few in Ahuacatlán with electricity, but Pilar must still haul water for cooking and washing up from the river, as the women of the village have been doing for hundreds of years. Promptly at eight Primitivo Pérez, a neighbor, drops by for his morning ration of Pilar's coffee. Lest a visitor think him lazy for being among the last in the village to rise, the old man explains that he is now officially retired. Like nearly all the old men of the village, he has spent his working life in the United States, most of it "with the railroad in Kansas City." In another corner of the kitchen, near an ancient pedal-driven sewing machine, fifteen-year-old Rafael Garay sits and listens to his stories.

A graduate of the sixth grade, the most the village school has to offer, Rafael is marking time until he can join his father and older brothers in Arizona. He wants to go now, he tells his mother, and Pilar smiles at his eagerness. "Perhaps next year," she says. With a husband and three sons working in the States, Pilar thinks she will be able to make ends meet and still have a little money left over. In the old days Bernabe by himself might have saved only $50 during an entire harvest. But with the beginnings of unionization in the Arizona citrus industry, wages have improved, and last season he brought home $1,200. This year Bernabe, Reginaldo, Kiko, and Bernabe, Jr., may save as much as $6,000 among them, but nearly a quarter of that sum must be set aside to finance next year's journey to Arizona. Pilar is sad that her husband and sons will not be home for Christmas—"*muy triste*," she says—but Bernabe has not been home for the last twenty-nine Christmases, except for the year he fell off a ladder in the lemon groves and broke three ribs.

* * *

"This Is the Only Way I Can Make Money"

As Bernabe and the others stood talking quietly in the vast, empty desert 1,000 miles to the north, bouncing across the sagebrush came a rattletrap blue Pontiac driven by a smiling young man named Ricardo, wearing the black leather jacket that is the unofficial badge of the alien smuggler. Ricardo—at least that is the name he is using tonight—is himself an illegal alien—"from Sinaloa," he says proudly, naming the northwestern Mexican state with a reputation for exporting marijuana, heroin, and fast operators. For $100 apiece Ricardo will drive the fourteen men to Phoenix, seven at a time, two trips that night and two the following night. For two days' work he stands to clear nearly $3,000. At those prices Ricardo could afford a much better car, and in fact, he used to have a shiny new Lincoln—he acquired his taste for junk heaps like the Pontiac after the Border Patrol began impounding vehicles used to smuggle aliens. Ricardo's profits are high, but he also has a lot of downtime. He was here most of last night, for example, waiting for the men who decided to stay in Sonoyta. It was just as well that they stayed put. An undercover Customs agent, wearing a silly-looking cowboy costume, was cruising up and down these back roads all night, stopping and searching every car in sight. But tonight the Customs cowboy is nowhere to be seen, and neither is the Border Patrol. Bernabe, his three sons, and three other men squeeze themselves into Ricardo's car, and Ricardo takes off toward Phoenix, his taillights glowing red against the jagged black Arizona mountains.

It was just north of Ajo, Arizona, that Ricardo ran out of gas. As his car sputtered to a stop, Bernabe and the other passengers burst out and scrambled up the hill, where they could hide in the brush overlooking the highway. Presently a policeman arrived, exchanged a few words with Ricardo, and then spoke into his radio microphone. A few minutes later a Border Patrol car drove up and took Ricardo away. As it was, Ricardo's arrest was only a minor inconvenience. Like most illegal aliens apprehended by the Border Patrol, Ricardo was permitted to return to Mexico "voluntarily" without a deportation hearing, a practice that saves the U.S. government much time and money. Had he been caught with Bernabe and the others, he probably would have been jailed and charged with alien smuggling. The next day Ricardo is back in Phoenix and back in business.

11

All night Bernabe and the others stayed hidden in the bushes, and they were very quiet. At dawn Kiko Garay carefully made his way down from the hillside and found a telephone. A 10-cent call to the underground transportation network, and another ride was on the way. When the group at last reached Phoenix late that afternoon, they went straight to the ranch where they had worked the year before. The lemons were not quite ready for picking, so Bernabe and his sons spent the evening setting up housekeeping, renewing old friendships, and playing cards. Not until that night, when the air began to chill, did Bernabe remember the blankets he had left with his friend Manuel Diaz the summer before. He resolved to get them first thing the next morning.

In years past the Border Patrol had raided the citrus ranches around Phoenix just often enough to keep the workers from becoming complacent, picking up a few dozen at a time and sending them back to Mexico. But this year, because of manpower shortages, such raids are few and far between—so few and so far between that once workers like the Garays reach the ranches, they are virtually immune from arrest. It is when they venture outside that they court some danger, as Bernabe and Kiko did the next morning when they went around to Manuel Diaz's house to retrieve the blankets. Manuel was not home, but as they walked away from his door, a lime green Border Patrol van rolled to a stop beside them. At that moment Bernabe Garay, father of nine, a man of respect and influence in Ahuacatlán, became an apprehension statistic. The next hours were unpleasant ones. Bernabe and Kiko were taken first to the Border Patrol station in Phoenix, then driven to a holding facility in Tucson. At nine that night they were ferried back across the border to Nogales and set free. A week after leaving Ahuacatlán, without having picked a single lemon, Bernabe was back in Mexico.

On Sunday morning he and Kiko took the bus to Sonoyta and set out again in search of José the driver. They finally found him and struck another deal, this time for $30 apiece. All day Sunday the two men retraced their steps along the border, through the desert, and back to Phoenix. Nine days after leaving home, $300 poorer and without having earned so much as a penny to take home to Pilar, Bernabe returned to the lemon groves. At eight o'clock the next morning he finally went to work. Bernabe worked furiously all day, hauling his heavy canvas bag up and down the stepladders propped against the tall lemon trees. By quitting time he had filled and emptied his bag eighty-two times, an impressive day's work for a man half his age. For his 3,690 pounds of lemons Bernabe was paid $41, slightly over a penny a pound, more money than he might have earned in Mexico in a week. Bernabe Garay was a happy man at last.

I met Bernabe Garay toward the end of 1980, the same year the United States finally lost control over who could come here and who could not. By the time we shook hands in the chilly Arizona desert I had been writing for more than a year about immigration in the United States, a project that began in the fall of 1979, when *The New York Times* assigned me to a team of reporters investigating what was then a relatively obscure Justice Department agency, the Immigration and Naturalization Service. Before moving to Houston, I had covered the Justice Department from *The Times*'s Washington bureau for more than five years. But with Watergate and then the CIA and FBI scandals to occupy my time, I knew virtually nothing about the INS except that it was rumored to be a particularly corrupt and brutal agency. What few even in the Justice Department then knew, however, was that it was also almost totally ineffective, that after decades of relative inattention to the control of immigration the United States could no longer defend its ports and borders. In 1979, according to even the most cautious estimates, something like half a million foreigners—the equivalent of the entire population of Vermont—had entered the United States illegally, roughly half of them by simply walking into the country, the other half by arriving at airports with temporary visas or forged papers and then losing themselves in the crowd. As boatloads of Caribbean islanders followed one another to South Florida, as Mexicans and Central Americans in search of work or political refuge streamed across the country's southern frontier, as phony "tourists" and "students" from dozens of countries passed unchallenged through the immigration lines, the INS, unprepared for the invasion and ill-equipped to combat it, could do little more than stand by and watch.

Partly out of simple neglect and partly because Americans and their lawmakers have always recoiled from such authoritarian measures as border fortifications and national identity cards, the immigration enforcement system that existed at the beginning of 1980 was never intended to deal with anything like the influx that confronted it. As the General Accounting Office was later to put it, "The INS simply does not know the number of illegal aliens, or who or where they are." Over the previous ten years the number of illegal aliens arrested had more than doubled, from about 420,000 to a few thousand short of 1 million. But the INS's resources had hardly kept pace; during the same period the number of INS employees had barely increased, from 7,000 to 10,000. There are barely 350 U.S. Border Patrol agents on duty at any one time, most of them concentrated across from the big Mexican border cities of Tijuana and Juárez, while the Canadian border, fast becoming a favored crossing point for uninvited visitors, is so sparsely guarded that in some places it is possible to walk or even drive into the United States unchallenged.

As I learned more about the INS's monumental shortcomings, however, it gradually became clear that inept as it was, the immigration agency was less a culprit than a victim of the nation's haphazard immigration policy and the historical reluctance to enforce it. Keeping unwanted immigrants from its shores, after all, has rarely been among the highest priorities of a nation that thinks of itself as a land of immigrants. For most of its two centuries, in fact, the United States has managed, sometimes eagerly, sometimes reluctantly, to live up to the promise chiseled into the base of the Statue of Liberty by sheltering the huddled masses fleeing poverty or less charitable governments. But in a postindustrial society bedeviled by a severely and perhaps permanently troubled economy, the question of what to do about illegal immigration was taking on an urgency equaled by few other issues. I wanted to find out why the new immigrants were coming and, more important, to try to gauge their impact on late-twentieth-century America.

I was surprised at how little I knew. I was a national correspondent based in Houston for *The Times*, and I had been traveling around the Southwest for more than two years. Although many of the people I encountered daily, including most of the maids who cleaned my hotel rooms and the young men who waited on me in restaurants, were illegal aliens, I had thought very little about them. For the next few months, as I criss-crossed the Sunbelt, from Miami to Los Angeles, I found that while most of the people I talked to knew as little as I did, they were clearly worried. The Jack Nicholson movie *The Border*, about the frustrations of a Border Patrol agent in El Paso, was something of a hit, and the polls showed that nine of every ten Americans supported an "all-out" effort to halt illegal immigration. But I wondered whether such sentiments were xenophobic or merely a reflection of the growing realization that the United States is a nation of crowded cities, persistent high unemployment, and finite resources.

I also wondered whether Americans were genuinely worried about the fragmentation of their society along ethnic lines or whether there was merely some cultural chauvinism at work. To many of those whose parents and grandparents had come here from abroad, it seemed that earlier waves of immigrants had been quicker to assimilate, to cast off the customs and languages of the old country for those of the new. But there was now a growing perception that unlike Hyman Kaplan, Leo Rosten's fictional turn-of-the-century immigrant who struggled mightily to subdue the English language at the American Night Preparatory School for Adults, many of the newest arrivals were less inclined than their predecessors had been to trade their culture for that of their adopted country.

Nor was it difficult to understand the reasons for such perceptions. Walking through East Los Angeles or along Miami's Eighth Street or even in downtown San Antonio, one can foresee a day when there will be not one but two Americas, neither of which can communicate very well with the other. According to several demographic studies, one U.S. resident in eight has grown up speaking a language other than English, the great majority of them Spanish, and for many their first language remains their language of choice. Within Miami's large Cuban community, for example, the language spoken most frequently in nine of every ten households is Spanish; more than half the Hispanic households in Los Angeles and New York City speak Spanish exclusively. As is the case in Canada, where everything from money to NO SMOKING signs is printed in French and

English, the potential for social stress brought about by such linguistic divisions is great, and I encountered more than a little animosity among non-Spanish-speaking residents of cities like New York and Miami, who find it impossible to communicate with their Hispanic neighbors. The same frustrations can be seen to a lesser extent in other cities, but it is in Los Angeles, amid the clamor of more than eighty languages and dialects, that the melting pot may have finally met its match.

The concerns I encountered were genuine, but so were many of the misperceptions. Largely overlooked, for example, was the fact that not all the new immigrants are "illegal aliens." In 1980, the same year it acquired perhaps half a million new illegal residents, perhaps more, the United States willingly opened its doors to an even larger number of legal immigrants and refugees: three-quarters of a million of them, more than were taken in by the rest of the countries of the world combined. No one, as I eventually discovered, really had the slightest idea how many foreigners were entering the country illegally. Nor was it widely understood that not all illegal aliens were Mexicans or even Hispanics. The majority of the newcomers do speak Spanish (the United States is now the world's fifth-largest Hispanic country after Mexico, Spain, Argentina, and Colombia), and more than half the Hispanics come from Mexico, where by some estimates 1 person in 5 now depends in part on money earned by a relative in the United States. But only about 6 percent of Mexico's 64 million people are thought to have migrated legally or illegally to the United States, compared with an estimated 7 percent of all Cubans and Haitians, 8 percent of all Dominicans, 12 percent of Trinidadians, 18 percent of Barbadians, and 22 percent of Jamaicans. Moreover, the Mexicans and the Caribbean islanders are fast being joined by Central and South Americans fleeing both economic hardship and political unrest, by Hong Kong and Taiwan Chinese, by Koreans and West Indians, Filipinos and Polynesians, Iranians and Thais, all of whom are bringing with them their own cultures, customs, and languages.

One fear, which I heard in Los Angeles, Miami, and New York but which is fast becoming evident all across the Sunbelt and in big cities to the north and east, was that the United States was somehow slipping backward, becoming poorer, less well educated, more fractious. Though a handful of the new immigrants, mainly Europeans and Arabs seeking tax exile, are wealthy, it is true that the vast majority are among the poorest peoples of the earth, ill-educated and largely without skills. Many Americans, including a few well-informed public officials, are afraid that the newcomers are bringing with them the seeds of a new and divisive civil rights struggle. As Ray Marshall, Jimmy Carter's secretary of labor, warned, "No democracy can flourish with an underclass outside of its basic laws. Perhaps the first generation of undocumented workers will endure their privations in relative silence. But you can rest assured that the children of these undocumented workers will be the focus of a civil rights movement of the 1980's." Marshall was not the only official to have expressed such concerns. William E. Colby, the former director of central intelligence and one who presumably ought to know, has termed the flow of Mexican aliens across the country's southern border "a greater threat to the future of the United States than [is] the Soviet Union."

For many Americans, the catalyst for their concern was the spectacle, replayed on millions of television sets each evening for weeks, of tens of thousands of refugees from Cuban communism landing by the boatload at Key West, while the United States government, at first unwilling and then unable to stop them from coming, looked on. As I stood on the docks at Key West during those first days of the boatlift, I was touched as the bedraggled-looking Cubans, many of whom had had no food or water for days, walked ashore and fell into the arms of waiting relatives, many of whom they had not seen for a decade or more. But the picture darkened considerably when it became clear that many of the Cubans were not fleeing communism at all but were being expelled by Cuba as "undesirable."

Angry Floridians reacted to the invasion by handing Carter an overwhelming defeat in the 1980 presidential election, and the former President later acknowledged that "the refugee question hurt us badly. It made us look impotent when we received these refugees from Cuba." But the 130,000 Cubans were only the most visible wave of the refugee tide. In the last few years as many as 100,000 Haitians have also come here, along with a quarter million Indochinese and hundreds of thousands of Nicaraguans, Salvadorans, and Iranians, some of them legally, some of them not. And now there are signs, almost certainly intensified by the Cuban debacle, that the growing animosity toward illegal aliens in this country has touched the legitimate refugees as well. The Vietnamese, most of whom fled the same Communist government the United States tried for years to prevent taking power, have perhaps the most compelling claim of all to refuge in this country, but a recent poll by the Roper Organization found that nearly 80 percent of those questioned disagreed with Carter's decision to double the annual quota of 80,000 refugees from Indochina and that nearly 50 percent wanted to see it reduced.

Unfortunately such sentiments were also expressing themselves in racism and violence. In Miami I saw bewildered-looking Haitians ridiculed for walking down the middle of busy streets (there are few sidewalks in Haiti). In Los Angeles I heard unkind jokes about the unfamiliarity of many of that city's new Korean residents with indoor plumbing. Friends in San Francisco laughed about the penchant of some Vietnamese refugees for dining on roast dog. Sometimes such sentiments have taken a nastier turn. Two years ago fishing boats were set afire and a man killed in Seadrift, Texas, not far from Houston, after local shrimpers and the Ku Klux Klan tangled with Vietnamese refugees fishing the same waters. In the suburbs south of Chicago gun battles are not uncommon between gangs of Mexican-Americans and the illegal Mexican aliens with whom they compete for jobs and housing. All those killed by blacks during the recent rioting in Miami were either Cuban or Anglo. In Los Angeles, gangs of black, Hispanic, and Asian youths do battle almost nightly in their quest for urban "turf."

At a minimum, each year has been bringing the country 1.25 million new immigrants, more than have arrived here in any other time in the nation's history. It is an immense number—greater than the population of Detroit—and it has lent itself to a lot of sobering predictions. If immigration to the United States were to continue at its current rate, say the demographers, the nation's present population of 226 million would surpass 260 million in just 20 years, would top 312 million in 50 years, would double by the end of the next century. In just 50 years 1 U.S. resident in every 5 would be either an immigrant who has yet to arrive here or his descendant. Moreover, the United Nations was projecting that during the next 130 years the world's population would double to 10.5 billion souls, with 9 of every 10 people being born in the poorer countries that are the prime source of immigrants to the United States. At current growth rates the population of Latin America, from which most of the new immigrants are drawn, will double in just 26 years.

The questions all this raised were manifold, but chief among them were the same ones that have always concerned Americans in times of economic distress: Were the new immigrants taking jobs when there were already not enough to go around? Was their thirst for welfare and other social services draining the public treasury dry? Were they dividing our cities into culturally and linguistically isolated—and potentially hostile—enclaves? Was America running out of charity and room? Or was the country simply experiencing another in the periodic waves of immigration that have made it what it is today?

Whatever the case, amid all the confusion, conflict, and anger a new and exceedingly difficult American dilemma was being addressed: Should the now somewhat tarnished golden door through which tens of millions of earlier newcomers have stepped in search of better lives remain open, and, if so, how wide? That was the question I wanted to answer.

CHAPTER TWO

"They're Like Peddlers Going Around"

One of the first things I found out was that although Bernabe Garay and the men from Ahuacatlán do not need anyone to help them find their way across the border, the romantic notion of a small band of men on a solitary passage through the desert is fast becoming an anachronism, a throwback to a simpler age. For as the number of foreigners desperate to live and work in the United States increases exponentially, the organized smuggling of illegal aliens into this country is becoming a big business—so big, officials say, that it is now one of the two predominant money-making industries along the Mexican border, rivaling in profitability even the smuggling of narcotics. Arrests in alien-smuggling cases have more than tripled in the last five years, and INS officials estimate that half of all illegal aliens who cross the Mexican and Canadian borders now do so with the assistance of a smuggler. Every day, they say, countless thousands seeking better lives, the majority of them from Mexico and the rest from virtually every country in the world, are infiltrated across this country's borders by the sophisticated, highly organized rings that traffic in human contraband.

Many of the smuggled aliens are neophytes, first-time visitors unfamiliar with the culture, customs, language, and geography of the United States, strangers in a strange land who are willing to pay those who know America well to guide them across its borders. But the smugglers also provide a relatively safe journey into the American interior, and even seasoned aliens willing to risk walking across the border on their own are now turning to the professionals for help with their travel plans. The professionals are good, but they are not cheap: Fees run $400 for delivery from the Mexican border to Denver, $600 to Chicago, $850 or more to Detroit or New York City. It is a great deal of money—half the annual income of some Mexican workers—but a small investment compared to what those workers can earn in the United States.

So competitive has the smuggling business become that some of the smugglers even give guarantees—a second crossing for free if the first one does not succeed—and the more sophisticated rings attract clients by offering packages of false documents as part of their service: birth certificates, Social Security cards, driver's licenses, whatever pieces of paper are needed for them to live and work in the United States. Others specialize, smuggling only prostitutes to big-city vice rings or Mexican babies to black-market adoption mills, where a fair-skinned infant can bring up to $10,000. Still others fill telephone orders from "labor contractors" or business people, supplying truckloads of workers on demand to apple ranches in Washington, feedlots in Colorado, citrus groves in Florida, garment sweatshops in Los Angeles, and factories in Chicago. Sometimes the companies at the other end of the pipeline are nationally known; several big construction outfits and at least one nationwide hotel and restaurant chain have alien smugglers on their corporate payrolls to ensure their operations a continuous supply of cheap labor.

"We do have some companies, big companies, who use large numbers of illegals," says Bill Chambers, the INS district director in Dallas. "They get a foreman and tell him, 'You get us a supply of workers here.' I think it's obvious that they know where their employees are coming from, but you would never be able to prove that anybody in the higher echelons of the company was involved." Even the Mafia has reportedly gotten into the act. According to federal investigators, for the past several years Cosa Nostra families in some eastern cities have been smuggling Sicilians across the Canadian border to serve as "soldiers" and to work in the Mafia's pizza parlors and other legitimate business interests. Now, the investigators say, the

Mafia has recognized the immense potential profit in the people-moving business, and at least one West Coast mob organization has been linked to some of the larger Mexican alien smugglers.

The smuggling process begins at the public "staging areas" that can be found in big cities and small towns all along the Mexican side of the border. Almost any day a visitor to Juárez can see the smugglers gathering at the Plaza Monumental, their gold Rolex wristwatches glinting in the bright sunshine. "They're like peddlers going around," says Bob Barber, who runs the Border Patrol's antismuggling unit across the Rio Grande in El Paso. "You can see negotiations being made all over the place." While the "coyotes," as the smugglers call themselves, trade prospective passengers back and forth like commodities on an exchange, each trying to assemble a full load for his particular destination, their *pollos,* or chickens, wait in shabby hotels along the Calle Mariscal that specialize in the rough trade. Once a group, or "load," is assembled, it is led on foot by the coyote across the border at a safe distance from town—because the Border Patrol tends to concentrate its resources closer to population centers, such crossings are usually successful—and when they are safely in the United States, the aliens are hidden again, in one of the "wetback motels" that are a feature of every American border city or in private houses or apartments rented by the smugglers. When the coast seems clear, the *pollos* are loaded, usually with little food or water to sustain them (the smugglers are low-overhead operators), into vehicles so crowded that there is often no room to lie down or even to sit. Then, preceded by spotters in radio-equipped scout cars, the vehicles—beer trucks, motor homes, moving vans, school buses, even horse trailers—set out from the border on their northward journeys.

So profitable has the people-smuggling business become—an average-sized ring moving 500 aliens a week across the border can easily gross $12 million a year—that it is now attracting criminal syndicates that once handled only marijuana and cocaine. "The big alien-smuggling operators make just as much as the drug smugglers," says Bert Moreno, who heads the INS's antismuggling operations in Washington. "There are hundreds of rings making money off this, and there are scores of them making big, big money." Bill Selzer, the deputy Border Patrol chief in Chula Vista, California, just across the border from Tijuana, estimates that at least a quarter of the narcotics-smuggling rings in the San Diego area are now "comingling their loads," bringing both aliens and narcotics across the border at the same time. The field is also crowded with thousands of smaller part-time operations, known to the Border Patrol as Mom and Pop shops, some headed by rather improbable amateurs like the wives of some naval officers stationed at Camp Pendleton, California, who were found to be hauling illegal aliens from Tijuana to Los Angeles in their station wagons. Others recently charged with alien smuggling include a U.S. Customs officer, a San Diego air traffic controller, and a Roman Catholic priest in Texas. The priest, one INS official said, "was looking at it as a humanitarian thing."

All this would have seemed inconceivable just a few years ago. During all of 1969, when alien smuggling was still in its infancy, the Border Patrol apprehended exactly 4,457 illegal aliens as they were being ferried into this country by smugglers; in 1981 it arrested more than that every week, and the reasons for the increase are not hard to understand. Unlike the smuggling of narcotics, in which it is necessary to deliver the contraband to a buyer before being paid, the smugglers of aliens usually collect from their clients in advance. If the narcotics smuggler is arrested and loses his load, he loses his investment, but if the aliens and their driver are seized, the smuggling ring already has its money. Smuggling aliens is also less risky since most judges tend to treat those involved, especially first offenders, far more leniently than drug smugglers. Only one alien smuggler in every ten arrested is ever convicted, and probated sentences are common; even without probation, the average time served in prison by alien smugglers is only nineteen months.

The great majority of the aliens smuggled into this country comes in across the 2,000-mile Mexico–U.S. border. But some of the rings are now beginning to recognize the advantages of using the even less well-guarded Canadian northern border, first flying their charges from Latin America and Asia to Canada, which, unlike the United States, does not require most visitors to have visas, then smuggling them south into New York and California. A favored crossing place for Chinese, Haitians, and other Caribbean islanders headed for the East Coast is the 800-mile stretch of heavily forested, sparsely patrolled border between Canada and New England, where many of the ports of entry on the American side are closed between midnight and morning for lack of money and manpower. On some roads running south from Canada, like those that snake across the border near the tiny village of Derby Line, Vermont, there are no border stations at all. Latin Americans who can afford the air fare to Toronto are taking advantage of the Canadian connection. So are Hong Kong Chinese and Taiwanese bound for San Francisco and Los Angeles, who fly first to Vancouver and are then smuggled across the border to Seattle to begin their trip south. Toronto police recently broke up a particularly aggressive smuggling ring that, not content to wait for aliens to come to it, was actually recruiting Caribbean islanders in their homelands, flying them to Montreal aboard Air Canada and Air France, then taking them south into the United States.

Like Bernabe Garay, about six of every ten illegal aliens entering the United States come from Mexico. But more are arriving every day from Central and South America, the Caribbean, Asia, the Middle East, and even Europe. In a single month in 1981 the Border Patrol station in El Paso arrested border crossers from *thirty different countries*, among them Italy, South Africa, New Zealand, Denmark, India, France, Jordan, and the Dominican Republic. Every year the INS sends illegal aliens back to practically every country in the world except the Soviet Union and China. But the major "sending" countries, as the primary sources of illegal aliens are known, number fewer than two dozen: Mexico, Guatemala, El Salvador, Colombia, Ecuador, Peru, Argentina (itself once a haven for immigrants but now, because of economic and political troubles, a net exporter of human beings), the Dominican Republic, Haiti, Jamaica, India, Hong Kong, Taiwan, the Philippines, Thailand, Korea, Greece, Iran, Nigeria, and Ethiopia. Many of the Salvadorans and Guatemalans and some of the Haitians are running from hostile governments, but most of the others are fleeing the same demons as their Mexican counterparts: poverty, soaring inflation, and the press of population. If the numbers of such OTMs (the Border Patrol's designation for "other than Mexican'') is smaller, it is only because the distance from their home-lands makes traveling here more difficult; Mexico is the only underdeveloped country in the world that shares a common border with a highly industrialized nation.

In most of the sending countries, as in Mexico, populations will double or nearly so in the next twenty years. In most a near majority of the population is under fifteen, the economy is stag-nant, per capita incomes are less than $500 a year, and the poorest quarter of the population earns less than 10 percent of the country's gross income. Under such circumstances, if mov-ing to the United States is possible, it is almost preordained. As New York's Senator Daniel P. Moynihan, a former U.S. ambas-sador to India, points out, ''You take a person's lifetime earn-ings in India and lifetime earnings in the United States and you have, probably, a $500,000 difference.'' For the OTMs, many of whom are making their first trip to the United States, the smug-glers' expertise is especially valuable. The first contact with the smuggling organization is usually made in the country they are preparing to flee, through the phony travel agencies and ''tour arrangers'' that can be found within a few blocks of most Amer-ican embassies, the signs in their windows advertising for ''passengers for New York and Los Angeles.'' From Central and South America the smugglers' prices are considerably higher than the POE (port of embarkation) fares quoted along the border; one ring charges $2,000 for the trip from Guatemala City to New York City, a sum that may easily be equal to the av-erage Guatemalan's life savings. Before it was broken up in 1979, a Los Angeles ring had grossed $25 million smuggling an estimated 25,000 Central and South Americans into southern California. Another ring, still operating in El Salvador, Mexico, and Arizona, is bringing 1,000 aliens across the border every month and banking $24 million a year in profits.

Alien smuggling is a violation of Mexican law, and though Mexican authorities have caused occasional problems for smug-glers operating along their side of the border, because of Mexi-co's continuing interest in sending its unemployed workers north, they have done relatively little to stem the trafficking of their own citizens. Mexico, moreover, has traditionally served as a ''trampoline'' for those from Central and South America who are making their way to the United States, allowing the "wet ankles," as those foreigners crossing its 800-mile southern border with Guatemala are jokingly known, to enter that country as tourists. Mexico gives the *trampolinistas* visas that prohibit travel farther north than Mexico City, but in the land of the *mordida*, the visas have done little to prevent the "tourists" from making their way to the U.S. border—one Phoenix-based alien smuggler told investigators that his organization was paying $2,000 a day in bribes to Mexican immigration officials at the Benjamin Hill checkpoint, about sixty miles south of the Arizona border, to ignore the restrictive visas. But now more and more of the *trampolinistas* are deciding to stay in Mexico, a Spanish-speaking country where they feel more comfortable than they might in the United States, and they are presenting Mexico with an illegal immigration problem of its own. Mexico may be the most economically advanced country in Latin America, but more unemployed workers is the one thing it cannot afford. So, like their counterparts in the U.S. Border Patrol, Mexican border guards are now conducting immigration checks along the Guatemalan border, and the Mexican government is preparing to issue its citizens identity cards.

Because the professional alien smugglers are so accomplished at what they do, the rise in the organized smuggling of aliens has dramatically increased the odds of making a successful border crossing, in favor of those aliens who employ their services, and has therefore made the INS's job all the more difficult. Realizing, however belatedly, that the smuggling rings are their biggest enemy, the INS is now devoting the bulk of its meager investigative resources to putting the rings out of business. So far they have had limited success mainly because many of the rings are run by interlocking groups of families that shun all contact with outsiders or by the amorphous multinational criminal syndicate known as the Mexican Mafia, whose territory extends from northern Mexico into the American Southwest. Because it has proved so difficult for immigration agents in this country to penetrate the largest and most successful smuggling operations, most of the INS's information about the smugglers comes from paid informants of dubious value, such as motel desk clerks and taxi drivers on both sides of the border. But a few Spanish-speaking INS agents have managed to pose as aliens wanting to be smuggled into the

United States. One of them recently spent three days with sixty-seven illegal aliens in an eight-by-twelve-foot El Paso drop-house before riding shoulder to shoulder with them in the back of a meat van on the ten-hour trip to Amarillo. "I was sick to my stomach for a month afterward," the agent said later.

Such penetrations are difficult to arrange, however, so the INS, which has only about 250 antismuggling agents around the country, tries to catch the smugglers in other ways, primarily at checkpoints on major highways near the border where suspicious vehicles are stopped and searched. The technique has not proved terribly fruitful mainly because the checkpoints are so visible and hard to move. In 1979, for example, searches of nearly 3 million vehicles by Border Patrol agents on highways from California to Texas yielded only a few thousand smuggled aliens. Bad weather and a chronic shortage of agents keep the checkpoints from operating continuously, and when they are "down," or closed, spotters posted nearby by the smuggling rings quickly flash the word. The big checkpoint about halfway between San Diego and Los Angeles on Interstate 5, a major alien-smuggling route, is normally closed on Sunday evenings both because of manpower shortages and because the flow of weekend traffic returning to Los Angeles makes stopping every car impossible without backing cars up for miles. The Sunday evening closing is well known to the smugglers in the area, who use it to their advantage. Precisely how much advantage, however, was not really clear until one Sunday last year when the Border Patrol, which had closed the checkpoint at 4:00 P.M. as usual, reopened it unexpectedly an hour later—just long enough for the word to go out that it was down. Over the next five hours the Border Patrol arrested 35 alien smugglers and 518 illegal aliens, hidden in everything from rented U-Haul trucks to the trunks of ordinary passenger cars. "The pipeline," said Don Cameron, the local Border Patrol chief, "was just about full."

The smugglers were caught unawares that day, but they usually manage to stay at least one jump ahead of the INS. In 1979, for example, the Border Patrol, believing that the loss of their vehicles would eventually put many of the smugglers out of business, finally acquired the authority to impound trucks and cars used by smugglers to transport their loads. The patrol seized so many vehicles that Cameron could joke that he had "more used cars than Cal Worthington," the southern California auto dealer whose silly self-advertisements are a fixture of late-night television there, but the impoundments put barely a dent in the smuggling traffic. Even though the loss of an aging truck or two is a small price for an organization that takes in $1 million or $2 million a year, many of the smugglers are now renting their trucks, and some of the more enterprising rings are moving their *pollos* north on Amtrak trains and even on commercial airlines.

The INS's antismuggling efforts have not been entirely unavailing: In 1980, it arrested more than 15,000 alien smugglers employed by some 300 rings. Unfortunately, however, such arrests have almost no long-term effect on the smugglers' operations since most of those who fall into the government's net are lower- and middle-class operatives—guides, drivers, arrangers: the buck privates of the smuggling trade—who know little about the organization that has employed them, probably not even the real name of the person who offered them the job. Meantime, the leaders of the rings, many of whom live abroad with their seven-figure bank accounts, remain beyond the government's grasp. Lately, in hopes that they will escape prosecution altogether, some of the rings have begun using teenagers and even children to guide the aliens across the border and drive them to their destinations in the United States. "The transporters," says Jerry Collins, an official of the United States Parole Commission, "are apparently telling these kids, 'You'll get a couple of nights in jail and the Feds will bounce you back across the border.' " As it happens, most of the younger smugglers are released without charges only to resurface a few days later with another load of illegal aliens, but such leniency from the Justice Department cannot always be relied upon. In 1980 the federal government convicted and actually sent to prison a sixteen-year-old Mexican boy, José Luis Ramírez, who was apprehended near San Diego at the wheel of a carload of illegal aliens. There has been a handful of similar cases since then.

Even when there are arrests in smuggling cases, prosecutions do not automatically follow. For one thing, it is not always easy to tell the smugglers and the aliens apart, and the aliens—the government's only potential witnesses—are frequently reluctant to point their fingers at those they may see not as victimizers but as benefactors. Indeed, for many Mexicans, the smugglers are folk heroes whose exploits are celebrated in the Mexican cinema, where they are portrayed as Davids who regularly best the Border Patrol's Goliaths. For these reasons and others, including the smugglers' pronounced tendency to jump bail, the current antismuggling campaign is a losing battle: Of the 15,000 individuals charged with alien smuggling in 1980, only 6,000 were ever brought to trial, and only 2,000 of those were ultimately convicted.

The antismuggling effort is aimed at only one species of illegal alien: the clandestine border crosser. But not all illegal aliens, perhaps not even the majority, come to the United States by slipping across its borders. The others enter the country openly—posing as students who never go to school and tourists who never take a tour, walking boldly through immigration inspection stations with counterfeit documents and credentials, even paying Americans to become their wives and husbands. In all of these ways and more, they take advantage of this country's tradition of welcome for foreign visitors, its fundamentally humane immigration laws, its heterogeneous, melting-pot society, which makes it easy for a stranger to seem to belong; its repugnance for any attempt to number and catalogue its citizens.

The ease with which a foreigner can gain official permission to enter the United States can be clearly seen in the line of visa seekers that, on most days, extends out the back gate of the cubelike American embassy in Mexico City and all the way around the block to the broad Paseo de la Reforma. Like the throngs standing patiently outside American embassies in dozens of other countries around the world, those who begin lining up in Mexico City before dawn hope to leave with one of the most sought-after pieces of paper in the world: a temporary visa allowing them to visit the United States as tourists or students, or on business. Some of those in line on any given morning are clearly what they seem to be: corporation executives with business in the United States or well-to-do families on their way to spend the weekend at Disneyland, skiing in Colorado, or lying on the beach in Miami. The others are hoping to get lucky, hoping that the visa officer will be in an expansive mood and not question them too closely about their plans, for unless they are caught, they have no intention of ever returning to Mexico, and more than likely they will never be caught.

The INS spends most of its time and money looking for illegal border crossers, not "visa abusers," as such bogus visitors are known. In 1980 it found only 64,000 foreigners who had overstayed their visas. Nobody knows how many it did not find, but indications are that their numbers were enormous; the same year 12 million foreigners entered the United States with nonimmigrant visas, but only 10.5 million were recorded as ever having left. Some of the 1.5 million shortfall is doubtless due to careless record keeping by the INS and the airlines that bring the visitors here and take them home—but not all of it. Daniel Vining of the University of Pennsylvania, who has calculated net migration to this country by air, estimates the number of overstayers at around 200,000 a year, and others think it may be twice that.

Either way, the contribution of visa abusers to illegal immigration is both significant and growing, and the inclination of the American government to encourage foreign visitors by not looking too closely at who the tourists are makes such abuses easier still. So does the active promotion of tourism by Mexicans to the United States, a particular priority because it offsets the balance-of-payments deficit created by the millions of American tourists who visit Mexico each year. "We've got a third of a million people a year who want to travel to the U.S.," says one consular officer in Mexico City. "They're spending a considerable amount of money there. Let's say we investigated all these cases. What would happen? We'd end up not being able to issue visas to people in a day's time the way we do now. We'd have to have a staff of investigators, and it would cost the taxpayers a lot of money."

Like their counterparts in nearly every country in the world, the American vice-consuls who hand out the visas in Mexico City—most of them young Foreign Service officers on their first tours of duty abroad—know that some of those standing in the hazy sunshine or sitting on the backless green benches in the embassy's courtyard are planning not merely to visit the United States but to live here. The problem is that they do not know which ones, and they have almost no way of finding out.

31

Whether those on line are legitimate visitors or not, most of them have brought with them documents they hope will convince the visa officers that they have good reason to return home: a bank statement showing a solid record of deposits, for example, or a letter from a longtime employer attesting to their reliability. Such documents are easily obtainable on the black market, and even those that were genuine yesterday need not be so today: Employees can quit their jobs, and savings accounts can be converted into travelers' checks.

With 1,200 visa applicants to process in an average seven-hour day, quick decisions are the rule, and the visa officers are forced to rely mainly on their instincts. "If the documents seem reasonable and reasonably current, what else can you do?" asks Allan Otto, who heads the Mexico City consulate. "It would take a tremendous effort and tremendous resources to check these things out." Adds Jim Kerr, the chief of the consular section, "We just don't have the people." The consuls are frankly guessing, and because of the press of time, they often guess wrong. "We tend to be a bit more generous than we should be sometimes," admits one young consul on her first overseas assignment, "because we need to make quick decisions." In the next five minutes she decides whether or not to grant or deny visas to a Mexico City woman who says she wants to take a trip to Puerto Rico, a German exchange student on a Mexican vacation from his studies in the United States, a well-dressed young man who wants to visit his brother in Texas, and a slight, shy young woman who says she has worked for a local doctor for four years and has always wanted to see Los Angeles. Granted, granted, denied, denied. The odds are better than even that at least one of the four is not telling the truth, but in a sense it does not matter. Anyone whose visa application is denied can always hop a bus to the border and find a coyote to take him across. "That's one factor we have to take into consideration," says Ruth McLendon, a former American consul general in Mexico City. "To refuse them a visa doesn't really stop them if they want to enter the U.S. If they're bad applicants, they can always walk."

So tempting a target for abuse has the visa process become that some alien smugglers are now actually securing visas for their clients and bringing them into the United States as members of "tour goups" rather than sneaking them across the border at night. Ted Giorgetti, the chief INS investigator in Chicago, says that "only God knows the number" of illegal Polish aliens living in that city who came there to visit relatives and never left, and an INS official in Detroit believes that at least half of that city's sizable Arab community came into the country the same way. In 1981 the INS uncovered a foreign-based ring that was smuggling Armenian "tourists" from Beirut to California, and earlier this year it broke up an organization in Los Angeles that was funneling Indonesian domestics to Beverly Hills housewives, providing them with passports, airline tickets, and enough "spending money" to convince the American consuls in Jakarta who issued them tourist visas that they were coming here for a vacation.

There was no evidence that any of the consuls in Jakarta were parties to the fraud, but knowledgeable State Department officials do not deny that a number of smugglers have operated with the complicity of American embassy personnel around the world. One who did was George Tajerian, a world-class cyclist and member of the Iraqi Olympic team who got his first taste of public attention on a hot July afternoon in 1968, when he stepped into the newly finished Olympic stadium in Mexico City, carrying his nation's flag. Before the games were over, Tajerian announced that he had decided to defect. George Tajerian was something of a national hero in Iraq, but he was also an Armenian Christian, a fact that made life for him in that Moslem country more difficult than it would otherwise have been. He thought that things might be better in Mexico, and Mexico was agreeable, so Tajerian married a well-to-do Mexican woman who owned a chain of drugstores, settled down, and fathered two children. Though he continued to feel concern for his Christian friends in Iraq who had not been able to follow him to the West, for most of the next decade Tajerian remained without the means to help them. When he finally found a way, it led him to a federal prison in Kentucky and to a life, at the age of forty, as a stateless person.

It was in 1976, or so Tajerian later said under oath, that he was first approached by a short, swarthy man with a mustache and glasses who invited him to have a cup of coffee at the American embassy in Mexico City. The man said his name was

Jorge García and that he was an American who worked in the embassy's security office. In return for money, García told Tajerian, he could produce anything—phony birth certificates, driver's licenses, marriage licenses, even genuine U.S. tourist visas issued by the embassy's consular staff. Tajerian thought immediately of the friends, and friends of friends, who had been pleading for his help in leaving Iraq. Over the next year, he said later, he bought some fifty visas for $500 apiece, thirty of them from García and the rest from García's friend, a mysterious "Mr. Enrique." Tajerian charged each Iraqi $1,000: $500 for the cost of the visa and $500 for a one-way airplane ticket to Mexico. From there all the Iraqis entered the United States at Dallas and then flew to Detroit, where they settled into that city's large Iraqi community. "All of my people got through with no problems," Tajerian said. According to the statement he later gave federal investigators, Tajerian paid García and Enrique their money in the men's room at the American embassy, and they in turn gave part of their cut to two consular officers there. He also identified for federal investigators photographs of the two consuls who, he said, had issued the visas. The investigation that followed, one INS agent said, "uncovered numerous irregularities" in the Mexico City embassy's visa section. "The indication we got was that consular personnel involved were on the take, and we were assured that corrective action would be taken by the State Department." Asked what that action had entailed, the investigator said, "I heard they shuffled some people around somewhere."

Among the worst of the visa abusers are the foreign students who flock to this country to take advantage of numerous exchange programs, which have been an important element of American foreign policy since the end of World War II. The theory behind the exchanges is sound. Apart from training the scientists and technocrats needed to raise the standards of living in developing countries, the programs, it is hoped, will give the students an understanding of American society and institutions that can be gained only by living in this country. But however well intentioned the efforts to open wide the doors of American schools and colleges to young men and women from other countries, such programs have also contributed heavily to illegal immigration. There are now more than 300,000 foreigners living in the United States on student visas, a figure that is expected to double in the next seven years. By 1990, unless restrictions are imposed, 1 U.S. college student in every 10 will probably be a foreigner. At the moment the overseas students are principally Iranians (about 50,000 of them currently enrolled and an equal number who have dropped out of school but are still living here), Taiwan Chinese, Japanese, Saudis, Nigerians, West Indians, and Latin Americans. A good many of them do come here for an education, but many others either come with no intention of studying or stay on after graduating or dropping out of school. A recent spot check in Los Angeles showed that more than a quarter of the foreigners holding student visas there were not enrolled at the schools they were supposed to be attending, and the same is probably true elsewhere. But just as the INS, with its nightmare record-keeping system, is unable to keep track of foreign tourists, it has no idea how many foreign students are "out of status."

Foreign students are not supposed to work while they are in school without special permission, but the majority do it anyway, waiting tables in restaurants or driving taxicabs (even in Washington, D.C., where many of the taxi drivers are Nigerians studying at Howard University), and officials concede that the prohibition against foreign students working is virtually unenforceable. The officials estimate that half the Iranians currently holding student visas came here not to study but to work, and the Iranians are not alone. INS agents who arrested 16 Guyanese "students" working in a Brooklyn factory said they suspected that at least 5,000 other Guyanese who had entered the country with student visas were also working in the area. The real concern, however, is the significant numbers of foreign students who stay in this country illegally after they are graduated. Despite all the concern over the taking of jobs by illegal Mexican aliens like Bernabe Garay, it is much more likely to be the erstwhile student from Europe, Asia, or the Middle East, not the unskilled Mexican worker, who is filling the well-salaried job for which unemployed American workers would be grateful—most of the foreigners obtain degrees in such highly paid fields as engineering, the physical sciences, mathematics, computer studies, and business administration and take jobs in these areas after graduation.

As with the issuing of tourist visas, the student visa system invites abuse because it has been set up to make things as easy as possible for all involved; foreign students, after all, bring an extra $1.5 billion into the country every year. When an American school accepts a student from another country, it issues him or her a copy of INS form I-20, which certifies that the student has been admitted to study. The student shows the form to an American consular officer, who issues a visa allowing him or her to live in the United States. Because the process is virtually automatic, the schools have essentially been granted the power to admit whichever foreigners they choose to the United States, an authority not delegated to any other private American institution. Before it can issue an I-20 form, a school must be approved by the INS, but such approvals can be had almost for the asking, not just by respected institutions of higher learning but also by vocational and technical schools that offer training, often of dubious value, in everything from barbering and auto mechanics to television and radio repair.

At the moment more than 3,000 schools have been approved to admit foreign students. Some, like Miami-Dade Community College, which has nearly 5,000 foreign-born students, more than any other school in the country, are perfectly legitimate institutions. Others are not schools at all but fly-by-night schemes that simply sell the sought-after student certifications to foreigners for the price of their "tuition." Typical of the breed, investigators say, are the two "language schools" in Washington, D.C., that admit large numbers of young Bolivians as part of a ruse to import cheap labor for Washington area restaurants. But even legitimate schools can become swept up in the fraud. As the tail end of America's postwar "baby boom" generation has graduated from college, the institutions to which they once flocked have watched in dismay as enrollments and tuition revenues have declined, and many, including some large state universities hit by declining tax revenues, have turned to educational "recruiters" for help in filling their empty classrooms. Even though the forms are supposed to be issued only after a student has been accepted, in their eagerness to attract paying students colleges often give the recruiters stacks of presigned I-20's to pass out to prospective candidates overseas. The recruiters sell the students to the schools, receiving as much as

15 percent of the first year's tuition as their commission. A few months before the takeover of the American embassy in Teheran by Iranian militants, Saeed Moorbakhsh, a recruiter from New York City's Hunter College, took 150 of the pre-signed forms to Iran to search for would-be scholars on behalf of both Hunter and Vermont's prestigious Bennington College. Joseph Murphy, Bennington's president, later admitted that giving Moorbakhsh the presigned forms probably "wasn't the moral thing to do."

Such schools are required to notify the INS when a foreign student stops attending classes. But one INS investigator said many schools were "very lax" in reporting changes in the status of their foreign students, partly through negligence but sometimes in an effort to keep their attendance figures up. A few years ago an INS investigation of a midwestern university found that dozens of Taiwanese students to whom the school had given I-20 forms were shown as in attendance, although they had never enrolled, and that several of the students had admitted to school officials that they had come to the United States not to study but in hopes of finding good jobs and marrying American citizens.

Fraudulent marriages are only one of a multitude of lesser-known but equally effective ways to gain entry to the United States, all of which only complicate further the nation's already losing battle to enforce its immigration laws. In keeping with the government's conviction that Americans should not be separated from their loved ones by international boundaries, marrying an American citizen entitles an alien to an immediate permanent resident visa, the so-called green card. (There are no visa number quotas for spouses, parents, and children of adult U.S. citizens as there are for all other categories of immigrant.) Although humanitarian in its intent, this law has spawned a false marriage racket of such proportions that "marriages of convenience" are now one of the most popular means of emigration for aliens who are otherwise inadmissible. In nearly every big city on the East and West coasts there are dozens of thriving marriage fraud rings, some run by shady immigration lawyers or alien-smuggling organizations as part of a package service, often using prostitutes as "wives" and seeking clients through ads in men's magazines (''Nice Mexican, Oriental ladies seek friendship and marriage . . .'').

In 1980 the INS received 115,000 applications for permanent residence status from aliens who had married American citizens. It interviewed 36,000 of them and charged more than 4,600—a record number—with having entered fraudulent marriages for immigration purposes. Among them was a young Nigerian named Israel Agu. Like many of his countrymen, Agu had come to America with a student visa and was in a hurry to become an American—so much of a hurry that three days after he arrived Agu married Mae Burns, a Dallas woman he had only just met, and promptly applied for permanent residency. Had he been a little more cautious, Agu's scheme might have succeeded. But INS agents, intrigued by the lightning speed with which he had tied the knot, investigated and found that Agu's brother, a permanent resident also living in Dallas, had offered to pay Mae Burns's living expenses if she married his brother. Mae Burns got an annulment; Israel Agu got six months and deportation.

Such cases are almost never quite so clear-cut because it is not easy for the government to say for certain if a marriage is bogus or ''real.'' What are the standards to be applied? There is no litmus test for love, and even if two people do not love each other, there is nothing to say they cannot get married or that they must stay married for a given length of time. (A foreigner who gains permanent residency through marriage keeps that status even after the marriage has been dissolved.) INS agents have been known to place a married couple under surveillance on their wedding night, not to observe what goes on in their bedroom but simply to see whether or not the pair actually spends the night together. In most alien marriage cases a divorce within two years will trigger an investigation, but even then proving fraud is far from simple—unless, as in Agu's case, one of the parties involved admits to a quid pro quo or unless, as also happens, the INS finds that the same woman is married to several aliens at the same time.

Many illegal aliens, on the other hand, come here in the boldest possible manner, flashing bogus passports and green cards at harried immigration inspectors as they stream through the turnstiles along the borders and at the nation's airports. David North, a highly respected immigration researcher, estimates that half a million aliens bearing fraudulent documents of one kind or another enter the United States each year, perhaps as many people as cross the Mexican border illegally in the same period of time. The immigration inspectors have some success at spotting counterfeits but, considering the vast numbers of entrants they must deal with, not nearly enough. The problem is now compounded by the INS's new "citizen bypass" procedure, under which an American—or an alien with a forged U.S. passport—can circumvent the immigration inspectors and go directly to Customs, whose officers are far less expert in detecting bogus documents than the INS. In 1978, 163 million people, aliens and citizens alike, entered the United States at official inspection stations from Mexico alone, and another 87 million came in from Canada. At airports, seaports, and along the border it is up to the person requesting admission to establish his citizenship or legal residency. But inside the country the burden of proof is shifted, and the proliferation of false documents makes the job of the INS even tougher than it is already. Under existing law, a U.S. immigration officer may, within certain broad limits, stop and question anyone believed to be in this country illegally. But because citizens are not required to carry any verifying credentials, the responsibility for proving illegality is on the officer, not on the suspected alien. An illegal alien, especially one who is newly arrived and has not yet learned the rules of the game, will frequently admit his or her illegal status after a couple of perfunctory questions. But if the alien asserts citizenship and backs up the assertion with documents, the officer has little choice but to extract a confession or to let him or her go.

The United States has never required its citizens to carry any kind of universal "identity card," the mere idea of which tends to evoke in most Americans the vision of a Gestapo agent stopping citizens on the street and demanding to see "Your papers, pliss." Even the recent rather modest proposal for the production of a new kind of "counterfeit-resistant" Social Security card has met with considerable opposition among civil libertarians, who fear that such cards may pave the road to a police state. It is therefore not surprising that when questions of citizenship are raised, and they are raised infrequently for most of us, the pieces of paper the average American carries in his or her wallet—a driver's license, a Social Security card, a Selective Service certificate, a voter's registration card—are usually accepted by most authorities as evidence, if not guarantees, that the holder has a right to be here. It is also not surprising that in cities like Tijuana, Juárez, and Matamoros—in fact, all along the Mexican side of the border—the same pieces of paper are being churned out by high-speed, high-quality printing presses.

The INS has files on more than 6,000 suspected sellers of fake birth certificates and other false identity documents, and there are at least 150 known sources of counterfeit immigration documents, like green cards and border crossing cards. But the magnitude of the traffic in false documentation was never really apparent until one afternoon in 1973, when agents stumbled upon the unheard-of quantity of 60,000 counterfeit green cards left in a locker at the Greyhound bus station in Los Angeles. The cards—such good copies that they even contained the secret identifying marks known only to immigration inspectors—could easily have commanded $500 apiece. Such a price is unusually high. All along the Mexican side of the border, buying a birth certificate or green card is almost as easy as buying a Coca-Cola, and almost as cheap. The document vendors, who tend to carry their inventories in their pockets and do business from back booths in bars and restaurants, can, in their favorite phrase, "get you everything for fifty bucks," not just the heavyweight credentials but the lesser ones that lend credence to the former: library cards; student identification cards; business and membership cards of all kinds. As a consequence, a well-documented illegal alien often has more "proof" of his identity than do most American citizens.

As if the task of detecting false documents were not enough —and Mike Williams, a Border Patrol agent in El Paso, is convinced that "the card can't be made that somebody can't counterfeit"—the authorities now must contend with the fact that not all the documentation floating around the border is counterfeit. A few years ago police discovered thousands of blank, genuine Social Security cards in the office of a Dallas "immigration consultant," and similar caches of driver's licenses and even American passports have turned up since. But why buy counterfeit documents when the genuine article is so easy to come by? With a birth certificate in hand, the illegal alien can readily obtain the plethora of credentials issued by federal and state government agencies. And there is nothing easier than getting a copy of somebody else's birth certificate.

In the last ten years INS agents have arrested three dozen illegal aliens carrying genuine birth certificates identifying them as the same dead California man. Since in most states birth and death records are not vetted against one another, there is nothing to prevent one's assuming the identity of a dead person and requesting an official copy of his or her birth certificate. Every year 10 million duplicate birth certificates are issued, most of them by mail on one of hundreds of different forms used by thousands of vital records offices around the country. In most states it is not illegal to ask for a copy of someone else's birth certificate, and in some there is even no law against impersonating a private citizen. For aliens with neither the time nor the expertise to follow the paper trail themselves, copies of other people's birth certificates can be obtained from brokers like Oscar, a Peruvian who was a genius at producing instant Americans. Before he was finally arrested, Oscar Elias Malca-Valdivia made millions of dollars by transforming Mexicans into United States citizens for $1,000 apiece. When the FBI grabbed Oscar, it found ledgers in the trunk of his Cadillac showing that he had taken in $232,000 during the preceding three months. He did it by taking advantage of laws that, in Texas as in most states, allow persons born there whose births were never registered to create a record after the fact. Oscar first typed a letter to the Texas State Registrar's Office stating that his "client" had been born there of illegal alien parents some years before, a fact that would, of course, make the child an American citizen.

When Oscar's letter arrived at the registrar's office, the files would be searched, and, of course, no birth certificate found, a fact that Oscar explained by saying the parents had feared that if they registered the birth, their illegal status would be discovered. Invariably the registrar wrote back to Oscar offering the opportunity to file a "delayed certificate of live birth" and even supplying the necessary forms. Oscar mailed the form back to the registrar's office along with the $2 fee and a couple of supporting documents attesting that the client had been born in

Texas: an affidavit from the client's "mother," say, or from the "physician" who had attended the birth, all of which Oscar himself prepared on letterheads he had printed up. Presented with such documents and never bothering to check their authenticity, the state registrar created a record of the client's birth and, ever helpful, even sent a copy to the clerk of the county in which the birth was claimed. All that remained was for Oscar's client to ask the county clerk for a copy of "his" U.S. birth certificate and—presto!—another instant citizen who could vote, hold public office, collect welfare, and, perhaps most important, bring his or her spouse into the country legally as a permanent resident alien. Oscar got thirteen years in prison, but the INS thinks it will never be able to track down the thousand or so Mexicans he turned into Americans, nor does it have the faintest idea how many other "Oscars" are still operating along the Mexican border.

For years Americans have associated Mexico with bargains. Americans cross the border to drink 50-cent beer and dine on $5 filet mignon, fill their cars with cheap gas, mail letters back to the United States for 9 cents apiece, visit cut-rate doctors and dentists, and stock up on staples—sugar, milk, coffee, fruits, and vegetables at a fraction of their U.S. prices. But Mexicans also come to the United States to buy, both because the quality of some products made here is better than those produced in Mexico and because items marked "Made in U.S.A." confer status on their owners in Mexico. Stores like those along Convent Street in Laredo, Texas, where $3 of every $4 are spent by Mexicans, sell more merchandise per square foot of floor space than anywhere else in America, even Beverly Hills' Rodeo Drive or New York's Fifth Avenue. For years a single Laredo grocery store has sold more Tide, Pet milk, and Kool-Aid than any in America.

Such cross-border commerce is encouraged by the United States, enhancing as it does the U.S. balance of payments with Mexico, which is now this country's most important source of foreign exchange. In 1981 more than 3 million Mexicans spent $2.5 billion here. Mexicans are now spending more money in the United States than Americans are leaving behind in Mexico. Americans need no special permission to walk across the border and shop in Mexican stores; no one assumes that they are likely to take up residence there. The same does not, however, apply to Mexicans, who must have a border crossing card, a pass that permits the holder to remain in the United States for up to seventy-two hours to shop or visit friends, for any reason except to work. As might be expected, the demand for such cards among Mexicans is fierce, and those seeking them often begin lining up outside INS offices at the border the day before they make their applications.

In theory, to get a crossing card, a Mexican must show convincing evidence that he or she is a "stable" resident of Mexico: a house, a bank account, a good job, or other viable reason to believe that he or she will not use the visiting privileges to move to the United States. As with everything else, however, the INS lacks the manpower to check an applicant's bona fides, and the cards are handed out almost as fast as they can be printed, an average of one every eight minutes in El Paso. There are perhaps 2 million such cards now outstanding, but the INS also has no way to monitor what the cardholders do after they enter the United States, to ensure that they observe the seventy-two-hour limit or the prohibition against working. So lax is the system, in fact, that the border crossing card has become one of the favored ways for Mexican workers to enter the United States illegally. Mexican women from cities like Tijuana and Juárez have used their cards for years to commute to their jobs as domestics on the American side of the border, but Mexicans headed for big cities in the north are also using such cards to cross the border, then mailing them back to their homes in Mexico before proceeding north to look for work. If they are captured, the aliens tell the INS that they slipped across the border illegally, and when they return home, their crossing cards are there waiting, ready to be used to make another trip.

For the few remaining foreigners who cannot find a coyote to smuggle them, a consul to approve their tourist visa, a phony school to accept them, an American citizen to marry them, an Oscar to sell them a birth certificate, or an immigration officer who will issue them a border crossing card, there is always a last resort, the United States Congress, which can pass a special law making a foreigner into a citizen even if he or she is ineligible to emigrate under existing laws. A private immigration bill, as such laws are known, can also expedite the naturalization process for an alien already living in this country illegally, delay impending deportation proceedings, or waive one of the basic requirements, such as the ability to speak English, required of naturalized American citizens. Between 1937 and 1973 more than 55,000 private immigration bills were introduced by members of Congress, 7,000 of them in the Ninetieth Congress (1967 and 1968) alone. Few of the bills—only about 6,000—were ever passed, but because of a quirk in the immigration laws, actual passage of the bills is not important. Until 1971 the mere introduction of such a bill in either the Senate or the House of Representatives was enough to stay deportation proceedings against its beneficiary; as long as the bill was pending, the INS was prevented from taking any action at all against the individual for whom it had been introduced. Even if the bill was never acted upon, as most were not, its sponsor could simply reintroduce it in the next session—and the next, and the next, thus keeping an alien who otherwise might have been deported immediately in the United States indefinitely.

Since 1971 a private immigration bill introduced in the House alone has not carried an automatic suspension of deportation. But a bill introduced in the Senate still does, and since many such bills are introduced in both houses simultaneously, the effect remains the same. When a private bill is introduced, the INS, an agency that has always prided itself on its congressional relations, takes a step backward. It will, for example, conduct a background check on the alien named in the bill only if asked by a committee of Congress—and even then the INS investigator's handbook makes clear that the inquiry is not to be overly thorough. "Information," it reads, "should never be solicited during private bill investigations concerning the payment of money in connection with the introduction of the bill."

Though the handbook does not say so, there is a good reason for such discretion. Representatives and senators do not always sponsor private immigration bills for humanitarian reasons. In fact, for years the private immigration bill has been one of the secret scandals of Congress. Among the most frequent beneficiaries have been foreign doctors, who come to the United States with temporary H-1 or H-2 visas (as foreign workers with skills that are in short supply) to serve their internships in American hospitals, then decide that instead of returning to India, Mexico, or Korea, they would prefer to remain in the United States, where the practice of medicine is far more lucrative. Many of the doctors make substantial contributions to the campaigns of members of Congress who have helped them obtain permanent resident status, but it is nearly impossible to prove the quid pro quo necessary for a conviction under federal bribery statutes.

Two New York congressmen who introduced their share of private bills—more than 200 apiece in one two-year period alone —were Mario Biaggi and Paul A. Fino, the latter now a justice of the New York State Supreme Court. One man for whom both congressmen sponsored such bills was Tulio Bellardini, who had been refused permission to emigrate to the United States because of his organized crime connections and reports that he was selling drugs to school children. The case was noteworthy because of evidence obtained by federal investigators that the Mafia, in addition to smuggling illegal aliens from Italy into the country, was using unnamed congressmen to introduce private bills on their behalf "to stall their departure from the United States." Biaggi and Fino were questioned by a federal grand jury in New York about the Bellardini matter as well as about what they knew about payoffs to congressmen in general, but neither was ever indicted. Fino later acknowledged that he had been offered money by immigration lawyers for whose clients he had submitted some of his private bills, but he said he had refused the bribes. The same federal investigation in which Biaggi and Fino were caught up produced information that three other congressmen had introduced private bills on behalf of aliens "close to organized crime." One of the three was Representative John J. Murphy, the Staten Island Democrat.

The last congressman indicted in connection with immigration bills was Henry Helstoski of New Jersey, who was charged in 1976 with having accepted bribes in return for introducing them. The Supreme Court eventually ruled that Helstoski could not be prosecuted because his congressional activities were constitutionally protected, and the charges against him were dismissed; one of his aides, however, was convicted of bribery. It had been thought until recently that private immigration bills, the introduction of which had been winding down since the Biaggi–Fino investigation and the Helstoski case, were no longer a serious source of congressional corruption. But in February 1980, the nation learned the bizarre story of six congressmen and a senator who were about to be charged with having accepted briefcases full of money from a mythical Arab sheikh seeking political favors in this country. As the world must know by now, the sheikh was an undercover FBI agent; the six congressmen and the senator, Harrison Williams of New Jersey, were subsequently convicted; and the word "ABSCAM" entered the American political lexicon.

What was largely lost in the considerable public attention paid to ABSCAM was the fact that in nearly every instance the favors being sought by the sheikh involved his supposed desire to emigrate to the United States. The ploy of seeking help from the congressmen for the sheikh's "immigration problems," one FBI agent said, was chosen by the bureau simply because "it was the one to which the congressmen responded most quickly." At least two congressmen, Raymond Lederer of Pennsylvania and John Jenrette of South Carolina, both Democrats, accepted $50,000 in cash in return for their promises to sponsor private bills, and the others, including John Murphy, were convicted for selling the sheikh the benefit of their "influence" with the immigration service. It was ironic, many veteran INS agents thought, that of the eight officials caught up in ABSCAM, only Senator Williams was not convicted of conspiring in any immigration fraud, for at one point in his career Williams had introduced more private immigration bills than any other member of the Senate—more than 220 of them, many for Chinese sailors who had jumped ship in New York Harbor. Around Capitol Hill Williams became known as the senator from Hong Kong, and he later received a number of campaign contributions from employees of various Chinese restaurants in New Jersey.

There were also a couple of noncongressional ABSCAM casualties. One was Maron J. "Babe" Sheehi, a fifty-five-year-old INS official who was overheard discussing shady immigration deals on an ABSCAM wiretap and who later admitted he had taken $22,000 in bribes from more than 100 wealthy foreigners, mainly Iranians, in return for helping them secure green cards.

According to the information the wiretaps picked up, Sheehi had secretly set up an immigration "consulting" firm, run by a former girl friend, that charged its clients fees of up to $10,000 in return for his help in shepherding their cases through the INS bureaucracy.

Another victim was Alexander Alexandro, Jr., a twenty-nine-year-old INS investigator in New York, who told the FBI's ABSCAM team that he would be delighted to help a friend of the sheikh gain entry to the United States for a $15,000 fee. As FBI videotape cameras in a hotel near New York's Kennedy International Airport recorded the scene, undercover agent Anthony Ameroso, posing as the sheikh's representative, counted out the first $2,000 of the bribe and put it on a coffee table. Alexandro picked the money up and put it in his pocket, but he was nervous. "I've got a prestigious position," he told Ameroso. "I can't afford to be put before a grand jury and the U.S. Attorney's Office because someone, you know, likes to talk." Alexandro's caution went for naught; both he and Babe Sheehi were convicted.

CHAPTER THREE

"We're Going to Have Every Boat in South Florida on the Way to Cuba"

Nineteen eighty was not simply the year of the illegal alien; it was also the year of the refugee. In that twelve-month period alone America took in at least 375,000 refugees: 225,000 Vietnamese, Cambodians, Laotians, Russians, and Eastern Europeans, who came at its invitation, and 150,000 Cubans and Haitians, who did not.

To anyone following the news reports, it must have seemed that every refugee in the world was making straight for the United States, but this was far from true. According to the United Nations High Commissioner for Refugees, about 12 million of the earth's people were seeking refuge in one country or another: Afghans in Pakistan; Palestinians in the Middle East; Cambodians in Thailand; Salvadorans in Mexico; Africans moving across that continent in search of relief from a withering drought (a quarter of the population of tiny Somalia, on the Indian Ocean, is made up of refugees from other African nations). Still, the notion of the United States as the world's refuge of choice was not without some basis in fact. In 1980 the U.S. took in twice as many refugees as the rest of the countries of the world *combined*, and it is doubtless true that if the Afghans, Cambodians, and others who settled elsewhere could have somehow come here, many of them would have.

America's desirability as a refuge from the ills and evils of the

world is due in large part to the warm welcome it has historically accorded refugees, a tradition that dates back to the nation's founding by Europeans fleeing religious persecution.
Whenever the peoples of the world have been displaced by politics or pestilence, it seems, the United States has managed to
find room for some of them, whether they have been fleeing a
Europe devastated by war, the Soviet invasion of Hungary, the
ascent of Fidel Castro, or the Communist victory in Indochina.
Since the end of World War II, in fact, the United States has
taken in more than 1 million displaced souls: 500,000 Cubans,
250,000 Indochinese, and hundreds of thousands of Nicaraguans, Chileans, Czechs, Poles, Hungarians, Armenians, and
Jews from Eastern Europe and the Soviet Union, for many of
whom California has replaced Israel as the promised land
(nearly one-fifth of California's 750,000 Jewish residents are recent émigrés). Like the Jews, most of those seeking refuge here
were escaping from armed conflicts or some sort of postwar political convulsion, but with the advent of the 1980's, the world
has begun to see a new species of refugee: the refugee from
starvation.

As the global economy stumbles, as inflation rises and
productivity falls, as the growth of the world's population out-
strips its ability to distribute food supplies, people are beginning to run from hunger as surely as from bullets and bombs.
John Oakes put it this way in *The New York Times:* "What is
new, and becoming rapidly more dangerous, is the rate of population growth in the most impoverished countries; exhaustion
of renewable resources in the most overpopulated countries;
and susceptibility to demagogic exploitation in the most unde-
veloped countries. This fatal convergence is not only a threat to
world peace but, if unchecked, an almost assured promise of
world convulsion." It may not be overstating the matter to say
that the long-range future trend in the movement of the earth's
people will no longer be along political lines from East to West
but along economic ones from South to North.

Ordinarily the accelerating movement of refugees around the
world would not be a major source of concern for U.S. policy
planners. The flow of refugees has always been accepted as the
single element of the immigration equation over which the
most control can be exerted. As is not the case with illegal

aliens, the number of refugees admitted by the United States was thought to be a matter to be determined in Washington. How, after all, could any refugee hope to come here, much less stay, unless at the express invitation of the American government? Refugees, by definition, were those who had made their way from their homelands to a temporary host country—known as the country of first asylum—and whose subsequent appeals for refugee status in the United States could then be carefully considered before they were allowed to proceed. But in the spring of 1980 this tidy theory of refugee resettlement collapsed utterly and completely when tens of thousands of Cubans and Haitians chose the United States as their country of first asylum, then piled into boats and came here.

Dick Gullage may have been the first to see them coming. In mid-April 1980 Gullage, the deputy chief of the INS's big Miami office, had picked up a rumor that "a couple of boats" from Florida had landed in Cuba, bearing cases of food for thousands of Cubans who had crowded onto the grounds of the Peruvian embassy in Havana in a bid for political asylum. The word now was that Fidel Castro was preparing to send a few of the dissidents back to Key West on the empty boats. "Boy," Gullage said, "if he does that, we're going to have every boat in South Florida on the way to Cuba, if they figure they can get their relatives out that way. If Castro does it for two, he'll do it for two hundred." Or, as it turned out, for 125,000.

A week or so before, more than 10,000 Cubans had stormed through the gates of the Peruvian embassy and had refused to leave until their safe conduct out of the country was assured; the incident was becoming an increasing embarrassment for the image-conscious Castro. As the unhappy Cubans remained barricaded on the embassy's grounds, a consortium of several Western Hemisphere countries began trying to work out arrangements to fly the dissidents to Costa Rica, which had agreed to serve as country of first asylum, and from there to several other countries, including the United States, which had agreed to take 3,500 of the refugees. But before the planning for the evacuation could be completed, Castro preempted it, deftly turning his problem into a problem for the United States by opening the Cuban port of Mariel, about twenty miles west of Havana, to the would-be exiles. If they wanted to leave Cuba so

51

badly, to forsake their role in his grand collectivist experiment, Castro seemed to be saying, then Cuba did not want them—let their families and friends in America come and take them away.

For many of the hundreds of thousands of Cuban-Americans who had fled to the United States since Castro assumed power, the first reports of the Mariel opening appeared to offer a slim chance, but one that might never come again, to be reunited with loved ones they had not seen, in some cases, for twenty years. In Miami, in New Orleans, in New York and Union City, New Jersey, wherever the Cuban-Americans had settled, they began making arrangements to go to Key West, the tiny island at the southernmost tip of America, to find out if the news was true. On Monday, April 21, the two boats Dick Gullage had heard about, the *Dos Hermanos* and the *Blanche II*, docked at Key West with forty-eight of the Cubans from the Peruvian embassy aboard. They were followed by a sixty-six-foot shrimper, the *Big Baby* out of Galveston, which had left Key West the day before and had returned with another 200 dissidents. As the word of the arrivals flashed across the country, the race to Mariel was on. When the sun came up over Key West the next morning, Highway 1, the causeway that runs from Miami through the slender chain of the Florida Keys, was clogged with autos towing everything from puny outboards to palatial cabin cruisers.

Key West wasn't ready. A week or so before, the last winter tourists had packed their bags, and the island was laying itself back to greet the slow, hot tropical summer, the time when the bartenders and waiters who service the winter trade quit their jobs and begin putting their boats back in shape. Now, in just a day, the lazy stillness had been shattered by a full-fledged invasion of Cubans, sightseers, boat owners, and a battalion of journalists who figured that something important was about to happen. Key West had seen nothing like it since 1962, when 5,000 American troops were dispatched there at the height of the Cuban missile crisis. Hotels that had been a quarter full at the same time the year before were suddenly filled to capacity. Supermarket shelves were quickly denuded by boat owners, provisioning their craft with cases of everything from canned beer to canned beans. Restaurants hastily added extra staff and began staying open around the clock to handle the overflow crowds, and within hours the inevitable commemorative T-shirt had made its appearance. FREEDOM BOATLIFT, it read. KEY WEST TO CUBA, 1980.

In hopes of staving off what it sensed, however dimly, might be the beginnings of a foreign and domestic policy disaster, Washington announced that any Americans who sailed their boats to Cuba and returned with some of the refugees were breaking the immigration laws and risked both sizable fines and the seizure of their boats. The warning, if not unheard, went unheeded. By Wednesday, April 23, the first rank of what would become a flotilla of thousands of boats on the Cuba to Mariel sealift was docking at the sun-bleached Key West naval base, their bedraggled-looking passengers stumbling down the gangplanks to the cheers of hundreds of Cuban-American families crowding the docks. For every boat that arrived, a dozen others were weighing anchor for Cuba.

The first contingent of refugees was shepherded into the converted USO building near the naval base, abandoned by the Pentagon in 1974, that had been pressed into emergency service as a reception center. After the 100-mile journey across the choppy Straits of Florida more than a few of the new arrivals looked pale and a little ill. The center was the scene of reunions both joyful and tearful, flurries of *abrazos* and *bassos*. But the families of most of the Marielitos, as the refugees were already being called, had not yet made their way to Florida, and for those like eighteen-year-old Adolfo there was no welcome to America. Adolfo was not expecting an *abrazo*: He had left the only family he had back in Cuba. In sad Spanish, he told of his sorrow at watching while his mother and nine brothers tried, without success, to join him on the grounds of the Peruvian embassy before the big iron gates swung closed. The nine days he spent crowded into the embassy's small compound had been pure hell—for the last week, he said, there had been no food at all—and when he finally climbed aboard the boat at Mariel, Adolfo understood that he would probably never see Cuba or his family again. Even so, he was glad to be in America, "for the *libertad*," he said. "There is no liberty in Cuba." Like Adolfo, most of those in the refugee center had been among the throngs at the Peruvian embassy. But a handful had not been there, and although the significance of this was not immediately apparent, to say the least, what it meant was that Fidel Castro was now releasing not just the asylum seekers but others who wanted to leave Cuba—and, as it would turn out, tens of thousands of Cubans whom he himself wished to be rid of.

The Justice Department, still hoping to dissuade the boat owners from making the trip to Cuba, announced that it planned to fine every captain $1,000 for each refugee he brought back. But the second threat made no more difference than the first. By noon on Thursday more than 600 boats, mostly local shrimpers chartered by wealthy Cubanos from Miami and a few smaller pleasure craft not really suited to such a voyage, had set out for Mariel from Key West. "They don't care," said Frank Veliz, the Key West harbormaster, with a shrug. "It's their family and friends they're going to pick up, and they'll worry about the fines when they get back." For most of those in the boatlift, bringing back their loved ones was the overwhelming consideration, but by now the spectacle had also attracted profiteers. One, giving his boat a final check in its berth at Garrison Bight, near the Key West Yacht Club, said he had "a couple of deals working" with Cuban-American families who had no boats of their own. They had offered him $4,000 to make the trip to Cuba, the man said, and he was not the least bit worried about the government's ultimatum. "If anybody asks me," he said, smiling, "I was just out fishing and I picked up these people out of the water after their boat sank." His price was cheap. That being quoted by other captains on the docks was running to $1,000 and more for each passenger brought back from Cuba. One young man with a fifty-foot cruiser pocketed $23,000 in cash from a group of families, and the owner of a larger charter fishing boat took in $75,000.

The trip from Key West to Mariel should have taken no more than twelve hours. But with nearly 1,000 boats clogging Mariel Harbor there was now a three-day wait to take on passengers. Then, on Friday, the weather turned bad. Despite warnings from the Coast Guard, another 200 boats had set out for Cuba that morning, and while the first boats to leave Mariel had been mostly owned and operated by Cuban-American lobstermen who could sail the Florida Straits blindfolded, there were now hundreds of Sunday sailors chugging their powerboats across

54

the dangerous waters. Roland Isnor knew the situation was ripe for a disaster, and he was very worried. Until that point Isnor, the ordinarily cheerful young executive officer at the Key West Coast Guard station, had thought he had pretty good duty. Key West is a pleasant place, and the Coast Guard's principal function there is chasing, and usually losing, the high-powered "cigarette boats" that run marijuana and other countercultural substances into shore from the big Colombian and Panamanian mother ships anchored out at sea. But as the increasingly heavy winds whipped what had been placid seas into waves of ten feet or more, the small Coast Guard station was being swamped with distress calls. "A lot of people are just buying boats and heading off," Isnor said, shaking his head. "Some are going in the wrong direction. Some run aground or get dead batteries or run out of gas, and they call us to come pick them up." The main problem, he said, was that most of the captains "don't have any experience beyond how to turn the engine on." The two Coast Guard cutters stationed at Key West, the *Diligence* and the *Cape York,* were zigzagging madly through capsized boats in the straits to pluck wet sailors out of the water. Three cutters from other stations were steaming full ahead toward Key West, and Coast Guard helicopters from Miami were making continuous patrols; but the chaos was still more than they could handle. "There are so many boats out there the Coast Guard just can't keep track of them," Isnor said.

While thousands of Cuban-Americans were making their way to Mariel or riding impatiently at anchor in Mariel Harbor, thousands more were spending their days, and much of their nights, scouring the docks in search of a captain with a boat—any boat—for charter. Luis, Juan, Gerardo, Rolando, Alberto, and José were six among the thousands who had come to Key West with their life savings in their pockets and a single dream: to see again the mothers, fathers, brothers, and sisters they had left behind in Cuba.

Luis and his group had no boat, and for them the consuming search was particularly grim. They had raised only $6,000 among them, half the going rate, and in the manic confusion of deals being made, broken, and remade, of tempers flaring into arguments and arguments into fistfights, of briefcases filled with tens of thousands of dollars in cash being passed from hand to hand, their money and their pleas for a vessel had gone all but unnoticed. There had been a moment of hope on Thursday afternoon, when the owner of a big boat at Marathon Key, fifty miles away, agreed to bring it to Key West and take them to Cuba. The six men, strangers whose common quest had made them friends, waited for the boat until well after midnight, but it never came, the owner having struck a deal with someone else for more money. Near where they waited in vain, John Gedart, a seventy-five-year-old retired carpenter from Cooperstown, New York, worked on his aging sailboat, the *Hilda Gerard*. It was past midnight, and Gedart was just heading home to bed when, on an impulse, Luis walked up and offered him the $6,000. For a long moment the old captain did not reply. The *Hilda Gerard*, a fifty-one-foot two-masted schooner built in Canada, had been a fine, fast boat in her day, but her day was a quarter century ago. Gedart had been working long hours to restore her, but it would be some time yet before she was up to a trip to Cuba. Her new sails had not even been fitted. Still, Gedart thought, $6,000 was probably more than the *Hilda Gerard* was worth, and the money would pay for a lot of repairs. He spoke with his wife and daughter, who had stepped down from the boat to see what the stranger wanted. Then, not without great misgivings, he agreed to make the trip. Gedart knew that what he was about to do was against the law, that he stood to lose twice the $6,000 in fines if the government carried out its threat. But like the other captains, he could not believe that it would, and he could surely use the money.

Luis and his friends were ecstatic. They had been waiting and watching while so many boats left, and now their frustration was at an end. The money was handed over. The boxes of food and jugs of water they had brought were loaded aboard the *Hilda Gerard* to sustain them for what was now reported to be a weeklong wait in the harbor at Mariel—and, they desperately hoped, to feed their relatives on the trip home. At noon the next day, to shouts of *"Arriba, Cuba,"* the *Hilda Gerard* eased away from the dock and into the glassy Key West Harbor at a sedate four knots. The bigger, faster boats plowing the sea around her could cover the distance to Mariel in ten hours, but it would take the *Hilda Gerard*, whose tiny engine would have to battle the Gulf Stream, the better part of two days to make the trip. There were also some advantages. Unlike many of the captains leaving for Cuba, John Gedart knew the Florida Straits and the Cuban port—he had sailed these waters as a young man—and Luis thought that going to pick up his family in a sailboat was somehow "more romantic."

The straits were also well known to some of the passengers. Alberto had escaped from Cuba in 1969 on a raft he had made out of inner tubes and had got far out to sea before he was caught by a Cuban patrol boat, taken home, and put in jail. He had left Cuba for good four months before under a government grant of amnesty, and now he was going back for his sister. Juan was even luckier. The raft he left Cuba on ten years before had made it all the way to Florida, and he was going in search of the two teenaged sons he had not seen since then. As the *Hilda Gerard* slid into the harbor channel, she was joined by the big, sleek Hatteras and Bertram cruisers, air horns blasting as they raced toward open sea, that had been hired by those with much more money. The sea lanes this day were a superhighway, and the bright sun, the smooth turquoise sea, the white-tipped waves, and the shouts of *hermano* ("brother") from those aboard the boats lent the scene the festive air of a regatta at Newport or Palm Beach. There was even an omen for a safe voyage: a school of dolphins that appeared briefly to dance across the waves. But as afternoon faded into evening, the other boats passed the *Hilda Gerard* by, and she found herself struggling alone against the swelling sea. The wind had picked up, and so had the waves, some of them now six feet high. In the last hour his boat had gone only two miles, and Captain John, as he had become known to his passengers, was worried. Gedart looked first at the darkening sky and then at his instruments. His boat was using too much fuel. He had tried to buy a reserve before leaving Key West; but he could find only an extra thirty-five gallons, and now that would not be enough.

An attempt to save fuel by hoisting the foresail failed, and there was also trouble with the rudder. The waves were topping eight feet and sometimes ten, and the *Hilda Gerard* was being tossed so badly from port to starboard that she was traveling farther sideways than straight ahead. Captain John knew his boat, what she could do and what she could not, and he knew she could not reach Cuba this day. Sadly he went to his passengers to tell them that he was turning back. *"Mucho peligro,"* he said. "Much danger."

Luis and the others were disbelieving at first, then angry. The prospect of finally seeing their families was overwhelming, and when the six men gathered for a conference at the bow, the talk was of mutiny. "We can take it," Alberto said in Spanish. "We can take it to Cuba."

But Juan, a mechanic by trade, pointed to the four-cylinder engine and shook his head. "Too little power," he said.

The others said nothing. They had been beaten by the sea, and now they knew it.

As the *Hilda Gerard* came about and pointed her prow into the breathtaking Key West sunset, Rolando put his head in his arms and wept softly. José, his mouth set in a thin line, re-treated to the stern and remained silent. Gerardo stared out to sea toward Cuba. Ten hours after she had departed, the schooner sailed back into Key West Harbor. A police car on the dock, its blue light flashing, mistook those aboard for arriving refugees. "Go to the naval base to land," its loudspeaker blared. "You must submit to inspection." For Luis, it was the final defeat. "I'm quitting," he said. "I'm going home to wait for a more civilized way to bring my family to Miami." But Juan remained undaunted. The previous Monday, he had made it out seventeen miles in a motorboat before the motor stopped. On the *Hilda Gerard* he had traveled twice that far. Perhaps the next day he would make it all the way to Cuba. Gradually his spirit began to revive the others. Rolando thought he might have a better chance on one of the boats that were now leaving directly from Miami and said he would try that. The four others agreed to return to the docks at Key West in the morning and try their luck again. Then Captain John broke the bad news. His wife had put their $6,000 in the bank, and it was now Friday night and the bank was closed. He could not give the money back until it opened again on Monday morning, but by then anything might have happened: There might be no boats left to charter, the Coast Guard might have begun a blockade, the Cuban government might have halted the exodus. Silently, their heads down, Luis and the others picked up their bags, walked off the *Hilda Gerard,* and went their separate ways into the tropical night.

Most of the boats were not so unlucky. A week after the sealift began, more then 2,800 refugees had been ferried from Cuba to Key West, where the island's small contingent of 10 INS officers was working around the clock to process them. For lack of any other alternative, the INS had decided at the beginning of the sealift to admit the Cubans to the United States as "conditional entrants" for sixty days, during which time their requests for political asylum would be considered. At least that was the theory. No one had anticipated anything like the number of refugees that were now arriving, and the immigration service had begun frantically rounding up its troops—INS investigators from Chicago and Detroit, Border Patrol agents from El Paso and San Ysidro, anyone who spoke Spanish and was not nailed down—and putting them aboard airplanes for Key West. It was only after they arrived that the agents, used to conversing with Mexicans, discovered that they could not understand the much faster-talking Cubans.

Since the ascent of Fidel Castro two decades before, South Florida had become a stronghold of virulent anticommunism; and because the general tendency among Cuban exiles there was to assume that anyone leaving Cuba was leaving for the right reasons, the first refugees were welcomed with open arms by the exiles, who not only donated tons of food and truckloads of clothing but left their jobs and families to work long hours as unpaid volunteers at the reception center to help smooth the refugees' arrival. The INS needed all the help it could get. The boatlift was gaining momentum by the day, and as it entered its second week, another boat was being launched from the Key West marina every ten minutes. To make matters worse, some of the returning captains were not landing at the naval base but, hoping to avoid being fined, putting in at one of the dozens of small private docks and wharves that dot the Florida Keys. The INS knew what they were doing, but it had nobody to go after them: It was all the INS and its volunteers could do to manage the influx at the naval base, where things were on the verge of chaos.

As each boat docked, disembarking passengers were herded

through a metal detector to check for hidden weapons, handed a cold Coca-Cola from a large bin, and then guided to the processing center, where a large sign on the wall assured them that CUANDO UN PUEBLO EMIGRA, LA TIRANIA TIEMBLA ("When a people emigrate, tyranny trembles"). With the help of one of the Cuban-American volunteers, each refugee filled out an INS form attesting to his or her arrival in the United States and was then guided to an INS officer for some perfunctory questioning: "Are you alone or with your family? Do you have relatives or friends in America?" If relatives were waiting, the refugee was released in their custody. If not, they remained wards of the U.S. government, which was fast running out of places to put them. Those with minor illnesses were seen to on the spot by a volunteer corps of Cuban-American doctors; more serious cases were taken to the local hospital. The others were given their first meal in America—a sandwich and a piece of fruit— then loaded aboard buses that took them to the Key West airport for transportation to the resettlement camp that had just been opened at Eglin Air Force Base in the Florida Panhandle.

Through it all, the Carter administration could not make up its mind how to respond to what had begun barely a week before as a trickle of political refugees but had now assumed the proportions of a mass exodus. On the one hand, the refugees were clearly coming in violation of the law, and not to dissuade them by ordering the Coast Guard to blockade the Florida Straits amounted to an admission that the administration's already haphazard immigration policy was a complete shambles. On the other hand, the public spectacle of thousands of Cubans fleeing communism, now available for viewing on television sets around the world, seemed to be a propaganda coup of the first order. The government's inability to decide whether to denounce the Cuban invasion or to encourage it created a paralyzing schizophrenia—on the same day that fines assessed against returning boat captains topped the $3 million mark, Vice President Walter Mondale was heralding the exodus as clear proof of "the failure of Castro's revolution."

It was now clear to officials in Key West, if not yet to those in Washington, that it was no longer just the refugees from the Peruvian embassy who were on the way to America. In order to bring back the friends and relatives they had gone for, returning boat captains were now saying, the Cuban authorities were requiring them to take on other passengers as well—some of them apparently criminals, homosexuals, and the mentally disturbed, whom the Castro government wanted to get rid of. Castro's use of the boatlift to cart away the refuse of Cuban society was still largely obscured, however, by the fact that like seventeen-year-old Leonor Chávez, most of the arrivals seemed to be genuine refugees from Castro's communism.

Leonor's odyssey had begun at five o'clock one morning the week before, when a nurse shook her awake as she lay sleeping in a Havana hospital room. Her baby was not yet due, and the abrupt awakening left the young woman confused until the nurse explained that Benito, her boyfriend, was waiting outside. When Benito walked in and announced that they were going to live in America, Leonor's confusion gave way to disbelief, but as he talked, she began to understand. It seemed that her twenty-eight-year-old brother, Germano, who lived in Miami, had come to Cuba on a fishing boat and given the authorities the names of Benito and Leonor; Pedro, her father; and her brothers Miguel and José as those he wanted to take back to America. Earlier that morning the police had come to the house where the couple lived and announced that they should get ready to leave Cuba at once. It had all happened very quickly.

At first Leonor was uncertain, but Benito told her she was crazy. He wanted very much to go to America, where he was sure he could find something better than the job he had in a Havana restaurant. Of course, she must come, too. Leonor checked out of the hospital and went home to pack her favorite clothes. For four days they waited at Mariel, hardly daring to sleep for fear that they would not hear their names when they were called for boarding. But when the call finally came, they did hear it, and as she lay exhausted on a mattress at the crowded refugee center in Key West, Leonor spoke of how she felt about leaving Cuba. She loved her country, she said, but not the government. In America she hoped to find the freedom she had lacked at home. Freedom—it was the same answer given countless times by the thousands of refugees who had stepped onto the Key West docks in the eight days the boatlift had been under way. But the freedom Leonor sought was largely economic.

Slowly, as if testing her newfound ability to tell a stranger frankly what was on her mind, Leonor ran through her complaints against Cuban communism: only one ounce of meat each week for her and Benito together, and only twice that much coffee; their diet had been mainly rice and beans. The government kept promising more and better food, but the promises were never realized. Nor had she been able to buy the things that, in America, were considered facts of ordinary life: a refrigerator, an air conditioner, an automobile. In Cuba she and Benito could afford none of those. Then, while she was pregnant, the government had ordered Leonor into the countryside to pick tomatoes. She had refused, hardly believing that the authorities would ask such a thing of an expectant mother. Moreover, she said, her brother Miguel had been a political prisoner. He had spent six months in jail, and for what? The police said he had stolen some clothes from a store, but that was not the real reason. It was that he sometimes told people he didn't like the government, that he wanted to leave Cuba. Even though Leonor had been born in 1963, four years after the success of Castro's revolution, she was certain that life in Cuba must have been better before; she didn't blame Miguel for saying what he said.

But wasn't there free health care for everyone in Cuba now, and free education? Weren't the buses and the public telephones also free? Hadn't she and Benito paid only $15 a month for their five-room house with its pleasant little patio, the kind of house that in Miami might cost them $500 a month or more? Did she know that even some Cubans who had lived a long time in Miami were having trouble finding work? Yes, Leonor said, she knew all that. But Benito had earned only $93 a month in Cuba. He would get a job in Miami; he was a good worker; he would make much more money; they would be all right. Most important, they would be in America, where Leonor had dreamed of one day going to live. Until the previous year these had been simply dreams, translucent images that floated across the night on the Spanish-language broadcasts from Miami, but then Germano's wife, Oneida, had come to Cuba to visit. Leonor remembered Oneida's clothes, her hairstyle, her jewelry, remembered listening as Oneida spoke of her life in America. After that it was more than just a dream; it was a life Leonor wanted, too.

Leonor's American life began when the *Capt. J.H.*, the Key West shrimp boat that had carried Germano Chávez to Cuba, arrived back home with more than 180 passengers on board, among them Benito, Leonor, her father and brothers—and six-pound, three-ounce Carlos Chávez, born at sea.

When the *Capt. J.H.* left Mariel, the harbor was full. The delay in taking on passengers had grown longer as the boats that now arrived by the hundreds each day were prevented from leaving by the storm, and none was more anxious to get under way than the *Viking Starship*, a huge charter fishing boat that had been one of the first vessels from Florida to arrive. A group of Cuban families from Miami had hired the *Starship* for $16,000 a day to bring their relatives back from Cuba, and the log kept by her captain, a taciturn twenty-eight-year-old named Bill Grimm, provided a dramatic record of the *Starship*'s choppy, twenty-hour voyage to Mariel, the maddening frustration of six days at anchor, and, finally, her dispirited trip home without the relatives she had gone for.

The voyage did not have an auspicious beginning. The crossing to Mariel had passed without incident, but the *Starship* had been in port only ten minutes when Cuban soldiers scrambled aboard, an event that Captain Grimm recorded tersely in his log. "Boarded by military," he wrote. "List of regulations —passport check and number—inform them we are licensed to carry 145 passengers." The *Starship*, Grimm is told, is the one hundred seventeenth craft to arrive, and there will be a wait before she can be loaded. In the meantime, the stern-faced Cuban officer says, her crew is not to take pictures of the harbor, to fish, or to leave the boat for any reason, not even to swim in the harbor. Most important, there is to be no radio communication with the other vessels. The Cubans do not want some kind of spontaneous counterrevolution hatched within walking distance of Havana.

At six o'clock Friday morning the soldiers are back, this time for the names of the 100 Cubans the *Starship* has been commissioned to carry to America. Police officers will try to find them; but that will take time, and there is another problem. "Military informs us they won't let us leave unless we take 200 passengers," writes Grimm. "We have no say." The Cubans are not tolerating any breach of regulations. At eight o'clock, when a crewman from one of the other boats dives into the harbor for a swim, soldiers cradling automatic weapons emerge from the bushes along the shore. The swimmer quickly leaves the water. The day passes slowly, and toward nightfall Captain Grimm decides to cruise the harbor in search of news. "Buy two cases of rum," he writes, "make rounds of other boats." But the news is not good anywhere. "Lots of boats haven't been boarded, have not received numbers." It looks like a long wait. Mariel Harbor is packed solid with boats, and only a handful, those, like the *Capt. J.H.*, that arrived much earlier in the week, have left with any passengers aboard. "Running short on food and water," Grimm writes. "Start to ration, no showers."

By Sunday morning some of the boats have been idle for four or five days. Their crews are beginning to chafe, and the Cuban authorities are also growing impatient. "Cuban officers very nasty," Grimm's log reads. "All boats that left yesterday are still sitting at the mouth of the harbor. No loading. Beginning to look like trouble." Now the Cubans tell Grimm that the *Starship* will carry not 200 passengers back to Florida, but 350, "and possibly leave tonight, or 0600 Monday." The news cheers Grimm and his crew, but by seven o'clock Monday morning nothing has happened. "Still waiting," the log reads. "Boats still coming in. They don't realize no one allowed to leave—like prisoners."

Grimm begins to think about forgetting the relatives altogether and making a run for open sea. But the northwestern sky is growing dark, and besides, he writes, "various boats have tried to leave and had guns pointed at them and ordered to return." Late Monday night the Cuban government sends a placating message to the boats at Mariel. The suspension of departures, it says, was only a precaution because of the weather. "No one here is a prisoner," writes Captain Grimm. "Anyone that wants to leave is free to do so." Early the next morning two small boats do leave, but they are empty, their crews having tired of the wait, run out of food, or both. By noon, however, there is a sign that the departure of the refugees may finally be under way. At twelve-thirty four boats pull out, overflowing with passengers. Captain Grimm is more eager now than ever to be gone, and at one-thirty he sets out to investigate the delay. "Went ashore with a couple of the Cubans to find out what was going on," he writes. "*MV Solana* was loading refugees—four more busloads came in. No *Viking* people on them. We talked to the colonel and a major—our passengers are supposedly in a concentration camp. They are supposed to be on the next buses." By seven o'clock nothing has happened. "Don't know when our passengers are coming," Grimm writes. "The Cuban runaround." The night seems to last forever, and when the sun comes up over Mariel, more than 3,000 boats surround the *Viking Starship*, and the stream of arrivals is unabated. At eight another 66 boats arrive in one group.

Concession stands have sprung up on the docks, selling supplies to the increasing number of vessels that have exhausted their provisions. "Big business," Captain Grimm writes. "Hundreds of people shopping. Prices sky high. Water $20 for five gallons. Carton cigs, $20." Cuban rum is only $5 a bottle, but American liquor is $35. At seven forty-five the *Starship* sends a final, desperate message to shore: "We must leave NOW." An hour later the long-awaited call to take on passengers finally comes. The *Viking Starship* kicks over her two huge Mercedes-Benz diesels and eases toward the dock. But when she arrives, none of the relatives of the families who chartered her are waiting. They could not be found, the Cuban officials say; perhaps they are already on another boat. Instead, Captain Grimm is told, the *Starship* will be bringing back 420 passengers chosen by the Cuban government.

Wearily Grimm gives his assent, and one by one, the disheveled Cubans climb aboard and settle into the plush reclining chairs in the *Starship*'s main salon that is usually the familiar ground of well-heeled sportsmen. By one o'clock the loading has been completed, and ten minutes later the *Viking Starship* clears the dock at Mariel. By three she has passed the twelve-mile limit and is out of Cuban waters and on the way home, loaded to nearly four times her capacity. In the galley, food is broken out, and the refugees are given ham and cheese sandwiches. Some tell the crew it is the first time in twenty years they have tasted ham.

It was just before midnight when the *Starship* finally pulled into a slip at the Key West naval base and cut her engines. Exhausted Border Patrol agents who had been at work since eight o'clock that morning began assembling her passengers on the dock. Many of them, it turns out, had been taken from a Havana prison that same morning and put aboard buses for Mariel without the slightest idea of where they were going, or why. They are having a little trouble understanding that they are now in America. In any event, Castro's intentions were now unmistakable. He was emptying his jails into South Florida.

The families who chartered the *Viking Starship* got neither their relatives nor their $16,000 back. They will never know whether it was true, as the Cuban police said, that the relatives could not be located. The *Starship*, which could have taken in more than that from a week of fishing trips, also lost money. ''If I had it to do over again, I wouldn't,'' says a disgusted Bill Grimm. Neither would the ship's owners. The next morning they were notified by the Treasury Department that they were being fined $1,000 for each of the Cubans they were forced to bring home—a total of $420,000, the largest fine assessed during the entire Mariel boatlift.

As the storm, which at the height of its fury had sunk at least thirty boats, gave way to calm seas and blue skies, the thousands of boats delayed in Cuba by the bad weather began streaming back to Key West, so many of them at once that five amphibious ships from the U.S. naval base at Guantánamo Bay were sent to help the Coast Guard control the rush-hour traffic in the Florida Straits. In just eleven days the number of refugees to leave Cuba had reached 10,000, prompting the now thoroughly alarmed Carter administration to send civil defense disaster teams from the Federal Emergency Management Agency (FEMA), whose main mission is to deal with the aftermath of a nuclear attack, to handle arrangements for food and shelter at Key West and Eglin and to begin searching for facilities for more resettlement camps. Another measure of Washington's alarm was that for the first time the INS began suggesting publicly that not all the Cubans were genuine refugees—that, as Bill Grimm already knew, some might not be coming to America of their own accord. It was by no means certain, the INS was saying now, that all requests for political asylum would be approved, but the agency did not say what it might do with the Cubans who were not granted asylum. In the two decades since Castro took power, the INS had been unable to deport a single Cuban back to Cuba, which would not accept the expatriates.

Those refugees who acknowledged having a felony record in Cuba were being sent to the minimum security federal correctional institution in Miami. Partly in recognition of the increasingly inescapable reality that it was stuck with the Marielitos and partly in keeping with President Carter's early and ill-advised promise that the United States would greet the refugees "with an open heart and open arms," the INS began giving those Cubans not locked up in jail halfhearted briefings about the history and customs of the country that looked as if it were going to be their new home. It also gave them new Social Security cards, $100 in pocket money, and help with such basics of American life as opening bank accounts. There was some question about how soon they would be able to make their first deposits. By May 5, two weeks after the first boat from Mariel had arrived at Key West, the Cuban refugees in Florida numbered more than 15,000, and several thousand boats were still waiting at Mariel to take on passengers. Ominously, more than half the arriving refugees were without family or friends in the United States willing to take them in—many of the friendless ones had simply run into the Peruvian embassy on an impulse, never thinking they would end up in Florida. The others were the *gusanos* ("worms"), the misfits Castro had discarded. Whatever they were, Washington was not about to turn them loose to walk the streets. When disaster officials at Eglin protested that they could warehouse no more bodies, the FEMA teams began opening more refugee camps in whatever facilities they could find—the Orange Bowl stadium in Miami; a blimp hangar in Opa-Locka; hastily requisitioned army bases at Fort Chaffee, Arkansas; Fort McCoy, Wisconsin; and Fort Indiantown Gap, Pennsylvania.

The mentally disturbed, petty criminals deemed not dangerous enough for prison, and the other "undesirables" were thrown in with genuine refugees, nearly 1,000 of them children who had joined the boatlift without their parents and who, it turned out, were not old enough to apply legally for political asylum. It was a formula for trouble. When riots broke out at Fort Chaffee, four of the converted army barracks used to house the refugees were set on fire and more then 50 people were hurt. Hundreds of Cubans broke out of the camp and set out for the nearby town of Fort Smith, Arkansas, where residents loaded their rifles and promised to use them if the Cubans made it into town. The refugees were rounded up in time. There were similar disturbances at some of the other camps, and when the instigators could be singled out, they were sent to the already crowded INS detention centers in El Paso, Brooklyn, and Port Isabel, Texas. When some of the Marielitos at El Paso were denied second helpings at dinner one night, they rioted again and ended up in the Pecos County jail.

By August 1980 nearly 100,000 of the Cubans had been released to sponsors, but more than 20,000 remained in federal custody in the five camps; sponsors were becoming increasingly difficult to find, largely because of the wide publicity given the Fort Chaffee riots and such relatively minor incidents as the arrest of two refugees who had escaped from Fort Indiantown Gap and had broken into a home in a nearby town. The publicity was fueled by attention seekers like Robert McIntosh, a black candidate for lieutenant governor of Arkansas, who set up a bed outside the main gate at Fort Chaffee and posted a sign that read, SLEEP ON, AMERICA, WHILE THE CUBANS TAKE YOUR JOBS. Taking the cue, the Ku Klux Klan began holding anti-Cuban rallies outside the fort's main gate.

The unfortunate message that all of the Marielitos were bad news traveled fast. When the government announced plans to settle 2,000 of the Cubans from Chaffee in three East Texas towns that already had nearly 5,000 unemployed residents, the local reaction was furious. "We are basically a union town and a union area," said Joe Skipper, the Morris County sheriff. "The workers don't like the idea of these men taking their jobs." Added Jerry Pratt, a county judge: "We're all good, hard-working, God-fearing people, and we don't want the type of people we understand these people are." A worker at the local Lone Star steel plant said, "We just don't need no more people that don't speak English." The resettlement plan was quickly abandoned.

As if the INS were not having enough trouble finding places to put the Marielitos, an alarming number of the Cuban-American families who had agreed in the early anti-Castro fervor generated by the boatlift to sponsor one of the refugees were now withdrawing their sponsorship, leaving their charges homeless and jobless. Other prospective "sponsors" proved to be simply looking for cheap domestic help and thought that sponsoring one of the Marielitos would get them a cook or a maid. The owner of a topless bar in Orlando, Florida, signed up to sponsor seven young women; it turned out he was short of dancers. Some sponsors proved to be pimps hoping to add comely young Cuban women to their stables. The owner of a Texas manufacturing company who took six of the Cubans, gave them jobs, and then refused to pay them explained he thought that anyone who sponsored a refugee got free labor for six months.

What to do with the Cuban criminals was an even more serious problem. More than 1,700 of the refugees had admitted committing crimes in Cuba that would have qualified as felonies in this country, and another 15,000 had admitted to criminal records for lesser offenses, including homosexuality and various political crimes. The nation's federal penitentiaries were already badly crowded, but room for the felons was somehow found in Atlanta and McNeil Island, Washington, and there they languished. Under the immigration laws the criminals were technically "excludable"; had convicted felons from any other country attempted to enter the country, legally they could simply have been turned away. But the presence of the Cubans was a *fait accompli:* How could the INS keep someone who was already here from coming? These Cubans were, of course, still subject to deportation, but deportation to where? Cuba certainly would not take them back. "Obviously," said Dave Crosland, the INS acting commissioner, "we have to send them to a country that's willing to take them."

At the same time the United States was making up its mind that it was stuck with the Cuban criminals, it was also becoming aware that it might have locked up many of the wrong people. The criminals had been separated from the other refugees largely on the basis of interviews with Spanish-speaking INS and FBI agents at Key West, but it seemed that the nuances of some of their case histories had been lost in translation. Although a good number of the Marielitos in jail were, in fact, serious criminals, some of them murderers and rapists, it now seemed that more than a few of them had been convicted of such offenses as stealing food or clothing and probably did not present much danger to American society. Theodore Jakaboski, one of the immigration judges assigned to hear the asylum cases of the Cuban convicts, discovered that some of them had been jailed in Cuba solely because their fathers had been officials of the Batista government that Castro had overthrown and that convictions for juvenile or petty offenses in other cases had often been recorded by the FBI agents as felonies.

Far more disturbing, however, was Jakaboski's suspicion that many of the tougher, hardened criminals among the Marielitos had managed to avoid prison by simply not telling agents of their criminal histories and without access to police records in Cuba, how else were the agents to know? The magnitude of the oversight may have been enormous; the State Department's Cuban task force estimated later that the number of hard-core criminals among the Marielitos was possibly ten times the official figure of 2,000, and suggested, further, that as many as 40,000 of the Marielitos had had some kind of criminal record in Cuba. The possibility that in the confusion attending the boatlift the government had let incorrigible criminals go free seemed to be borne out by crime statistics. In Miami, where the bulk of the Marielitos had settled and where thousands had subsequently been turned out by their sponsors, the number of burglaries doubled and the violent crime rate jumped. By the end of 1981 a quarter of those in jail in Miami were Marielitos, and other cities were reporting similar statistics. Nearly 1,000 Marielitos were arrested in New York City during 1981, and half the 47 Cubans who settled in Amarillo, on the Texas Panhandle, were charged with such offenses as burglary, driving while intoxicated, and even rape.

Most Americans were convinced by now that anyone who had come from Mariel was a criminal, gay, or crazy, and the tens of thousands of Marielitos who had had genuine reasons for wanting to leave Cuba and were prepared to become productive members of American society were encountering an antipathy they had never expected. From Miami, where the food stamp office was taking on 200 new Marielitos a day, to Los Angeles, where nearly 6,000 of them were receiving welfare payments in one form or another, skilled Cubans with marketable trades—welders, carpenters, electricians—were finding it impossible to get jobs.

Fidel Castro, no doubt satisfied with the havoc the Cuban boatlift had wreaked, eventually closed the port of Mariel. When the last boat to leave docked at Key West, the tally of the Cuban refugees stood at close to 125,000, and the sorry episode represented a devastating setback for this country's relations with Cuba and for its immigration policy as well. The newly minted Refugee Act of 1980, which increased the number of refugees the United States was willing to accept each year from a paltry 17,400 to 50,000, had been widely applauded as an important and necessary reform. But just as the new law took effect, it had been devastated by the arrival of 125,000 Cubans, and Jimmy Carter had been presented with one of the most serious dilemmas of his presidency.

Carter had initially agreed to accept 3,500 Cubans from among the 10,000 who had sought asylum at the Peruvian embassy. He had ended up with all 10,000 and another 115,000 to boot, perhaps 40,000 of whom were in one way or another undesirable, and he could not send a single one of them back. Fidel Castro, whom no one had ever accused of being slow-witted, had turned a potential public relations disaster for his government into a genuine disaster for the United States, and under the circumstances Carter did the only thing he could do: He invoked the presidential parole power to "admit" the Cubans formally by overriding the immigration laws, then asked Congress to pass another law allowing those who were not locked up in jail to become permanent residents. In the end, the Carter administration's handling of what was by then being called the Cuban refugee crisis was so inept and halfhearted that it pleased almost nobody. And unnoticed in all the commotion at Key West another crisis was waiting just offstage. For while the nation's attention was riveted on the boats landing at Key West, other boats were limping ashore practically unnoticed on the beaches around Miami and Fort Lauderdale, and the passengers they carried were not refugees from Cuba but from the steamy, impoverished Caribbean island of Haiti.

The Haitians are America's other boat people, and they have been coming here for far longer than the Cubans. The first leaky sailboat to make the dangerous 600-mile voyage from Port-au-Prince, the Haitian capital, arrived in Florida in 1972. But it was not until 1978, when the Bahamas government, concerned about unemployment, began expelling thousands of Haitians who had sought refuge there, that their numbers in South Florida began to increase dramatically. Now, in the spring of 1980, several hundred more were arriving by boat every week on the golden beaches that lay within sight of the posh hotels and expensive condominiums along the Florida Gold Coast. Many of the refugees managed to sprint across the hot white sand and make their way to the Little Haiti section of Miami's all-black inner city without attracting the attention of immigration agents. Many others did not, but they ended up in Little Haiti anyway; after arresting and "processing" them, including physical examinations, the INS simply turned the Haitians loose in the city to await their deportation hearings.

The appearance of the gray army bus and its load of new arrivals from the INS processing facility was the event of the day in Miami's rapidly swelling Haitian community, and although the bus came at unpredictable times, word that it was on the way spread so quickly that when it finally pulled into view, dozens of Haitians had gathered in hopes of seeing someone they knew, perhaps even a relative, step off. Each night for nearly a week Antoine Charles had waited outside the seedy storefront community center for the bus to arrive, and on the fifth night of his vigil his persistence was rewarded. One of the first to climb down from the bus was his cousin Garry, who had landed in a homemade boat the Sunday before, the same day a record 700 Haitians had walked ashore on the beaches of South Florida. Garry looked apprehensive, his eyes scanning the crowd for a familiar face, but he was doubly lucky. Not only was his cousin Antoine waiting there, but with him was Jean-Claude, a friend from the old colonial capital of Cap-Haïtien.

Like most of the new arrivals, Garry had brought nothing

with him but the clothes he was wearing when he left: a faded green paisley shirt, tattered denim trousers, and a sorry pair of shoes. As he stepped inside the community center, a smiling black woman in a Red Cross uniform handed him a small bag filled with soap, deodorant, and a few other toilet articles. With his clothes, they marked the sum of his earthly possessions, but Garry was happy enough just to be alive and in Florida. As he sat on one of the center's backless benches, he spoke in excited Creole to Antoine and Jean-Claude of his agonizing journey from their homeland, of twenty-two seemingly endless days with 140 other people in a boat so small it had been impossible for him to lie down or stand up. For the first few days, he said, the voyage had reminded him of a movie he had seen about slave trafficking in the eighteenth century. But then the food on the boat ran out, and the water, and the movie dissolved into a horrid nightmare. Toward the end Garry watched as a passenger named François starved to death.

Garry had had no job in Haiti—not, he said, because he was lazy but because he had been out of favor with the Tontons Macoutes, the fearsome Haitian secret police who had once beaten him terribly. After ninety-six lashes with a whip, his left buttock was without any feeling. Garry had run away and hidden in the countryside for seven months, until he could arrange passage on one of the refugee boats. He knew, he said, that his prospects of finding work in Miami were not the best. Even if he could obtain a work permit from the immigration service, like most of his countrymen, Garry would still face a number of obstacles. Not only do most of the Haitian boat people speak no English or Spanish, the twin *linguas francas* of Miami, but most also are illiterate and bring only the barest of nineteenth-century agrarian skills to a city that, until recently, liked to think of itself as a place where the twenty-first century had arrived early.

At least half of Miami's Haitians have been unable to find work, and most of those who have must be content with washing dishes in restaurant kitchens. Twenty years ago Miami's Cubans worked in some of those same kitchens, and today they own the restaurants. But many of the Cubans were well-educated, experienced entrepreneurs before they came here; most of the Haitians had never seen a telephone or a flush toilet before arriving in Florida. Treated with disdain and contempt, isolated by their Creole patois that no one outside Haiti understands, the Haitians have settled in the middle of Miami's black inner city, where the only splashes of color against a dismal background of sun-bleached concrete are the bright reds, blues, and purples of its residents' native costumes.

At the refugee center near where Garry sat chatting with his cousin, the bulletin boards were filled with lists of available job openings, among them positions for secretaries, firemen, clerks, comptrollers, and chemists. But the notices were a bad joke; the Haitians who worked at the center as volunteers had difficulty operating the push-button telephones. Those who did find work in Miami had to settle for the worst jobs the city had to offer: hauling garbage, washing dishes, emptying bedpans. Thousands of Haitians who had gone north in search of work found themselves picking vegetables alongside Mexicans in Florida's winter produce belt or in the fields of eastern Maryland, living the primitive life of the migrant farmhand that was no better than what they had known in Haiti. Garry's job prospects might be grim in America but no grimmer than they had been at home, and at least the policemen in Miami did not carry whips.

Following his release by the INS, Garry was taken to the house in Little Haiti that his cousin Antoine shared with a group of other exiles. Inside, blankets had been hung from the ceiling to partition living spaces, and the strong, sharp fragrance of Creole cooking was everywhere. Over the clamor of *Mission: Impossible* reruns on a battered television set, Garry was greeted warmly and given a plate of *bouillon*, the watery Haitian soup that was the household's evening meal. It looked insubstantial, but Garry attacked it greedily. "It's been a long time since I've seen that kind of food," he said between mouthfuls.

Moise, one of Garry's new roommates, had lived in Miami for three years, surviving on occasional work as a house painter. But Moise's passion was another kind of painting, and the walls of his shabby room were hung with a bright array of primitive oils he had produced, many of them showing women picking cotton in the homeland of his memories. One of his better efforts, of which he was especially proud—it took him four days to finish—he offered to sell for $22, a fraction of what it would have brought in a New York gallery. But Moise did not know any gallery owners, so the painting and its companions added some badly needed color to the glum room.

The startling physical beauty reflected in Moise's paintings, the breathtaking green mountains and azure seas that serve as a backdrop for the most desperate poverty in the Western Hemisphere, remains vivid in the minds of most visitors long after they have departed that tortured island. But the tens of thousands Haitians like Garry, Antoine, and Moise who have fled their lush homeland for South Florida paint a starker verbal picture: of a frightened nation of 6 million caught in the grip of a government whose rule is enforced through extortion, terror, censorship, and arbitrary arrest. Among the signs that clutter the walls of the refugee center is a somber testament to the continuing struggle. EN HAITI, it reads, IL Y A DES CHOSES TERRIBLES QU'ON NE VOIR SUR LES AFFICHES TOURISTIQUES ("In Haiti, there are terrible things one does not see on the travel posters"). But Haiti's vital statistics also make grim reading: a life expectancy of 52 years, 150 babies out of every 1,000 dead in infancy, 4 out of 5 adults illiterate and trying to survive on annual incomes of less than $500, half the adult residents of Port-au-Prince without work and the other half earning an average of $2 a day. So insensitive is the Haitian government both to world opinion and to the suffering of its people that Jean-Claude "Baby Doc" Duvalier, the country's baby-faced president for life, had no qualms about spending more then $1 million on his gala wedding to a fashion model.

In deciding what to do with the Haitians, the INS had chosen to focus on Haiti's poverty, and at the same time it was paroling the Marielitos into the country, Washington was taking the position that the Haitians were coming to America not to escape political repression but to flee the country's shattered economy. No matter that the U.S. State Department had acknowledged Haiti as an authoritarian society—it was not a Communist one, and President Carter's promised welcome for the Marielitos would not be extended to the Haitians.

Washington, the leaders of the Haitian exile community in

Miami thought, had failed to grasp the subtleties of their situation, had failed to comprehend that in Haiti politics and economics were so intertwined that the only prospect for a young man who was not "in with the government" was to run and play in the mountains, to "catch a breeze." Many of the Haitians frankly admitted that they had come to Miami to look for jobs, but they also made the point that without paying tribute to the gun-toting Macoutes it was impossible to get any kind of job in Haiti. The Macoutes—the name punctuated nearly every conversation in Little Haiti, but it was always spoken softly— were essentially an unpaid volunteer police force. In return for their loyalty and protection the late Haitian dictator François "Papa Doc" Duvalier had allowed them to carry guns and given them what amounted to a license to extort money and property from the citizenry. If a Macoute wanted a new house, he simply rounded up several young men from the village and ordered them to build one. If he wanted your money, or your bicycle, or your chicken, or your daughter, you complied—or else for you there would be no money, no work, no food, perhaps no daughter. If you refused a second time, your life became worth little, but when you ran away to America, you became an economic refugee. How, the Haitians wondered, could the bureaucrats in Washington be expected to understand such things? There were also to be found in Miami Haitians who had had no apparent economic motive for leaving Haiti. One, a young man who gave his name only as Arthur (like the whisperers, he was convinced that Baby Doc had arms long enough to reach to Miami), said that in Haiti he had "lived in a nice, beautiful home in a place where you have no freedom, no freedom of speech, no freedom of the press, where you do not even say what you think or they will put you in jail." Arthur was living in a hovel in Miami, but he would never go home, he said, as long as Baby Doc was alive. His friend Christian, who was earning $80 a week bagging groceries in a Miami supermarket, agreed. He had made that much in a single day in Port-au-Prince as a guide for "rich American tourists," Christian said, but he had come to America anyway, "so I can talk. In my country, I cannot do it."

No one who was visited or studied Haiti in recent years has mistaken it for an open society, but the degree to which persecution and repression exist there today is a matter of contention. One American businessman who has traveled to Haiti for years says he has noticed "a tremendous relaxation of surveillance" since the death of François Duvalier in 1971. Under Jean-Claude, the man said, "there is still a certain degree of fear, but nothing like what it was under the father." Indeed, some small steps toward political liberalization in Haiti have been undertaken in recent years, but without much real effect. A brief period of freer speech ended in the fall of 1979 with the enactment of a strict press censorship law and the arrest of Sylvio Claude, the leader of a short-lived opposition political party. The dreaded Tontons Macoutes were officially dissolved and replaced by another paramilitary police organization, the Volontaires de la Sécurité Nationale (Volunteers for National Security), but the VSN counts many former Macoutes among its members. There were even a couple of human rights rallies in Haiti, but they stopped after American and other diplomats attending one were beaten by men armed with sticks who were later identified as from the VSN.

Yet Washington, ever concerned about the rise of yet another Communist government in the Caribbean and recognizing a prerevolutionary society when it saw one, continued to send the thoroughly corrupt Duvalier regime tens of millions of dollars in economic assistance each year. Still, continued American aid had been loosely linked to Baby Doc's promise to begin restoring some human rights, and the Haitian government, fearing that the flow of dollars might be threatened by the publicity surrounding the refugees, hired former Massachusetts Governor Endicott Peabody to plead its case before the American public. "The government of Haiti," Peabody said, "respects the basic right of any of its citizens who may aspire to come to America for whatever reason."

When Fénelon Rosemond heard about this, he laughed. His arrival in Miami a few months before, Rosemond said, had been his second try at an escape from Haiti. The first time, he said, the Tontons Macoutes had fired on the little sailboat in which he and his friends were crouching as they tried to make for open sea. The passengers, he said, were arrested and beaten. Rosemond escaped and was hidden by friends until a second voyage could be arranged. Peabody's remarks notwithstanding, Fénelon Rosemond wondered what the Macoutes would do to him if he were deported back to Haiti.

So did Amnesty International, the highly respected London-based human rights organization, which hotly disputed the claim by the Haitian government that those refugees who returned home would not be "prosecuted or detained for illegal departure." AI noted that it was illegal to leave Haiti without the government's permission, so that every Haitian now in America had already broken Haitian law. Political imprisonment and torture, the group asserted, were still taking place in Haiti, and AI would be concerned for the safety of any returning refugee until the administration of law there had been brought "into conformity with even minimal international standards."

The exiles in Miami were equally convinced that those of their countrymen who had been forcibly returned home by the INS were being punished severely. One, Max Julien, said his brother had been arrested and imprisoned for four months at the notorious Fort Dimanche prison after being deported by the INS. Jean Louis, another refugee who had actually been a member of the Tontons Macoutes, said he had received "standing government orders that anyone and everyone deported back to Haiti was to be arrested and imprisoned.

"The rationale," Louis said, "is that if you left Haiti, you must be against the government. Many die in prison, and the length of stay in jail varies from weeks to months to years. If the person survives."

As they wait for the outcome of their deportation hearings, the Haitians huddle in the shabby bungalows of Little Haiti, a ghetto within a ghetto for which the word "squalid" seems a wholly inadequate description. "When you put twenty people in a house with the capacity for five or six, garbage piles up," says a worried Dade County health official. "Septic tanks overflow. In certain areas of Little Haiti, sanitation has been set back fifty years." Miami, already overburdened by the influx of Cubans, could do precious little to relieve the unrelieved misery of the Haitians, except to try to make sure that none of them was put out on the street by the INS, and even at that the city was not always successful. "There are people here with nowhere to stay," said the Reverend Gérard Jean-Juste, a soft-spoken Roman Catholic priest who has become the unofficial mayor of Little Haiti. "They are sleeping in cars, garages, and parks or just walking the streets at night." They were also starving, in such numbers that Jean-Juste's main concern has become collecting food; the day before, he had taken some flour and vegetables to a family that had eaten nothing for two days. But despite his public appeals for such staples as tomatoes, plantains, and grits, the only food that remained in the center's storehouse was a few cartons of stale marshmallow bunnies left over from Easter that some merchant had donated rather than throw away.

More than anything or anyone else, it was Father Jean-Juste who held the frightened community together. The first Haitian to be ordained by the Catholic Church in the United States, he liked to describe himself as "a priest without a parish." In fact, his parish was all of Little Haiti, and as he walked its streets, he was recognized by everyone, greeted with waves and smiles and shouts of *"Mon père,"* and also barraged with problems and complaints. Don't worry, Jean-Juste told his flock, be strong, help will come. Privately he was not at all certain that it would, and though he did not like to admit it, he himself was not without fear. He was constantly followed, Jean-Juste said, by men he was sure were agents of Duvalier, and his fear of Duvalier is widely shared. At the community center that same afternoon, word had begun to circulate among the new arrivals that a Duvalier spy, a black man, had slipped into the room. All talk ceased as a hundred pairs of cold eyes focused on the stranger, who quickly left. Later the appearance of a white visitor in a Haitian neighborhood sent a whisper rippling ahead of him down the block, followed by a slamming of doors and a dousing of lights.

As Jean-Juste set off on his evening rounds, his first call was on a young woman named Alcien, who sat dejectedly in what passed for the living room of the tumbledown shack she shared with her four young children. In the faint, eerie glow of the room's single blue bulb, Alcien looked half again as old as her thirty years, and as she spoke to the priest in a dull monotone, she sounded enormously tired. In fact, she was starving. Her rent, Alcien said, was $100 a month, a sum she could barely afford when she was working in a factory that made lamp polish. But then she had been fired, her job given to a Cuban woman, and now that there was no money for rent, the landlord had told her to leave. There was almost no money for food either. That night she and her children had had some rice for dinner. Breakfast that morning had also been rice. For dinner the previous night, "a little plantain, that's all." It was, Father Jean-Juste observed, "the same diet as in Haiti." So why, a visitor wondered, had Alcien made the difficult and dangerous journey to Miami? She seemed scarcely better off there than she had been in Port-au-Prince. "Duvalier," she said, her voice dropping to a whisper. "The Macoutes." Pressed for details, Alcien shook her head. All she would say was that her husband's parents had "disappeared." The refugee center had given Alcien a little food from time to time, but that night Jean-Juste had nothing to bring. "We've run out of resources," he told her. The conversation was interrupted by a scurrying noise that seemed to come from inside the ceiling. "Rat," said Alcien, and her children cowered in a corner. Outside the grimy windows the soft, warm dusk was turning to dark, and in the distance the chrome and glass towers of Miami Beach gleamed softly.

Maurice Ferre, the Miami mayor whose heritage is Puerto Rican, was sympathetic to the Haitians' cause. Miami, Ferre said, had somehow absorbed more than half a million Cubans, and he doubted that another 50,000 Haitians were going to put the city under. The government's distinction between the Cubans and the Haitians, Ferre thought, was tragic. "There was a time when there were 50,000 freedom fighters from Hungary that President Eisenhower decided should be immediately accepted into the United States, and there wasn't much trouble with that." But if Ferre wanted the Haitians, no one else did, not even Haiti. As long as the world believed that Alcien and those like her were fleeing poverty and not political persecution—and Washington was doing all it could to foster that impression—Jean-Claude Duvalier was happy to see them go. For him it only meant that many fewer mouths to feed. Miami surely did not want them. In a city where whites looked down on Cubans, where Cubans looked down on blacks, and where blacks from the Bahamas and other Caribbean countries had their own intricate system of castes, the Haitians were at the bottom of everybody's list, and their arrival in Miami had been met with a far greater degree of animosity than had confronted even the Marielitos. White Miamians living near Little Haiti feared the exotic diseases they believed the Haitians had brought with them, and they complained of the trash that was left on the ground, of vandalism, marijuana smoking, lawns used for parking junked cars, and dwellings left in a fetid state.

For most of the postwar period, the only refugees the United States was willing to accept were those fleeing Communist countries like Hungary, Vietnam, and Cuba. But the new Refugee Act of 1980 did away with the Cold War approach to refugee resettlement. Now the only requirement for political asylum would be a "well-founded fear of persecution" upon returning home, no matter whether from a government of the right or of the left. The Haitians' real problem, however, was that they were the first large group of refugees who were fleeing a non-Communist authoritarian government. No one had expected such a swift test of the new law, and at the State Department some officials were privately uncertain whether the Haitians were the right group to use as guinea pigs. They were, after all, coming from a country that was officially a friend of the United States, not to mention a key strategic bulwark against the spread of Caribbean communism. Their fear of the Haitian government did seem a bit nebulous, having to do with these Macoutes and all, and on top of everything else they were, well, black.

The country's continued ability to accept refugees, these earnest officials confided, depended largely on a degree of public sympathy for the plight of the refugees in question. Public opinion polls had shown that only 1 American in 5 supported President Carter's decision to double the number of refugees from Indochina to 168,000 a year, and the Indochinese had been our allies. It might be better from a policy standpoint, the officials suggested, to wait for some refugees from another right-wing government before putting the provisions of the new law into effect. But then they would always add, "If I had my way, you understand, I'd let them all stay. . . ." It was not that they were unsympathetic to the Haitians' suffering, they explained; it was just that turning the United States into an open-door refuge for the world's poor was impossible. Where would it all end? To permit the Haitians to remain in this country simply because they were starving in Haiti might even erode the government's legal authority to expel the hundreds of thousands of Mexican aliens who were coming here illegally in search of work. "If we're going to let the Haitians in because they're hungry," said Ray Morris, the INS chief in Miami, "then how can we stop people from India and China from coming in?"

On its surface, the "Haitian problem" seemed far easier to solve than the one presented by the Cubans. Castro would not take back the Marielitos, but Haiti had no grounds for refusing to take back the Haitians. In sending them home, however, the INS was bound by the terms of the United Nations Protocol Relating to the Status of Refugees, which required that "every precaution" be taken to ensure that anyone requesting political asylum "is given an opportunity to fully present his case." Any Haitian who wanted to file a claim for asylum had the right to a hearing, but for the INS such hearings were merely an annoying prelude to eventual deportation, to be disposed of as quickly and painlessly as possible. Dick Gullage, the INS deputy chief in Miami who had forecast the Cuban invasion, issued a memorandum ordering his agents to "take whatever action they deem necessary to keep these cases moving through the system." But as was soon to become apparent, in its haste to send the Haitians home the immigration service simply ignored many of the rights accorded them by law, neglecting to tell some of their right to be represented by a lawyer and returning others to Haiti without ever advising them of their right to apply for political asylum. When the Haitian Refugee Center sent representatives to the Miami INS office to inform arriving Haitians that free legal counsel was available to them, a guard was posted to keep them out. Steve Forrester, an intense young man and one of a tiny group of Berkeley, California, lawyers who had moved to Miami to help the Haitians plead their case, was told by some of his clients that INS officers had warned them that retaining a lawyer would only "get them in trouble."

Forrester also had evidence that some of the documents relating to the Haitians' cases had been falsified. INS records showed, for example, that Jean Supris, who arrived in Miami in

1978, had declined the offer of a lawyer. But Supris swore in a subsequent affidavit that he had never been asked if he wished to be represented by a lawyer. Another refugee, Urile Pierre, said he had been asked if he wanted a lawyer and had told the INS that he did, but Pierre was listed in INS records as declining legal assistance. "I could not understand why they were continuing to ask me questions after I had told them I didn't want to answer before I had a lawyer," he said later. Two-thirds of the several hundred Haitians the INS had sent home were listed as "voluntary returnees"—that is, those who had waived their right to asylum and deportation hearings and had agreed to leave the U.S. forthwith. But many of the returnees who were interviewed later by State Department representatives in Haiti said their departures had not been voluntary at all, that they had been told by the INS that unless they agreed to leave without a hearing, they would spend the rest of their lives in a Miami jail—something, of course, that was not true. One refugee, Fritz Charles, said that when he arrived in Miami, he had been ordered by the INS to sign a standard form requesting that he be allowed to return home voluntarily. Charles said that when he refused to sign, explaining that "I was a member of the Haitian navy and they might kill me if I go back," the INS interviewer forged his signature on the paper. "I never so much as put my hand to it," he said. Immigration officers were preparing to take Charles and his wife, Louisanne, to the airport and put them aboard a plane to Haiti when Louisanne became hysterical. A lawyer witnessed the scene and telephoned Steve Forrester, who telephoned the immigration service. The Charleses remained behind, but Forrester wondered how many other Haitians recorded as having returned home "voluntarily" had been the victims of similar coercion.

In its determination to get rid of the Haitians as quickly as possible, the INS tried other sleights of hand. It began scheduling a dozen or more asylum and deportation hearings at the same hour, making it physically impossible for Steve Forrester and his small cadre of lawyers, each of whom was representing several different Haitians, to appear on behalf of all their clients. Running from hearing to hearing, the lawyers often had only thirty minutes to prepare complicated asylum cases that normally would have taken them twenty hours or more, and the hearings themselves, which ordinarily averaged ninety minutes, were abbreviated to less than half an hour. The INS interviewers, hastily recruited from duty stations at Miami's airport and untrained in the evaluation of asylum claims, were angry and intimidating. Some Haitians who tried to invoke their Fifth Amendment privilege against self-incrimination were thrown in jail. Five-minute answers to such crucial questions as "What do you think would happen if you returned to Haiti?" were reduced to a single sentence, and the recorded answers often bore a remarkable similarity. On more than half the written asylum forms Steve Forrester had seen, the question "Why did you come to the United States?" was answered with the identical phrase "I came here to find work."

Other answers were simply fabricated. Gracia Carida's asylum application showed that she had answered no when asked whether she had been politically active in Haiti and that she did not want to return home because it was "impossible to make a living" there. Actually, Carida said, she told the INS "that I could not go back to Haiti because the government had killed my cousin, that the government was looking for everyone in my family." Ludicrously, one of those listed as having come to the United States "to work" was Jean Louis, the former Tonton Macoute who had had an excellent job in Haiti paying him $87 a month, a relative fortune. What Louis had really told the INS, he said, was that "If I go back, they'll kill me" for having defected from the Macoutes.

No matter how long and hard the Haitians' lawyers labored, it seemed, no matter how impassioned their clients' appeals for asylum, the result was always the same: the arrival of a form letter declaring: "The record of proceedings concerning your asylum request indicates that you have not presented sufficient information to support your claim." The letter was followed by a one-way airplane ticket to Haiti. Frustrated and incensed, Steve Forrester and his crew collected affidavits relating these and dozens of similar incidents and used them to file a class-action lawsuit against the immigration service. Their evidence was persuasive. In July 1980, just as the Cuban exodus was beginning to taper off, Federal Judge James King ruled that the INS had knowingly violated "the constitutional, statutory, treaty and administrative rights" of thousands of Haitians who had sought political asylum in this country.

In one of the sharpest rebukes ever handed an executive agency by the courts, Judge King declared that such treatment "must stop," and he ordered that the Haitians' asylum claims be reconsidered by the INS in a way that eliminated "the wholesale violations of due process" that had taken place. "Haitians who came to the United States seeking freedom and justice did not find it," the judge wrote in his 180-page decision, but were confronted instead "with an Immigration and Naturalization Service determined to deport them, irrespective of the merits of their asylum claims." The agency, he added, had also "demonstrated its failure to grasp the fundamental rules of Haitian politics and economics."

His courtroom, Judge King said, had become "populated by the ghosts of individual Haitians who have been beaten, tortured and left to die in Haitian prisons." He had been shown "a stark picture of how these plaintiff-immigrants will be treated if they return to Haiti" and "an equally stark picture of the treatment of Haitians by the INS"—treatment, he suggested, that had been motivated to some degree by racial prejudice. The Haitians, the judge noted, "are part of the first substantial flight of black refugees from a repressive regime to this country," and he said he could place no other interpretation on an internal INS memorandum asserting that the presence of the Haitians threatened the economic and social "well-being" of Miami.

Gérard Jean-Juste, the Haitian priest, was in the courtroom the day Judge King delivered his opinion, and as he walked out into the bright Miami sunshine, he was smiling. "This is the first time in history the INS has had to deal with black boat people," he said. "In times past they needed them to work here as slaves. But we are not the modern slaves."

In a single stroke Judge King's decision had altered entirely the political topography of the government's Haitian dilemma. In the face of the court order to reconsider thousands of asylum claims at a time when the INS's resources were stretched to the breaking point by the Mariel crisis, the easiest course seemed to be simply to let the Haitians stay. In October 1980 Jimmy Carter granted most of the Haitians already in the country the same status as the Marielitos, admitting them under the newly created category of "Cuban-Haitian Entrant," which entitled them to Medicaid, to various welfare benefits, and, if Congress agreed, to eventual citizenship.

Carter's action made a mockery of the new refugee law, of American immigration policy in general, and of the notion that the United States could formulate any kind of rational policy specifying which foreigners, and how many, it would permit to come here. The U.S. had begun by agreeing to accept 3,000 Cubans and no Haitians. By the end of 1981 it had become home to 132,000 "Cuban-Haitian entrants" (and perhaps another 40,000 Haitians who had arrived surreptitiously), whom it frankly had no workable means of sending home. Carter's order also failed to take account of the fact that unlike the Marielitos, the Haitians were still coming—and, as word of what seemed to amount to a blanket amnesty from the American government filtered back to Port-au-Prince, coming in ever greater numbers. Those arriving after what had become known as the Carter cutoff were not entitled to the status accorded the earlier exiles, and the INS had no choice but to begin again to process and to deny their asylum claims. Nothing in Judge King's decision or the President's order had altered the immigration service's essential view of the Haitians as economic refugees, and the result was the worst sort of Catch-22 bureaucracy at work. If you came on Tuesday, you were home free. If you came on Wednesday, you got a free trip home.

This time, however, the INS was determined not to repeat its earlier mistake of permitting the Haitians to go free during the months, and in some cases years, their claims for asylum were pending. Allowing the Haitians their freedom had originally been thought a humanitarian gesture, a way to permit them to work if they could find a job, to earn a little money during what was assumed to be nothing more than a stopover in the United States. But many of the Haitians had simply disappeared into the depths of Little Haiti, and in a community whose residents were experienced at evading the police, where the common language was incomprehensible to most Americans, where everyone's name sounded vaguely like everyone else's, and where few carried any sort of identifying documents, tracking them down had proved virtually impossible.

A few months after Jimmy Carter left office, the INS began

locking up arriving Haitians, mainly to avoid losing track of them but also in hopes that when word of the incarcerations reached Haiti, it might deter others from coming. The only problem was where to put them. The most obvious choice was the Krome Avenue detention center on the outskirts of Miami, an abandoned army missile base at the edge of the Florida Everglades that had been taken over by the INS for use as a processing center for the Marielitos. When the Krome camp became full, as it quickly did, the government began looking for other facilities. A disused air force base in Montana was considered and rejected as too expensive to reopen. Then Washington decided that 2,500 of the Haitians could be sent to Fort Drum in upstate New York, a cold-weather combat-training facility thirty miles from the Canadian border, where winter temperatures reached thirty below and snowdrifts of twelve feet were common. No place in the continental U.S. was less like Haiti than Fort Drum, and the American Civil Liberties Union attacked the INS's decision as a move to place the Haitians, none of whom had ever even seen snow, in "cold storage." Maurice Ferre said he believed Washington was trying to tell the Haitians that "if they come here, it won't be easy for them," and Steve Forrester pointed out that since the legal group working on the Haitians' cases was in Miami, moving the exiles to New York would leave them "without any legal representation whatsoever." All these issues had doubtless occurred to the INS, which began laying plans to send the next contingent of Haitians to Fort Allen, in a desolate corner of Puerto Rico. But Fort Allen filled as quickly as had Fort Drum, and by the end of 1981 the Haitians were being held in seventeen different camps and facilities around the United States, including the federal prison at Lexington, Kentucky. None of them liked it a bit. They had left a society where freedom was an illusion and ended up without even the illusion of freedom. From the frigid cold of Fort Drum to the mind-numbing heat of Fort Allen, the Haitians grew ever more restive as they waited behind barbed-wire fences and prison bars for the INS to process their asylum claims, an enormous job for which it was thoroughly unequipped. (During all of 1981 the INS managed to render final decisions in only 50 asylum cases, leaving a backlog of more than 5,000 still undecided.)

The Haitians at Fort Allen had come to America for the same reasons as those Haitians who now walked the streets of Little Haiti, and the rationale behind the official policy that had allowed the earlier arrivals to go free escaped them. Several of the Haitian women locked up at Fort Allen threatened to commit suicide if they were not released soon. They weren't, and they didn't; but the inevitable finally did happen: The Haitians stormed one of the camp's outer fences and staged a two-hour riot, throwing rocks and empty bottles at security guards. Word of the rioting at Fort Allen quickly spread to Camp Krome, where hundreds of Haitians were confined in quarters intended to hold half their number and where facilities were so inadequate that the inmates were forced to bathe in urinals. But the worst deprivation of all at Krome was the suffocating boredom.

"We get up and we eat," Milius, one of the Haitians there, told Greg Jaynes of *The New York Times*. "Then they put us in the yard. The sun boils us. At midday they send us to eat again. Then after we eat they send us inside. Then we lay on our beds. There is a policeman at the door, and you cannot go out. You have no freedom. When I was in Haiti I thought I could work much more here and support my children. Everywhere in Haiti they speak of Miami. If they would release me, even if there is no work outside, I will find work. In Haiti you put your head upside down trying to find ways to get money for your family. Can I clean your car? I will carry your garbage. Anything." Asked about the Haitians' plight, Attorney General William French Smith replied, "They can leave voluntarily any time they want to—all they have to do is go home."

It was not quite that simple. Lawyers for the Haitians filed another lawsuit challenging the Reagan administration's incarceration policy as both inhumane and racially motivated, and in June 1982 a federal judge in Miami ruled that locking up the Haitians was unconstitutional. The Justice Department appealed, but the court ordered the 1,900 or so Haitians under detention in Miami and Puerto Rico freed anyway. Resettlement agencies began searching for Miamians who would sponsor them.

The INS might have learned something from its experience with the Haitians, but it did not. A few months later another federal judge, this one in Los Angeles, ordered the INS to stop threatening and abusing refugees from El Salvador and to begin advising them of their legal right to seek political asylum in the United States. The immigration agents, the judge ruled, had been using "verbal and physical abuse" to coerce the Salvadorans into waiving their right to seek asylum, and he added, "Salvadorans who resisted were told that their refusal would be of no avail and eventually they would be deported to El Salvador anyway."

CHAPTER FOUR

"Gossip About Gossip Is Still Gossip"

Nineteen eighty was a far cry from 1820, the first year that immigration statistics were kept by this country. That year the United States admitted precisely 8,385 foreigners to residence here, among them 20 Danes, 3 Swedes, 5 Poles, 14 Russians, 6 Asians—and a single Mexican, whose name, regrettably, has been lost to history. America, as we like to teach our schoolchildren, is a nation of immigrants—American Indians joke that if their forebears had had stricter immigration laws the country would still belong to them—and over the past 160 years the United States has welcomed, sometimes gladly and sometimes grudgingly, nearly 50 million immigrants. The first great wave of transatlantic immigrants, mainly Germans, began arriving in the 1850's. The Germans were followed by the British and the Irish, then by Russians and Eastern Europeans, and, in the early part of this century, by Italians. Annual immigration, barely 100,000 in 1842, had surpassed 500,000 by 1881 and reached an all-time annual high in 1914 of 1.2 million. Like the Mexicans, Cubans, and Haitians of a later era, most of the early immigrants were running away—from poverty, famine, depression, political upheaval—but there was an important difference. When they arrived in New York Harbor, those who were healthy enough to walk found an open doorway.

Until the early part of this century, in fact, immigration to the United States was virtually unrestricted. The nation's first real immigration law was not passed until 1877, when the Forty-third Congress barred the admission of convicts and prostitutes and, hoping to reduce the number of Chinese being forcibly imported to this country to help build the railroads, of Asians brought here "without their free and voluntary consent." The anti-Chinese provision was cloaked in humanitarianism, but the motives behind it were darker. Samuel Gompers, the founding father of the American Federation of Labor, declared that 99 out of every 100 Chinese were gamblers, and he spoke of "little girls no older than 12 found in Chinese laundries under the influence of opium" and speculated that the other crimes "committed in those dark and fetid places [were] too horrible to imagine." It was the barest attempt at regulation, but from that unprepossessing start has grown a body of immigration law that today, with the arguable exception of the tax code, is the most complex of all the federal statutes. Once it had begun to restrict immigration, however, Congress lost little time in embroidering its handiwork. In 1882, beginning an era of racial and ethnic selectivity that was to last for more than half a century, Congress enacted outright restrictions on the arrival of Chinese, idiots, and lunatics. But as Congress was to discover repeatedly in the century to come, most recently with the Refugee Act of 1980, legislating immigration curbs and halting immigration are two very different things. The "Chinese exclusion statutes" did not stop the flow of Chinese to the United States; they merely diverted it from the nation's seaports to the then-unpatrolled Mexican border.

As E. P. Hutchinson has pointed out in his definitive *Legislative History of American Immigration Policy*, it was the changing character of the transatlantic exodus, the gradual displacement of immigrants from Northern and Western Europe by those from Southern and Eastern Europe, that gave rise to increasing public pressure for more restrictive measures. Among the laws proposed during the late nineteenth century were those prohibiting the purchase of property by immigrants, denying them public employment, and forbidding them entry into the armed forces. Congress was able to resist enacting severe restrictions until after the turn of the century, with the result that in the years before the First World War, legal immigration to the United States was higher than ever before or since. Not until

1917 did Congress succumb to the growing exclusionist sentiment by passing, over Woodrow Wilson's veto, a law requiring
a literacy test for arriving aliens that had the intended effect of
barring immigrants who spoke no English.

The Immigration Act of 1917, as the law became known, also
provided for the rejection of immigrants on several other
grounds, among them constitutional psychopathic inferiority,
chronic alcoholism, vagrancy, and advocating the unlawful destruction of property. Even though its terms were narrowly
drawn, the 1917 act established the general concept of exclud-
ing undesirable aliens that exists to this day (the list of excludable offenses has been expanded to include bigamy, homosexuality, and drug addiction). The next year, in response to fears
that the Marxist revolution in Russia might be contagious,
aliens who belonged to groups advocating the forcible overthrow of the United States government were added to the exclusion list; that authority was later used to deport Emma
Goldman to the Soviet Union and to justify the notorious
Palmer Raids, in which, on orders from Attorney General A.
Mitchell Palmer, thousands of suspected Eastern European
"radicals" were arrested and deported.

Though the 30 million immigrants who arrived here between
1860 and 1920 contributed immeasurably to the nation's economic growth and to the expansion of its physical frontier, by
1920 Congress had wholeheartedly embraced the antialien furor that was sweeping the country. As Hutchinson suggests,
such xenophobia seems to have grown in part from fears that
America might be overrun by refugees from postwar Europe
and from the eugenicist theories then at the height of their pop-
ularity, but it had at its roots many of the same concerns being
heard today: that the immigrants were unhealthy, were taking
jobs from Americans, and were somehow diluting the nation's
values and culture. The result was the watershed Immigration
Act of 1921, which established for the first time a set of "national immigration quotas," annual limits on the number of
aliens permitted to emigrate from each foreign country (except
for Asian nations, which had no quotas) equal to 3 percent of
the number of immigrants from that country residing in the
United States according to the census of 1910. The effect of the
law was to favor newcomers from the fairer-skinned nations of

Northern and Western Europe, from which the majority of the pre-1910 immigrants had come. Great Britain, for example, which then had about 2 percent of the world's population, was given nearly half the total number of places. Three years later, in an effort to refine the strain of arriving immigrants to even greater purity, Congress substituted the 1890 census, taken before most of the immigration from Italy, Russia, and Austro-Hungary had occurred, as a basis for figuring the national origin quotas. It also appropriated $1 million for the creation of a "Border Patrol" to keep the growing number of undesirables out of the country. Making no secret of its motives, Congress declared that with this newest law it "hoped to guarantee, as best we can at this late date, racial homogeneity in the United States."

The Quota Acts of 1921 and 1924 had the expected impact. Total immigration, which had topped 800,000 in 1921, fell to 309,000 the next year and dropped to 241,000 by the end of that decade. During all of the 1930's, in fact, total immigration numbered only 528,000—fewer immigrants than had arrived the year the first Quota Act was passed. The ethnic composition of the immigrants changed as well. Between 1911 and 1920, more than 1 million Italians, Bulgarians, and Greeks had been admitted to the United States, but between 1931 and 1940 only 68,028 Italians, 938 Bulgarians, and 9,119 Greeks were permitted to enter the country. As had happened with the Chinese exclusion laws, however, by establishing ever-smaller categories of admissible aliens, Congress also created ever-larger numbers of potential illegal immigrants, and many of them were quick to realize their potential. In the ten years before the passage of the Quota Acts, a scant 27,000 aliens were deported from the United States as inadmissible. Over the next ten years the number of deportations increased nearly five times, to 126,000.

In 1940, as war once again broke out across Europe, and with it fresh concern about subversives and saboteurs, Congress moved to require the annual registration of all aliens living in the United States, a requirement that was suspended only last year. The Alien Registration Act of 1940, as it was called, also provided for the first time for the "voluntary departure" of illegal aliens who agreed to forgo deportation and return home at their own expense, a procedure still widely employed, particularly for illegal aliens from Mexico. The next major additions to the rapidly expanding body of immigration law came in 1950, and they had a distinct Cold War flavor. That year Congress approved the Internal Security Act, which provided for the deportation of aliens believed to be "politically dangerous," and followed it two years later with the landmark Immigration and Nationality Act of 1952, popularly known as the McCarran-Walter Act, or simply the McCarran Act, passed by Congress over President Harry Truman's veto. The McCarran Act, which expanded the categories of excludable aliens to include "subversives," has in recent years been attacked as a product of anti-Communist hysteria. It was, but the law contained so many other provisions, some of them admirable, that it also amounted to a virtual rewriting of American immigration law.

The McCarran Act established for the first time an annual limit on the number of immigrants the country was willing to accept, but it also removed the barriers to Asian immigration that had existed since the 1920's. It reduced the national immigration quotas and authorized the admission of refugees fleeing Communist persecution. And, again for the first time, it required all permanent resident aliens to carry the certificate of registration still universally known as a green card (though the latest edition is red, white, and blue). Finally, the new law gave the attorney general the authority to "parole" into the country on an emergency basis aliens who were otherwise ineligible, a power that has since been used to admit a wide variety of foreigners, including the shah of Iran after his overthrow in 1979, and that serves only to emphasize again that the exceedingly fine line between a legal and an illegal alien may be no more than a stroke of the pen. The McCarran Act remained in force until 1965, when the basic immigration policy that exists today, and that in retrospect has not served the country very well, was set in place. But the 1965 reforms, largely inspired by the increased sensitivity in Congress to civil rights, did soften some of the law's harsher provisions and, in general, marked a major liberalization of American immigration policy, by doing away with the racist national origins quotas altogether. As he signed the reforms into law in a ceremony at the Statue of Liberty, Lyndon Johnson declared his hope that they would "repair a deep and painful flaw in the fabric of American justice." The era of unrestricted immigration, Johnson said, was gone forever, but at least now those who came here would come "because of what they are, not because of the land from which they sprung."

The 1965 law retained an overall ceiling on immigration, but under it the distribution of immigrant visas was far more equitable than before. Henceforth total annual immigration to the United States could not exceed 290,000, with 120,000 of the immigrants coming from Western Hemisphere countries (the first numerical limit ever on Western Hemisphere immigration) and the other 170,000 from the more numerous countries of the Eastern Hemisphere, including the Asian nations so long accorded second-class status. No Eastern Hemisphere country could provide more than 20,000 immigrants in any year (there were no such country-by-country ceilings for Western Hemisphere nations), and for the first time visas were to be awarded according to seven "preference categories," which emphasized the reunification of families by reserving three-quarters of each year's visas for relatives of resident aliens and citizens and which admitted spouses, parents, and children of U.S. citizens without numerical limit. First preference went to unmarried children of citizens, for whom 20 percent of the visas were reserved. Next in line were spouses and unmarried children of resident aliens (20 percent), members of the professions, scientists, and artists (10 percent), married sons and daughters of citizens (10 percent), brothers and sisters of citizens (24 percent), skilled and unskilled laborers whose services were certified by the secretary of labor as being in short supply (10 percent), and finally refugees from Communist and Middle Eastern governments (6 percent).

The 1965 law had several results, some intended and some not. As expected, it did increase the total number of immigrants. In the five years preceding its enactment, legal immigration had averaged around 283,000 a year, but in the five years that followed, the average climbed to 373,000 and hovered around 400,000 through the 1970's. Most of the immigrants admitted over and above the 290,000 ceiling were family members exempted from the numerical limits of the preference system. But because only one-fifth of the visas were reserved for persons with needed talents or skills, many of those who did get visas were unsuited for all but the most menial work. And, just as its sponsors had hoped, the 1965 law also enriched the makeup of legal immigration. The year the law was passed, the United States admitted 113,000 immigrants from Europe and only 71,300 from Asia, Mexico, Africa, and Latin America (exclusive of Argentina, Brazil, and Colombia, the "big three" sending countries on that continent). By 1977 the number of European immigrants had fallen to 70,000, while the number of Asians, Africans, Mexicans, and Latin Americans had risen to 231,000.

In 1976, in an effort to increase the equitability of visa distribution still further, the 20,000 annual ceiling on immigrants from each Eastern Hemisphere nation was also imposed on all Western Hemisphere countries, including Mexico, which until then had by itself accounted for about half the Western Hemisphere's quota of 120,000 visas a year. The 1976 amendment to the Immigration and Nationality Act was pushed through in the final hours of the Ninety-fourth Congress after some members, having been assured that the bill would not be presented for a vote, had retired for the evening. The amendment was passed at two o'clock in the morning, and it may have done more to exacerbate illegal immigration than anything except the end of the Bracero Program, which abruptly left hundreds of thousands of Mexican farmhands who had been working in this country legally without jobs. In attempting to erase entirely the racist and exclusionary precepts that had guided immigration policy since the 1920's by making the scarce visas more uniformly available to all citizens of the world, Congress had placed at a great comparative disadvantage would-be immigrants from the larger, poorer nations of Asia and Latin America, particularly Mexico. Canadians, for example, never use all of the 20,000 visas available to them in a given year; Mexicans could easily use ten times that many, and while the new restrictions limited legal immigrants from Mexico to a third their former number, they did nothing to diminish the number of Mexicans who wanted to come to the United States. It was no accident that in 1977 apprehensions of illegal aliens, 90 percent of them Mexicans, topped 1 million for the first time since 1954.

As it turned out, the preference system itself proved to be a spur to illegal immigration. In 1980 the United States admitted the maximum of 290,000 legal immigrants, as well as another 100,000 spouses, parents, and children of U.S. citizens. But because there were far more aliens who were eligible for such visas than there were visas available, many of those who applied for one were told that they would have to wait for years. Between 1978 and 1979, to take just one example, the backlog in the fifth-preference category alone doubled from a quarter million to half a million. In some "prime source" countries, such as Hong Kong, the waiting lists for some visa categories are so long that they are officially closed—no more names are being accepted. For the young Mexican wife of a resident alien who is told she must wait eight years to join her husband in Texas, for the Hong Kong brother of a San Francisco Chinese with whom he will not be legally reunited for a decade, the obvious alternative—easy, cheap, and quick—is illegal immigration.

Whether immigration policies are racist, like the Quota Acts, or well intentioned, like the 1965 reforms, whether they achieve their aims or have unintended effects, those who make them cannot escape the fact that at the bottom of every debate over immigration policy there is a fundamental question: How many foreigners are living in the United States without permission? One might as well ask an astronomer how many stars are in the universe. The answer is not only that no one knows but that no one can ever know. Because illegal aliens are in the country illegally and because they take some pains to keep themselves invisible, no record exists of who or where they are. If they could be counted, after all, they could also be deported. Estimates proliferate; but they are only estimates, and the confusion that has resulted from claims by competing interests has contributed neither to understanding the new immigration nor to mapping realistic policies to control and shape it.

A few authorities recognize the dangers inherent in the numbers game. Among them is Lawrence Fuchs, the distinguished Brandeis historian picked to head the Select Commission on Immigration and Refugee Policy, who dismisses the existing research on the number of illegal immigrants with the admonition that "Gossip about gossip is still gossip." Such cautions, however, have done little to prevent a number of responsible officials, academies, and institutions from using such figures as exist to try to quantify illegal immigration. Douglas Massey, the Princeton demographer, puts the number of illegal aliens in the United States at around 4 million. So does the CIA. The State

Department says it is 7 million. *The Washington Post* estimates that between 250,000 and 500,000 are coming here each year. Maxwell Taylor, the retired chairman of the Joint Chiefs of Staff, thinks the number is a cool 1 million. The Environmental Fund assures subscribers to its newsletter that "The Border Patrol knows that for every illegal alien who is apprehended, perhaps four go uncaught" and that "those who are caught eventually get in." Zero Population Growth warns that "one-fourth to one-half" of the nation's population growth is attributable to immigration. The Federation for American Immigration Reform (FAIR) declares that the number of illegal aliens who have come here over the past decade totals more than 4 million.

All these assertions share two things in common: there is no evidence that any of them is true. There is also no evidence that any of them is not true. There is no evidence, period. Not that those who debate the immigration issue can be blamed for tossing such numbers around. So many of the questions that surround illegal immigration depend for answers on how many illegal aliens there are. And the government, after all, has been playing the immigration numbers game ever since 1972, when the INS first put the number of illegal aliens in the country at an even million. Three years later, Leonard F. Chapman, the commissioner of immigration, touched off an alien "scare" when he spoke of "a vast army" of 4 to 12 million Mexicans. The INS refused to make the basis for either of the estimates public—for the simple reason, officials conceded later, that neither had any basis in fact. But it hurriedly reduced its "official" estimate to between 5 and 8 million, a figure it obtained by the highly unscientific method of asking its regional directors for their best guesses about the number of illegal aliens living and working in their jurisdictions. Then, in 1978, the INS lowered the number further still, to somewhere between 3 and 6 million.

The only certainty in all this was that while the government's estimates of the number of illegal aliens were decreasing, the number of aliens was increasing; no one suggests that there were fewer illegals in the country in 1978 than in 1975. Leonel Castillo, Jimmy Carter's immigration commissioner, himself called the 1978 estimate "soft," and it may have been no accident that it came in the midst of an economic recession, at a time when the Carter administration might have wished to play down the potential impact of illegal aliens on the job market. Nor was it a coincidence that when the Mexican government, acutely sensitive to the rising antialien sentiment in this country, released its own estimate in 1980, it was the lowest of all, a mere 488,000 to 1.22 million.

The U.S. Census Bureau countered with a figure of 3 to 5 million that, though much higher, was still well below the Chapman era estimates. Although both the Census Bureau and Mexican government estimates received considerable publicity at the time, like those that had come before, neither had any foundation in fact. The INS and the Census Bureau both have since acknowledged the obvious—that you cannot count what you cannot see, that there is simply no way of knowing how many illegal aliens are entering the United States or how many are already here.

One of the principal difficulties with all such estimates is that the number of foreigners living illegally in the United States at a given moment is changing continuously, not only because more are coming all the time but also because some are always leaving. Aliens from the more distant nations of Asia and Latin America, particularly those fleeing government oppression or political turmoil, tend to come here with the intention of remaining indefinitely. But many others, especially Mexican workers, come for a few months at a time, arriving in the late winter and early spring and then returning home in October and November to spend the Christmas holidays with their families. Many of the Mexicans are "target earners," who quit their jobs after accumulating enough money to see their families through the year; for them the United States is a place to work, not to live, and like Bernabe Garay, they are always coming and going.

Wayne Cornelius, the noted University of California researcher who has interviewed hundreds of Mexicans returning home from the United States about their experiences here, believes that for every illegal Mexican alien who settles in this country, as many as eight others "commute" between their homes in Mexico and their jobs in the United States. Largely for that reason, Cornelius argues, the number of illegal aliens living permanently in the States is relatively small, somewhere between 1 million and 3 million. Other experts dispute his estimate as too low, suggesting that while he does have some good data, they do not support all his conclusions; even Cornelius agrees that "no one can estimate with any precision what the total numbers of illegals of all nationalities are."

Amid all the confusion, however, one important fact seems clear: At the moment more people from other countries are attempting to enter the United States—legally or illegally, to visit or to stay—than ever before in the nation's history. Over the past decade alone, the increase in their numbers has been little short of spectacular. According to INS statistics, in 1970, 2 million temporary visas were granted to foreign visitors, primarily tourists, students, and business executives; by 1980 the number had grown to 12 million. In 1970, 373,000 foreigners were admitted to the country as legal immigrants and refugees; in 1980 such admissions totaled 760,000. Two and a half times as many foreigners applied for and were refused nonimmigrant visas in 1978 than were denied them in 1970, and nearly three times as many arriving passengers were turned away at airports or along the border for "lack of admissibility." Such statistics are not precisely accurate; one immigration inspector has said that while he and his colleagues were supposed to record the number of aliens they admitted or turned away, the figures were largely guesses. "People just put down whatever they felt like putting down," the inspector said. But the orders of magnitude are roughly accurate, and one does not have to be able to count illegal aliens to conclude that illegal immigration is on the rise. If one accepts that some more or less constant percentage of nonimmigrant visitors overstay their visas and that some constant or even increasing proportion of foreigners who are denied legal admission then enter the country illegally, it stands to reason that there are more illegal immigrants today than there were ten years ago, probably several times as many.

That assumption is supported by yet another statistic: the startling increase in the immigration service's arrests of aliens who are in the country without permission. In 1961 only 80,000 illegal aliens were apprehended and sent home by the INS. In 1970 the immigration service caught 325,000, or four times as many. In 1977 it arrested three times more than that, just over 1 million. (Of those aliens 90 percent were Mexican, most of them seized at or near the border after having been in the country less than seventy-two hours and before finding work. The other 10 percent were arrested in cities during immigration raids on restaurants, factories, and other workplaces. The reason for the disparity is not, as one might suspect, that most aliens are stopped and turned back at the border but rather that there are far fewer immigration agents looking for aliens in the cities than patrolling along the border. This also accounts for the fact that while 9 of out every 10 aliens arrested are Mexicans, they do not make up 90 percent of all illegal aliens living in the United States.)

The apprehension statistics, which have fluctuated greatly over the years, did not begin their geometric increase until the mid-1960's. Despite the high unemployment rates that prevailed during the Great Depression, for example, only 14,000 illegal aliens were caught, on the average, in each of the depression years. During most of World War II, when thousands of Mexican farmworkers were imported under the Bracero Program to offset the agricultural labor shortage caused by the drafting of domestic workers, the number of apprehensions was even lower. It began to rise again following the war, averaging around 500,000 a year until 1954, when the notorious Operation Wetback raids netted just over 1 million illegals, most of them Mexican workers in California and the Southwest. Over the next decade the number of apprehensions dropped again, to around 100,000 a year. But after the Bracero Program was ended in 1964, many of the Mexicans who had worked in this country under its auspices began returning to the United States illegally. As a result, between 1965 and 1969 apprehensions of illegal aliens averaged 200,000 a year, reaching 345,000 in 1970. Two years later apprehensions passed 500,000, and in 1976 they numbered 866,000. The million mark was reached in 1977, and the total has hovered near there ever since: 1,057,977 in 1978; 1,076,418 in 1979; 910,000 in 1980.

Like visa approvals and denials, the apprehension statistics are a good crude indicator of the order of magnitude of illegal immigration, but they contain some gaping holes. One, mentioned earlier, is that because the bulk of the INS's resources are concentrated along the Mexican border, it is there that most of the apprehensions occur. Meantime, the far more sparsely guarded Canadian border remains wide open to illegal alien traffic, and the relatively small number of apprehensions made there each year is probably no longer indicative of the true scope of the cross-Canada border traffic. A far more important statistical problem, however, is that many of those arrested along either border are repeat offenders. Because the Border Patrol lacks the resources to detain, deport, or prosecute all but the tiniest fraction, when it catches an illegal alien, he is almost always permitted to return home, usually within a few hours, free to try his luck again. (Fewer than 5 percent of the illegal aliens apprehended in this country are ever formally deported.) When the same alien is caught crossing the border a second time, or a third, or a fourth, he becomes a separate statistic. Because of the INS's chaotic record-keeping system, and because many aliens never give the Border Patrol the same name twice, there is no way to separate repeat offenders from first-time border crossers. One INS inspector says, "I've got one friend from Mexico who's been arrested thirty times over the years, and each time he's recorded as a completely different guy. The records don't ever cross." The inspector's point, frequently lost in the debate over illegal immigration, is that the number of apprehensions of illegal aliens in a given year—a statistic that has become a favorite of everyone on both sides of the debate—is probably larger, and perhaps considerably larger, than the number of living, breathing human beings who tried to cross the border in that year.

The problem is that no one knows how much larger. On the average, 1 apprehended alien in 3 admits during questioning that he has been arrested before. But how many times before and in which years are not recorded, and even if they were, there would be no reason to accept such answers as truthful. Nor is there any reason to believe that the 7 aliens in every 10 who deny prior arrests are telling the truth. The result, a most unfortunate one from the standpoint of the policymakers, is that the number of aliens apprehended trying to enter the country each year tells us nothing. A million apprehensions might mean anything: It could represent 500,000 aliens, each of whom was arrested twice; or 250,000 aliens, each arrested four times; or only 100,000 aliens, each arrested ten times. And even if the answer to *that* question was known, there is no way of knowing what happened to those aliens in the end. Did all of them finally succeed in evading arrest and enter the United States successfully, or did only half succeed and the other half give up and go home, or what?

Because the Border Patrol's manpower has not increased by anything even remotely matching the increase in apprehensions, however, it is safe to assume that the ever-increasing number of illegal aliens caught over the past decade probably means that more of them are coming than before. But despite the appeal of apprehension statistics to headline writers (ILLEGAL IMMIGRATION UP 34%), despite the INS's use of them to back its pleas for more funds, despite the temptation for academicians to use them as a basis for suggesting improvements in immigration policy, even knowing exactly how many illegal aliens were caught in any year would be of no use whatever in determining how many were not caught. And that, of course, is what we need to know. One might, for example, interpret the drop in 1980 apprehensions as representing a lessening of the cross-border flow when, in fact, that flow was probably greater than ever; central Mexico was hit by a severe drought that year, ruining crops and forcing many small farmers, who in other years would have stayed home, across the border in search of work. The drop in apprehensions occurred because of gasoline and manpower shortages that resulted when hundreds of Border Patrol agents were pulled off the Mexican border and sent to Key West to handle the Mariel crisis.

Even INS agents cannot agree on how many illegal aliens there are. Some veterans are convinced that they catch only 1 illegal alien in every 10. Others put the figure at 1 in 5, the most cautious at 1 out of every 2. Not knowing how many aliens are caught to begin with makes such impressionistic estimates worthless, but some scholars have nonetheless relied on them in trying to "count" the illegal alien traffic, an enterprise that is even more futile when one considers that illegal border crossers are by no means the only illegal aliens.

Hundreds of thousands of inadmissible aliens enter the country each year with bogus passports and other documents, not to mention the visa abusers, who come as tourists or students and overstay their visas. As with the border crossers, no one knows how many visa abusers there are, and only by making a number of impossible assumptions do the available data lend themselves to the formulation of "upper" and "lower" estimates.

Assume, for example, that every illegal alien apprehended last year by the INS was caught nine other times that same year and decided to go home following his tenth arrest. Assume, further, that the INS catches 1 alien out of every 2 who come here and that of those who escape detection, only 1 in 8 settles permanently in the United States. Assume, finally, that of the 1.2 million foreign visitors last year who were never recorded as leaving the United States, 9 out of 10 are nothing more than record-keeping errors and that of the remaining 10 percent half eventually leave on their own. In that case, the number of illegal aliens taking up permanent residence in the United States last year was a mere 72,500. Assume, on the other hand, that every alien apprehended is a first-time offender, that the immigration service catches only 1 alien in 10, and that 1 out of every 2 aliens who get by the INS remains here permanently. Assume, also, that all of the 1.2 million foreign travelers unaccounted for are still here and plan on staying. In that case, the country gained 5.7 million new illegal alien residents last year.

It can therefore be stated with near-absolute certainty that the number of illegal aliens who entered the United States in 1980 is somewhere between 72,500 and 5.7 million. As with the number of stars in the universe, any other number is just a guess. For whatever they are worth, however, most guesses by what are commonly referred to as responsible observers suggest that there were between 1 million and 3 million illegal aliens living in the United States in 1975 and that there have been half a million new arrivals each year since then. Such an assumption would put the current number of illegal aliens at between 4 million and 6 million, or about 3 percent of the nation's current population of 226 million, not a very large number. But as should now be clear, even that estimate is not worth very much. None of this is meant to suggest, by the way, that the current concern over illegal immigration and its effects on the American economy is unfounded, only that those who play the numbers game are at risk. Clearly a good many people from other countries now wish to live and work in this country. Just as clearly many more of them are coming here now than ever before. Almost certainly the new arrivals number at least a couple of hundred thousand a year, and there are probably several million people now living in this country without official permission.

Such uncertainties have not prevented demographers from attempting to predict the effects of illegal immigration on the nation's future population. One imaginative study compared the increase in the population of Mexico between 1960 and 1970 with the increase that, given the average birth and death rates there, might have been expected. The difference of 1.6 million was assumed to be the number of illegal aliens living in the United States. One of many flaws in the study, however, was that not all illegal immigrants are Mexicans. Another study compared U.S. census data with federal income tax and Social Security records. Using what is called the capture-recapture technique, it assumed that the 3.9 million people living in the country but not paying income or Social Security taxes were here illegally. (In fact, most illegal aliens have both kinds of taxes withheld from their paychecks.) A third study compared deaths in selected regions of the United States with U.S. census data, hypothesizing that death rates for areas where illegal aliens were concentrated should be considerably greater than the average expected rate. The study assumed that the census had failed to count most illegal aliens, that the deaths of illegal aliens were always reflected in official figures, and that the life spans of those aliens were not much different from those of the U.S. population as a whole; however, there is no evidence to support any of those suppositions.

In the late 1970's the Mexican government, worried about the eventual effect of continuing illegal immigration on its relations with the United States, conducted several surveys of its own. Thousands of Mexican citizens who had worked in this country and had either been apprehended and sent home or returned on their own were interviewed. Among the study's conclusions was that many Mexicans who entered the United States illegally remained for only a short time and that fewer than 1.5 million of them had taken up residence here. The most recent Mexican study involved interviews in which Mexican families were asked if any member of the household was currently living or working in the United States. The estimate that resulted was lower still, about 400,000. Apart from the presumed reluctance of at least some Mexicans to acknowledge that a relative was living in the United States illegally, the study also overlooked instances in which an entire family had emigrated to the United States. Moreover, the study was conducted in December and January, months in which many Mexican workers are home with their families.

In 1980 three U.S. Census Bureau demographers, Jacob Siegel, Jeffrey Passel, and J. Gregory Robinson, examined these and other demographic studies of the illegal alien question and concluded that "there are currently no reliable estimates of the number of illegal residents" in this country. Most of the so-called statistical studies, their report said, depended "on broad untested assumptions." But the three authors were unable to resist the temptation to make some assumptions of their own. The total number of illegal U.S. residents, they said, was "almost certainly below" 6 million and might be substantially less, possibly between 3 and 5 million. Furthermore, they suggested, the "Mexican component" of that total was "almost certainly" less than 3 million and might be as small as 1.5 million. But Siegel, Passel, and Robinson presented no empirical basis for their conclusions, and a few months later Vincent Barabba, chief of the Census Bureau, acknowledged: "We have no method at present to measure the number of illegal residents."

Even though it has no answer, the question the demographers are addressing is of supreme importance, for at the moment arriving legal immigrants and refugees make up a far larger proportion of the nation's population increase than ever before. In the first decade of this century immigration accounted for about 40 percent of population increase; today, mainly because the fertility rate of native Americans has declined in recent years to a record low of 1.8 children for each adult female, it makes up about half. Indeed, immigration is now the key to this country's future population growth. If all immigration were halted tomorrow and the fertility rate of American women remained unchanged, the U.S. population would eventually begin to decline.

But immigration will not be halted tomorrow, and despite the paucity of hard numbers, it is at least possible to estimate the effect of various levels of immigration on the nation's population.

For example, if annual legal immigration were to remain at 760,000—the number of immigrants and refugees admitted in 1980—the country's population would reach 262 million by the end of this century and top 300 million by the year 2090. If a comparatively modest annual addition of 250,000 illegal border crossers and visa abusers were added to the total, the U.S. population would pass 268 million by the year 2000 and 312 million by 2030. Assume a million legal immigrants and another million illegals each year, and the increases are staggering: 293 million people by the end of the century, just eighteen years away, and 379 million in just fifty years.

Partly in hopes of finding out what it could about which of these projections might come true, the Census Bureau announced in 1979 that it would try to include as many illegal aliens as possible in the following year's head count. It even produced a series of Spanish-language radio and television messages to encourage illegal alien participation, around the theme of *No tenga mideo, conteste el censo* or ("Don't be afraid to answer the census"). Such reassurances were necessary because of the understandable reluctance of illegal aliens to expose themselves to any authority, even the Census Bureau. They could hardly be blamed; in Galveston, Texas, two Border Patrol agents convinced an illegal alien from Greece to open his door by identifying themselves as census takers. Vincent Barabba offered guarantees of "protection" to illegals who cooperated with his enumerators, assuring them that census data would not be made available to the immigration service or other federal agencies. The Census Bureau, Barabba said, had a long history of protecting the confidentiality of its data no matter how compelling the request; it had even refused to give the FBI information on the whereabouts of Japanese-Americans in the days after the attack on Pearl Harbor. Securing the participation of illegal aliens in the census was important for another reason. The allocation of federal funds for more than 100 public programs is based largely on census data, and to the extent that illegal aliens are undercounted by the census, programs that serve communities with large numbers of illegal residents are shortchanged—by some estimates, every resident overlooked by the census represents $150 to $200 in federal funds lost to local institutions.

The Census Bureau counted 9.1 million Hispanics in 1970; but it readily acknowledged that it might have missed half a million or more, the majority of them illegal aliens, and some authorities guessed that the "undercount" was as high as 5 million. The bureau's plans to reduce the undercount in 1980, however, resulted in a lawsuit by FAIR, the anti-immigration group, charging that it was illegal to count illegal aliens because they were not entitled either to the use of public programs funded with tax dollars or, because they cannot vote, to congressional representation. If 8 million illegal aliens were included in the census, said FAIR, New York would lose only one congressional seat instead of two and California would gain eight seats instead of five. FAIR's argument made sense to many members of the House of Representatives who did not like the idea of representing constituents who could not vote to reelect them, and by a vote of 222 to 189, the House passed a resolution forbidding the counting of illegal aliens by the census.

The Census Bureau replied that it was required by the Constitution itself to count "the whole number of persons" in the country, whether they were here legally or not. It also pointed out that ever since the first census was taken in 1790, the government had simply counted everyone without making any distinctions and that until the first immigration laws were passed in the late 1800's, the concept of an illegal alien had not even existed. On behalf of the Census Bureau, the Justice Department argued that illegal aliens, like other people, required fire and police protection, emergency medical care, and other municipal services funded in part with federal money, which partly consisted of taxes paid by illegal aliens. The government also pointed out that other considerations aside, it would be practically impossible to count illegal aliens separately from other residents since they could not be relied upon to acknowledge their illegal status. Moreover, it said, there was nothing wrong with including illegal aliens with citizens in allocating seats in the House of Representatives, since the drafters of the Fourteenth Amendment "had deliberately rejected proposals that the apportionment of representatives be based on the number of citizens."

The legal wrangling threatened to scrap the 1980 census altogether; but the Supreme Court rejected FAIR's request for a delay, and the decennial head count began on schedule. Despite efforts to include as many illegal aliens as possible, however, the 1980 census promises to be of little help in estimating how many of them are in the country. The Census Bureau believes it counted "a sizeable but unknown number of persons in the country in other than legal status," as one demographer there put it, but it unfortunately has no way of knowing how many. The 1980 census forms had a number of built-in biases that made the counting of Hispanics in general, and illegal Hispanic aliens in particular, all the more difficult. The forms included a "Spanish-origin" question in which a resident could identify himself as Mexican, Puerto Rican, Cuban, or Mexican-American. But the question and, in fact, the entire form mailed out by the Census Bureau, were written in English, not Spanish. A note at the bottom of the form advised recipients to send away for a form in Spanish. Moreover, the forms, whether in Spanish or English, had room for only seven residents of each household. Larger households had to wait for an enumerator to come to take the rest of the information. Finally, the Census Bureau, which went so far as to ask the INS to suspend raids on neighborhoods and workplaces to facilitate its counting of illegal aliens (yet another reason for the decline in apprehensions in 1980), did not ask those it counted to identify themselves as living in the country illegally. There were three other questions that bore on citizenship, but none of them will be very much help in identifying illegal aliens. The first asked whether the individual was a U.S. citizen; the second, his country of birth; and the third, the year, if he was born elsewhere, that he entered the United States. A preliminary scan of the answers to these questions, however, suggests that a significant number of individuals did not answer them truthfully. Some of those immigrants who claimed to be American citizens, for example, also said they had been in the country for less than five years, the period of residency required before one can apply for naturalization. Another difficulty is that because the Census Bureau does not know how many illegal aliens it counted in 1970, it will not be able to estimate the number of illegals counted in 1980 by extrapolating from the previous census—by predicting, for example, the degree to which, given known fertility rates, the

Hispanic population should have grown in the intervening ten years and then attributing the difference to illegal Hispanic immigration. A third problem is that the 1970 census data cannot be compared directly with those from 1980, since in 1970 some residents who identified themselves as "Mexican," "Venezuelan," or some other Hispanic designation were counted as "white," while in 1980 they were not.

Just as the Census Bureau does not know how many illegal aliens it counted in 1980, it has no way of knowing how many it did not count that year—the so-called miss rate. Still, according to Jeffrey Passel, if data such as the number of legal immigrants and refugees, the number of naturalized citizens, the mortality of aliens, and the outmigration of legal aliens (foreigners who have emigrated here and then for some reason gone back home) are juggled, it may be possible to put a "lower bound" on the number of illegal residents. Passel's guess is that the lower limit will be somewhere around 3 million, a number equal to the population of Los Angeles. He agrees that the upper bound is unknowable, but he is quick to add that "three million people is a lot of people."

CHAPTER FIVE

"They Have a Sort of System of Non-Management Over There"

By all accounts Jimmy Carter was furious. His decision to let Mohammed Riza Pahlevi, the deposed shah of Iran, into the United States for emergency medical treatment had angered thousands of the young antimonarchist Iranians attending colleges and universities here, and day after day crowds of shouting Iranians were gathering to demonstrate in cities across the country—even outside New York City's New York Hospital-Cornell Medical Center, where the hated man himself, attended by a battalion of high-priced physicians, was undergoing radiation therapy.

Carter suspected that while many of the demonstrators might have come to America to study, they had since dropped out of school and were therefore living in the United States illegally. If this were true, he could send them home, back to the land of the Ayatollah Khomeini, whose name they now so rudely shouted in the streets. So the President told Attorney General Griffin Bell to see to it that the troublemakers were expelled.

Like every attorney general since the early 1940's, when the Immigration and Naturalization Service was shifted to the Justice Department from the Department of Labor (a move prompted by the refusal of Frances Perkins, Franklin Roosevelt's secretary of labor, to send the radical labor leader Harry

Bridges back to Australia), Bell had paid the INS little attention. Just how little he was soon to find out. When Bell called Leonel Castillo, the commissioner of immigration, to convey the President's order, he could scarcely believe what Castillo told him. The INS, the sole federal agency charged with admitting qualified foreigners to the United States and keeping unqualified ones out, had no idea how many Iranians were in the country, how many of them were students, or who or where they were.

"They have a sort of system of non-management over there," the attorney general ruefully reported back to Carter, and everyone seemed to share the President's astonishment. Everyone, that is, except the 12,000 employees of the INS and the several million foreigners who had had dealings of one sort or another with the agency. As they knew only too well, the INS had been teetering on the brink of collapse for most of a decade. Overwhelmed by an enormous influx of legal and illegal aliens that had crippled its frail bureaucracy, hampered by a bare-bones budget, a victim of decades of inattention from Congress and successive administrations, shot through with nepotism, incompetence, corruption, and brutality, the INS was suffocating beneath a mountain of paper work, its harassed staff badly demoralized by the hopeless task of plugging holes in a boat that was continually shipping water.

Had it not been for the politics of the moment, the White House might never have noticed that the INS was the worst-managed, least-effective federal agency in Washington. Certainly most Americans had never thought much about the immigration service one way or the other, for the INS is the only entity of government that has no jurisdiction over the daily affairs of its citizens. But though no one could have foreseen it in the fall of 1979, its anonymity was about to evaporate; the next twelve months would focus the nation's attention not only on the Iranian student debacle but on the spectacle of boatload after boatload of refugees from Castro's Cuba and Duvalier's Haiti arriving in South Florida with the Carter administration virtually powerless to stop them.

As 1980 began, the INS's problems were far worse than anyone on the outside could have imagined. Not only could it not tell the White House where the Iranian students were, but it also had not kept much better track of the rest of the nation's foreign visitors and immigrants. Each day tens of thousands of aliens entered the country legally, leaving behind them a paper trail of 48 million files, with which the INS simply could not hope to cope. As one INS official put it, "We have no idea who came, who left, and, of course, who's here."

"The agency is a shambles," Representative Elizabeth Holtzman, who headed the House's immigration subcommittee during 1980 and who knew what she was talking about, told Bernard Weinraub of *The New York Times*. "It's an agency out of control, with 19th century tools. Record-keeping is a disaster. There's not one part of the place that seems professional to me." Charles Gordon, the agency's former general counsel, agreed. "They're overworked and understaffed," he said. "They don't have the ability to cope with the influx. It's sort of like putting your finger in a leaking dike. The pressures by people who want to come here are enormous, and they just can't handle them."

Holtzman and Gordon were being kind. The reality—and it really was a remarkable state of affairs for an immensely rich and technologically advanced nation in the late twentieth century—was that the United States of America was no longer able to keep out those from other countries who wished to come here, and there were many who wished to come. Anyone who possessed the physical strength, it seemed, could walk across the Mexican border into Texas, Arizona, or California. Anyone with access to even the most bedraggled little boat could sail it into the Gulf Stream and land on some deserted Florida beach. Those who had the price of a one-way airline ticket could enter the country as tourists or students and then lose themselves in the crowded ethnic communities of some big city, and bogus visas and counterfeit immigration permits were for sale the world over. Once they were physically inside the country, the chances of being caught and sent home were slim, and should such misfortune somehow befall them, the long string of hearings and appeals to which every alien was entitled could delay their departure for months, even years. Then, if and when they were actually deported, they had only to begin the process over again, and better luck next time.

As the General Accounting Office put it after studying the immigration service and its problems, "An illegal alien, once safely into the United States, has little chance of being located and deported." Some politicians in Washington, sensing the beginnings of concern among the electorate, began warning that the country was rushing headlong toward the day when its ports and borders would be open to all comers. But the joke was that at that very moment the nation's ports and borders could scarcely have been open wider.

In addition to being the most mismanaged federal agency in Washington, no mean distinction in a city that is home to the General Services Administration and the Agency for International Development, the INS is the most archaic. At a time when the number of legal and illegal immigrants flooding the United States is greater than ever before in the nation's history, most of the INS's records are still being kept by hand, in torn manila folders stuffed into old-fashioned filing cabinets. It is as if, one bureaucrat there said, the Internal Revenue Service were still using quill pens and ledgers.

The INS now inspects some 270 million people a year as they enter the United States at airports, at seaports, and along the Mexican and Canadian borders. It catches 1 million more who enter the country illegally, but it does not have the faintest idea how many it is missing. It is not just the Iranian students who have escaped the immigration net. Because of lost or misplaced files, as 1980 began, the INS did not know for sure whom it had caught, whom it had sent home, whom it had made into citizens, whom it had turned down, or where any of them lived and worked. It had numbers—reams of statistics on apprehensions, deportations, and naturalizations that it presented to Congress every year at appropriations time—but when it came to attaching names and faces to the numbers, it was hard put to comply. No one at the INS, moreover, was bothered by such blind spots. One Justice Department official recalled a meeting between Attorney General Bell and several top INS officials called to try to resolve some of the agency's multitude of problems. "It was incredible," the man said. "All they cared about was more overtime. People were worrying about everything but the substantive concerns of an immigration agency."

When Leonel Castillo took over the INS in early 1977, not one cent of the agency's $318 million budget had been earmarked for computerization. There were millions of dollars set aside to pay bloated overtime salaries but precious little to hire more badly needly personnel at stations like Calexico, California, one of the principal ports of entry on the Mexican border, where thirty-six INS inspectors were madly trying to monitor 20 million crossings a year—one every two seconds. Chief among its shortcomings was the agency's list of aliens visiting the United States, which was at least six months, and probably closer to a year, out of date. Visitors filled out one form as they entered the country, another as they departed. But the two sets of forms had never been merged, and while the INS might, after a long and painful search, be able to say whether a particular person had, in fact, come here—that is, if some clerk could read the handwritten form the visitor had scrawled before landing—it could not say with any certainty whether he had ever left. In early 1980 INS officials were saying that it would be 1983 before they knew for sure who had entered or left the country during the previous two years. (This was part of the problem with the Iranian students; a further problem was that neither the arrival nor the departure records had ever been meshed with a third set of forms, frequently incomplete because of lax college administrators, showing whether aliens holding student visas were still registered or had dropped out of school.)

Sometimes the immigration system seemed to those who ran it as though it had been designed to fail; even when the INS was able to do its job, it only created more work for itself. Castillo recalled what happened after a naturalization ceremony he attended in Baltimore. "We swore in about seven hundred people," he said. "They became new citizens at noon, and by one o'clock our office in Baltimore was jammed with the same people who were now petitioning for other members of their families to come to the United States. Rather than clearing up work loads, we added work loads."

The supreme confusion and frustration of trying to check the flood tide of aliens across the Mexican border, coupled with the dual mission of attending to the hundreds of thousands of foreigners a year who wished to obtain labor certifications, change their immigration status, or become permanent residents and naturalized citizens, seemed to have nearly paralyzed the agency, often with tragicomic results. In February 1977 a Hong Kong merchant whose business in New York was taking longer than expected asked the service for a routine three-month extension of his visa. The request was never acknowledged, so the businessman went home early. Nearly three years later his lawyer received a letter from the INS saying that the request had been granted. Then there was the Iranian doctor whose application for permanent residence in the United States had been approved after many months. But when the doctor was told that he would have to return to Iran to pick up his new visa at the American embassy there, his lawyer telephoned the INS. "How can he go to the American embassy?" the lawyer asked. "Everyone's being held hostage there."

The official to whom he spoke was unmoved. "Those are the rules," he said. "No one's given us any other instructions."

The lawyer was lucky even to have got through. In the INS's thirty-seven district offices around the country telephones usually rang unanswered, and when they occasionally were answered, callers—including, in one embarrassing instance, the agency's general counsel, Dave Crosland—were placed on hold indefinitely. Special "search teams" assigned to locate urgently needed files looked high and low without success. Bags of mail were left unopened for months, sometimes for years, no matter who the senders were. A box filled with 200 unanswered letters from members of Congress, some of them postmarked a year earlier, was found stuffed into one INS file in Washington. Laughable, except that for every lost or misplaced file, for every unanswered telephone or letter, for every delay in acting on a request there are human consequences, sometimes tragic ones: deportation proceedings that never should have taken place; parents and children kept needlessly apart; impoverished refugees denied public assistance because they could not officially establish their right to be here. One such case was that of Janos and Edith Hagl, two Hungarian émigrés who owned a dry-cleaning shop in Miami. Though the Hagls had filed their application for permanent residency upon arriving here in 1971, they heard nothing until nine years later they were notified by the INS that because their application could not be found, they would have to leave the country. The Hagls' only alternative, the INS said, was to return to Hungary, file another application, and wait their turn.

Several weeks after its receipt of President Carter's order to send the Iranian students home, the INS told the White House that it knew of at least 50,583 Iranians in the United States who had been admitted with student visas. But that number had been obtained a year before by asking schools and colleges for a head count of Iranians and did not include those who had not reenrolled since then. Privately, INS officials said, the real number was probably closer to 100,000, but there was no way of knowing, and even if it had known, the INS did not have the personnel to track down more than a fraction of them. Nor, the officials added, did they have the slightest idea how many of the other 244,000 foreign students thought to be in the United States were similarly "out of status." Since it was unable to go to them, the INS was reduced to issuing a public appeal for all Iranians in the United States to come to it—to present themselves at the nearest office of the immigration service to have their student status verified. (Two years later, an INS official said that 6,500 of the Iranians who had come forward had been living in the country illegally. But the service would never know how many others had simply stayed hidden. "I still couldn't tell you how many Iranian students are here," the official said.)

In fairness, it was a nearly impossible job that the INS had been handed. With a total staff of fewer than half the number of police officers in New York City, the immigration service is responsible for:

*Guarding the nation's 2,000-mile border with Mexico and its 3,750-mile frontier with Canada, nearly 6,000 miles of unfortified boundary between friendly nations, with barely 2,600 Border Patrol agents to watch over them (only 400 of the agents are actually on duty at any one time, about the same as the number of officers assigned to police the New York City subway system).

*Thwarting the illegal entry of ineligible aliens into the United States and apprehending, questioning, detaining, and deporting all those it catches trying to slip into the country illegally.

*Inspecting and admitting, or denying entry to, more than a quarter *billion* citizens and visitors arriving each year at dozens of ports of entry around the country, not just the landlocked ports on both borders and the major international airports and sea-

119

ports but a number of smaller entry points, such as Raymond, Montana, and Presidio, Texas.

*Investigating violations of the Immigration and Nationality Act; receiving, recording, filing, and producing documents of entry, departure, and naturalization of aliens; and maintaining a registration record of all aliens who enter the United States, including files on where all permanent resident aliens are living and working.

*Extending visas held by visiting foreigners, acting on requests for changes of immigration status, emigration, and naturalization, all after conducting background investigations to see if the aliens are qualified for whatever they are seeking.

A number of the INS's difficulties stem from its bifurcated role as both a law enforcement and a service agency. On the one hand, the INS is supposed to monitor aliens streaming into the country and turn away those not qualified for admission; on the other, it is responsible for offering all possible assistance to aliens who wish to visit or emigrate here legally. It is the agency responsible both for keeping aliens out and for helping them get in. When the INS encounters an arriving visitor who does not have a proper visa or finds someone it thinks is here illegally, it is obligated by law to afford him or her a hearing at which he or she can argue his or her right to be here. And if the visitor has such a right, it is the INS that guides him or her through the maze of forms and petitions that will ultimately allow him or her to remain. What, then, is it: a police officer or a social worker? Many of the service's employees are never quite sure, and the two different functions are often in conflict.

The enforcement part of the job, which consists largely of saying no, is by far the easier of the two tasks. The service side is governed by more than 5,000 pages of rules and regulations, topped by three hefty volumes of statutes that devote 36 pages alone to the procedure for dealing with crew members of foreign vessels that stop over in the United States. The section on naturalization law itself is more than 200 pages long, and for every statute there are myriad judicial decisions that determine how it should be interpreted. Many INS employees, most of whom are not lawyers and some of whom are semiliterate, never fully comprehend either the immigration laws they are sworn to enforce or the arcane notions of civil rights to be preserved in the process. (Few Border Patrol agents, for example, understand the ever-changing limits the judiciary has placed on their fundamentally broad powers of search and seizure.) In the end it is usually simpler to throw somebody out of the country than to pore over the laws and regulations in hopes of finding a clue to whether or not he should be allowed to stay. Under such circumstances mistakes are inevitable. The Los Angeles County Bar Association estimates that one of every ten people deported by the INS's office there, now unofficially renamed Ellis Island West, has a legal right to be in the United States.

Given the immense numbers of arriving aliens, however, even under the best of circumstances the job of the immigration service would be next to impossible. Immigration offices around the country are literally overrun by new arrivals seeking assistance with immigration problems. In Houston, where the INS can handle only 200 applicants a day, people line up before dawn in front of the red-brick federal building in hopes of being served before nightfall. In El Paso the lines begin forming at 3:30 in the morning; in Miami, at 1:00 A.M.; in Los Angeles, at midnight. By noon tempers are usually running high among those who have been standing in the same place for hours. Pushing, shoving, and shouting are commonplace. Full-fledged riots occasionally break out, and instead of using all its resources for their intended purpose, too often the INS is reduced to crowd control. An apt analogy might be Charles Dicken's Circumlocution Office, where files were passed from room to room but nothing ever happened.

Some of those in the lines at the doorstep of the immigration service are in the country illegally, but they know no fear. It is not unusual for someone to walk into the district director's office in Los Angeles and announce that he or she has been smuggled into the country and wants to apply for a green card. The harassed secretaries only send them away. A couple of years ago Dhanajay Paranjpe, a student from India who wanted to return home but had no money, went to the Washington, D.C., office of the immigration service to announce that he was an illegal alien and wished to be deported. He was ignored. The INS, Paranjpe said later, "wants to do the opposite of what people want." In fact, it is all the agency can do to keep the

121

lines moving through the most Kafkaesque labyrinth thus far devised by government, a system in which people in one line are given numbers that allow them to get into other lines to receive other numbers that might or might not guarantee that their cases will be heard, their questions answered, their problems resolved, before the big glass doors swing shut for the day. It takes hours, sometimes days, for an immigrant to make contact with another human being, and then it is likely to be with an overworked, ill-trained official who has learned to detest the numbing job that pays him perhaps $12,000 a year and who, chances are, cannot even speak the applicant's language unless it is Spanish, and even then probably not very well. Yet such petty bureaucrats have nearly total power to decide the fates of those who appear before them. "The INS just can't be compared to any other agency," says an immigration lawyer who has done daily battle with the service for years. "They operate with a great deal of discretionary power. Other agencies have specific regulations, but the immigration people are their own bosses. Each one, each immigration officer, is a little king. Each has tremendous discretionary power. No other agency in the government is like this—it's a zoo." Or, as another immigration lawyer put it to the *Los Angeles Times*, "The aliens who attempt to play it straight with the I.N.S. are the ones that get screwed. They whip you around, telling you one thing one day and another the next. I can't tell my clients this, but sometimes I think they'd be better off if they stayed away from I.N.S., remained undocumented and got false papers."

On the enforcement side things are not much better, and nowhere are they worse than in San Ysidro, California, where the INS presides over the busiest port of entry in the country (and, for that matter, the world), sixteen miles south of San Diego and just across the border from Tijuana, Mexico. There are twenty-four lanes for vehicles at San Ysidro and five more for pedestrians, and there is a force of 104 immigration inspectors, thirty-four per shift, to man them twenty-four hours a day, seven days a week. It is an immense job. Last year, some 40 million people entered the United States at San Ysidro alone, in cars and on foot, 75,000 of them on a typical weekday, twice that number on weekends and holidays. Many were Americans who have been to Tijuana for the day, but many more are aliens, the great majority of them Mexicans. Every one of them has to be asked the same litany of questions, which always begins with "Of what country are you a citizen? Where do you live? Why are you coming to the United States?"

Though many of the arrivals have valid nonimmigrant visitor's visas or carry border crossing cards, which permit them to visit the United States for up to seventy-two hours if they stay within twenty-five miles of the border, many more simply tell the inspectors that they are American citizens or permanent resident aliens, perhaps producing an official document like a passport or a green card to back up their claim, perhaps not. The problem confronting the inspectors is that many such claims are untrue, and many of the documents proffered to support them counterfeit, and it is up to the inspectors to decide which is which. If the first set of questions does not provide a clue there are others: "Where did you go to high school? What's your mother's maiden name? What's your home telephone number?" Such questions might trip up the casual border crossers, those who try to make it through the gates on a lark, but not the more determined ones. Even so, it is exceedingly difficult to tell in thirty seconds—which is the average time a line inspector has to question each individual—if he or she is telling the truth.

It would be a difficult job if the inspectors were sitting in a quiet room somewhere, but they often work under the most trying conditions, surrounded by swirling exhaust fumes, buffeted by wind, rain, and snow, trying to make themselves heard over the honking horns of impatient motorists stuck in a line of cars that might be backed up for blocks. There are, to be sure, little tricks of the trade—watch the carotid artery at the base of the throat to see whether the pulse rate quickens; watch the pupils of the eyes to see if they dilate—but none of them is infallible. On an average day at San Ysidro, something on the order of eighty false claims to American citizenship are detected. No one knows how many other bogus citizens get by; but there are many, and the scene at San Ysidro is repeated day and night at other ports of entry along both borders and at dozens of airports and steamship docks around the country.

The low priority that the immigration service's mission, particularly its enforcement function, is accorded by the government is most clearly seen in the amount of money the INS has been given to spend. In 1978 the agency's overall budget was $283 million, about half that of the FBI and less even than its sister agency, the U.S. Customs Service. By 1980 it had grown to only $298 million—an increase of 5 percent that, in a year of near double-digit inflation, was a substantial decrease. During the same period the INS's enforcement budget grew by less than 2 percent, a smaller increase than had been given to the U.S. Marshal's Service, the Secret Service, or the Drug Enforcement Administration. To the policymakers in Washington, guarding federal prisoners, protecting the President, and stemming the flow of illegal narcotics into the country all seemed more important than slowing the alien influx, but that was because official Washington had not noticed how high the tide had risen, had not noticed that at the same time the immigration service's resources had been shrinking its work load had grown at an exponential rate. Nearly 10 million nonimmigrants, for example, were inspected and admitted in 1978, compared with 4 million in 1970. During the same period the number of illegal aliens arrested while entering the country illegally increased by more than 300 percent, from 325,000 to just over 1 million.

Perhaps the most serious shortcoming of the INS's budget, however, remained its failure to provide the funds to help the agency dig out from under the blizzard of paper that was blowing its way. When Castillo made a stab at computerizing his agency's files shortly after assuming office, he was forced to appropriate money set aside for vehicle maintenance and other purposes. But the computer system he set up was a classic case of too little too late. For a variety of technical reasons, Castillo's computer never worked properly; and while it was being tinkered with, the INS's records, so vital to the agency's performance, remained in near chaos. Although the INS continued to ask the public to let it know the whereabouts of illegal aliens and even set aside special hot line telephone numbers for this purpose, tens of thousands of tips and leads called in by citizens, labor unions, and others who knew where illegal aliens were working or living were simply thrown away. "There was nowhere for the information to go," one INS inspector explained.

Businesses that asked the INS for guidance on whether a job applicant was in the country illegally had to wait months, sometimes a year or more, for an answer. By that time the employee was likely to have moved on. State and county welfare agencies that had the same question about people seeking public assistance grew tired of waiting for a reply and began passing out benefits to all who asked. For refugees seeking certification of their resident status, something they needed in order to obtain special relocation funds, waits of six months to a year were routine. In the INS's Houston office, which Castillo tried to turn into a model operation that would prove to Congress and the Justice Department that the immigration service could be made to work, the waiting time to become a citizen was two years. Anyone who lost an immigration document such as a green card would be lucky to have a replacement within a year, and in the meantime, a permanent resident alien who had no way to verify his or her status with the INS might end up being deported.

In Los Angeles, as in other big cities, visitors applying for routine six-month extensions of their visas were not likely to receive a reply until after the six months had gone by. "Even by the time I get a denial out," said Joe Howerton, the weary district director there, "they've probably got their six months plus some more." The case of an ordinary illegal alien presented for deportation there might not be heard for years, and Howerton was wondering why such cases should be assembled at all. "There's no reason for us to pump out work for the courts," he said, "when there's nothing there." As he spoke, more than half a million requests for visa extensions had yet to be entered in the INS's computers because they could not be matched, by hand, to the original arrival forms. But half a million was a trifling number. By September 1981 the backlog of handwritten, smudged, often illegible I-94's—the arrival and departure forms filled out by visitors—numbered 30 million. The same year the INS simply gave up attempting to register resident aliens, something it had done each January since the beginning of World War II. INS officials later acknowledged that it didn't much matter, that the alien registration requirement had been mostly for show, that the registration cards had never been matched up with the aliens' files anyway.

* * *

One reason was that the files themselves, the so-called A (for alien) files, the backbone of the service's record-keeping system, were so frequently lost. "The way the system is set up, it's totally unmanageable," said Lynda Zengerle, a Washington immigration lawyer who has frequent dealings with the INS. "It's programmed to fail. You're talking about a mountain of paper. Last week I called to check on three of my clients. All three files were lost. At some stage of the game one out of every two files is lost. Sometimes they're recovered, sometimes not. If you're a poor immigrant and you can't afford a lawyer, you've had it."

For most of its existence the INS has paid scant attention to its constituents' needs, because it has not had to. Aliens, after all, cannot vote and have no clout with Congress, and it is Congress that has asked the questions and controlled the purse strings. Or, in the case of the INS, two members of Congress. One was Senator James O. Eastland, the Mississippi Democrat and cotton planter who served for years as chairman of the Senate Judiciary Committee. A product of the southern agrarian aristocracy, Eastland was more sensitive than some in Congress to the needs of farmers and in particular to the need, which his own family sometimes felt, to employ illegal alien labor. The other was the late Representative John Rooney of Brooklyn, for many years the head of the House subcommittee that passed on the agency's budget.

Together Eastland and Rooney controlled the agency's top appointments, in return for protecting the INS from meddlers, reformers, and other outside interference. Though the INS, like any branch of the administrative tree, was in theory subject to congressional oversight, it operated for years as a closed system, which is just the way Eastland, Rooney, and the INS higher-ups wanted it. Until quite recently the top INS brass, with the exception of the commissioner, had almost to a man begun their careers in the Border Patrol. Service on the Mexican border was a requisite for membership in the INS insider's club; and as those men rose through the ranks, they took with them the night-stick-and-six-gun mentality they had acquired there, as well as the belief that their sole mission was to keep undesirables out of the country—with the understanding that field hands who worked for some of the wealthiest ranchers or maids who cleaned the homes of the nation's better families were not necessarily undesirable. Neither were those well-connected foreigners with a little pull in Washington. "Frequently," an internal INS memo from the Eastland–Rooney era declared, "a 'humanitarian' parole has been obtained by a Congressman, Senator or the White House for some favored person. Normally the person is inadmissible for some reason, but we would be subject to criticism if the person were not allowed to enter the United States." Under the parole authority, senior INS officials have acquired the power to admit anyone they please into the United States, and the power has traditionally been subject to considerable abuse. When a Mexican woman, holding her baby girl fathered by an immigration officer, appeared at the California border a few years ago and threatened to create a scandal unless she was admitted, an INS supervisor quickly paroled in both the woman and her baby.

During much of the 1950's the INS was headed by a retired army general, Joseph May Swing, a West Point classmate of Dwight Eisenhower's who began his career as a young lieutenant with the Pershing expedition pursuing Pancho Villa across the Southwest and who ended it, as he liked to say, still chasing Mexicans. Swing ran the INS the way his counterpart, J. Edgar Hoover, ran the FBI, which is to say, like a private preserve. He put his daughter on the agency's payroll and made no apology when newspapers printed the story. He took hunting trips to Mexico at government expense, and when a congressional subcommittee asked him about such improper use of federal funds, Swing said the trips had been "liaison visits" with Mexican immigration officials.

Swing's successor, Raymond Farrell, a bureaucratic nonentity handpicked by Rooney, was followed by another military man, Leonard F. Chapman, a former commandant of the Marine Corps who, in the best leatherneck tradition, spoke of illegal aliens as though they were the enemy, muttering about the "silent invasion" as though he were referring to Chinese Communist regulars slipping across the 40th parallel. It was an inspired departure from such tradition, then, when Jimmy Carter chose Leonel J. Castillo, a thirty-seven-year-old Mexican-American from Houston, as Chapman's replacement. Castillo, a former Houston city controller whose grandfather had paid 50 cents to walk into Texas from Mexico early in the century, proved to be both a brilliant appointment and, through no real fault of his own, a disastrous one.

Because Castillo was the first Hispanic ever to head an agency that dealt mainly with Hispanics, his perspective on the immigration problem differed sharply from that of his predecessors. As a civilian, Castillo had been critical of the INS's treatment of illegal aliens—a term he disliked, preferring, to the consternation of most of his subordinates, who still spoke of ''wetbacks,'' the more cumbersome ''undocumented worker.'' Castillo had been a high school football star, a campus leader during his college days in San Antonio, and one of the first Peace Corps volunteers. But he knew how unpleasant life in America could be for people with brown skin, and he was determined not to add to their suffering. He also refused to be drawn into the illegal alien numbers game. ''My God,'' he said once, ''I've got official figures that range from two to twenty million. Who knows how many there are?'' Castillo was also unsure just how much of an economic threat the illegal aliens really posed. ''Some of them clearly perform important functions,'' he said. ''But even if you could somehow miraculously round up eight million illegal workers, you'd then have to find eight million U.S. workers who were willing to go into jobs that are low-paying and to do work that is very menial.''

Despite the conventional wisdom, Castillo didn't think those workers existed, nor did he think there was any truly desirable way of keeping the aliens out. ''You cannot seal the border,'' he said. ''The only long range answer is world economic development. If a guy's making $4 a week in Mexico and he can come to Houston and be a dishwasher for a dollar an hour, that's a tremendous increase in his economic status. In the short run, there will have to be some better enforcement. But in the long run, the United States cannot afford to have itself walled off from all the poor people of the world. It's not practical. It's not sensible. It's not going to happen.''

To many in the immigration service, Castillo was beginning to sound as if he were, well, soft on illegal immigration. If any doubt remained, such suspicions were confirmed the day he announced that he intended to shift his agency's focus away from its preoccupation with enforcement to more emphasis on its service role. "The INS doesn't exist just to keep out people who want to enter this country illegally," the new commissioner told his subordinates. "We also exist to provide a whole variety of services for immigrants who are legally here."

Remarkable words from the nation's chief immigration enforcer, and there would be more. He was aware, Castillo warned, that the human rights of aliens were being disregarded, even abused, by the INS, that not every alien was being told of his right to a deportation hearing or to a lawyer. His deputies, he said, had assured him that the abuses were due not to malice but to the administrative overload, that his agents "simply don't have time to give everybody a hearing, to go through all the necessities of due process." But Castillo thought that was no excuse. "We've got to give an alien in this country as many protections as are offered under the Constitution," he said. Castillo ordered the Border Patrol to keep "hands off" the ad hoc private schools that had sprung up around Texas to educate the children of illegal aliens who had been denied free admission to the public schools. "You don't want to raid a school with a lot of little children," he said. "It's very short-sighted to deny them schooling." The Border Patrol, to whom the children were just little wetbacks, chafed. When farmers in the Presidio Valley of Texas could not find American workers to help them harvest their onions and melons, Castillo approved the temporary admission of a few hundred Mexican field hands from across the border who were glad to do the backbreaking work. The Border Patrol agents watched them come and ground their teeth.

After touring the service's sweltering, flea-infested detention center in El Paso, Castillo bought some soccer equipment for the detainees, who had had nothing to do while waiting for their deportation hearings but play checkers and watch television. Among Border Patrol agents in El Paso, who had been told there was not enough money in the INS budget to buy them a single helicopter, the gesture was not popular. Castillo was also concerned about the multitude of immigration lawyers and counselors, many of them retired INS personnel, who took advantage of their connections with the service to secure preferential treatment for their alien clients, sometimes going farther than the law allowed by arranging sham marriages for immigration purposes, running dubious "travel agencies," and other rackets. The counselors usually made far more money in retirement than they had in active service; a note to an in-service friend saying "please take care of my client," known within the INS as a *por favor*, could bring a fee of several hundred dollars. But Castillo knew the system was rotten. "When we start picking priorities," he said, "I think that's one of the key areas to crack down on." He never got around to it, but to those in the service who were looking forward to joining the ranks of the immigration counselors, they were not pleasant words.

One of the commissioner's most controversial ideas was Operation Outreach, a part of something Castillo called his absorption program. Like everybody else, Castillo had no idea how many aliens were living in the country illegally, but he suspected, given the vast complexity of the immigration laws, that quite a few of them might unwittingly be eligible for some variety of permanent visa. One way to reduce the number of illegal aliens, Castillo thought, was to turn into legal residents those who could qualify. He recorded a number of radio announcements in Spanish to be broadcast around the country. "Attention, attention," they began. "Many people are under the false impression that foreign nationals have no rights while in the United States. If you are a visitor, student, or in doubt about your immigration status, it may be possible for you to stay in this country." Listeners were advised to telephone the nearest INS office for assistance.

Castillo also favored an amnesty for those aliens whose status could not be regularized in some other way. "I think the law clearly has to allow for some persons who have been here illegally a long time to adjust their status," he said. "They have worked here, paid taxes here, and lived decently. We have done this three times in our history before; we can do it again." The reaction from Congress and the ranks of the INS was withering. Here was the immigration commissioner, whose job was to throw illegal aliens out of the country, offering to find ways to help them stay, even suggesting that some of them had somehow earned the right to citizenship. It was a far cry from the knock-heads-and-take-names-later attitude the INS had grown accustomed to under Generals Swing and Chapman, and few in the service liked it. To his troops, Castillo's message seemed to be that they were no longer expected to enforce the immigration laws, that the service had capitulated to the enemy. Before long he was being referred to within the ranks as the wetback commissioner.

Castillo was surprised by such reactions. Again and again he insisted that there had been no lessening of enforcement during his tenure, pointing out that during his first year in office the service had apprehended and sent home a record 800,000 illegal aliens, the next year 1 million plus. Hadn't he been the one to push for the unprecedented assault on the alien smugglers who often preyed brutally on their countrymen? Hadn't he been an outspoken supporter of the controversial plan to replace the aging border fences with new, impermeable barriers? Castillo didn't think he had been antienforcement; he had just been trying to strike a proper balance. But his appeals fell on mostly deaf ears, and before long whatever chance he had had to shape and mold the INS evaporated. Among his subordinates he was ignored, laughed at, derided, his directives disobeyed, his reforms sabotaged. In the El Paso Border Patrol station, somebody put a cartoon on the bulletin board that showed four Mexicans in sombreros crossing the Rio Grande. Across the top somebody else had written, "Castillo's cousins." Everybody there thought it was very funny.

Nor, it seemed, could Castillo garner much support from Hispanic Americans. Even though he had recommended both an amnesty and a doubling of the quota of 20,000 immigrants a year from Mexico, he was bitter about the fact that everywhere he went "I get picketed by Chicanos because I'm deporting too many people." In September 1979, realizing that he was destined to have little lasting impact on the agency and weary of what was surely the most thankless $50,000-a-year job in Washington, Leonel Castillo resigned and went home to Texas. His departure left the INS leaderless at the most crucial moment in its history, and it was to remain that way for more than two years. Jimmy Carter, who had pledged to fill as many key posts as possible with women and minorities, insisted that Castillo be replaced with another Hispanic, even though Dave Crosland, the INS general counsel who had been hastily elevated to acting commissioner, was everybody else's choice for the job.

White House talent scouts scoured the country in search of candidates but with little success. There were able people who fitted the President's prescription, among them Henry Cisneros, the impressive young mayor of San Antonio. But like Cisneros, most of them realized that it was a no-win game. "It's a very demanding, difficult job," admitted Benjamin Civiletti, who had replaced Griffin Bell as the attorney general. "It's not as if there are hundreds of people seeking to become INS commissioner." Herman Sillas, the United States attorney in Sacramento, was briefly considered, then discarded after it was alleged (though never established) that he had once taken a $7,500 bribe. Next in line was Matt Garcia, the fifty-two-year-old son of an illegal Mexican alien, a Texas state legislator with a strong civil rights record but no particular knowledge of immigration or the immigration service. During his confirmation hearings Garcia made the mistake of telling the Senate Judiciary Committee that he thought the INS had done a "respectable" job of tracking down the Iranian students. "I worry about your being head of INS, if you think the job the INS is doing now is respectable," said Senator Thad Cochran of Mississippi. "That place is a disaster area." After a routine FBI background check discovered that he had been late in filing his federal income tax returns for several years, Garcia's nomination languished in limbo, and on November 4, 1980, the day Ronald Reagan started Jimmy Carter back down the road to Plains, the Senate had yet to act on it. The next day a disgusted Matt Garcia withdrew his name from consideration.

The search began anew, but it proved no easier for the Republicans, and as Ronald Reagan celebrated his first year in office, there still was no permanent commissioner. The Reagan White House had approached William B. Kolender, the respected police chief of San Diego who at least knew something about the subject at hand, but Kolender turned the job down. Reagan's second choice was a millionaire Miami Cadillac dealer named Norman Braman, who, not coincidentally, had been a major fund raiser for the President's 1980 campaign. Apart from the fact that his father had emigrated to the United States from Poland and his mother from Romania, Braman had no visible qualifications for the post. When the public and congressional reaction proved to be adverse, Braman quietly withdrew, explaining that "the current depressed market" in the auto industry required that he devote full time to his business. In the meantime, the INS, like a rudderless boat, was cruising in ever-widening circles out to sea.

To be fair, not all of the INS's problems were of its own making. As 1980 began, the agency became the victim of a bizarre string of events, foremost among them the springtime invasion of Florida by Cuban refugees, an unexpected, unbudgeted emergency that placed a nearly intolerable strain on its paper-thin resources. As scores of overworked Border Patrol agents were plucked from the Mexican border and sent to Key West to help process the boatloads of arriving Cubans, vast holes were opened in the nation's already meager border defenses. Two-thirds of all illegal border crossings occur in and around San Ysidro and El Paso, and it was from there that most of the officers were taken. The El Paso station lost thirty agents, a fifth of its total force, and San Ysidro gave up fifty. Some of them would not return for months.

To make matters worse, scores of INS investigators from big cities like Denver, San Antonio, and Chicago, men who in normal times would have provided the service's second line of defense by scouring neighborhoods and businesses for illegal aliens who had made it past the Border Patrol, were also being detailed to Florida to help with the Cuban influx, and most of those who remained were busy interviewing Iranian students, tens of thousands of whom were still unaccounted for. The losses hurt. In Los Angeles, Phil Smith, the chief INS investigator who might have had forty or fifty men on the streets on a normal day, was now down to eight. Ironically, it made little difference. The transportation budget was so low that Smith's eight investigators could catch enough aliens in an hour to fill up the three buses that set out each night for the border. In San Francisco the monthly apprehension rate dropped from close to 1,000 to fewer than 500. In Chicago it was down by 25 percent. If the aliens could make it across the border and into the big cities, said Dick Staley, the long-suffering Border Patrol chief in El Paso, they were "home free." And by the tens of thousands every week, they were making it.

In fact, according to all reports, they were coming in unprecedented numbers. Mexico was experiencing its worst harvest in three decades, the result of an unusually dry autumn and an early frost, and the drought had hit hardest at the small farmers in the central and northwestern parts of the country, where crops lacked irrigation. In normal times such men probably would not have made the long trek northward across the border, preferring to eke out a subsistence living at home, but they were not going to sit in their villages and starve. And as if it did not have troubles enough, the Border Patrol was also running out of gasoline, thanks to a budget that had made no provision for the soaring cost of fuel.

The patrol had always operated on the theory that a significant percentage of illegal border crossers would get through its frontline defenses, which was why it conducted secondary operations farther to the north, such as stopping cars at checkpoints along major highways and raiding farms, ranches, restaurants, and other places where aliens might be found. But now there was no gasoline to conduct the secondary operations. Those Border Patrol vehicles that were not incapacitated by the lack of spare parts were limited to three gallons per eight-hour shift. The Iranian student project had eaten up what contingency funds were left, and the problem now became one of pure economics. ''If you have less fuel to transport people and to transport officers to their areas, you're just not going to make as many arrests,'' one INS official said. In some places the Border Patrol reverted to riding horseback along the border. A horse, one patrol chief explained, cost the service only about $50 a week, a third the cost of operating a motor vehicle. But for the most part the patrol could do nothing except mass its remaining officers in more or less stationary positions along the border in hopes that potential border crossers would be dissuaded by a show of force.

It was called a high-profile strategy, and it was a disaster. A month after it went into effect, apprehensions in San Ysidro and El Paso were down 50 percent. Stationary officers, it seemed, were simply that much easier for the border crossers to get past. All along the border, agents told of watching aliens walk into the United States a few hundred yards away. There was no gasoline for going after them or for hauling them to detention centers, and anyway the centers were full. It was a holiday for illegal aliens. In New Orleans, vanloads of Mexicans were being put back on the streets because there was no money to pay for their transportation to Mexico. In Laredo, when a smuggled load of 150 Mexicans was spotted three miles outside the city limits, the Border Patrol made no move to intercept it. "We haven't got enough gas to go out and get them," one agent said.

After years of begging, the Border Patrol had finally acquired eight badly needed helicopters—not new ones but Vietnam surplus machines scavenged from the army. But there was no money to outfit the helicopters with floodlights or radios, rendering them next to useless. Then, just when it seemed as though things could not possibly get any worse, the Justice Department ordered the immigration service to stop its random searches of homes and businesses for illegal aliens so as not to interfere with the counting of aliens by the impending 1980 census. Those immigration investigators and Border Patrol agents left in the big cities told of driving past restaurants and construction sites and seeing the aliens wave at them. "We've created a sanctuary in this country for illegal aliens," an INS official said. "The word has gotten back to Mexico about our relaxing our standards. It used to be that when we'd come around, they'd all scatter, but now they don't even notice us." By far the sharpest blow, however, was the INS's growing realization that the Justice Department, which since the Iranian student mess had been paying close attention to the immigration service and its problems, was less and less convinced that simply throwing more manpower and money at the border was the way to stop the alien traffic. More border guards, the department thought, might simply mean that the same aliens would be apprehended more often before finally making a successful entry. Surveys of Border Patrol agents showed that most of them disagreed, believing that the addition of another 3,500 agents to the existing force of 2,600 would enable them virtually to seal the border. From Los Angeles to Houston the refrain was the same: Just give us the people and we can do the job. But Civiletti had made clear that he had his doubts, and they were reflected in the Carter administration's 1981 budget, which allocated $347 million to the immigration service, a piddling increase of 4 percent and, after subtraction for inflation, a decrease of 6. To top that off, the administration was also ordering the elimination of 262 INS personnel, including 199 Border Patrol agents. The INS was now officially a "lower-priority" agency.

As 1980 wore on, apprehensions were down dramatically, by as much as 400 percent in South Texas alone; this meant not that fewer illegal aliens were trying to get into the country but that more were succeeding. But as the INS well knew, not all the illegal visitors could be attributed to its own shortcomings, and the knowledge served only to increase its sense of hopelessness and frustration. In 1968 250,000 foreign business people had visited the United States. In 1978 there had been 800,000. During the same period the number of tourists jumped from just over 2 million to 6.6 million, and the number of students from 73,000 to 187,000. In 1980 temporary foreign visitors for all purposes totaled 12 million, and it was possible that more than 1 million of them had not gone home when they were supposed to. The problem was that, more and more, the State Department, which is responsible for issuing nonimmigrant visas, was granting them to "bad-risk" applicants, and for familiar reasons: Like the INS, it simply did not have enough money or people to do its job properly. But the overstayers were not the State Department's problem; once they were in the United States, it was up to the immigration service to make sure they left on time. This, of course, the INS could not do. By counting the I-94's, it might be able to determine that 12 million people had entered the country and that only 10 million had left, but because it did not have the resources to match the forms with each other, it had no idea who had stayed behind.

In addition to driving INS personnel up the wall, such laxness was costing the taxpayers dearly. According to David North, the noted immigration researcher, the average time an American Foreign Service officer spent deciding whether to issue or deny a visa was four and a half minutes, a decision that cost the government $3.37. The cost to the INS of inspecting the arriving passenger was even less, 42 cents. But North estimated that once the visa overstayer was in the country, it cost the Border Patrol $43.38 to catch him, if indeed it ever did. In addition, the INS was spending some $12 million a year to "repatriate" the visa abusers it did catch, to send them back to Latin America, Asia, or wherever they had come from. (When the repatriation funds ran out, aliens who spoke Spanish and had brown skin, whether they were from Argentina or the Philippines, were often transformed into what the service called quick Mexicans and put on a cheap bus to Mexico.)

There was another reason for the flood of visa overstayers, one that almost nobody at the State Department wanted to talk about. It had to do with the fact that though many of the 650 American consuls abroad were earning as little as $17,000 a year, they were nevertheless expected to dress well and to move through the upper levels of local society. At the going black-market rate of $1,000, a junior consular officer could double his annual income by selling fewer than twenty visas a year, an average of one every two and a half weeks. Too many of them, it seemed, were doing just that. In the capitals of nearly every Third World country—in Mexico City, in Seoul, in Kingston, in New Delhi—the waiting lists for immigrant visas were backed up for years. But for $1,000, if one knew to whom to speak, one could obtain a nonimmigrant visa. Usually the go-between was a travel agent who "knew somebody in the embassy," but it might just as easily have been a policeman or a taxi driver. And what did it matter that the visa might cost a year's salary? The little red stamp was a ticket to a whole new life.

Such corruption was naturally more prevalent in poorer countries, where there were more people desperate to start their lives over. A Japanese businessman or a British tourist could have a visa for the asking; there was little reason to doubt that either would return home when the holiday or business was finished. But it was harder for the visa officer to justify such assumptions about the average Paraguayan, and to acquire a tourist visa, such people often found it necessary to provide some incentive.

As economic and political pressures have intensified around the world, as more and more people have become willing to pay for the privilege of coming to the United States, visa fraud has grown worse. In a given year, some State Department officials estimate, between 20,000 and 50,000 American visas are sold, by either American diplomats or local employees of American embassies. Until recently the American consulate in Hong Kong was notorious for its corrupt local staff, and the same is unfortunately true in India and several Latin American countries, among them Brazil and Paraguay.

"The U.S. is an island of security compared to a lot of countries," says Hume Horan, a deputy assistant secretary at the State Department's Bureau of Consular Affairs, "and people will do anything to come here. Foreign Service officers are fallible. They're not made of any different substance from anyone else. They come under pressures, subtle pressures, and sometimes the younger people don't know what's happening until it's too late."

A woman who worked in the American consulate in Port-au-Prince describes the pressures as enormous. "Almost as soon as you arrive you're tested," she told Bernie Weinraub of *The Times*. "First off, someone handed me an envelope with eight hundred-dollar bills for some visas. On several occasions people offered me money flat out. I was intimidated and harassed. If I went to a restaurant or a nightclub, people would appear out of the woodwork and ask me about visas. People followed me home and hung around my house. It was all pretty weird."

That woman was able to resist the offers and suggestions, but some of her colleagues were not. Two years ago Carolyn King, an American vice-consul in Port-au-Prince, was sentenced to prison for selling visas. A short time later the Miami law firm of David M. Walters, a former United States ambassador to the Vatican, was charged with having illegally obtained visas for thirty-four of its foreign clients from A. Stephen Vitale, then chief American consul in Nassau. At one point in 1981, State Department security agents said, there were investigations of criminal visa fraud under way in thirty-five American embassies and consulates around the world, including the Dominican Republic and Colombia. In a significant number of cases the suspected bribe takers were not locally hired employees but career American Foreign Service officers like King and Vitale. Though the State Department, with its pinstripe-suit mentality, is reluctant to acknowledge that some of its highly educated, carefully selected personnel are susceptible to corruption, a confidential department report acknowledged: "Unfortunately, too many of our officers have succumbed to the temptation of easy money."

The State Department must shoulder another share of the

blame for the immigration mess. Thousands, probably tens of thousands, of the United States passports being flashed at INS inspectors by arriving passengers each year are frauds—that is, they are genuine passports issued by the Passport Office, but to foreigners not entitled to carry them. The incidence of passport fraud is higher than the State Department cares to admit, and it is on the increase. At a minimum, department security agents estimate, some 30,000 passports are issued to ineligible applicants every year, and the number might well be much higher. Contrary to the storybook image of the foreign spy who painstakingly forges his counterfeit passport, all that is needed to obtain the real thing is a birth certificate, a document that can be purchased for a few hundred dollars on the black market or, given some time, obtained free from any county clerk's office in the country. The State Department reluctantly agrees that some passport fraud exists but argues that trying to eradicate it would be too expensive, involving extensive background checks on every applicant. The INS considers this attitude unfortunate. Most immigration inspectors are fairly good at spotting counterfeit or altered passports—a few inspectors, known as fraudulent documents experts, are absolute whizzes—but when confronted with the genuine article, they can do little except allow the bearer to walk through the turnstiles.

By 1980 the 12,000 men and women of the immigration service were beginning to think that they alone cared about controlling illegal immigration, and many of them were also beginning to wonder why they should care, why they should struggle to hold back the tide at the border when, all across the Caribbean, the Coast Guard was rushing to assist foundering boats filled with Cubans and Haitians and escorting them to Florida. As the absurdity of the government's immigration policy began to sink in—a Mexican caught walking across the border would be sent home but a Haitian walking ashore in Florida became a "Cuban-Haitian entrant"—immigration inspectors around the country were simply giving up on the job, "retiring in place." "They're just waiting for that retirement check," said one inspector at San Ysidro. "If an alien's breathing, if he's got shoes and socks on, they just wave him up the road." The San Ysidro port, he said, was now one of the easiest places in the country for illegal aliens to enter the United States.

"Just keep trying," he advised, "and you'll find some inspector who's asleep at the wheel." The malaise was catching. At Miami's airport, INS supervisors were overheard telling their subordinates, "Don't defer anyone. We're too busy downtown." At Kennedy, in New York, the word was: "Don't deny any extensions. We'll just have to grant them on motions to reconsider." An ancient INS dictum declared, "No inspector ever got in trouble for letting someone into the country," and in the summer of 1980 it was being followed with a vengeance.

Yet it was the inspectors who were eating up what was left of the INS budget. Under a remarkable provision in the 1931 immigration act, inspectors were paid double for overtime—and they worked a lot of overtime, $20 million worth every year. The average overtime pay for each of the service's 2,700 inspectors was $5,500 a year, but senior officers made far more. In 1979 one supervisor at the Honolulu airport earned $58,826 in overtime alone, and several others as much as $40,000. During the Mariel crisis some senior INS employees in Key West were making an extra $10,000 a month. Some of the overtime was justified, but much was not. "I saw a lot of overtime that was absolutely unnecessary," said Ed Begley, a former inspector at San Ysidro. "In a number of cases when I worked overtime on Sundays and at night, there was absolutely nothing to do, just sit around occupying time and space and drawing double time for it. There were jokes about the number of Mercedes-Benzes and Cadillacs in the parking lot—take a look, it'll amaze you. These guys are civil servants." One of the Cadillacs, Begley said, belonged to a supervisor who collected double time for coming in on Friday nights to make popcorn for the other inspectors. But the overtime was the one bright spot in the inspectors' unrelieved misery, and they were prepared to fight for it. When the Reagan administration, determined to reduce the cost of government, proposed an amendment that would have repealed the double time provision, the inspectors at San Ysidro threatened a work-to-rule slowdown that would have backed up traffic into Mexico for miles. "We will inspect at least one compartment per vehicle, which will add thirty seconds to the average vehicle-inspection time of twenty-nine seconds," said Mike Swanson, president of the American Federation of Government Employees local there. "We can inspect every compartment in a vehicle, too. All this is legal. The only reason we don't do this all the time is for the convenience of the traveler."

In the district offices and in the central office in Washington, morale was at an all-time low. INS employees in the Washington, D.C., office, said one lawyer who was a frequent visitor there, "sit and drink coffee and smoke cigarettes all day. Everything they do for you is a big fat favor. Go into one of the offices and you'll see GS-threes and GS-fours yakking on the telephone and polishing their nails. I have to call an immigration officer fifteen or twenty times to deal with one applicant. Your people are treated as files, pieces of paper, numbers. I don't like to go there. It's depressing, dirty, and ugly. They've got a new computer now—so fifty percent of the time I call to check on the status of a client and they say the computer is down. It literally does not work. They don't know what they're doing. They're dealing with foreigners, poor people, people who don't speak the language, and they just don't give a damn."

By now the Justice Department knew how bad things had become, and it was worried. "It has got to the point," one senior department official said, "where after a while there's no enforcement and no service either. An awful lot of offices have just given up. Everybody is basically dissatisfied." Worrisome as that was, the official had a far more serious concern. Under the circumstances, he said, "There's bound to be corruption." He was right, for in addition to being the most inept and mismanaged of the federal agencies, the INS was also the most corrupt.

CHAPTER SIX

"The Best Proof of Eligibility Is Money"

For months the United States Attorney's Office in San Diego had been collecting evidence in what, for the federal government, was the most unusual case. Frank Paul Castro, an immigration inspector at San Ysidro, had been taking bribes from inadmissible Mexicans and then looking the other way as they walked through the clicking turnstiles that separated Tijuana from California.

So overwhelming was the evidence against Castro that the Justice Department, whose main role was the prosecution of federal crimes by private citizens and which had always been reluctant to accuse its own employees of wrongdoing, could find no way to ignore it. In May 1971 the department, which at that point had not prosecuted an officer of the Immigration and Naturalization Service in something like thirty years, presented the Castro case to a federal grand jury.

In due course the jury charged both the forty-eight-year-old Castro and his wife, Nena, with twelve counts of accepting bribes and four more counts of having lied about it. Privately the prosecutors whispered that the scope of Castro's illegal activities had been far broader than the skeleton indictment suggested. In just four years, the government's attorneys estimated, Frank Castro had supplemented his $24,000 annual salary with more than $250,000 in bribes and proceeds from the sale of fraudulent U.S. immigration documents—visitor's visas, border crossing cards, even green cards—to Mexican aliens. But just as the Castros were preparing to stand trial, the government's case hit a crucial snag. A good deal of the evidence against the pair had come from an FBI wiretap, and the Justice Department's request for the court order authorizing the tap, along with dozens of similar requests in other cases around the country had, incredibly, been signed by the wrong official in Washington.

In more than a few of the fifty-nine U.S. Attorney's offices, prosecutors watched helplessly as months and sometimes years of work went down the drain, all because somebody had taken a bureaucratic shortcut. In San Diego, Brian Michaels and Howard Frank, the two assistant U.S. attorneys who had developed the case against the Castros, were equally glum. Without the wiretap transcripts, the government would simply have to dismiss the charges—unless, that is, the Mexicans who had paid the bribes could somehow be produced to testify. But how? All but a few of the potential witnesses had already been sent back to Mexico, released by the government with thanks in the expectation that their testimony would not be needed. Rounding them up and flying them to San Diego in time for the trial seemed an impossible task.

In late December a telephone rang at the American consulate on Avenida Constitución on the outskirts of Monterrey, Mexico's third-largest city. The man who picked it up was Alan Murray, a veteran INS investigator serving as officer in charge of the consulate's immigration section. *"Bueno,"* Murray said, expecting a question about the current availability of a particular visa or a plea for help with some other kind of immigration problem from one of the millions of Mexicans who, as Murray had come to learn during his three years there, desperately wished not to be living in Mexico. Frankly Murray was bored. Things had been slow in Monterrey the last few months. The most interesting call in weeks had come from the INS office in Mexico City, asking him to travel to the capital of Chihuahua and search through the files for a birth certificate issued there forty years before. Murray dutifully got a copy and sent it on, thinking no more about it until a few days later, when the person to whom it belonged was named to a high-level post in the Nixon administration. The official, it appeared, had been born in Mexico and was living in the United States illegally, and though Murray never knew what happened to the copy he pulled from the files, he suspected that someone in the White House had found a use for it.

Today, however, the voice on the other end of the telephone belonged to Brian Michaels, and the young prosecutor sounded frantic. There were, Michaels told Murray, a number of witnesses in Mexico, perhaps a dozen altogether, who were absolutely essential to the success of an upcoming criminal case. Several of the witnesses were living in the western Mexican state of Durango, but the others had scattered to God-knew-where. He was aware, Michaels said apologetically, that what he was about to ask was impossible, but it represented the government's only hope. Would Murray try to run these people down?

Anyone who knew Al Murray could have guessed the answer. In his twenty-odd years with the immigration service, Murray had ruffled his share of official feathers, but as far as anyone knew he had never turned down a tough assignment. He had made some enemies among higher-ups who could not control his freewheeling style, but Al Murray also had a lot of friends—not a few of them in the upper reaches of the government, partly why he was now enjoying a pleasant assignment in Mexico instead of chasing Peruvians through the streets of Brooklyn. Murray also knew the immigration service inside out, having joined the Border Patrol as a young man just out of Naval Intelligence in the early 1950's—the days when the patrol agent's uniform consisted of blue jeans, cowboy boots, and a Stetson hat—and learning Spanish and immigration law on the job in dusty border towns from Yuma to El Paso. Though he grew to detest the corruption he saw around him, by the time he left the border there wasn't much Al Murray hadn't learned about how to take bribes and cheat the government.

As Brian Michaels was soon to find out, he had called on the right man for help. As soon as Murray hung up the telephone, he and a young Mexican lawyer named Saul Rodríguez, whom he had borrowed from the local district attorney and put to work as his local investigator, set out on the trail of the missing witnesses. Michaels's call for help had come just before Christmas, and by February 5 Murray and Rodríguez had located all thirteen witnesses. Murray impressed each of them with the importance of telling the truth in an American court of law, and Rodríguez hauled them to Laredo and loaded them aboard planes for the three-hour trip to California. As the steady stream of Mexicans began arriving in San Diego, the prosecutors, amazed and delighted, placed the witnesses in protective custody and made arrangements to go ahead with the trial of Frank and Nena Castro.

Then more trouble. One by one the witnesses reported that they had decided not to testify after all. Some talk about reprisals had reached them in jail, and they were afraid of Castro. Al Murray's telephone rang again, and when the next plane left for the United States, he was on it. When Murray arrived at the old federal courthouse in San Diego, the prosecutors were threatening the witnesses with such niceties of American law as perjury and contempt of court. Telling the prosecutors to relax, Murray took each of the thirteen men aside for a little talk. "Look," he told them, "you can bullshit the gringos up here, but you can't bullshit me, because I'm going back to Mexico, and if you don't tell the truth now, your ass is mud." Just to make sure there was no more backsliding, Al Murray posted himself in the courtroom, his eyes focused steadily on each witness as he took the stand, silently daring him to falter or recant. Frank Castro got six years.

During his sojourn in San Diego, Murray had been staying at the Royal Inn Motel, the best he could afford on the $25 a day the government allotted its employees for travel expenses. In the next room was George Barnitt, an immigration investigator in San Diego who had worked the Castro case from that end, and the two men passed the long evenings together, drinking beer and telling stories about their early days in the INS. One night about eight, just as they had broken into the first six-pack of Budweiser, there was a knock at Murray's door. Standing outside was an INS officer from the big port of entry at San Ysidro, where until lately Frank Castro had worked. The officer managed a bluff greeting, but he looked worried. Murray offered him a beer, and the three men settled into a discussion of the Castro case, which was then making headlines across Southern California.

The man had been one of Castro's most ardent defenders,

and with good reason. Until his indictment, Frank Castro had been widely thought of as a model immigration officer, the sort of man the INS would not hesitate to make available to visiting newspaper reporters wanting to write about life on the front lines at San Ysidro. Castro was a wizard at detecting false documents and a human bloodhound when it came to ferreting out concealed narcotics—the sort of officer, or so the INS had believed, that the agency needed more of. Patiently Murray and Barnitt hammered away at the third man's defense of Frank Castro. They could understand, they said, why it was difficult for him to abandon a man he had supported publicly, in whose behalf he had testified to the grand jury, but there was just no getting around the fact that for more than four years Frank Castro had been providing an alien smuggler named Ezequiel Castrellón with forty or fifty immigration permits a week—in return for immunity, Castrellón had told the grand jury all about it.

The man nodded tiredly. Then he changed direction. "You guys," he told the two investigators, "don't mind going after the Indians. But you're afraid to go after the chiefs." Murray and Barnitt said nothing, sensing that they were about to learn the real reason for the officer's visit. The government, the man went on, was throwing its full weight behind the prosecution of Frank Castro, yet Castro was not guilty of anything that many other officers, some of them high-ranking seniors, were not doing. In fact, the man said slowly, there were a number of INS employees in the all-important Southwest Region, which stretched from California to Texas, who had committed equally serious crimes. Murray and Barnitt could not believe what they were hearing. Here was one of the highest-ranking officials in the immigration service telling them that the Castro case was just the tip of an iceberg they had not even known existed. The man began to name names. When he finally left, it was after one o'clock, but Murray and Barnitt were wide awake.

Quietly Murray and Barnitt enlisted the help of two other men—Herb Grant, another INS investigator they had met on the Castro case, and Gene Flynn, an FBI agent assigned to the bureau's San Diego office. On their own time and without telling their bosses, the four men began to run down the information the INS officer had provided. Not only did the tips check out, but one seemed to lead to another. Within a month Al Murray's little team was convinced that the corruption within the INS was far worse than even his late-night visitor had imagined.

Before long Alfred Hantman, the deputy chief of the Justice Department's general crimes section in Washington, and Steve Weglian, his young assistant, were boarding a plane for San Diego to find out what was going on out on the West Coast. What they found was Al Murray, George Barnitt, Herb Grant, and a pile of investigative files, and while Hantman and Weglian listened in amazement, the three investigators laid out the evidence they had assembled. Shaken, the two lawyers returned to Washington to prepare their report. "After listening to the various people in San Diego," Hantman wrote to Attorney General Richard Kleindienst, "one comes away with a feeling of complete disgust concerning the activities of the Immigration and Naturalization Service in the Southwest Region." The matter was serious enough, Hantman told Kleindienst, that the Justice Department should begin "a major investigative effort" into the INS as soon as possible. The evidence gathered thus far, he said, included "numerous allegations involving the illegal sale of entry permits and registration cards" by INS personnel and physical brutality against illegal aliens. Moreover, mismanagement seemed to be everywhere. So much high-priced overtime was being worked by the San Ysidro inspectors that Joe DuPuis, their boss, was earning less than most of his subordinates, while the Border Patrol agents there were having to siphon gas from illegal aliens' cars to keep their own vehicles running.

Kleindienst read what would later become known as the Hantman report, then fired off a memo to Henry Petersen, the head of the department's Criminal Division, ordering an "investigation of all allegations of administrative mismanagement and possible criminal misconduct by persons presently or formerly employed by the Immigration and Naturalization Service." The INS, he added, was also "to be advised that experts within the various INS fields which you desire to be detailed to this probe are also to be furnished forthwith." That meant Murray, Barnitt, and Grant, who were now officially attached to the U.S. Attorney's Office. The three investigators had been given what amounted to carte blanche to ferret out wrongdoing within their own organization, and they talked to everyone who would talk to them: old friends who remembered things they had seen, heard about, and in some cases done; INS employees whose grudges against superiors had led them to keep "little black books" noting their bosses' transgressions; fellow officers and investigators who acknowledged some impropriety and then, in hopes of avoiding prosecution, "gave up" somebody who had done something worse; wives, ex-wives, and girl friends who, jilted, two-timed, or discarded, could be persuaded to tell what they knew about their men.

The file folders piled up, and before long Steve Weglian could report that Operation Clean Sweep, as somebody in Washington had named the investigation, had opened criminal cases on 217 past and present INS officers, 146 of them involving the taking of bribes from illegal aliens, the others assorted violations of the civil rights laws, fraud against the government, and administrative wrongdoing. Considering that the targets were federal law enforcement officers, the information in the files was devastating. There was evidence of alien and narcotics smuggling, fraud, perjury, rape, robbery, extortion of money and sex, influence peddling, misappropriation of government funds and equipment—"every federal crime," Al Murray said, "except bank robbery."

Of a senior Border Patrol agent the investigators wrote: "Subject is a known associate of various narcotics smugglers and a business partner with one such smuggler." Of another: "Subject is involved in the smuggling of marijuana from Mexico." Of a supervisory immigration inspector: "Subject sells permits to aliens and his wife smuggles aliens through him when he is on the vehicle line at SYS [San Ysidro]." Of another inspector there: "Subject gives permits for sex." Of a deportation officer: "Subject arranges fraudulent marriages for immigration purposes—fee $300." Though the list went on and on, some of the cases stood out as particularly remarkable, like the Border Patrol agent in New Mexico who owned a ranch in partnership with a major narcotics smuggler. The ranch's landing strip was being used as an airdrop for the smuggler's cargo. Or the antismuggling agent who hung out at a Tijuana bar with a handful of prestamped entry documents he used to pay for drinks. Or the wife of an SYS inspector who was caught with a load of smuggled aliens at the San Clemente checkpoint and allowed to proceed on her way, the load intact.

To Murray, Barnitt, and Grant, what the files meant was that the INS, to which they had devoted most of their adult lives, was not only a far less effective obstacle to illegal immigration than it might have been but also a major contributor to the problem it was supposed to help resolve. How else could one interpret case after case in which federal officers, most of them with years of service, were breaking the same laws they were sworn to uphold? Even if the investigators' gut estimate that 90 percent of the INS's 8,000 employees were honest and hardworking was correct, that still left 800 corrupt and dishonest officers. "The best proof of eligibility," Murray said in disgust, "is money, I guess."

Equally disturbing, it appeared as though the INS had known about, or at least suspected, much of the wrongdoing by its personnel and had either looked the other way or meted out token punishments. One case that particularly bothered the Clean Sweep team was that of a Texas Border Patrol agent who had been charged three times with sexually abusing his fifteen-year-old Mexican maid but had never received more than a five-day suspension from duty. Another case involved an inspector in San Francisco who, despite having been caught stealing jewelry and other valuables from arriving passengers, smuggling pornographic films, and selling immigration documents, was somehow still on the job. Four Border Patrol agents in Laredo found to be employing illegal aliens as maids had been given ten-day suspensions. Two INS officers who had permitted aliens to "escape" had been suspended for two days. An officer who had "used his official position to seduce a female alien" was sent a letter of reprimand. A Border Patrol agent who had accepted bribes from aliens was not disciplined at all. Two patrolman in El Paso, charged with raping a Mexican woman in their custody, were suspended for three days. A patrolman at San Ysidro who raped a female alien was permitted to resign. None of the rapists was ever prosecuted.

Most of the scams uncovered by the Clean Sweep team were fairly primitive, involving brute extortion or the outright selling of documents, but one showed flashes of imagination. The INS had long been bedeviled by the problem of what to do with the hundreds of thousands of illegal aliens it apprehended each year inside the United States. Entering the United States illegally, or "without inspection," is a misdemeanor under federal law, unless the alien has been previously deported. Then it is a felony. But before he can be prosecuted or deported, any alien has the right under the law to present his claim to citizenship or residency at a formal deportation hearing before an immigration judge.

The theory behind the law is admirable. Rather than act preemptorily, the government is in effect telling the alien, "We think you're here illegally, but we're going to give you a chance to convince us that we're wrong." It is more than most countries do for illegal border crossers, and such hearings can be of great value. Although an alien may appear to be in the United States illegally, and may even think he is here illegally, without knowing it, he may fit into one of the manifold categories that make him eligible to become a resident. Among the factors that can bear on his case are the year and country of his birth, whether a close relative is an American citizen or permanent resident, even whether a previous application for admission was rejected during certain years. As a practical matter, however, hearings for all but the tiniest fraction of apprehended aliens are a physical impossibility; even if the nation's 6,600 prisons and jails were emptied entirely, there would be enough cells to hold only half the aliens arrested in 1980 alone.

Knowing that there are not enough jails to hold them, not enough immigration judges to hear their cases, the government encourages the vast majority of aliens it catches to plead guilty on the spot and return home. The concept is known as voluntary departure, and for illegal visitors from, say, Peru or Hong Kong, the idea makes sense. It will take most of them years to save enough money to finance a return trip to the United States. But 90 percent of the aliens the Border Patrol was catching were Mexicans, and it soon became apparent that simply loading Mexicans aboard buses and dropping them off on the Mexican side of the border was no solution at all—the aliens were beating the buses back to the U.S. After pondering the problem, the INS came up with a refinement, which it called interior repatriation. Mexican aliens would still be returned to

Mexico, but rather than being offloaded just across the border, they would be flown—at their own expense if they had the funds, at government expense if they did not—to a place deep in the Mexican interior, hundreds of miles to the south. It might not stop them from coming back, but it would certainly slow them down. Apart from its dubious legality—it was not clear how the United States government could contravene the Mexican constitution, which guaranteed freedom of movement, by forcing Mexicans citizens to travel to a place in their own country where they did not wish to go—the scheme had a certain appeal.

On alternate nights between eleven and twelve o'clock those aliens earmarked for interior repatriation filed past a table at the Border Patrol headquarters in San Ysidro, where each of them paid $39 to a man from a Mexican charter airline. The Mexicans were then put aboard Border Patrol buses and driven three miles to the Tijuana airport, where they boarded an aging DC-6 for the 1,200-mile flight to the central Mexican state of León. The DC-6 usually took off approximately on schedule, but instead of turning south, it circled the airport while a crew member announced that the plane was preparing to land again at Tijuana. Those passengers who had enough money left for a *mordida*, he said, would be allowed to get off. Most nights about half the passengers paid extra for the "short trip" and were back in the United States before daybreak. The others ended up a long way from anywhere. American immigration officers, the Clean Sweep team soon established, not only were taking kickbacks from the Mexican transportation company but were aware that the aliens were being shaken down and were sharing in those proceeds as well.

Through the long Watergate summer of 1972, Clean Sweep plodded ahead, with Al Hantman and Steve Weglian virtually commuting from Washington to the West Coast to keep an eye on the investigative team, which now included, at Al Murray's insistence, Saul Rodríguez. Unshaved and dressed in old clothes, Rodríguez was posing as an illegal alien in order to make "buys" of immigration documents from INS officers along the border. Murray was crisscrossing the border as well, filling dozens of the brown spiral tablets he always carried with careful, well-phrased notes.

The information now being developed by Clean Sweep went far beyond anything Murray and the others had expected to find. Some 326 criminal investigations had been opened, and apart from the massive wrongdoing at San Ysidro, serious corruption had been uncovered along the entire Mexican border: There were other cases at Tecate, Calexico, Andrade, San Luis, Nogales, El Paso, Laredo, Hidalgo—wherever, it seemed, INS personnel were stationed. Not even tiny Columbus, New Mexico, the smallest INS station on the border, was immune. "There were ten guys there, and they all were crooked," Murray said.

Most of the Clean Sweep cases were still in the investigative stage, but a few were beginning to find their way to the grand jury. In October, two immigration inspectors at San Ysidro, Walter O'Donnell and Joseph Byrne, were formally charged with having accepted $60,000 in bribes to allow twenty-four tons of marijuana to pass through the port of entry. Both were convicted; Byrne got six years in prison; O'Donnell, five. The Clean Sweep investigation also led to the breaking of what was then the biggest alien-smuggling ring ever uncovered in the Southwest, run by a group of sixteen bewigged Mexican women known as Las Hueras ("the Blondes"). At its peak the ring, which charged $225 for the trip from the border to Los Angeles, was grossing $9,000 a day.

The San Diego grand jury was being kept busy as well. INS officials were waiting in line to answer its questions, and as the transcripts of their testimony grew into a tall stack of neatly bound blue folders, it was becoming clear that the corruption was by no means limited to the service's rank and file. The INS, for so many years a bureaucratic stepchild of successive administrations in Washington, an agency whose mission was not thought to be crucial to either national security or domestic tranquillity, had been all but ignored by the government's watchdogs, and those who ran it had taken advantage of their low profile. The Clean Sweep team was reporting to Washington that top INS officials had shared a $25,000 bribe to sidetrack the deportation of the head of a Mafia family, had entered into questionable business associations with their counterparts in the Mexican government, and were taking lengthy pleasure trips to Mexico, in the best tradition of General Swing, at government expense. INS airplanes, boats, and other vehicles had been used by officials for their personal recreation—much of which seemed to include, according to one report, "sexual misconduct arranged for by INS personnel." Two senior INS officials on the West Coast were supplying members of the Los Angeles Rams with young Mexican women in return for season tickets.

A top official in Washington, Clean Sweep learned, had arranged for the regular delivery of illegal Mexican farmworkers to the LBJ Ranch while its owner was living in the White House. Following his lead, several other officials were doing the same thing for other large farms and ranches across the Southwest, paroling the farmworkers into the country under the pretense that they were "informants" providing intelligence about alien-smuggling rings. The day before the workers were due to be paid, the Border Patrol, which had been under orders to stay away from the ranches thus favored, would appear and send them back to Mexico. The ranchers got their crops harvested for free, the INS men got fishing and hunting privileges on the ranches, and the Mexicans got nothing.

Four senior INS officials, the Clean Sweep team learned, had been promised $1 million by a real estate developer from whom the INS leased a West Coast office building at an exorbitant rent. The four were planning to travel around the world together after they retired. Another senior official in San Francisco had actually taken such a trip, paid for by a wealthy Chinese "labor importer." Yet another senior official, it was discovered, had entered the United States illegally as a young man and had never adjusted his status, and two others had criminal records, one for robbery, the other for murder. "It began to look," Al Murray said, "like if you didn't have a criminal record, you shouldn't be in immigration."

But always the higher-ups remained just out of reach. Murray, Barnitt, and Grant had begun to despair of ever turning the allegations against their superiors into grand jury indictments when they received what seemed at the time like an incredible stroke of luck—their own Deep Throat. An immigration investigator in New York, a man well connected throughout the service because of his prominent position in the federal employees' union, "dropped a dime" and put in a call to his friend Al

Murray. There was, the New York investigator said, an inspector in charge at the tiny port of entry at San Luis, Arizona, who was just the sort of man the Clean Sweep team was looking for. Moreover, he had reason to believe that this inspector could deliver many INS higher-ups to the prosecutors. His name was Norman David Summers.

Murray was interested. He called Norm Summers, who agreed to drive the three hours from San Luis to San Diego for an interview, and it proved to be the most promising Murray had so far conducted. Summers, he wrote later, "has indicated a willingness to cooperate, and it is felt that he may lead to the successful prosecution of at least 10 others." Though the prosecutors had no interest in convicting Summers himself, but rather in his potentially incendiary testimony, they opened a file that could be translated into an indictment in case he decided not to talk. "Summers is believed to have been receiving kickbacks from the Estrella Blanca bus line," it read. "He has been selling INS passes . . . and has been allegedly supplying girls to other INS personnel." And here was the kicker: "Summers indicated that he had information on higher INS officials. He is going to discuss his situation with his lawyer and get back to us." For nearly twenty years Summers had been "making book," keeping detailed records of the favors he had done and for whom. Not only was he the most important witness the Clean Sweep team had yet developed, but as things were to turn out, he would be the last. Though no one knew it then, Norm Summers was a ticking time bomb, and he was about to go off.

One of Summers's functions, as he eventually acknowledged, had been to use his sterling connections along the border to provide Mexican prostitutes for various high-level visitors—not just INS officials but congressmen, even federal judges—whom the INS wished to have in its debt. The women, Summers said, had been compensated, at the direction of his superiors, from confidential INS funds earmarked for paying informants. Among those the INS had systematically compromised, he said, were an assistant attorney general (who soon thereafter resigned), an auditor from the Office of Management and Budget who was investigating waste within the immigration service, and a staff member of the House Judiciary Committee.

An INS official in Washington called Summers "the service's chief pimp in the Southwest corridor," and Summers's lawyer, Robert Hirsh, concurred. "Norm's job," he said, "was to get the officials laid."

As a prelude to forcing Summers to testify under oath, the Clean Sweep team had him indicted on multiple counts of fraud and bribery—charges, it was understood, that would gladly be dropped in return for his full and frank testimony. Then the time bomb went off. In a brief letter to his lawyer, dated June 15, 1973, Summers warned that if INS officials were "going to be indicted for going with prostitutes in Mexico they [will] have to get a lot of higher-ups, including Rodino. Don't be surprised if Rodino doesn't stop any probe . . . and try to impeach me as a witness."

The man Summers was referring to was the Democratic chairman of the House Judiciary Committee, Representative Peter W. Rodino of New Jersey, and his timing could not have been worse. Now, in the summer of 1973, it looked very much as though Rodino would soon take on one of the most sensitive assignments ever conferred upon an elected official in the nation's history. For even as Summers typed his letter, the Judiciary Committee was gearing up to hear the evidence on which it would ultimately vote a bill of impeachment against Richard Nixon. This was all the Democratic-controlled Congress needed. An effort that could not now be abandoned was under way to unseat an incumbent Republican president, and in their zeal to clean up their own little agency, a ragtag team of *immigration investigators* was threatening to derail the whole impeachment effort by compromising the man behind it, perhaps by leaving him open to criminal charges.

The allegation against Rodino, accompanied by his firm denial that any visit to a Mexican whorehouse had ever taken place, was briefly reported by the press, and the prevailing opinion in Washington was that the rumor was a lame attempt by the Nixon White House, now notorious for its "dirty tricks," to smear the man who held the President's fate in his hands. Al Murray, who had spent precious days scouring Juárez before finally finding a prostitute who said she remembered Rodino, was livid. But the effect of the flap on the Clean Sweep investigation was fatal. Suddenly, so suddenly that it took them some time to realize what had happened, the prevailing winds changed direction. The inquiry had been proceeding slowly for several months, but Murray and the others had put Washington's sluggish responses down to the city's single-minded preoccupation with the political future of Richard Nixon. A few scattered newspaper stories about the probe had spurred things for a time, but most of the press, like most of the Congress and the Justice Department, had eyes only for Watergate. "How the hell," Murray asked his colleagues, "are we going to compete with a President going down the tubes?" But now somebody was actively winding down the investigation. Several of the FBI agents who had worked on the case had been transferred out of San Diego, taking with them the specialized knowledge and investigative techniques they had developed. The INS was even putting pressure on Saul Rodríguez, who, upon returning to Monterrey, had been told he no longer had a job in the consulate there "because you and Mr. Murray are causing too many problems."

Murray intervened, and Rodríguez was allowed to remain on the job—fortunately, as it turned out, for Murray's fourteen-year-old daughter, Alison, who was living in Monterrey, Mexico. One afternoon a few weeks later a senior INS officer visiting the consulate recruited Rodríguez to drive him to the airport, where they picked up another immigration official who had just flown in from California. In the car the two men, both of whom were Clean Sweep targets and neither of whom realized that Rodríguez spoke English as well as he did Spanish, began discussing in hushed tones how Murray and the investigation might be stopped. Rodríguez could make out the words "grab the kid," and no sooner had he dropped the two men off than he telephoned Murray in San Diego. Murray called a friend, the head of Mexican immigration in Monterrey, who immediately drove young Alison Murray to McAllen, Texas, where he handed her over to an American immigration officer. Within minutes the terrified girl was safely aboard a plane for San Diego.

The fatal blow to Clean Sweep came precisely as Norm Summers had predicted it would in his letter to his lawyer. Late in the summer of 1973 he had appeared before a federal grand jury in Phoenix and told the whole sordid story. But Summers came away with the strange feeling that he had somehow become a hostile witness. "It was a farce," Robert Hirsh said later. "The government did everything it could to discredit him." Summers, Murray said, fuming, "could have given us several congressmen, at least one senator, the top of the immigration service. Now, what they would in turn have given us, that's what I'm curious about."

Clean Sweep sputtered on. No new cases were being developed, but there were some outstanding indictments to try. Another immigration inspector at San Ysidro had been caught taking a bribe, and a second officer there had been charged with offering to murder potential witnesses in the smuggling case against Inspectors Byrne and O'Donnell. But for all intents and purposes, the investigation was over, and somebody, probably somebody who knew Al Murray well, was afraid he would not get the message. On the afternoon of September 25, 1973, as Murray parked his car in front of the federal courthouse in San Diego and climbed out, he noticed what looked like another government car halfway down the block. When the driver spotted Murray he pushed the accelerator to the floor. Murray's body flew through the air, bounced off a parked car, and hit the curb. With two of the disks in his back splintered, in terrific pain, Murray managed to drive himself to a hospital, but a few minutes after checking in, he thought better about staying any longer in San Diego.

Having checked out, Murray grabbed a cab to the airport and boarded a plane for New York, where he was met by an old friend, an intelligence agent with the Internal Revenue Service, who drove him to the public health hospital on Staten Island. Murray had a lot of friends in New York, and he figured he was as safe there as he could be anywhere, maybe safer. As he discovered upon waking one morning to find some worried-looking doctors hovering over him, he had almost been dead wrong. A few days before, a male nurse, who since had not shown up for work, had increased the amount of Demerol flowing into Murray's veins to far beyond the danger level. Murray had blacked out and gone into a coma. Had the mistake—or was it?—been discovered a few minutes later, he would never have awakened.

As soon as he was able to dial a telephone, Murray called his

IRS friend and a second man he knew, an agent with the Drug Enforcement Administration. Late that night the two officers, flashing their badges at the government security guards, carried Al Murray, still in his body cast, out of the hospital and slid him into the back of a station wagon. As the sun rose over the East River, Murray arrived at Newark Airport and was loaded aboard a nonstop flight for Miami. By now he was taking no chances; when the plane landed, his nephew, an army ranger captain, was there to meet him.

Murray had long since used up his accumulated leave, and by now his government paychecks had stopped. Nearly broke, dejected, in great pain, he checked into a cheap hotel, where, a few minutes after midnight, he placed a long-distance call to George Barnitt in Los Angeles. For some reason, he also tape-recorded the call. "What the hell," Barnitt said when he heard his friend's voice, "are you doing in Miami?" Briefly Murray went over the events of the past few weeks. "Without doing any unnecessary bleeding," he said, "let's just say they're doing a good job on me."

Then Murray brought up their mutual friend, the San Ysidro officer who more than two years before had provided the impetus for Operation Clean Sweep. "You know they gave [him] the business, don't you?" he told Barnitt. "They called him up and said, 'You're the guy who caused all the trouble, and you're going to be transferred to Minnesota or else you can retire.' "

"Yeah, they gave him the business," said Barnitt, who had since been assigned to area control operations in Los Angeles. "They're giving you the business, they're giving all of us the business. I think we lost the ball game, Al."

The game was over, and the final score was dismal. Out of more than 300 potential criminal cases against past and present INS personnel, 7 officers had been indicted and 5 convicted. In addition, 30 civilians, mostly aliens and alien smugglers, had been sent to jail. "Allegations were easy to come by," Al Hantman said later. "Proof was not that easy. It was like trying to pick up mercury."

Barely a month before, Richard Nixon had resigned the presidency and left Washington, taking Watergate with him, and now Leonard Chapman, the new commissioner of immigration, was determined to put Clean Sweep to rest as well. "For more than two years,'' Chapman said, seething, ''the immigration service and its 8,000 employees have been under a cloud of suspicion brought about by charges of widespread corruption. Further charges have been made, recklessly, that immigration officers and Border Patrol agents are in collusion with ranchers, farmers and others to permit illegal alien labor to enter this country for employment. I welcome a thorough investigation of all charges by any bona fide authority, including [a] grand jury. I believe that such an investigation will reveal that virtually all of the employees of the INS are honest, dedicated, hard-working and loyal public servants.''

There had already been a grand jury investigation, but Congress and the Justice Department seemed content with Chapman's conclusion. Of the scores of immigration officers who, thanks to Norm Summers and Watergate, had escaped prosecution, most were able to continue their careers in government service. Some were even promoted. An immigration inspector at San Ysidro who was in cahoots with an alien-smuggling ring is now officer in charge of a station in Arizona. Another inspector alleged to ''admit female aliens and subsequently meet them at a prearranged location to indulge in immoral activity'' was promoted to criminal investigator. So was a Border Patrol agent who raped a female alien. The inspector who ''arranged fraudulent marriages for immigration purposes'' became a supervisor. A Border Patrol agent ''involved in the smuggling of marijuana from Mexico'' is now a criminal investigator. A motor pool mechanic ''involved in the theft and sale of INS permits'' became a Border Patrol agent. The immigration investigator whose wife was caught smuggling aliens is a senior INS official in California.

By the fall of 1979 the government's official memory of Clean Sweep had nearly faded. Al Murray, recovered from his injuries, was retired and living in San Diego, fleshing out his pension with the fees he earned from an occasional job in Central America for a government agency he was reluctant to talk about. The administration in Washington had changed as well, and with it the top and middle-level personnel of the Department of Justice, including most of the nation's fifty-nine United States attorneys. The new U.S. attorney in San Diego was Mike Walsh, a young California lawyer and Stanford trustee typical of the breed of activist prosecutor that then populated the Justice Department, men and women who had come of age during the 1960's and whose sensitivity to civil rights went beyond that of their predecessors in the Nixon and Ford administrations. Although Mike Walsh was later to have an impact on the immigration service beyond anything uncovered by Operation Clean Sweep, at the moment he had never heard of Clean Sweep and had no idea that its files were gathering dust in an unused corner of his office.

As one seemingly inconsequential event was shortly to establish, however, while Clean Sweep had gone away, the corruption that soiled the immigration service had not. A few days before Christmas 1978 a young Chinese woman, newly arrived in the United States from Hong Kong and taking in the neon glitter of Reno, Nevada, obediently produced her green card for a curious immigration officer there. Something about the document piqued the officer's curiosity. He checked the files and found that although the card was a genuine one issued by the INS, the number it bore had been assigned to someone else. Puzzled, the officer confiscated the card and began typing a report to Washington.

A few months later Al Murray picked up a newspaper and was startled by what he read. William Van Tubbs, a supervisory immigration inspector assigned to the San Francisco International Airport, had been arrested and charged with selling, for up to $20,000 apiece, green cards to thirty-six aliens from Hong Kong, among them the woman whose card had been questioned in Reno. As he scanned the article, Murray felt the old anger welling up again. What bothered him was not just that a corrupt immigration officer had been caught red-handed; Murray and the Clean Sweep investigators had known Bill Tubbs was a crook, had given Al Hantman and the prosecutors what they considered hard evidence that the same man had been taking bribes from a group of Samoans just as he had apparently been taking them from the Chinese. But the prosecutors had simply put the file away with the others marked "Prosecution declined."

Though he did not know it, Al Murray had not been alone in his suspicions. Another INS investigator working in San Francisco recalled that when "we used to catch wets out in the fields, they'd present their citizen's ID cards, and within half an hour we'd break them to being illegal. The funny thing was, all the cards had Tubbs's name on them." The investigator reported this coincidence to headquarters, but nothing was done. Nor, probably, would any action ever have been taken against Bill Tubbs except for a Hong Kong seaman named Joe Seung Chui. A decade before, Chui had jumped ship in New York Harbor and disappeared into the shadows of Manhattan's Chinatown, taking a job as a cook in a Chinese restaurant. He had chosen that route, he said later, because the list of Hong Kong Chinese awaiting immigrant visas was very long and he was eager to come to America.

For several years he worked and saved his money, glancing always over his shoulder for the immigration agents who prowled the alleys around Mott Street. Then, one day in 1978, Chui heard from a friend that it might be possible to obtain his own green card. It would not be cheap—the card would cost him $15,000, the friend said—but it would put an end to his constant terror of being caught and sent back to Hong Kong. Or so he thought. Chui gave his friend the money, every cent he had managed to save, and soon he held in his hands what, though he could not read the writing it bore, was a genuine INS Form I-151, an alien registration receipt card issued at the request of one William Van Tubbs. "This is to certify," the card read, "that Joe Seung Chui was admitted to the United States as an immigrant and has been duly registered according to law."

Joe Chui must have felt as though his heavy burden had been lifted. After so many years of hiding he could walk the streets in daylight, see something of the country where he had been living as a nonperson. So Chui could scarcely believe his bad luck the day the FBI agents came to tell him that the piece of plastic for which he had paid a fortune was no good, a fraud, that not only was he now penniless, but he was still an illegal alien. Joe Seung Chui, his anger rising, resolved to do something Bill Tubbs had not counted on. Yes, he told the FBI men, he would tell his story in court.

Just about the time that Tubbs's operation in San Francisco was beginning to break apart, Juan Espinal, a clerk in the INS's big New York office, heard an intriguing rumor from some fellow employees. There was a man in Brooklyn, they said, who was willing to pay much money for blank immigration permits and other favors. It was a good deal, and a lot of people in the office were in on it. Was Espinal interested? The young clerk wasn't sure. He had never done anything illegal before, and he wanted some time to think it over. A few days later Espinal was back. Yes, he said, he would like to meet the man from Brooklyn. Like any other civil servant trying to make ends meet in the big city, Espinal could use some extra money.

The man Juan Espinal was sent to meet was Isidore Markowitz, a budget analyst with New York City's Community Development Agency. But Markowitz had another job on the side: He was one of the scores of "immigration fixers" who circulate through the large immigrant and refugee communities of any big city, offering to help resolve complicated immigration problems for a healthy fee. A number of refugee and immigrant organizations in New York knew about Markowitz, knew that for $50 he could obtain a work permit, could secure an extension of a temporary visa for $450, could come up with a green card for a couple of thousand dollars. For larger sums, it was said, Markowitz could even have a derogatory immigration file destroyed. The man, it seemed, had some amazing connections inside the INS, but his clients knew little about how he operated. Although they may have suspected that part of the stiff fees he charged was being used to bribe INS employees, they didn't know for sure. All they knew was that Markowitz had a reputation as a miracle worker where immigration matters were concerned.

Someone, however, did want to know more. After hearing about Markowitz, Juan Espinal had gone straight to the FBI to report what appeared to him to be serious corruption in the INS office in New York. The FBI convinced Espinal to act as its undercover agent, to go ahead with the Markowitz meeting and see whether the man offered him a bribe. So that their conversation could be overheard and recorded, the agents wired the clerk, attaching a small radio transmitter to his body. There were several meetings and telephone conversations between the two, more than twenty hours altogether, all recorded by the FBI and all most illuminating. Markowitz, it seemed, had no reluctance to talk about his activities. He named a dozen INS employees in New York, not just clerks but immigration inspectors, deportation officers, and detention guards, to whom he claimed he had paid thousands of dollars in "gratuities." Then came what the FBI had been waiting for. How, Markowitz asked, would Espinal like to make some money?

In November 1979, the same month Bill Tubbs was convicted in San Francisco of having unlawfully reproduced immigration documents, Izzy Markowitz was found guilty in New York of having paid Juan Espinal $2,800 for a sheaf of blank immigration permits. In the investigation that followed, six other INS employees were also convicted of having accepted bribes from Markowitz, but that was just the beginning. The Tubbs case, it seemed, had broken the rancid crust that had begun to congeal over the cesspool of Operation Clean Sweep, and now corruption was bubbling up everywhere. In Chicago the top INS official, David Vandersall, was demoted and transferred after having accepted gifts, including a $2,000 oil painting and free meals, from restaurant owners who employed illegal aliens. "He ate dinner at places teeming with illegals," one INS official said. "The busboys who'd serve his table were illegal aliens, and he knew it." And Vandersall was only one of nine district directors under investigation.

In Buffalo, New York, rock star Peter Frampton, who is British, and Olivia Newton-John, the Australian singer, were subpoenaed by a federal grand jury investigating allegations that INS inspectors there had "expedited" visas for big-name entertainers entering the United States from Canada. In Texas the Justice Department was trying to find out how 653 Mennonite pilgrims had managed to emigrate to the U.S. from Mexico with tourist visas. In San Ysidro two inspectors, Charles Morgan and Robert Worrell, were sent to prison for conspiring to allow illegal aliens into the country in return for cash bribes and sexual favors. Richard Harvin, an immigration inspector in Palm Beach, was charged with having sold immigrant visas for $3,000 to Argentinian prostitutes wishing to ply their trade along the Florida Gold Coast. Jack Chestnut, another SYS inspector, was convicted of aiding and abetting the entry of illegal aliens. Some of the cases never made the newspaper, like that of the two California inspectors who were selling citizen's ID cards for $1,000 apiece. Or the inspector who was caught passing his Mexican girl friend and the two pounds of cocaine she was carrying through the line at San Ysidro. Or the Mexican-American inspector there who was found to be working in tandem with an alien-smuggling ring operated by his Mexican cousins.

But those inside the INS knew about those cases and others, and the impact on morale was severe. "What's the point," a Texas Border Patrol agent asked, shaking his head, "of going out night after night arresting wets when all these other guys are letting them in?" The Justice Department was wondering the same thing. "There's no other agency like it," one senior Justice official said. "It's a target for corruption." Added another: "It's the worst component of the department. It's so bad we don't know how corrupt it is. What we're frightened about at INS is what we don't know."

Though much of the corruption was hidden, its roots were easy to trace. They grew out of the wrenching economic disparities between the United States and the Third World nations of Latin America, Asia, and the Caribbean, disparities that had created a tremendous black market for any piece of paper that could guarantee admission to the country. For a Mexican, a Chinese, a Jamaican, permission to live and work here might mean the difference between borderline starvation and a college education for one's children. If a bribe of a few thousand dollars could purchase such a document, it was gratefully paid, and there seemed to be a disturbing number of immigration officers who were happy to take the money.

The privilege of emigrating to the United States was for sale to the highest bidder, but for those who could not pay the price, an encounter with the INS could be brutal. Ed Begley had seen the brutality firsthand, and it had horrified him. Begley, whose stature and bulk belied his gentle and compassionate nature, had spent an unhappy fifteen months as an immigration inspector at San Ysidro, and he was convinced that the immigration service actually encouraged a disregard for civil rights and the law. "That's what disturbed me most," Begley said, "the continual admonitions to trainees to violate the law." The admonitions had begun during the eighteen-week training course all new INS officers were required to undergo at the Federal Law Enforcement Training Center at Glynco, Georgia. Begley remembered one instructor there who "told us about handcuffing illegal aliens to the patrol cars and making them run alongside all the way to the border.'' The instructor, Begley said, told his students, ''A Mexican can run thirty-five miles an hour if he has to.''

''I was mature enough at the time to understand that this was an idiot talking,'' said Begley, who spent ten years as a Marine Corps physical training instructor before joining the immigration service. ''But most of the kids in the class were twenty-one or twenty-two years old. They thought it was really great that this kind of conduct was allowed.'' Another instructor, he said, told of ''pushing illegals off cliffs'' merely because they had been found with pocketknives in their possession. ''It's been done,'' the man said, ''so it would look like an accident.'' The future immigration inspectors were also taught hand-to-hand combat, something Begley found absurd. ''Teaching somebody to jab somebody in the eyes is one thing in mortal combat,'' he said. ''But when you're trying to prevent somebody from resisting arrest, blinding them is not acceptable.''

Begley was equally distressed by the caliber of some of his fellow inductees, who lent the training program what he called an *Animal House* atmosphere with their nightly antics. ''Vandalism, destruction, throwing furniture through the windows, false fire alarms, you name it,'' Begley said. ''One of the trainees, a woman, had her front teeth knocked out in a drunken brawl one night, and we had a rape in our barracks while I was there. A bunch of immigration investigators got some drunken girl into a squad bay downstairs. She was completely passed out, so they just took turns raping her.'' One trainee, Begley said, ''even had his illegal alien girl friend living in a motel outside the gates'' of the training center. Nor was the academy's faculty without its problems. While Begley was there, one of the instructors, the son of a retired regional INS commissioner, was fired after he was arrested and charged with making obscene telephone calls. But what bothered Ed Begley the most was the undercurrent of racism that ran through much of his training. ''It was at the academy that I first heard the word 'tonk,' '' he said. ''According to one of our instructors, that was the term used to indicate an illegal alien in the immigration service, even in official documents.''

In addition to their studies in immigration law, Spanish, firearms training, and police procedure, INS and Border Patrol trainees are required to receive instruction in "human relations" and "Mexican culture." But Begley called the four hours of human relations training a joke and said that the cultural classes were used to practice Spanish. Even the language course, he said, conveyed a picture of aliens as fundamentally dishonest. One test Begley remembered asked students to translate from English to Spanish such phrases as "Did he ask you to sell him the birth certificate?" and "That Cuban and his wife have been here illegally for a long time." Despite the fifteen-week Spanish course, many of the agents graduate from the academy barely able to speak the language. One Border Patrolman told of a colleague whom he discovered "pushing an alien around, trying to ask the guy his name, and naturally he was asking in Spanish. '¿Como me llamo yo?' he kept saying, and the alien wouldn't answer him. Finally a Mexican-American officer took him aside and said, 'You're asking him your name, and he doesn't know it.' " The communications barrier, the man said, only intensified the frustrations many immigration officers encountered in their dealings with aliens, usually to the aliens' disadvantage. "A lot of the Anglos learn the Spanish language only by the book and the forms they give you," he said. "You memorize the forms, and if you forget, you don't get anywhere. You get frustrated." The Border Patrol publishes a Spanish-language handbook, but the sample phrases it contains, not the sort to inspire rapport and goodwill, include "You're lying," "Where did you get these papers?" and "Besides this last time, how many times have you been arrested?"

When he began his INS service in October 1976, Begley quickly discovered that the principal function of an immigration inspector was not to assist arriving aliens in establishing their eligibility for admission but to coerce them into admitting their inadmissibility. "The degrading of the aliens disturbed me," Begley said, and Leonel Castillo knew what he meant. Shortly after becoming immigration commissioner, Castillo, whose face was not widely known, took an unannounced tour of some INS facilities, standing in line with arriving aliens along the border and at airports to see firsthand what sort of treatment they were accorded. To several of the inspectors Castillo encountered he was just another Mexican claiming to be an American citizen.

"It was an enlightening experience," the commissioner said later. "They were a little brusque with me."

At San Ysidro, Ed Begley said, aliens from Europe or Canada were treated politely while their requests for admission were being considered and allowed to wait in one of the public areas in the immigration building. But aliens from Mexico and Central and South America were thrown into holding cells that were usually "so full they all had to stand up—whole families, kids, parents, babes in arms, it didn't matter."

Because U.S. citizens are not required to carry documentation attesting to their status, the only way to detect a false claim of citizenship is through a confession, and one of the things that kept Ed Begley awake at night was the way such confessions were obtained. "We used to hold people in those cells for hours," he said. "It was like a joke. 'We've got one that's been in there nineteen hours, or twenty hours, or twenty-four hours.' People were held incommunicado, had not had any rights explained to them, no right to telephone for assistance or for somebody to bring their documents to them or whatever. They were even held without food, no food at all, no provision for it. When I found out how long these people had been there, I snuck out and bought hamburgers for them. On my break, I'd go over across the street to the Jack-in-the-Box and buy them a hamburger. It almost got me fired."

To make things as uncomfortable as possible, Begley said, the air conditioning in the holding cells was turned down until it was "ten or fifteen degrees colder than the rest of the building. The term they used was 'freezing them.' They'd send these people in there stripped of their clothing, left with just their shorts. I happened to walk by once, and this guy said, 'Señor, would you please bring me my clothes?' His clothes were stacked outside the door, so I just opened the door and handed them in. Another inspector came along and said, 'What the hell are you doing, letting him have his clothes back? I'm trying to freeze him.' " That technique, other officers said, was equally popular elsewhere along the border—at INS stations where there was no air conditioning, aliens were dragged naked from the showers and thrown into Border Patrol cruisers whose air conditioners were running full blast.

When freezing did not elicit a confession, humiliation and

even physical violence might be employed. Ed Begley remembered one alien who was "made to stand for about thirty-five minutes with his nose up against a concrete slab as punishment for having lied. I got kind of upset about the public humiliation this gentleman was having to go through. He was an illegal, but it wasn't our job to punish him for that." Another day Begley sat in the inspectors' lunchroom while two other inspectors "beat the living hell" out of an alien who had continued to insist that he was a U.S. citizen. "One of them locked the door so no one could see in," Begley said. "It went on for two or three minutes. When I tried to get in to stop it, they told me, 'You don't belong in here. Get your ass back to work.' " Begley withdrew to the sounds of the man "being slammed against the wall, screaming and begging."

Several of Ed Begley's colleagues confirmed his accounts and added some details of their own. "I'll tell you another technique we use," one San Ysidro inspector said. "When we're trying to break an alien and we catch him in the daytime, we'll hold him until after four o'clock [when the courts close], and then take him down to the MCC"—the federal Metropolitan Correctional Center in San Diego—"and book him, knowing that when he comes up for arraignment the next day, the U.S. attorney is going to decline prosecution. I don't know if that's legal or illegal, but I have done it myself. I know the investigators do it without even thinking about it. Their feeling is that if the guy spends the night, he might think twice about the way he talks to an officer again."

Under the immigration laws, aliens denied entry at the border are entitled to a formal "exclusion" hearing, at which they can appeal the denial and argue their cases for admission. But because such hearings simply make more work for the immigration service, the aliens are often simply shoved back across the border into Mexico. No one denied entry at San Ysidro while he was there, Ed Begley said, was ever told of his right to remain silent, to have a hearing, or to be represented by a lawyer. "I myself unwittingly violated the civil rights of a number of persons," Begley said, "including U.S. citizens, by requiring they confess to crimes without counsel and under threat of abuse and detention. I never told anybody they had any rights. Nobody did. The most common statement a person with brown skin hears during interrogation is: *'En este lugar, Usted no tiene derechas.'* That was one of the first Spanish phrases they taught me—'In this place, you have no rights.' ''

Often, Begley said, entire families would arrive at the port of entry and claim citizenship, and a favorite method of extracting a confession was to separate the children from their parents. ''That's against the official policy of the immigration service,'' he said, ''but they're always separated for interrogation. A lot of times you can get information out of a four- or five-year-old kid: 'What's your name? What's your mama's name? What's your daddy's name?' If you browbeat them enough, tell them, 'We're going to leave your mama locked up forever if you don't tell us the truth,' the kid will tell you anything.'' Another San Ysidro officer said the opposite technique was also used. ''I've heard guys use the ploy that they would separate the child from the mother forever to get the mother to break,'' he said, ''and she would always break.'' Ed Begley heard such threats made ''many times—in fact, I made them myself a couple of times, I'm ashamed to admit.'' The last time, he said, he was ordered by a supervisor to ''break'' a thirteen-year-old girl named Julia Pérez. After being detained for several hours, repeatedly questioned and threatened with arrest and detention without food, the girl ''confessed'' that she had been born in Mexico, and the U.S. birth certificate she carried with her was confiscated as counterfeit. The young girl was fingerprinted and photographed, officially catalogued as an illegal alien, and sent back to Mexico by herself without money or papers.

Though he was certainly not the first immigration officer to send a child back across the border alone—a few weeks before in El Paso, an eight-year-old Colombian girl had been deported to Juárez, and a few weeks before that a five-year-old had been released alone into the streets of Tijuana—Ed Begley could not stop thinking about what he had done to Julia Pérez. She had finally admitted to being illegal, it was true, but something about the confession bothered Begley. His suspicions were confirmed a couple of days later when the girl reappeared at the border with her angry father in tow and undeniable proof that she was indeed an American citizen. Horrified at what he had done, Begley tried to amend the record he had made showing Julia Pérez to be an admitted immigration violator but was told that "the system did not allow for correcting a mistake of that kind." The INS, Begley said, "was not going to tolerate me taking this kind of attitude on behalf of what they thought of as just another Mexican, but I had to go ahead and do it. I couldn't let this little girl be treated like that, let her spend the rest of her life in the computers as an illegal alien." Begley went ahead and made the necessary changes, and that, he said, "was the beginning of the end of my civil service career."

In a memorandum explaining Ed Begley's dismissal from the immigration service, his supervisor noted that "Begley is highly critical of the way INS treats people, that we do not follow the Commissioner's directive of viewing the alien's problems in a humanitarian light, and that we often border on harassment of those aliens . . . he tends to over-empathize with people trying to get into this country legally or illegally. Mr. Begley does not have the proper attitude to become a successful immigration inspector."

But the harassment and brutality that had so disturbed Ed Begley were nothing compared to the treatment illegal aliens received at the hands of the quasi-military Border Patrol.

CHAPTER SEVEN

"This Is About as Frustrated as I Ever Want to Be"

It was a few minutes after seven o'clock in the morning when across the hills and canyons that dot the landscape near San Ysidro the Motorola radios in a dozen Border Patrol cruisers crackled with a cryptic transmission.

"One-eighteen, two-seventy" went the metallic squawk. Jeff Otherson, a Border Patrol agent assigned to the big Chula Vista station, was trying to raise his buddy, Patrolman Bruce Brown.

A couple of miles away Brown reached for his microphone. "Go ahead, Jeff," he said.

Otherson's voice came back: "Are you Delta Henry?"

"Affirmative," replied Brown, a former army officer.

"OK," Otherson answered, putting his vehicle in gear. "I'm on my way."

To anyone eavesdropping on the Border Patrol's radio frequency the morning of July 3, 1979, the brief conversation would have been meaningless. Nor would it have been any clearer to many of the other Border Patrol agents who overheard the odd call. Had any of them taken the trouble to look through the patrol's radio code book, they would not have found the phrase "Delta Henry." But as the Justice Department was later to prove in court, the exchange was indeed a code, and a chilling one. Delta Henry, it turned out, was shorthand for "designated hitter"—not the baseball variety but, among what federal prosecutors later termed an outlaw group of vigilante Border Patrol agents, the officer of the day responsible for administering brutal beatings to certain illegal aliens caught trying to slip across the border.

A few minutes earlier thirty-one-year-old Jeff Otherson and his partner, a Border Patrol trainee named Gino Freselli, had monitored a radio transmission from the patrol's single-engine aircraft, known to the Mexicans as the mosquito, flying watchdog duty along the sixteen-mile slice of border that is the responsibility of the Chula station. "Zulu," the aircraft's radio designation, was reporting that a young Mexican border crosser wearing a dark jacket and a baseball cap had just given the low-flying pilot the finger. Dirk Dick, a twenty-five-year-old patrolman and a friend of Otherson and Brown, dropped what he was doing and set out to look for the disrespectful alien. So did agent Ronald Gamiere, who soon came across a young man wearing a dark jacket but no cap. Figuring that he might be the culprit anyway, Gamiere took his prisoner to the loading dock where aliens arrested in the field were held until there were enough to fill one of the big transportation vans that shuttled back and forth between the dock and the processing center. Otherson and Freselli were working transport that morning, and when they pulled their green van to a halt at the dock, Freselli said later, he heard Ron Gamiere tell Otherson that one of the young men in custody there appeared to be the one who had made the obscene gesture.

"This guy," Otherson replied as he shoved the alien roughly into the van, "maybe he ought to see Bruce. He needs talking to." He started his engine and reached for his microphone to put out the call to Brown. But as he drove toward Brown's position, an observation post known as E-1, Otherson began to have some misgivings about his young partner. "I don't know if I should bring you up here," he told Freselli. "You're just a trainee." Gino Freselli might have been a trainee, but he was no tenderfoot. A Vietnam veteran, Freselli had had eight years' experience in law enforcement before joining the Border Patrol, two of them as a deputy U. S. marshal. But nothing in his background prepared him for what he was about to witness. As he told the story later, when the van arrived at the spot where

Bruce Brown's car was waiting, Brown calmly put down the newspaper he had been reading and pulled on a pair of tan gloves, picked up his lead-weighted night stick, and got out of the car.

According to a trial memorandum prepared by the government:

> Brown and Otherson talked about the fact that they thought the alien in the van was the one who had been "flipping the bird" at Zulu. Expressing their mutual displeasure, Brown and Otherson opened the door of the transport van and called the suspect to the door. Before he reached the door, Brown grabbed him by the shirt, jerked him out of the van and stood him straight up against the van, holding him at attention. The interrogation began. Brown accused the alien of flipping the bird to Zulu. The alien did not respond. Brown proceeded to slap the subject, first with his right hand, then with his left. Right, left, right, left. Each time, Brown would straighten the man up and slap him again, each time with an open, gloved palm. Just before the beating began, Otherson cautioned Brown: "Hit him with the palm of your hand so it won't leave any marks."
>
> Right, left, right, left. The strength of the blows was strong enough to knock the man two feet to each side. The interrogation continued. Had he flipped the bird to Zulu, Brown demanded to know? The man refused to give the desired confession, steadfastly maintaining his innocence instead. Not satisfied with the alien's denial, the punishment continued. The alien offered no resistance. His arms lay limp at his sides. Brown then took the alien's hand and placed it down on the floorboard of the van and struck it, five or six times hard and fast, with his nightstick. The hands started to swell. "Be careful," Otherson warned. "Be careful not to break his hand."

Though it was not clear what he had to lose, the young Mexican, tears streaming down his reddened cheeks, still refused to confess. The beating continued. Otherson hit him in the stomach. Brown battered his shins with the night stick. After six or seven minutes the two Border Patrolmen, having grown tired, threw the alien back into the van, and Otherson, a shaken Gino Freselli by his side, drove off to answer another call for transport. As they rode, Otherson must have sensed the question on

Freselli's mind. "Sometimes," he said slowly, "we find it necessary to do things like this because the criminal justice system doesn't do anything about these assholes."

Gino Freselli had not yet survived the ten-month apprenticeship required to become a journeyman Border Patrol agent, and he decided at first to say nothing to anyone about what he had seen. "If you want to pass your exam and remain an agent," he explained later, "you observe and you don't say nothing." For all Freselli knew, what had happened that morning was standard procedure along the border, and even if it wasn't, whom should he report it to? When eight o'clock came, he signed out and went home.

The next day, the Fourth of July, Jeff Otherson and two other trainees, Steve Iverson and Blake Brown, chased a pair of teenage Mexicans through downtown San Ysidro before finally cornering them in an appliance store. Next to showing a Border Patrol agent disrespect, trying to run away was the greatest of sins. Otherson took the two young "runners" to meet Bruce Brown. Out came the tan gloves, and then the sound of blows. The government later charged that as Iverson and Blake Brown watched, Otherson and a third agent, a thirty-year-old former high school French teacher named Dan Charest, joined in the beatings. After a couple of minutes Otherson took one of the young men's shoes, a precious commodity to most Mexicans, and threw it down a nearby canyon for good measure. It really burned his ass, Otherson said, that the Mexicans had had the gall to sneak into the United States on Independence Day.

Otherson, Brown, Charest, and Dick were all assigned to Unit Five of the Chula Vista Border Patrol working the increasingly dangerous territory in and around San Ysidro, the busiest transit point on any international boundary in the world. In San Ysidro the Border Patrol was being overrun, and lately it had come under armed attack as well.

For months scarcely a night had gone by that the four agents or someone they knew had not been the targets of rocks, bottles, even gunfire from across the rickety chain-link fence that divided the tiny hamlet from the bustling, million-plus border metropolis of Tijuana. As John Munch, one of their colleagues who worked the dangerous four-to-midnight shift, eased his darkened cruiser through the rugged foothills outside town, he shuddered as he talked about the night a week before when he and two other officers had been pinned against the border fence by rock throwers. They were not hurt, but other Border Patrol agents had been badly wounded. One carried a steel plate in his head as a reminder, and there were places along the border now where Munch would not drive, even though out here he was far from alone. Above him Border Patrol helicopters, searchlights blazing and loudspeakers blaring a warning in Spanish to "go back," wheeled and dipped in the inky night sky. Scattered through the hills behind him were other agents, many of them Vietnam veterans, wearing flak jackets and peering closely at the border through special night-vision starlight scopes.

Like a defensive football squad, the agents waited for the offensive rush from the Mexicans they could see in the distance, clustered around their faintly flickering campfires. If there had been a point spread, the aliens would have been heavy favorites. The previous day the Chula sector had apprehended 936 aliens coming across the line, and the Border Patrol knew that several times that number had gotten through. So far the deployment of 430 agents and all the technology the Border Patrol could muster, including the electronic body sensors buried along the border, had failed to stop them. The body sensors were Vietnam surplus, identical to those once sown in the demilitarized zone between North and South Vietnam. Back at patrol headquarters, red dots winked on a room-size map as the sensors recorded the tentative footsteps of illegal border crossers—and, all too often, of cows, dogs, and jackrabbits as well. Even when one of the thousand or so sensors that now stood guard between San Ysidro and Brownsville was triggered by a human being, the intruder was usually gone by the time a Border Patrol cruiser arrived—that is, if one had been available. Because of manpower shortages, about a third of the sensor signals were going unanswered, and the sensors were moved so often that even the agents sometimes forgot where they were and triggered them inadvertently. But the aliens always seemed to know. It was not uncommon for the patrol to arrest an alien smuggler and find a map of the sensor location in his pocket. One Border Patrol agent spoke for many when he called the system "a big fraud."

The truth was that nothing the patrol could come up with was likely to make very much difference. Tijuana, the largest city on either side of the border, second in size only to Los Angeles on the Pacific coast of North America, had in the past few years become the primary way station for Mexicans from tiny, dirt-poor villages on their determined journey to the United States. Each month brought Tijuana another 30,000 temporary residents, swelling its *colonias* to overflowing, straining its Spartan social services far beyond capacity, raising street crime and violence to what its residents said were terrifying heights. Sensors or no sensors, the Mexicans streamed across, making San Ysidro the Border Patrol's most frazzled outpost. Upward of 1,000 illegal entrants were being apprehended (the Border Patrol disliked the word "arrested") in the sector every day, ten times as many as a decade before, and for every 1 it caught, perhaps 2 more, perhaps 5 or 10, managed to evade its threadbare defense. In San Ysidro even more than elsewhere, it was now undeniably clear that the border was an obsolete myth, a farce, a sieve that anyone with a modicum of perseverance could eventually overrun, blitzing the outnumbered *migras* in their forest green uniforms like so many halfbacks around a lugfooted defensive line. So open was the Mexican border, in fact, that the KGB, the Soviet secret police, which for years had infiltrated its undercover intelligence operatives into the United States from Canada, was now sending them in from Mexico.

In Arizona the desert, scorching by day and freezing by night, provided some kind of physical barrier, and east of El Paso there was the Rio Grande to be crossed. But here there was nothing between the United States and Mexico: no river, no desert, no mountains, no natural obstacle of any kind except a nearly dry cement canal, all that was left of the Tia Juana River, and a sorry, decrepit fence, in some places no more than a sagging steel cable slung so low between its cockeyed posts that a car could drive across it without even slowing down. And now, as though the task of guarding the border were not already difficult enough, the sixteen-mile stretch of frontier that ran east from "border beach" on the Pacific Ocean had become the most turbulent piece of international boundary in the world. There had been outbreaks of violence at other key crossing points, like El Paso and Calexico, but those stations had seen nothing to match the trouble here, where Border Patrol cars had been attacked by bands of aliens and brush fires set along the border. Just a few days before, one of San Ysidro's precious helicopters had been brought down by a rock thrown at its tail rotor, seriously injuring the pilot and his observer. They were only two of nearly sixty SYS officers who had been attacked and hurt on the job.

Most of the officers assigned to patrol the San Ysidro strip were quick to admit that they were afraid—so afraid that at one point they collectively refused to set foot in a 300-acre no-man's-land on the American side of the border that had been taken over for use as a staging area by the alien smugglers or to patrol anywhere else except in pairs. (Months later the forbidden area was reclaimed by the Border Patrol in a surprise tear-gas attack.) Nor did the danger subside altogether when they went off duty. Many of their neighbors in the tiny bedroom communities between San Diego and the border were themselves alien smugglers, or related to alien smugglers, or friends of alien smugglers, or simply aliens—and they all considered the Border Patrol their natural enemy. Even though the agents were careful not to wear their uniforms to and from work, they would come home to find that their houses had been vandalized, the tires on their family automobiles slashed, a couple of them even firebombed. In the summer of 1979 all of them were having trouble remembering why they had ever wanted to join the Border Patrol.

If the FBI, highly trained and well paid, was at the top of the federal law enforcement ladder, then the Border Patrol, which was neither, was near the bottom, and duty at San Ysidro was the bottom, period. The average tour there was only nineteen months compared to ten or fifteen years on the relatively placid Canadian border. All that most of the agents in San Ysidro wanted was to be somewhere else, and the constant turnover created by early retirements and transfers to saner posts had left the force made up of men like Otherson and Brown who did not have enough seniority to transfer out, agents who were largely young, green, and frightened. Yet the ill-trained, inexperienced, and underpaid agents—the starting salary of $12,500 a year was enough to qualify some of them for food stamps—were called upon daily, or rather nightly, since the invasion always waited for darkness, to make split-second decisions that could affect the freedom of movement, and often the economic futures, of tens of thousands of people of foreign birth. It was a tough job anyway, and given the combat-zone atmosphere in which they had to work, some of the officers assigned to San Ysidro thought they could understand—not justify, maybe, but understand—why Jeff Otherson and his friends had taken the law into their own hands. The aliens, they said, had started the war along the border. The Border Patrol was just fighting back.

Except that it was not the illegal border crossers, few of whom ever were armed with knives, much less guns, who were responsible for most of the violence. Guns are a particularly difficult commodity to come by in Mexico, certainly well beyond the scope of the average worker's income, and as intelligence reports later showed, some of the trouble during that difficult summer had been orchestrated by alien smugglers in hopes of diverting the Border Patrol and leaving holes in its defenses. Much of the rock and bottle throwing was attributable to the roving gangs of unemployed youths who lived in and around the desperately poor Tijuana neighborhood of Colonia Libertad, and the gunplay was mostly from the Mexican ''border bandits'' who lay waiting to rob and rape the aliens on their way across the border.

The bandits had become a real problem only in the past couple of years, after Bill Kolender, the San Diego police chief, had withdrawn a special squad of Spanish-speaking decoys that had roamed the border in hopes of attracting and arresting the bandits. (There was some talk that international relations had played a part in the squad's demise. A couple of years before, a Mexican police officer named Horacio Fuentes was shot half a mile inside U.S. territory by two of the squad's members when he leaped from his hiding place and pointed a .45-caliber revolver at what he assumed was a pair of illegal border crossers. By the time the decoy squad was disbanded, it had apprehended five other Mexican policemen under similar circumstances.)

Conditions along the border were now drastically different from what they had once been, of that there was no doubt. But so, some Border Patrol veterans thought, were many of the patrol's new recruits, who seemed to lack a good deal of the maturity and dedication that had once been the patrol's hallmark. Too many of the younger men, the old-timers grumbled, were products of the Vietnam War who had either come to the Border Patrol directly from the army or after spending a few years with a police department somewhere, and they all seemed to want to play combat or cops and robbers. Nor did they seem particularly committed to the patrol, often making no secret that for them it was simply a stepping-stone to a more glamorous job with Customs or the Drug Enforcement Administration. This was unfortunate, because for most of its fifty-plus years, the Border Patrol, which was a branch of the INS but liked to think of itself as an independent agency, had attracted an uncommon sort: a self-reliant, adventuresome outdoorsman, the archetypal flinty-eyed man of few words. Most of the earlier agents had grown up in the Southwest and for them the patrol had not been a stopping-off place but an opportunity to stay with the land they loved. Whether they had patrolled rugged stretches of border in jeeps or on horseback or had followed a faint line of tracks moving north, the job had suited their rustic natures, and it had been a satisfying one. The old days were gone now—take sign cutting, tracking an illegal alien by following his trail, a skill of which the old time Border Patrol agents were proud. But following a single border crosser, or even a dozen, for days and miles through the desert and the sagebrush made no sense anymore, not when there were thousands more right behind.

There was something else, something the older agents found difficult to talk about. Many of the newer recruits were city kids with fifteen weeks of conversational Spanish under their belts, young men who might never have seen a Mexican before coming to San Ysidro, much less gone to school or played baseball with one. The old-timers might refer to the aliens as wets, but not with any harshness or cruelty—wasn't that how the border crossers jokingly referred to themselves, as *mojados* ("the wet ones")? No, it was the younger agents who had invented the term "tonk"—the sound, they laughed, that a night stick made when it connected with a Mexican's skull. It was, perhaps not coincidentally, one of the same epithets American soldiers had applied to their enemy during the Vietnam War. (Within the Border Patrol, Leonel Castillo was Supertonk.)

For all its problems, however, the Border Patrol still seemed sometimes to call a special kind of man. One of them was Mike Williams, the son of a literary scholar who had passed up the tame academic life to become one of the Border Patrol's brightest and most promising young officers. Williams was assigned to El Paso, which sat squarely at the midpoint of the border and, after San Ysidro, was the busiest station in the patrol's network. The year before, the 130 agents there had caught 125,000 illegal aliens, nearly 1,000 apprehensions per man, and this year they would catch even more. In contrast with San Ysidro, El Paso was the closest thing the patrol had to a model station, the best on the border, and one of the reasons for its success was Mike Williams.

It has already been a ten-hour day, but Williams, a supervisory patrol agent, is pointing his cruiser away from home and dinner and toward the big Southern Pacific freight yard on the outskirts of El Paso. "Got anything yet?" he radios to the agents who have the yard staked out, but the answer comes back that it is still too early. The northbound freight of the Rock Island Line, a favorite conveyance of border crossers heading north to look for work, is still being made up in the yards. If the aliens are lucky, tonight the train will be hauling some shiny new automobiles to dealers on the West Coast. Find one with an open door and spend the rest of the trip reclining on the back seat, listening to the radio. As it is every evening, the freight will be searched, not before it leaves the yard but by Border Patrol agents waiting a few miles up the line; and after a brief spin around the yard Williams heads for the intercept point. There is already some action when he arrives. Herb Gordon, an affable, baldish man who left a well-paying job as a stagehand with CBS in New York to join the Border Patrol, has found three young Mexicans waiting for the train inside a junked Pontiac next to the tracks. Noe, an earnest seventeen-year-old wearing an iridescent purple shirt over torn Levi's jeans, seems a little taken aback by the forest of green uniforms that has him surrounded, but he manages to answer Williams's questions. He and his friends, he says, came to El Paso from Cuidad Chihuahua, about 200 miles to the south, hoping to ride the freight to a big city where jobs are waiting with no questions asked.

As a slow-moving train rounds a bend—the engineer knows the Border Patrol will be waiting here and gently applies his brakes—Noe and his companions are locked in a transport van while Williams and his "train crew," wearing heavy railroad gloves, leap aboard the engine. They start by opening the hot, cramped compartments along its sides, then peer into boxcars and even along the tops of the wheel carriages, checking every hiding place they can think of. The night before last, they pulled nineteen aliens off the train here. Tonight it appears empty, but last night it was empty too and when it arrived at Alamagordo, New Mexico, forty miles to the north, a backup team found ten illegal aliens on board. The train checks are part of the unending game of cat and mouse; every month, it seems, the aliens board the train farther up the line, and the Border Patrol is playing hopscotch with them.

As the red lights of the caboose fade in the darkness, Noe and the two other boys are driven to the Border Patrol's processing center and loaded aboard a bus for the short trip back to Mexico. They will try their luck again tomorrow night or the night after, and eventually they will make it. Mike Williams knows this, and the young men know he knows. There is an unspoken acknowledgment between them that tonight is only the end of an inning, not the end of the game. "Believe me, I understand why they come," Williams says as he follows the van back to the patrol's cinder-block headquarters building near the El Paso airport. "They're starving to death down there. They have everything to gain and nothing to lose. You have a rich country alongside a poor country, you're going to have an illegal alien problem. But every country has to protect its sovereignty. You have to have some control over who comes and who goes."

Williams and Gordon have been working freight trains tonight, one of several strategies the Border Patrol pursues to keep illegal aliens from moving north once they have crossed the border. Meantime, other officers are watching departing passengers at the airport and the bus station and searching suspicious cars at several "vehicle checkpoints" on key highways leading out of town. The checkpoints have been a feature of southwestern highways since 1927, three years after the Border Patrol was founded. The idea behind them is to catch illegal aliens who have somehow evaded the patrol's frontline defenses and are heading for Denver, Chicago, Detroit, New York, and other big cities to the north and east. Because they are a second line of defense, most of the checkpoints are 50 to 100 miles away from the border, but the one at Truth or Consequences, New Mexico, is 122 miles from El Paso, and another, at Miami, Oklahoma, is 600 miles from Mexico. They all do a brisk business. At the Sarita, Texas, checkpoint, 705,000 vehicles were stopped last year, an average of better than one a minute, and they often yielded more narcotics than illegal aliens. Some civil rights lawyers are bothered by the legality of the roadblocks, at which any passing vehicle can be stopped and searched and its occupants questioned, whether or not the officers have probable cause to believe they have committed some crime—powers denied any other police agency in the country.

One of those most concerned about the practice is Jim Harrington, an attorney with the American Civil Liberties Union in the Rio Grande Valley. A couple of years ago, Harrington was driving a friend's mobile home when he was stopped by the Border Patrol just outside Falfurrias, Texas, a few miles east of Sarita. The agents, Harrington recalled, "went through the drawers and the closets," places where no grown human being, or even a child, could possibly have hidden. "I asked one of them if he had a warrant or any probable cause to search us. He said, 'No, but we can search you if we want to.' This has been going on so long that people think it's normal and permissible, but it's atrocious." Among Harrington's fears is the one that the Border Patrol is misusing its authority to enforce the immigration laws to search for drugs, and he may be right. Last year the checkpoint searches turned up twenty-seven tons of marijuana, thirty pounds of hashish, four pounds of cocaine, and 57,000 pills, all carried by unsuspecting travelers who were not guilty of any immigration violation. Checkpoint duty—standing in the wind and rain, assaulted by noise, exhaust fumes, and reckless drivers—is among the least sought-after details in the Border Patrol. It is also one of the least productive. Of the aliens taken into custody by the El Paso station, about half are caught at or near the river, and tonight, as most nights, the real action is taking place on the border itself, where

"This Is as Frustrated as I Want to Be"

Hector Sena and Lew Moss are working the linewatch. El Paso is where the Rio Grande, which marks the border between Texas and Mexico, turns north toward its source high in the Rocky Mountains. From here south to Brownsville on the Gulf of Mexico, the river is the only impediment the border presents to an illegal immigrant, and, because much of its water is siphoned off for irrigation, some days it is almost no obstacle at all—in fact, the river is so shallow in places that it is possible to walk across it on stones.

Moss and Sena have stationed themselves on the American side of a small steel railroad trestle known as the *puenta negro* ("black bridge") that spans the sluggish river. It is a critical crossing point. Should anyone make it past the bridge, he will be barely two blocks from the South El Paso barrio, from streets crowded even at night with thousands of Hispanics, so it is here that Moss and Sena watch and wait. Of the pair, Sena has the best "night eyes," and he shields them carefully from the sudden glare of a flashlight, a cigarette lighter, an oncoming car. "The worst enemy," he says, "is light." In a fraction of a second the night vision he has acquired during the first few hours of his shift could be lost for precious minutes, and on the linewatch, night vision is everything.

Sena can see clearly the shadowy groups of Mexicans standing at the other side of the bridge. "Not many tonight," he says, counting fifty or sixty. "They're waiting for Hector to leave," says Dale Cozart, Sena's supervisor, with a laugh, but the laughter has a nervous ring. The day before, some Border Patrolmen were stoned by an angry crowd of Mexicans after one pulled a drowning alien from the swift-flowing irrigation canal that parallels the river. The agent attempted artificial respiration, but the alien died, and from the other side of the canal his ministrations must have looked like something else. "You murdered him," one of the rock throwers shouted. "Now you are going to have to murder us." There have been a few other violent incidents here, but yesterday's was the most dramatic. During the first few hours of darkness Sena, Moss, and the dozen or so other officers on linewatch duty farther down the river play a waiting game, chiefly to establish their presence. As the two agents pace back and forth, a few of the Mexicans on the other side of the bridge venture out toward the invisible line at the middle that marks the U.S.-Mexican border. One or two of the braver souls urinate across the line, but when Sena makes a move forward, they scurry back.

It is a game, and the Border Patrol is the first to tire of it. "We can't stand around waiting to catch them at the bridge," Moss says. "Obviously time is on their side." He and Sena climb into their cruiser and head for the freight yard. Moss brakes to a stop at a spot where he can watch a slice of the riverbank without being seen. "If they come across tonight, maybe some of them will come through here," he says, lighting one of the many cigarettes he will smoke before his shift ends at midnight. While he waits to hear from Hector, who has taken a walkie-talkie and hidden himself near the bridge, Moss ruminates on his never-ending job. "The only way they'll ever eliminate this problem is for Mexico to create employment for its people," he says. "I don't believe any fence will keep them out, not as bad as some of these people want to come to this country." But in the meantime, the frustrations are overwhelming, particularly for those who have come to the Border Patrol from police departments around the country where they grew used to putting lawbreakers in jail. For them, Moss says, "the whole idea of grabbing somebody and sending them back is hard to take."

His musing is interrupted by Sena's voice, crackling from the cruiser's radio in an amplified whisper. "There's some accumulation over here," Sena says. A minute passes, then another, before he reports that a young man "wearing a white shirt with big squares on it" has just stepped off the bridge and into the United States, followed in short order by a younger boy wearing a white sweat shirt and "an older kid about eighteen in blue pants."

"Ten-four, Hector," Moss responds. As he replaces the microphone, the boy in the sweat shirt steps into view at one end of a dimly lit street leading from the river. Moss eases his cruiser into the light and pulls up, but the boy makes no move to bolt. A few polite words are exchanged in Spanish. His name is José, and he is fourteen years old and from Juárez. Moss nods and opens the rear door. "Sí, señor," José says obediently as he jumps inside and curls up behind the steel-mesh screen that separates the driver from the back seat. He came over, José says, just to see what El Paso was like, but now he is worried.

He has to be in school in Juárez at nine o'clock tomorrow morning, and he wants to know if the *migra* will have him back home in time. Plenty of time, Moss says, and drives back to his hiding place to wait for the shirt with the white squares to emerge. When no one has appeared after fifteen minutes, Moss decides that "they probably waited to see what would happen to José here, then went the other way when we pulled out." By now it is raining heavily, and Moss and Sena agree that the rain will probably do what they cannot: stop the border traffic for the rest of their shift. Once, Moss says, he and another agent caught 102 aliens in six hours, but tonight he and Sena will have to settle for their one small prisoner.

Back at the detention center, 110 illegal aliens have been processed since the shift began at four o'clock that afternoon. José will be number 111. But before being put aboard a bus that will deposit him on the Mexican side of the border across from Ysleta, about seven miles down the river, José is questioned briefly. He gives his full name, his age, his occupation (*alumno*—student), his place of residence. Then he is shown a paper and asked in Spanish if he wants to waive his right to a formal deportation hearing. The "advice of rights" form, printed in both English and Spanish, acknowledges that he has been told of his rights to a hearing and a lawyer but has agreed to waive them and return to Mexico voluntarily. Even though Moss knows that José would not stand a chance in an immigration hearing—the boy has no conceivable claim to residency—he goes through the prescribed procedure anyway. José, who realizes that to ask for a hearing would mean being locked up at the INS's detention center for weeks and that he would only end up back in Juárez anyway, signs the form. "I am a citizen of Mexico," it reads, "and admit that I am illegally in the United States."

Though José has technically committed a federal crime—to be precise, a violation of Title Eight, United States Code, paragraph 1325, for which the maximum punishment is six months in jail and a $500 fine—no one thinks for a moment about actually prosecuting him. The Justice Department prefers to reserve the crowded federal courtrooms for alien smugglers; there are not enough judges in the country to hear a fraction of the cases like José's, not enough prosecutors to try them. Nor does the government want to spend the money to have José formally deported: The equally crowded deportation dockets are filled mainly with smugglers and multiple repeaters, aliens who have been caught and who have returned home "voluntarily" many times before. But unless those apprehended give the Border Patrol their real names, and few do, there is no way to check on the number of prior entries. As a result, many aliens are sent home dozens of times a year without facing deportation. Nor is a deportation record any guarantee of prosecution. The patrol regularly picks up aliens with two, three, and even four prior deportations who have never spent a day in jail. The immigration system is verging on terminal overload, and for nearly everyone who comes here uninvited, illegal immigration has become a crime without punishment. As one El Paso Border Patrolman put it, "There is no deterrent for the illegal to try it again and again."

Partly because they know that to do so will only burden the system further, not all Border Patrol agents are as scrupulous as Lew Moss has been tonight in advising José of his rights. Oftentimes, says a prominent Houston immigration lawyer, "they pick them up and they say, 'I'll tell you what: Either you go to jail, or we'll let you go back to Mexico voluntarily.' They say, 'Sign right here,' and if the fellow says, 'I want to talk to my attorney,' they say, 'You can talk to him when you get back to Mexico.' " Legal aid and Hispanic rights groups around the country have compiled endless lists of instances in which immigration officers have not only failed to tell aliens of their right to a hearing and a lawyer but have insisted instead that the aliens have no choice but to return to Mexico or wherever their home may be. One such case is that of Everardo Guiterrez, who was arrested and interrogated in January 1979 by INS agents in Chicago. According to a lawsuit filed by the Legal Assistance Foundation there, Guiterrez told the INS that he had a brother who was a United States citizen living in Denver and asked the agents to call him, but they refused and put the young man on a bus to Mexico. An even more egregious case was that of Tomasa Butiom, who entered the United States illegally from Mexico in 1961 and married an American citizen in 1975. Mrs. Butiom, who was called last year as a witness by the U.S. Civil Rights Commission, happened to mention during her testimony that she was under orders from the INS to leave the country within six weeks. When one commission member asked whether she knew that being married to an American citizen qualified her to become a permanent resident, she replied that the INS had never told her that.

"The Supreme Court says you can't throw anybody out of the country without a hearing," says Theodore Jakaboski, a Yale-trained immigration judge who sits in El Paso and who has serious doubts that every alien is properly advised of his right to a hearing. "But they catch about ten thousand aliens a month here, and we (he and the two other immigration judges there) only get about three hundred who want deportation hearings." Even when an alien does request a hearing, says Jakaboski, the Border Patrol sometimes pays no attention. "I had a case in Lubbock where a guy had filed his petition to be classified as a relative of a U.S. citizen. They picked him up while the petition was being adjudicated and sent him back to Mexico. Then his petition was denied because he failed to show up for the hearing." Because immigration judges have no contempt powers, Jakaboski says, their orders are often simply disregarded. "A guy came up before me for deportation. He had a citizen wife, so I let him go without bond and gave him sixty days to consult a lawyer and get his affairs in order. They picked him up and deported him anyway, but I have affidavits that show he showed them the papers with my orders."

As Moss escorts José to the waiting bus for the short ride down the river, the boy promises solemnly that he will not try to sneak back across the border again. Moss nods, but he is trying to suppress a smile. "We'll catch him again," he says when the boy is out of earshot, "either tomorrow or the next night." As the bus pulls away, Moss picks up a telephone and calls the Border Patrol's records center. He gives the duty officer José's full name and birthday, waits, then shakes his head. Hector Sena and Lew Moss just spent six hours and $200 of the government's money to catch a fourteen-year-old boy on his twenty-ninth illegal visit to the United States.

It rains most of the night, and the next morning the thin mountain air—El Paso is more than 4,000 feet above sea level —is crisp and clear. Today Mike Williams is working city patrol, in charge of a squad of six plainclothes patrol agents who will comb hotels, restaurants, and other businesses around town in hopes of surprising aliens at work. As he drives to the first stop, Williams talks about the unwritten rules of the border game. ''If a guy is willing to walk to the outskirts of town, he can pretty well get by us,'' he admits. Some, Williams says, cross the border 50 or even 100 miles from El Paso, but they are mostly ''country people'' from the rugged Mexican interior, men who are used to the heat and deprivations of the desert. ''Your city people wouldn't be able to make it,'' he says. Just after sunrise this morning, in fact, a man was found facedown in the sagebrush near Fort Hancock, 60 miles south of here. Next to his body were some cans of beans and sardines that he had hammered against a rock in a futile effort to break them open.

Many of the more timid border crossers who enter the country in and around El Paso venture no farther, preferring to remain close to the families they have left behind in Juárez. ''There's a lot of jobs available to them right here,'' Mike Williams says. Driving past a downtown café, he slows and points through the plate-glass window. ''See that gal behind the bar? She's illegal.'' He will come back later to see if she is still there. Turning east along the Rio Grande, which separates downtown El Paso from its sister city of Juárez, Williams sees a middle-aged Mexican man standing on the American side of the river. ''He's just fishing, so I'm not going to bother him.'' As he passes the Bridge of the Americas, one of three that link the twin cities, he points to a jagged hole that someone cut long ago in the chain-link fence atop the bridge. The concrete abutment below has been worn smooth by the friction of countless bodies sliding to the ground, but the hole has never been repaired. ''As long as it's there,'' Williams says, ''we know where they come in. We're operating on our terms, not theirs.''

In late 1978 the fence between El Paso and Juárez, like those dividing San Ysidro from Tijuana and Nogales, Arizona, from Nogales, Mexico, was replaced with what the Justice Department described as new, ''impregnable'' twelve-foot-high metal barriers topped with barbed concertina wire. The new fences quickly became known as the Tortilla Curtain—the Mexicans, people said, would eat them for lunch—and many in the Border Patrol, including Mike Williams, were frankly skeptical of their value. ''You figure that somebody comes all the way to the border from the interior of Mexico, say Michoacán or Guana-juato," Williams says, "he's not going to turn around and go home when he sees a little twelve-foot fence." The new fences nevertheless touched off protests from Hispanic groups after their manufacturer was quoted as saying that the wire strands of which they were made would be so sharp that anyone who tried to scale them might lose his fingers and toes. The controversy intensified when Bill Selzer, the deputy Border Patrol chief in Chula Vista, predicted that the six-mile-long fence at San Ysidro would divert illegal border crossers into the California desert to face "death from exposure or thirst." Among those offended by the fences was the Mexican government—Gaston de Bayona, a government official in Juárez, called them "very much like the fence that exists between East and West Berlin"—but no one need have worried. Within a week after the fences were finished, they were full of holes, some large enough to drive a truck through.

Considering that the country on either side of it was first settled more than 400 years ago, the international border between El Paso and Juárez is a relatively recent development. Until the Treaty of Guadalupe Hidalgo was signed in 1948, the two were a single city, and despite the Border Patrol's best efforts, in many ways they still are. A lot of people in El Paso have relatives in Juárez and vice versa, and it is not unusual for a family to have a wedding in Juárez and the reception in El Paso or a funeral in El Paso and the burial in Juárez. The cities share the same culture, language, and direct-dial telephone service, even the same pollution. Juárez, with more than 900,000 permanent residents, is far poorer than the booming Sunbelt city of El Paso, whose population is now close to half a million, but together they make up a metropolis that outranks all but four American cities in size.

Every day, tens of thousands of Juarensas, flashing their laminated border crossing cards, stream into El Paso to shop, to visit friends, and, although it is against the law, to work as maids, cooks, nannies, gardeners, at whatever jobs are available. The immigration inspectors at the American end of the bridges know that many of those entering with crossing cards are coming to work, but short of following each to his or her job, there is no way to prove their suspicions, and anyway, finding them and sending them back home is the job of the Border Patrol. Instead, some of the inspectors take advantage of the young women, fondling them as they walk through the turnstiles and taking some into back rooms to be "searched." The women generally endure such humiliations as the price they must pay to get to their jobs, but on the morning of March 9, 1979, hundreds of them decided that they had had enough. Gathering on the Mexican side of the Paseo del Norte Bridge, the women blocked the traffic and complained to anyone who would listen about their treatment at the hands of the American immigration officers. "We're here protesting the abuse they hand out," said Petra Rayes. "The immigration inspectors have been mauling the young women. They take us in the office and make us undress; then they feel us all over." The INS investigated and reported finding "no indication that any INS personnel acted in a wrong manner or misused authority, or searched anyone illegally," but one El Paso immigration lawyer dismissed the investigation as a fraud. "I've had several cases where women tell me of improper propositions at the bridge," he said, adding that most of his clients were "too embarrassed or too ashamed" to report the abuse.

But it is not the crossing-card violators Mike Williams is concerned with today. He is looking for the other thousands who do not have the cards and who are forced to wade the river each morning to make money any way they can. First stop for the "city patrol" is a blood plasma center a short distance from the bridges, one of nine centers in South El Paso that buy blood from Mexican border crossers for $8 a pint—the equivalent in Juárez of a good day's wages—then sell it for $20 to hospitals and research labs. The centers advertise in their windows that a regular donor can earn up to $81 a month, and for not a few in Juárez the blood banks are their sole source of income.

Williams frequently finds donors at the centers who have been coming over from Juárez twice a week for years to sell their blood. Earlier this week he found fifteen of them waiting on dirty plastic chairs when he walked into one center a few minutes before noon. The aliens were taken into custody and sent back across the river, but when the city patrol returned to the center after lunch, eight of the fifteen had beaten them back. It was one of those days, Williams says, when he thought:

"This is about as frustrated as I ever want to be." Something only he understands keeps Mike Williams coming to work in the morning.

Besides the plasma centers, the city patrol will check several other places it knows it can find illegal aliens working or relaxing: car washes, construction sites, lumberyards, bars, and cafés. Last night the game was cat and mouse; today it is foxes and hounds. One plasma center has stationed a lookout, and by the time Williams and his crew arrive the place is empty. After circling the block a few times, Williams decides that the donors are being hidden in an apartment over the center. Quietly he and three of his men leave their cars and tiptoe up the stairs. The building is fetid, its peeling, apple-green walls covered with obscene graffiti in Spanish—*Chinga tu madre,* someone has written. Loud norteno music blended with some salsa blares from a dozen radios, each seemingly a different station. It is a typical barrio tenement, one-room apartments decorated with colorful swatches of cheap fabric, each crammed with a stove, hot-water heater, television set, and beds until there is almost no room to walk.

A Mexican-American girl of about twelve hears them arrive and leans out the door of her apartment to nod silently toward the communal showers at the end of the grimy hallway. The patrolmen knock on the shower door, and after a minute the running water is turned off. "Come on, get out of there," Williams shouts in Spanish, and four would-be blood donors file out, fully clothed and looking sheepish. They are handcuffed and led away. It is not unusual, Williams says, for Mexican-Americans to turn in illegal aliens, whom they see as unwanted competition for jobs and lebensraum and as interlopers who have taken the easy route into the United States. Just a few minutes before, two teenage Mexican-American girls in a white Mustang stopped Williams's car and gave him an address where they said five illegal alien women were living. From what Williams could gather, two of the women had stolen the informants' boyfriends. The tip will be checked out. Knowing he has the support of the barrio makes Williams feel a little better about his job.

On the way to visit a body and fender shop notorious for employing illegal workers (and also notorious for its low prices),

Williams turns a corner and spots three young men standing on the sidewalk a block away. "There's one there," he says, pointing out a man wearing an electric-blue shirt and a Zapata mustache, as his foot stamps on the accelerator. "I caught that guy yesterday." Williams swerves to the curb and leaps from the car to block the man's path. "U.S. Immigration," he shouts, as though he might have been mistaken for a forest ranger. "Where are you from?" Smiling, the man climbs into Williams's car without even answering the question. He is an experienced player who knows the rules, but not all apprehensions are as easy. By law, the most the Border Patrol can do to a suspected illegal alien is ask questions. "If you claim you're a citizen," Williams says, "it's up to me to prove you're not. It's a hard job. It takes training and a little skill. Sometimes I can do it, but sometimes I have to let them go." In practice, however, the Border Patrol has other weapons it uses to loosen tongues, among them the threat of a full body search, a prospect that Hispanic women find particularly traumatic. A twenty-two-year-old Mexican woman, seized in a raid on an El Paso garment factory, became hysterical and had to be hospitalized after Border Patrol agents ordered her to undress, saying, "You'll talk better if you're naked." (The INS later told the woman's lawyer that the search had been necessary to look for "concealed weapons.")

Because the man Williams spotted a few moments ago recognized him, too, there is no need for a lengthy interrogation. On the way to the detention center the man, who says his name is Rubén, tells Williams that he has been earning $15 a day at the same body shop the city patrol was on the way to search—as much, he says proudly, as he could make in a week in Juárez, if he could find a job. Last night the Border Patrol caught him and took him sixty miles downriver before it dropped him off in Mexico, but when the body shop opened this morning, Rubén was back. He returned, he says, because he had a job he hadn't finished; besides, he enjoys the work. His job was cut short today—Rubén had been on his lunch break when Williams drove up—but he will probably be back again tomorrow. For Rubén it is not a bad arrangement. "The odds are definitely in his favor," Williams admits. "Even if he gets caught one day a week, he's still paid very well."

"This Is as Frustrated as I Want to Be"

Near the end of a longer day than usual (he didn't get much sleep after his late tour at the railroad yards last night), Williams tries to explain the sixth sense that helps him pick out the illegal border crossers trying to blend into El Paso's large Mexican-American population. He is not sure himself exactly what it entails, but it has to do with their clothing, their haircuts, how they respond to his initial questions, even the way they walk. "Sometimes," he says, "they try too hard to look nonchalant." But there is also something indefinable. Two blocks away, two attractive, stylishly dressed young women carrying shopping bags are sauntering along a freeway access road. To the untrained eye they look for all the world like a pair of middle-class El Paso housewives on their way home from the shopping mall, but when Williams sees them, he guns his engine. "There's what I mean," he says, "they're definitely illegal." In less than a minute the two women, who readily admit that they have crossed the river from Juárez, are in the back seat of Williams's cruiser and on their way home.

As he drives, Williams points out several other likely candidates, but his car is full, and he does not stop. "Catching them isn't that difficult," he says. "It's what you do with them after you catch them. You just run out of places to hold them. You have to pick your priorities." Serious criminals, alien smugglers, incorrigible recidivists—by any measure those ought to be the immigration system's priorities. Yet it is the blood donors, the body and fender men, the schoolboys, and the casual visitors who most often fall into the Border Patrol's net. It is as Diogenes described the law: "All the little and helpless things get caught, but the heavy and giant things break through."

It might have been a romantic and fulfilling job in an earlier time, but Mike Williams has trouble finding much glamour or satisfaction in what he does, and he is not alone. The Border Patrol seems to be caught in an insane, mindless contest of wills, a feeling that many of the younger agents can remember from Vietnam. Most Americans do not appear to care much about what kind of job the patrol does, or whether its job is done at all. In fact, the only group that has supported the patrol publicly is the Ku Klux Klan, which announced in 1977 that its members would begin assisting the patrol by hunting aliens in their spare time. Driving automobiles with "KKK Border

Patrol'' painted on the doors, Klan members actually took up positions at San Ysidro and several other points along the border. Officially the Justice Department was horrified, and Attorney General Griffin Bell issued a stern warning to the Klansmen to leave enforcement of the immigration laws to the immigration service. But the Klan's leaders refused to desist, and one, a San Diegan named Tom Metzger, who later ran a losing race for Congress, confided that his Klavern had several members who were themselves Border Patrol agents.

Unofficially, however, the Klan's offer was welcomed. Ed Begley, who was then an immigration inspector in San Ysidro, recalled that when Metzger and his Klansmen arrived at the port of entry building, they were well received by the officers on duty. ''They came down there on a Sunday,'' Begley said. ''They came into the port wearing 'White Power' T-shirts. The officer in charge met them at the door and gave them the red-carpet treatment, a tour of the port, an explanation of how aliens should be handled, very graphic descriptions of what their rights were as far as apprehending aliens.'' The Klansmen were even told, Begley said, ''that if they brought somebody in and said he was an illegal, it would be investigated.'' Followed by reporters, the Klan cruised the border for most of one weekend, but without success. Finally, in desperation, some Klansmen seized a passerby who appeared to be Mexican, threw him in their car, and drove to the nearest Border Patrol station, where they handed the poor man over. It turned out that he was in the country legally. ''The Klan actually kidnapped a resident alien,'' Begley said, ''and the Border Patrol held the man and let the Klan go.''

Troubled by the effect that such lopsided odds were having on his troops, concerned by the nightly incidents of violence around San Ysidro, and shocked by reports that hundreds of aliens were dying on their way across the border, Leonel Castillo ordered an investigation into the causes of the growing turmoil. ''We've had more deaths, more shootings, more incidents of rock-throwing in the last six months than people have seen in years,'' Castillo said. The study confirmed the Border Patrol's suspicions that the rock and bottle throwers were, in the main, not illegal entrants themselves. But it also suggested that the increasing numbers of aliens, along with what many

Border Patrolmen were convinced was a less than total commitment by the federal government to stopping them, had combined to produce tremendous stress that contributed to the shootings and beatings the patrol was handing out in retaliation. In a word, the Castillo study said, the Border Patrol felt "overwhelmed." The practice of permitting captured aliens to return voluntarily to Mexico made illegal reentry "almost certain" and only heightened frustrations. The study also questioned the "quality, dedication and maturity" of the new recruits who were replacing the veteran agents now resigning or retiring in droves. Finally, it recommended psychological testing for applicants that might identify officers emotionally unsuited for such work. (The INS has yet to make such tests a part of its hiring procedures, explaining that psychological assessments are not permitted under civil service regulations.)

Whether such a test would have singled out Jeff Otherson as a potentially violent or brutal man can, of course, never be known. But even if Otherson had been denied a badge and a gun, it would have made little difference, for the fact was that the incidence of violence perpetrated by the Border Patrol had attained the proportions of an epidemic.

The month before the Fourth of July beatings, Mike Walsh, the U.S. attorney in San Diego, had begun meeting with each shift of Border Patrol agents about to go on duty at San Ysidro, cautioning them to use "the utmost restraint" in apprehending illegal aliens. "Violence begets violence," Walsh warned. "Avoid resort to force if at all possible. The use of your weapon should be the absolute last resort."

The warnings had been occasioned by an incident at San Ysidro a couple of months earlier. As Benito Rincón remembered it, he and a friend, Efren Reyes, had been sitting on an embankment overlooking Tijuana and drinking some wine when a pale-green automobile pulled up beside them. Although they had no intention of going anywhere, the two young men were about fifty feet inside the United States and technically in violation of the immigration laws, so the driver of the car, a veteran Border Patrol agent, took them into custody.

For the agent, it had already been a bad night. A few hours earlier he had been hit by a rock thrown from the Mexican side of the border, and now he was wearing a protective helmet with a plastic face shield. The vehicle he was driving was a "war wagon," one of the Dodge Ramchargers at San Ysidro whose windows had been reinforced with sturdy wire mesh as protection against the rock throwers. Like most of the Border Patrol agents working the "combat zone" that night, the man was a little jumpy. He had only one pair of handcuffs, and following standard police procedure governing a lone officer arresting two suspects, he used it to bind Reyes and Rincón together. But as he led the pair back to his vehicle, urging Rincón forward with a kick to the backside, Reyes bolted and began running back toward Mexico. "I had no choice but to follow," Benito Rincón remembered later. "About three-quarters of the way down the embankment I heard a shot from the Border Patrolman's gun. I squatted down. Then another two shots were fired. At first I did not realize I was hit, but after a few minutes I felt an intense pain in my shoulder. I laid facedown for twenty or twenty-five minutes before anyone came. Reyes was dead as soon as the bullet hit him."

When the coroner arrived at three o'clock the next morning, he found Efren Reyes lying at the bottom of the twenty-eight-foot embankment next to a patrolman's black night stick, his cheap shirt soaked with blood. From his right wrist hung a pair of Smith & Wesson handcuffs. According to the coroner, the cause of death was massive hemorrhaging of the heart, right lung, and liver, "due to gunshot wound, chest, right." Reyes was twenty-four years old when he was killed for trying to run away.

In the inquiry that followed, the Border Patrolman said he fired at the two young men in self-defense. But Edwin Miller, the San Diego district attorney, said his investigation showed that "neither of the handcuffed men made any move to strike or kick the agent" or to reach for his weapon. Under California state law, Miller said, an officer who had made such a misdemeanor arrest would not have been permitted to use deadly force to prevent his prisoners' escape. But the man was a federal officer, and after "long and painful reflection" Miller decided against prosecution. The chances of convicting a Border Patrol agent in a city where every second or third car sported a red, white, and blue bumper sticker reading "Stop the Silent Invasion" were not good.

The case of Reyes and Rincón attracted the attention of Herman Baca, an indefatigable young man who heads the San Diego-based Committee on Chicano Rights and who deplores the Border Patrol's helicopters, flak jackets, tear gas, electronic sensors, and night-vision devices as the Vietnamization of the Southwest. "You talk about people throwing rocks," Baca admonished the Border Patrol, "but you never ask yourselves, 'What do these rocks mean? What are the people who throw the rocks responding to?' " In hopes of finding out, Baca sent his followers into the community to talk to Mexicans and Mexican-Americans about their experiences with the Border Patrol, and before long he had compiled a list of a dozen alleged abuses that he said was just "the tip of the iceberg."

Among those on Baca's list were Margarito Balderas, shot in both forearms by a Border Patrol agent as he stood with his hands in the air; sixteen-year-old Martin Zarate, shot in the legs from a Border Patrol helicopter as he stepped across the border into San Diego County; Mario Medina, kicked repeatedly in the testicles by a Border Patrol agent when he refused to admit he was an alien smuggler; and nineteen-year-old Guillermo Carrazco, shot in the back by a Border Patrol agent who said he thought Carrazco had been about to throw a rock at a group of officers standing guard along the border. Nor was Baca's list the only one. The federal defender's office in San Diego, which supplies lawyers to indigents and therefore handles a large number of complaints brought by both aliens and citizens against the Border Patrol, combed its files and came up with another twenty-five cases in which Mexicans arrested by the Border Patrol had suffered serious, even severe beatings, most of them while "resisting arrest."

Such incidents were by no means confined to Southern California. One of the most disturbing had taken place near Laredo, Texas, when Estela Salazar, age six, and her fifty-five-year-old uncle were killed by shotgun blasts while the pickup truck in which they were riding was being chased by two Border Patrol agents. The Border Patrol denied that its officers had fired at the truck, and though it was not clear where else the shots could have come from, no indictments in the case were ever returned.

Then there was the case of Elfego Mendoza, a twenty-eight-year-old Mexican who, accompanied by two friends, entered the United States illegally at Sonoyta, Mexico, just across the border from Lukeville, Arizona, on a spring day in 1978. "I came," Mendoza said later, "because I heard that what you make in one month in Mexico you can make in one week here. And things weren't going well at home. I had no idea what type of work I'd get when I came. Maybe in a factory, perhaps in the fields, or washing dishes. Whatever." His wife, Adela, understood. "It was hard to see him go," she said, "but if he was to go, I wished him well."

The trio had walked as far as Sweetwater Canyon, about ten miles north of Lukeville, when Mendoza heard the first shot. He remembers nothing after that, nothing until he awakened a few days later at the Maricopa County Hospital in Phoenix to discover that he could not move his arms or legs. According to testimony later produced in court, Mendoza and his companions had set off one of the Border Patrol's body sensors, and William D. Manypenny and his partner, Jerry Hjelle, had been sent by the patrol's Gila Bend station to investigate. As Manypenny called out to the three men to halt, they began running toward the border. A double-ought shotgun pellet hit Mendoza in the neck, severing his spine. But after Mendoza had been rushed to a nearby hospital, Manypenny told the attending physician that he had found the Mexican in his paralyzed condition. Mendoza, he said, must have slipped somehow on the rough walls of the canyon and hurt his neck.

A short time later the agent changed his story, admitting that he had fired his shotgun, but only at the ground. The buckshot, he said, must have ricocheted. The story kept on changing. Manypenny's foot had slipped and the gun had gone off accidentally. He had meant to shoot in front of the man but had misjudged his speed. He had believed that Hjelle, his partner, was in danger and had shot at Mendoza to protect him. His gun had jammed, causing the first shot that struck Mendoza; then he had tripped, causing the second. A Pima County grand jury indicted Manypenny on one count of assault with a deadly weapon. The case was transferred to United States District Court, but when the jury found Manypenny guilty, the judge threw the verdict out, saying the county had lacked jurisdiction to bring charges against him in the first place. Manypenny was fired from the Border Patrol, not for shooting Elfego Mendoza but for having carried an unauthorized shotgun while on duty. The general feeling among Border Patrol agents at Gila Bend, one of them says, is that Bill Manypenny, who is now raising strawberries in Arkansas, got a "raw deal" from the immigration service.

Elfego Mendoza, a quadraplegic for life, is living in Tucson with his wife and three children in a small, neat house surrounded by the concrete ramps needed to accommodate his wheelchair. He sued the government and won $953,333 in damages, at the time a record settlement, but the Mendoza family received only $190,000. The rest went to his lawyer, William Piatt, and to a trust fund set up to pay Mendoza's medical bills. "He's just a poor, ignorant alien," Piatt said. "We're protecting him from himself."

By their own standards, the Mendozas are rich. "We have more things here, and we can pay for what we need," Adela said. "But it was better back in Mexico because Elfego was fine. We were poor, but we were all healthy." Elfego, who was granted permanent residency by the government and passes most of his days watching television programs beamed to Arizona from Mexico City, misses his village in Mexico. "I'd like to take a stroll down my street," he says. "I miss hearing the rooster crow when I'd get up early to go to work in the fields."

As case after case of violence was uncovered along the border, it became clear that most of them fitted into a standard pattern in which the Border Patrolmen involved claimed they had acted in self-defense after being attacked or threatened. Usually, the self-defense claims were supported by fellow officers, but there was some reason to question their veracity. "If there ever was a fraternal group, they're it," says one INS man who has worked closely with the Border Patrol for years. "I know of a couple of instances where guys really did do something wrong, and they had 'witnesses' who were five miles away. One Border Patrolman I know recognized a coyote as a guy he'd had a fight with. He didn't waste any time—he just rapped the guy upside the head with a flashlight and knocked him out cold. Several other guys popped up and said they were there when they weren't.''

Over a couple of beers in a local tavern, some of the San Ysidro Border Patrol agents acknowledged that inflicting brutality on illegal aliens was an unavoidable part of their job. ''The whole thing about this brutality,'' said one, ''is that too many times we have to bring in as many as thirty aliens at once. If one of them gets tough, they all will, unless we do something about it. It's to save our own ass that we maybe punch the guy who gets out of line. Sometimes it takes a baton to do it.'' But older agents scoff at such excuses. ''These aliens,'' one says, ''are law-abiding people. We have had cases where a Border Patrolman who has caught more people than he can move puts one of the aliens in charge of fifty others. He goes and calls for a bus, and when he gets back, they're still sitting there. They grow up believing that authority equals blind obedience. They are very fatalistic people. They all know the old saying, 'Eso es mi pinche vida' ('This is my bad-luck life').''

Fred Drew, the only black Border Patrolman at San Ysidro when he was assigned there, agrees. ''All the illegals I ever saw were very meek and extremely respectful of authority,'' he says. ''But I've seen Border Patrolmen beating aliens over and over again, almost to death.'' Only 10 or 15 percent of his fellow agents were genuinely brutal, Drew says, ''but the big problem was that the rest of the patrolmen tolerated it.

''Most of the people in the United States don't live here,'' he says. ''They don't see what goes on here, and they don't want to see, especially if it's cruel.'' Fred Drew will remember some of what he saw for the rest of his life, like the day he watched his supervisor walk across the border to the pond where the women of Tijuana gather each morning to wash their clothes, drag one of the young girls back across the border, and rape her. ''She couldn't have been more than twelve or thirteen,'' he says. ''When it was over, she went back across and she was crying.'' Drew reported the rape to his superiors, but nothing was done. Nor, he said, was anything done about the group of San Ysidro agents who were smuggling aliens across the border for $20 a head. Equally distressing to Drew was the virulent racism among his colleagues, most of whom, he says, viewed Mexicans as ''the lowest form of life. It's a feeling that gets taught to them from the very first day, when they're told what *cabrón* means.'' The epithet, interchangeable with "tonk," is Spanish for "goat."

The same sort of attitude, other officers say, also applies to Mexican-Americans in the Border Patrol, who are valued for their command of Spanish but treated as second-class officers in every other way. More than half the agents at the Laredo Border Patrol station are Hispanic, but not one had ever been promoted to supervisor until Leonel Castillo became immigration commissioner. Castillo also made a few high-level Hispanic appointments at INS headquarters, among them Humberto Moreno, whom he placed in charge of the elite Anti-Smuggling Unit. But with Castillo's departure, few Mexican-American officers are destined to rise beyond the level of journeyman agent.

Though the problem of race is ever-present, it surfaces only rarely. In 1981 a group of seven Mexican-American Border Patrol agents in Tucson publicly charged that they had been discriminated against in assignments, promotions, and job evaluations by their superiors, and had been "repeatedly harassed, badgered, and bullied" by other Anglo officers. "I see and hear racist comments all the time," said Victor Ochoa, one member of the group, which also accused their colleagues of having mistreated Mexican aliens in their custody—refusing to give water to those apprehended in the desert and stealing valuables from them. Many of the problems encountered for years by Hispanic Border Patrol agents also exist for the patrol's new women recruits, for whom the INS was forced to modify its physical qualifications test after it was sued by a group of thirty female applicants who claimed the tests were discriminatory. The Border Patrol began accepting women soon afterward, but they were not made to feel welcome. Like male police officers everywhere, Border Patrol agents say they are reluctant to work with female partners on whom their lives might depend, and their wives say they do not want their husbands to have women partners for other reasons.

One who suffered the worst of both worlds was Ernestine Lopez, the only Mexican-American among the first six women admitted to the Federal Law Enforcement Training Center, the same place that Ed Begley began his abbreviated career as an immigration inspector. Lopez, who had been working as a secretary for the Ventura, California, Sheriff's Department, said that when she decided to change careers a few years ago, her thoughts turned immediately to the Border Patrol. "I used to see the Border Patrolmen come into the jail," she recalled, "and I thought they looked so professional." Lopez applied and was accepted, the beginning of a traumatic experience that was to leave her angry and embittered, "a completely different person." Among the male trainees at the academy she quickly became "the Mexican hot tamale." More than one instructor suggested that she could improve her grades in bed. One night at dinner her classmates, encouraged by one of the instructors, auctioned her off to the highest bidder. "I wasn't embarrassed," she said later. "I was mortified."

All that she might have endured, but not what followed the knock on her dormitory door that interrupted a late-night study session. The visitor was a fellow trainee, and he had been drinking. "He pushed his way in," Lopez said. "He tried to put his arms around me and kiss me." As she resisted, her attacker grew more determined, ripping off her pajamas. In the struggle that followed her bed was broken. After the man passed out, Lopez reported the attack to the academy's administrator, who took one look at her broken bed and laughed. No charges were ever filed against her assailant. Instead, Lopez said, "I was made to feel like I was the guilty one." An hour before the graduation exercises that marked the close of the eighteen-week training course, Ernestine Lopez, her name already printed in the graduation program, was told that though her grade average of 71 was above passing, she would not be graduated with the rest of her class. As the other trainees filed into the auditorium to receive their diplomas, she packed her things and headed for the airport. It was not until her separation letter arrived a few weeks later that Ernestine Lopez learned that she had been terminated "for poor judgement in your handling of an alleged rape incident at the academy." She appealed the dismissal and was eventually ordered reinstated with back pay, but she does not consider it a victory. "I'll just never be the same," she says.

Another who will never be the same is Nicholas Estiverne, one of Ernestine Lopez's classmates at the academy who spent his ten-month probationary period at the McAllen, Texas, Border Patrol station in the lush Rio Grande Valley near the eastern end of the Mexican border. Nick Estiverne was not an ordinary Border Patrol agent. Born in Haiti, he became an American citizen in 1971 and had acquired three university degrees, including a law degree, before joining the patrol at the suggestion of one of his professors. An earnest, scholarly, highly principled young man, Estiverne began to have second thoughts about his decision almost from the day he joined the immigration service. "They teach you to hate aliens," he said. "They keep telling you every day, 'Here's the wet coming at you. He's going to stab you. You better shoot him.' They teach you karate because the wet's going to hit you, teach you to use all the force you can because the wet's hostile to start with. But they're just poor guys. They're not hostile at all."

His superiors, Estiverne said, urged the Border Patrol trainees to obtain an extra, unregistered weapon and carry it with them while on duty. "They explained that if you shoot an alien by accident, all you have to do is throw the gun next to him and say he was shooting at you." Estiverne said that many of the Border Patrol agents he knew had carried such weapons, and other officers confirmed his account. "I had that taught to me, too," one Anglo agent said, "wrapping cloth tape on the handle to prevent fingerprints from getting on the gun, the whole thing." In 1979 Border Patrol agent Daniel Krohn was charged with murder by a Texas grand jury after he had shot an alien twice in the back. Krohn initially claimed self-defense, but at his trial admitted that he had placed a "throw-down" gun next to the body after the shooting. The jury acquitted him anyway.

At the McAllen station, Estiverne said, the brutalizing of aliens was "a common thing, an everyday thing. Everybody was doing it—serious punching I'm talking about, kicking, hitting with a stick in the stomach, all of which is not considered a big thing in the Border Patrol." Such beatings, he said, were not only administered gratuitously or out of frustration but also to extract confessions. "Let's say a group of ten people comes through," he said, "and the agent who catches them says, 'Tell me who the smuggler is.' Nobody talks, so they pick somebody out and say, 'You're the smuggler.' The guy says, 'I'm not the smuggler,' and so they walk him into one of the back rooms and just beat the hell out of him to make him say he is the smuggler. Then the Border Patrol ends up with a smuggler who's not a smuggler.'' It also ends up with a criminal case since the Justice Department almost always prosecutes those against whom the Border Patrol brings felony alien-smuggling charges. Needless to say, the Miranda warning that the Supreme Court has said must be given to those suspected of breaking the law—the advice of their right to remain silent, to a lawyer, and that anything they say can be used against them in court—is not normally administered by the Border Patrol under such circumstances. As one INS agent put it, ''The officer can always say, 'Well, until he confessed, I didn't know I had a criminal case.' ''

''I used to come home every day with tears in my eyes from what I saw on the job,'' Estiverne said. ''I've seen many shootings. I saw shootings regularly. And these are unarmed people, people who come across just to get jobs.'' Nick Estiverne also saw his share of corruption. Some Border Patrol agents at McAllen, he said, were smuggling aliens into the country and then renting them out to local farmers for a few dollars a day. One agent ran a male escort service on the side that employed good-looking young men he imported illegally from Mexico. ''Smuggling is easy for the Border Patrol,'' Estiverne said. ''You come across the border with three people in your car, nobody asks you any questions because they know who you are. You just pass by and wave.'' One of the agent-smugglers told him, Estiverne said, that if he mentioned the practice to anyone outside the patrol, ''I would be a dead man with my throat cut.''

Nor, he said, were some Border Patrolmen reluctant to use their authority over aliens to extort sex from Mexican women. ''There's a restaurant in McAllen,'' Estiverne said, ''that's a haven for female aliens, beautiful-looking girls. Every time you wanted something from one of them you'd just go into the restaurant and say, 'Hey, if you don't go with me, you know what's going to happen.' Those women knew the whole Border Patrol, practically, because everybody was doing it. They talked about what they did. They'd say, 'Hey, you want a piece? Just go to this restaurant. Just pick them up and they won't resist.' '' The practice is also common elsewhere. In San Ysidro, several officers there said, a group of Border Patrol agents actually rented on a monthly basis a motel room to which they repaired with female aliens they had taken into custody.

It was also his impression, Estiverne said, that many of the Border Patrol agents in McAllen were less interested in catching illegal aliens than in seizing the narcotics smugglers who use many of the same routes of entry along the border. (In 1979, the same year that agents in McAllen caught some 40,000 aliens, they also turned up 84,375 pounds of marijuana.) Simply catching another illegal alien, Estiverne said, counted for nothing. But seizing a smuggler and his load of marijuana won the officer a mention in the National Intelligence Report and, more important, the chance of a job with the Drug Enforcement Administration. "Most of the guys were looking forward to going into DEA, because DEA pays more money than the Border Patrol," Estiverne said. "So if you make so many drug busts, when you go to apply for a DEA job, that gives you a plus. That's why we have so many illegal aliens now. The Border Patrol will let the aliens come in because they're waiting for a load of marijuana to come across. They might stay there all night hoping that a marijuana load will come, and by that time two hundred illegal aliens will walk right in front of them and they won't pick them up." In their zeal to make narcotics arrests, Estiverne said, some Border Patrol agents hid part of a captured shipment of marijuana before turning the rest in. "Then a couple of weeks later they'd go out and pick up three kilos from the stash and try to catch a couple of aliens. Then they'd match the kilos with the aliens. The aliens don't speak English, they don't know what's going on, so they're brought in as mules carrying three kilos and the aliens don't even know they're being charged with marijuana smuggling." A couple of agents he knew, Estiverne said, simply kept the marijuana and sold it.

There were other perquisites. Restaurants that employed illegal aliens as waiters, cooks, and busboys, he said, provided free meals to the Border Patrol agents in return for being left alone, while those that refused to let the agents eat for free were raided frequently. The same treatment, he said, was accorded growers who did not regularly provide agents on "farm and ranch" duty with baskets of fresh fruits and vegetables. (But then, the Border Patrol has never been noted for its eagerness to raid friendly ranchers. A few years ago William Toney, a deputy Border Patrol chief in Del Rio, Texas, wrote a memorandum to his superiors complaining that dozens of illegal aliens had been working for months on a ranch owned by a prominent cattle and banking family, even though the ranch was being "traversed frequently by Border Patrol agents." Toney said he called for an investigation of the lack of enforcement but was told, "Most of the guys disagree with you about cracking down on all the wets around here." When raids are necessary for the sake of appearances, ranchers and business people are sometimes tipped off by the Border Patrol in advance. One member of the Texas Civil Rights Commission testified last year that a businesswoman he knows was almost always given such warnings. "She told me that the immigration and the Border Patrolmen would come by and check her business, but that she was always forewarned before they came, that she would get a call from the agents saying, 'Look, we're coming, get rid of the people that don't have papers.' One day the agent came without calling, and he later called to apologize and said that because his inspector was with him, he did not have a chance to call."

In the fall of 1976, as he was approaching the end of his probation, Nick Estiverne wrote a letter to Leonard Chapman, the immigration commissioner, outlining everything he had seen and heard. He received a note of appreciation from the commissioner for "bringing these matters to my attention," but nothing happened. Nothing, that is, except to Estiverne, who was fired. The reasons given for his discharge—his inability to speak Spanish and his failure to keep his shoes shined—made no sense. On his mid-probation evaluation report, both his language ability and his personal appearance had been rated "above average."

Had it not been for the United States Commission on Civil Rights, the INS might have been able to dismiss the allegations of former employees like Ed Begley, Fred Drew, Ernestine Lopez, and Nick Estiverne as the grumblings of soreheads and malcontents. But in November 1980, after an extensive, nationwide study of immigration practice and procedure, the commission concluded in a report that "in the process of immigrating to and remaining in the United States, persons can be and sometimes are deprived of their constitutional rights." The commission found that the INS's raids on homes and businesses often amounted to "unconstitutional searches and seizures" and that the right to counsel and to immigration hearings were not being "provided to suspected immigration law violators at all crucial stages of the deportation process." On too many occasions, it said, aliens had been denied altogether the "expeditious and impartial" hearings to which they were entitled. The commission's Texas Advisory Committee, which held a year's worth of hearings in connection with the study, went even further. Illegal aliens, it said, were being subjected to frequent physical and psychological abuse by INS and Border Patrol personnel, abuse that was "exacerbated by the inability of some INS officers to communicate effectively in Spanish." But of all the Civil Rights Commission's 157 pages of recommendations, findings, and conclusions, perhaps the most significant was its assertion that the INS's "procedures for investigating and eliminating employee misconduct were neither efficient nor effective."

Even when examples of such wrongdoing were brought to its attention, the INS appeared to care little about how its personnel behaved, and more often than not such incidents were simply never reported. A central reason is the profound reluctance of illegal aliens to complain to the authorities in a country where they are uninvited visitors about their treatment at the hands of the INS. They will talk to those they trust, but they do not trust men with badges and guns. "We hear many complaints from aliens," says Al Velarde, an official of the United States Catholic Conference in El Paso. "But they won't pursue action against the individuals involved because they don't want to expose themselves to deportation." Unlike most police officers, immigration agents are able to get rid of the witnesses against them by sending those aliens whom they have brutalized, extorted from, or otherwise mistreated out of the country. "A doctor can bury his mistakes," one immigration agent says. "A Border Patrolman can deport his to Mexico."

Like most federal agencies, the INS has a branch, called the Office of Professional Responsibility, that is supposed to uncover and punish internal wrongdoing. But the OPR has rarely seemed eager to take the action such cases appear to warrant. In recent years it has frequently taken no action at all, and even when it does, the INS much prefers to hand out administrative punishments, such as reprimands, suspensions, and dismissals, rather than seek criminal charges. Examples abound: An INS employee who "assisted an alien smuggler" and then refused to testify about the incident was fired, but not prosecuted, even though smuggling aliens is a federal felony; seventeen INS employees who allowed a group of aliens to "escape" were sent letters of admonition; an employee who extorted money from illegal aliens was permitted to resign; an INS detention officer who raped a female alien at knifepoint was fired but not indicted; a Border Patrol agent who shot an alien and then deported the man in an attempt to conceal the incident was permitted to resign; another agent who beat an alien was suspended for three days; an INS investigator who "placed a wastebasket over the head of an alien and pounded on the basket" was suspended for five days; an officer who shot an American citizen by mistake was fired; a Border Patrolman who beat a female alien with his night stick was "admonished"; two immigration inspectors who opened fire on an unarmed motorist were given fifteen-day suspensions. The list goes on and on.

An INS official who for a time headed the OPR blamed the apparent indifference to internal wrongdoing on his superiors, who, he said, had displayed an almost total absence of support for his efforts. "No one liked to clean his own linen," the man said, "but they were threatened by it. All we did was put out little brush fires. I almost had an ulcer over the brutality cases. They sickened me." Echoing one of Nick Estiverne's assertions, the official said a major impediment to his investigations of suspicious shootings had been the widespread use of throwaway guns by immigration officers. He had had to borrow wiretapping equipment from other federal agencies, the man said, because the INS would not buy any of its own. Nor would it allocate funds to pay informants who helped gather evidence of internal corruption—the informants were paid with collections taken up from other officers. Despite his appeals for more internal investigators, he said, he had been forced to use regular INS employees as ad hoc investigators, with the result that they were often asked to look into the conduct of colleagues with whom they worked every day. Though many of the service's victims were aliens from Mexico and Latin America, he had no investigators at his disposal who spoke fluent Spanish.

An INS agent who has worked as one of the OPR's part-time investigators lays the blame for the lack of internal discipline on immigration officials in Washington, who he says were oblivious to his appeals for action. "I'm a pain in the ass to everybody," the agent admits, "because when I see something wrong, I tell them. The service doesn't like that. They don't like things out in the open. They like to sweep it up." Even when it was confronted with unassailable evidence that one of its employees was breaking the law, the agent said, the INS often failed to inform the Justice Department. He mentioned the case of a deputy chief of a medium-sized border station in the Southwest who had been caught giving entry permits to female aliens in exchange for sexual favors, a felony offense. The man was demoted one grade and transferred, but the INS never brought the matter to the attention of federal prosecutors. Asked how such a lapse was possible, the agent said, "When you get to be an assistant officer in charge, you've got a rabbi someplace."

In another case he knew of, the agent said, the INS actually obstructed the prosecution of a San Ysidro immigration inspector also known for giving permits to females in return for sex. "He was a slime," the man said. "I personally caught him on a couple of occasions wrapped up with girls in dark corners right there at the port." But the inspector's activities were tolerated until the night the agent discovered him forcibly abusing a thirteen-year-old girl. "It was about twelve-thirty at night when I walked in," he said. "He had told her he was going to frisk her. He had one hand under her sweater and the other up her skirt. Her breasts and crotch were being frisked very thoroughly." The agent filed a criminal complaint against the man and would have pressed charges, but the INS refused to allow the girl, who had since been deported, back into the country to testify against her assailant. The inspector involved was permitted to resign.

Though some officials in the Justice Department had long suspected that something was wrong with the investigation of internal wrongdoing at the INS, they were not certain just what it was until the department ordered a study that came up with some disturbing conclusions. There was "confusion," the study found, over which offices within the INS were responsible for investigating which kinds of misconduct, with the result that many internal investigations had remained unresolved for as long as two or three years. Most dismaying, however, was the discovery that senior INS officials were ''not reporting all allegations of serious misconduct to the Attorney General's office'' as required by law. The findings troubled Dave Crosland, the INS general counsel who had taken over as acting commissioner after Castillo resigned. ''If the system doesn't work,'' said Crosland, ''I'd like to make it work.'' He revamped the OPR and recruited a tough New York City police inspector named Walter Connery to run it. That Connery was serious about his job quickly became evident, and among all the musty files filled with unresolved cases that were waiting for him, one especially intrigued him. The file was filled with complaints of abuse by Border Patrol officers at the San Clemente checkpoint, including one from a fifteen-year-old boy who had been removed from a northbound bus by agents who beat him until he confessed that he was a citizen of Mexico and agreed to go back. The forced confession was bad enough, but it was also untrue: The boy was really an American citizen.

For Mexican-Americans, confrontations with the Border Patrol, which is frequently unable to distinguish between illegal aliens and American citizens of Hispanic descent, are an unfortunate fact of daily life. Some, like Al Velarde, have learned to take them in stride; whenever Velarde is challenged by the patrol to produce his green card, he pulls his American Express card from his wallet. For those not so sanguine, however, the experience can be most traumatic, as it was for Margarita Guiterrez. A member of the San Ysidro school board, Guiterrez was accosted by a Border Patrol agent while walking near her home. When she protested that she was not only a citizen but an elected local official, the agent told her, ''You Mexicans are all a bunch of liars,'' and threw her into his cruiser. Velarde and Guiterrez are educated and speak perfect English, and sooner or later such individuals are usually able to convince the Border Patrol that it has made a mistake. Millions of other brown-skinned Americans, like Norberto Gautier, are not so lucky. Gautier, an American citizen born in Puerto Rico, was arrested and deported to Guatemala because an immigration officer "thought he had a Guatemalan accent." When he arrived in Guatemala City, he was charged with emigrating illegally to that country and thrown in jail. After the mistake was discovered and Gautier was released, he had to pay his own way back home to Newark.

Angel Jimínez, a native of South Bend, Indiana, had never even been to Mexico. But during a bus ride from Texas to Louisiana, Jimínez was grabbed by the Border Patrol, locked up for eight days, and threatened with "a couple of years in prison" unless he agreed to "return" to Mexico. He signed the agreement simply to get out of jail and found himself in the Mexican town of Dolores Hidalgo, 400 miles south of Brownsville. But that was nothing compared to what happened to Daniel Cardona, another U.S. citizen who was swept up off the streets of Clovis, California, in an immigration raid and sent "back" to Mexico. Cardona, who is emotionally disturbed, walked the streets of Tijuana in a daze for five months before his family finally tracked him down.

A few weeks after Walt Connery took over as the INS's chief internal watchdog, Border Patrol agents working the San Clemente checkpoint routinely stopped a bus headed for Los Angeles, ordered its passengers to step down, and marched them inside the checkpoint's office for questioning. Agent J. G. Wood began badgering one of the passengers, a Mexican farmworker judging from his appearance, demanding that the man admit he had crossed the border illegally. No, the man insisted in Spanish, he was an American citizen. When he still refused to confess, Wood hit him with a metal flashlight, then with a pair of lead-lined gloves. Nearby Wood's partner, Border Patrolman José Barker, was having the same problem with another passenger who was continuing to maintain that he, too, was a citizen. Cursing, Barker picked up a metal chair and threw it at the man. Three months later J. G. Wood, the same agent who had beaten the fifteen-year-old boy a year before, was charged by a federal grand jury in San Diego with nine counts of assault and deprivation of civil rights. Among the charges was an unusual one: assaulting a federal officer. The "farmworker" Wood had beaten with the flashlight and the gloves was Juan Espinal, the young INS clerk from New York who had gone undercover for the FBI in the Markowitz case and was now working for Walter Connery in internal affairs. José Barker was charged with eight counts of assault, also including assault on a federal officer. Javier Dibene, the man he had hit with a chair, was another of Connery's undercover men. Barker got a year in prison, Wood three years' probation. The case marked the first time the INS had used its own agents in an undercover capacity to ferret out wrongdoing within its ranks, but it would not be the last. Dave Crosland thought such prosecutions were useful. "People will think twice before they push people around if they see somebody else being indicted," he said.

The only problem was that most of the U.S. attorneys around the country were reluctant to bring such charges. The courtroom spectacle of an illegal alien accusing a federal law enforcement officer from the witness stand, the prosecutors thought, was not likely to win them much support from the local citizenry. Nor were most prosecutors eager to present such a "pissing contest" to a jury, whose natural sympathies probably would be with the man who wore a badge and a gun. And what alternative was there, given the near impossibility of inducing Border Patrol agents who might have witnessed corrupt or brutal acts to testify against their brother agents? It was, most prosecutors agreed, a no-win situation, so they chose to go after tax cheats, drug smugglers, and other cases more certain to bring convictions. Which made it all the more remarkable when Mike Walsh, the young U.S. attorney in San Diego, made up his mind to seek charges against Jeff Otherson, Bruce Brown, and Dan Charest for the Fourth of July beatings—for having, as the government would later assert in court, "formed themselves into a vigilante outfit for the purpose of meting out their own brand of punishment to aliens who violated U.S. immigration laws." Indicted along with the three was Border Patrol agent Dirk Dick, another member of the group, who a few weeks later had kicked an elderly Mexican man in the face with his boot while the man lay on the ground, helpless and exhausted.

Walsh's case, it was true, was stronger than most. For one thing, it had the willing testimony of someone besides the victims—the four Border Patrol trainees who had witnessed the various beatings. But that did not detract from the fact that for the first time in the Border Patrol's fifty-five-year history the government was prosecuting its own agents for brutalizing illegal aliens. The indictments hit the patrol like a thunderbolt, instantly evaporating whatever morale had remained at San Ysidro. Suddenly the entire patrol was being portrayed in the newspapers and on television as a bunch of brutal, bloodthirsty savages, and the agents thought that was most unfair. "I never saw any real abuse," one told the *Los Angeles Times*. "Oh, maybe sometimes when we'd catch a bunch of wets and nobody would talk, then maybe somebody's foot would get stepped on or we'd stick a guy's head in the toilet and flush it a few times until he'd start to talk." But no real abuse.

Like many of the inspectors at the San Ysidro port of entry, the Border Patrol agents there responded to the indictments by giving up on the job. "I was out at the Border Beach State Park," one INS officer recalled, "and I had an informant working these smugglers. I walked over and told a Border Patrolman, 'When this girl gets off in a blue Ford, she's going to be loaded. All I want you to do is call in at San Clemente and give them the license plate, tell them to watch for her.' It was right after the indictments. All he said was: 'Don't you read the headlines?' Hell, there were wets running all over his car, coming across in droves, and he was sitting there watching the waves. He didn't want to catch any. He never made the call."

In the days that followed the Fourth of July beatings, the four trainees who had witnessed them talked among themselves about what they had seen and what to do about it. They went to the prosecutors to tell their story, then told it again to a federal grand jury. After word of their visit to the grand jury began to circulate, Steve Iverson, one of the trainees, found the lug nuts on a wheel of his car unaccountably loosened. The wife of Gino Freselli, who had been with Jeff Otherson on the morning of July 3, was followed to the supermarket and menaced by a man she later identified as Otherson. Alarmed, Mike Walsh placed the four trainees in protective custody, a procedure normally reserved for those who have agreed to testify against the Mob. Though he could have assigned the case to Pete Nunez, his first deputy, or any one of several other capable assistants in the San Diego office, Walsh chose to spare them the grief he knew such a role would bring and to prosecute the case himself. What bothered him more than the beatings or even the vigilantism, he said, was the fact that the brutality had been tolerated, even condoned, by many of the other agents at San Ysidro. "Nobody's kidding anybody," he said. "We know this goes on. I had no choice but to jump on the case, to let everyone know that that sort of behavior will not be tolerated." As things stood now, Walsh said, "I'd be afraid to go down to the border at night."

At the trial, lawyers for Otherson and his group at first tried to argue that the civil rights statutes under which their clients had been indicted did not apply to illegal aliens. Since the victims had been in the country illegally, the lawyers said, how could they have any rights at all? The judge, Howard Turrentine, disposed of that argument in short order. "So long as the American flag flies over the United States Courthouses," he said, "the Federal courts and the Federal justice system stand as bulwarks to assure that every human being within the jurisdiction of the United States shall be treated humanely." It was the first time that a federal judge had affirmed the idea that illegal aliens also had civil rights. Then the prosecutors began to play their trump cards. Before joining the Border Patrol, they disclosed in court, Jeff Otherson had been fired from the Covina, California, Police Department for having taken marijuana from suspects he arrested and given it to his girl friend, then lied about the reason for his discharge on his application to join the Border Patrol. The government also produced a surprise witness, a thirty-four-year-old legal resident alien named Apolinar Rivas-Aguilar, whom Otherson had one day mistaken for an illegal alien and forced to kiss the ground. Otherson, Rivas said under oath, had ordered him to sign a paper admitting he was in the country illegally and agreeing to return to Mexico or else take "a bullet between my eyes." Rivas testified that Otherson had said he was not worried about killing him "because he could always drop me in the water."

The trial ended in an anticlimax when the all-white middle-aged jury, after having deliberated for more than a week, reported that it could return no verdict except in the case of Dan Charest, whom it acquitted. The jurors said later that they had stood eleven to one for convicting Otherson and Brown, and ten to two for convicting Dick. The government agreed not to retry Dick if he resigned from the Border Patrol, which he did. Over Christmas 1979 Mike Walsh struggled with the question of whether to prosecute the remaining defendants again, but Jeff Otherson and Bruce Brown saved him the trouble. In a scene rarely played in any federal courtroom, the two waived their right to a retrial and agreed to let Judge Turrentine decide their fate—"a slow plea of guilty," as the judge described it. Both received three years' probation and fines of $1,000. Both Brown and Otherson were fired from the Border Patrol.

Mike Walsh, drained by the ordeal, left the Justice Department soon after to take a job in private industry, and the INS seemed content to regard the case of *U.S.* v. *Otherson, et al.*, as an isolated instance of wrongdoing. Except, that is, for the INS investigator who had characterized himself as "a pain in the ass" to the immigration service and who told a far different story. "If they'd tossed me on the stand," the agent said, "those guys would have got convicted the first time. It was a much bigger conspiracy. There was another group, code-named Charlie-Charlie. I'd hear it over the radio: 'Charlie-Charlie to the loading dock,' and they'd go over and thump themselves a wet. Bigger, much bigger, but I haven't told anybody. I've thought about it, but I'm not sure it would make any difference. They won't do anything down here about the really big stuff."

CHAPTER EIGHT

"Nothing Happens Before Its Time"

For most illegal aliens, *la vida americana* is in many ways indistinguishable from the lives of the indigenous poor. Illegal aliens may work a little harder, six or seven days a week instead of five or six. They own cars, but usually not the houses in which they live. Sunday mornings most of the Hispanics among them are likely to attend services, probably at a neighborhood Roman Catholic church. They shop in ghetto supermarkets, where, like many Mexican-Americans and blacks, they pay high prices for cheap food. Their children probably go to public schools. Since they do not understand most of what they read in English-language newspapers or what they see on American television, they are largely cut off from the official business of the country. They know or care little about politics and government; that does not matter much since they cannot vote.

But there is one profound, consuming difference in the way they lead their lives. Their unrelenting fear of attracting the attention of the authorities makes them easy prey for endless numbers of predators—dishonest landlords, gouging merchants, employers who charge them "hiring fees," immigration lawyers who take their money and then do nothing—all of whom are free to cheat them in the nearly certain knowledge that they will not complain. Typical of the breed is the owner of an East Los Angeles house, a crumbling shack with a leaky roof, drafty broken windows, no electricity or water, and every pest and vermin known to science, who was charging fifteen Mexicans $9 a day each to take turns sleeping in shifts on the sagging, mattress-covered floor—a rent of $4,050 a month. "At those prices, they could have rented a penthouse on Wilshire Boulevard," one INS agent said. "But they didn't know that. They thought it was the going rate."

Among those quickest to take advantage of illegal aliens are dishonest immigration lawyers who parlay their knowledge of the convoluted INS bureaucracy into a license to steal. "Your client comes to you," says Peter Hirsch, who practices immigration law out of a storefront office in Manhattan, "and right off you see how ignorant he is of the law, of the way of life in this country, and even of the language." Hirsch is one of thousands of decent and honorable immigration lawyers, some of them equal in skill and dedication of any of their colleagues in the loftier reaches of the legal profession. But immigration law is not particularly satisfying work, and it does not attract many of the brightest legal minds. Not only are the immigration statutes among the most obtuse in the federal code, but immigration lawyers must deal exclusively with the maddeningly inept bureaucracy of the INS. And most immigration cases are hardly challenging, involving filling out the same petitions and applications and making the same arguments and appeals to immigration judges day after day.

But the practice of immigration law can also be highly lucrative, and it is perhaps for this reason that the field seems to attract more than its share of shysters who promise clients more than they or any lawyer could ever deliver, do little or nothing on their client's behalf, and then threaten to have the client deported if he or she does not pay up. Until recently the undisputed king of the immigration lawyers was a man named Gerald Kaiser. In his heyday, which was only a couple of years ago, Kaiser was opening branch offices of his law firm, Kaiser, Heller & Rogers, like so many McDonald's hamburger stands and spending millions on nationwide television advertising to fill his offices with clients. In one commercial, shown incessantly in several big cities around the country, Kaiser was seated behind a big desk as he assured a client that "in many cases" a green card could be obtained in as little as three to six months. As the commercial drew to a close, Kaiser turned toward the camera and intoned, "It is possible that we can help *you*."

Of course, it was also possible that he could not, but the advertisements worked. Kaiser's firm handled more than 5,000 cases in 1979 alone. "To make money in immigration law," he told Howard Blum of *The New York Times*, "the answer is to handle a large volume of cases. That's why we put so much money into advertising, to bring them through the front door, and that's why I've gone nationwide."

Kaiser's theatrics attracted the enmity of many of his fellow immigration lawyers, who felt that he was misleading his clients into believing that he could secure green cards or certain kinds of resident visas for individuals who had no conceivable claim to them. "He takes the money and doesn't do things," said Mike Weiss, an immigration lawyer in Miami, where Kaiser lives. Some of Weiss's colleagues have gone farther, accusing Kaiser of outright deceptive practices. One is Donald Lindover, a member of the Ethics and Standards Committee of the Association of Immigration and Nationality Lawyers, who points out that Kaiser advertises that among his specialties is obtaining "investor status" for prospective immigrants. The immigration laws do make provision for the admission of foreigners who are willing to invest substantial sums of money here, but Lindover notes, "There has been no investor number granted by the immigration service for the past two years. He's advertising implicitly that he can get this for a client, and to me that's unethical. He's a hustler." In response to the criticism, Kaiser acknowledges that his ads contain "a certain amount of poetic license," but he insists that he agrees to take the case of only one client in every eight who walk through his door, telling the rest that they do not "have a chance for residency." But in the course of investigating Kaiser for the "unethical practice of immigration law," the New York office of the INS obtained affidavits from several unhappy Kaiser clients like Leonora Neal of the Bronx, who stated that although she gave Kaiser a $400 down payment on his fee and agreed to pay the balance of $1,100 in monthly installments of $100 each, after fourteen months "the law firm of Gerald Kaiser has failed to take any legal action on my behalf."

"Anyone can produce affidavits criticizing a specific case,"

Kaiser says. "I can get you hundreds of affidavits saying what a great job I've done." Kaiser is still in business, minus the erstwhile Heller and Rogers; but his operations have been vastly scaled down, and in 1981 he filed for bankruptcy. Immigration lawyers are practicing attorneys subject to bar association discipline, which at least provides their clients with some protection. But the self-anointed "immigration consultants" who circle in their wake are virtually free from regulation. "Just about anyone can say he's an immigration consultant," says Allen E. Kaye, a New York City lawyer. "The only thing is, these consultants don't know anything about the law, and they're playing with people's lives. One error on an immigration form and a person can be deported."

A number of the consultants are retired INS employees like Dallas's Jim Kelley, who has been accused by the Texas State Bar of selling to aliens for up to $1,500 "highly specialized and technical legal advice" that he is not qualified to provide. Kelley prefers to see himself as performing a needed service. "Aliens don't get any help from immigration," he told the *Dallas Morning News*. "You can spend an hour down at the federal building any morning—just see how long it takes a single person to get any help." Kelley may have a point, but most of the immigration consultants are not acting out of compassion for the immigrant. Consultants handling as few as ten clients a week at fees of $200 to $500 apiece can gross hundreds of thousands of dollars a year in return for little or no work, and by the time the client realizes that he has spent his money for nothing it may be too late, as it almost was for Roggerio, a Peruvian national who paid $860 to a New York City consultant who promised to help him remain in New York with his wife, an American citizen. The case should have been open and shut: Spouses of U.S. citizens are automatically entitled to permanent resident status upon filing the appropriate application. But Roggerio's case dragged on for more than two years, and he was on the verge of being deported by the time he sought competent legal counsel.

Many of the consultants, particularly those in the Southwest, advertise themselves as *notarios publicos*, a term that in Mexico is applied to lawyers who have been certified to practice by the government and have standing before the bar. In this country, of course, a notary public is not usually an attorney or a specialist of any kind, just someone who notarizes documents for a small fee. Many Mexicans, however, do not understand the distinction, and the consultants are happy to take advantage of their ignorance. All that most of the *notarios* ever do is help their clients fill out the standard immigration applications that can be picked up at any federal building. Then when the applications are rejected, as they usually are, the consultant assures the hapless client that he did his best.

Police departments in several large cities say that in addition to being bilked and cheated, illegal aliens are also the most frequent victims of violent crimes, principally murders and robberies, many of them committed by Mexican-Americans who live in the same communities and see the illegals as easy marks, which, in fact, they are. Nearly all illegal aliens do not have bank accounts, for example, since opening one involves making a record of one's existence and whereabouts, something most of them strive to avoid. Instead, they cash their paychecks at bars and liquor stores and often carry with them hundreds of dollars. Such total liquidity, while risky, is necessary since all their purchases and transactions must be accomplished with cash. Moreover, if an alien is picked up by the Border Patrol, at least his savings are in his pocket, not stuffed in a mattress somewhere or stuck in a bank account. Unfortunately this also makes aliens tempting targets for strong-arm robbers, like the five armed men who recently burst through the front door of a Dallas duplex shared by six Mexican construction workers, beat the men, took their money, and killed twenty-two-year-old Manuel Aguilar. Aguilar's friends called the police, but most such crimes go unsolved because aliens fear that reporting such attacks will attract the Border Patrol and result in their being sent home. So intense is the aversion of the aliens to the police, in fact, that robbers often turn it to their advantage; an example is the two Texas men with dime store badges who placed a group of Mexican aliens ''under arrest,'' drove them to a deserted park, took their money, and shot one to death.

The fear of the police, known among Mexican aliens as the *cárcel azul* (''blue jail'') is not without foundation. For even though they have no authority to enforce the federal immigration laws, local police and sheriff's departments for years have made a practice of stopping Hispanics and asking to see their papers, arresting anyone who cannot produce a birth certificate or green card on an "immigration hold," and calling the Border Patrol to come pick them up. In 1978 Attorney General Griffin Bell, concerned about the legality of such arrests, pointed out that enforcing the immigration laws was the responsibility of the federal government and asked that state and local law enforcement agencies no longer "stop, question, detain, arrest, or place an 'immigration hold' on any person not suspected of a crime, solely on the ground that they may be deportable aliens." Several big-city police departments changed their policies in response to Bell's request, but many smaller ones did not, unfortunately for Gerardo Rivera, an American citizen whose car was stopped by police in Grand Prairie, Texas, a suburb of Dallas, on suspicion of speeding and drunken driving. When those charges were dropped, the arresting officers decided that Rivera looked like a wetback and put an immigration hold on him. Rivera spent a weekend in jail before INS agents arrived and verified his citizenship. Worse yet was the experience of Ezequiel González, a legal U.S. resident who was stopped by San Diego County sheriff's deputies late one night as he was walking home from work. The officers threw González into the back seat of their car, drove him sixteen miles to the Mexican border, and pushed him across.

Police are not the only authority figures aliens have to fear, nor even the ones they have to fear the most. That distinction is reserved for their natural enemies, the agents of the Immigration and Naturalization Service. Even those illegal aliens who have made it past the Border Patrol's first-line defenses must contend with raids by INS agents on places they think illegal aliens might be living or working. Almost every day in any big city INS vans can be seen pulling up to bus stops, homes, businesses, even playgrounds, disgorging armed agents who stop and question any passerby with brown skin, and the raids are not always carried out with great regard for the law, as Guillermo Olvera knows. The way Olvera, who owns La Chiquita restaurant in Fullerton, California, recalls the evening of September 18, 1979, a dozen people were having dinner when two INS agents burst through the front door. "They entered the premises without a warrant of any kind," Olvera testified later. "They did not have my consent to enter. They searched the entire restaurant, including the kitchen. A number of my employees and myself were detained and questioned about our immigration status. All my Latino patrons were questioned, while none of the Anglo patrons were questioned."

Such raids, which the INS calls area control operations, have long been a feature of daily life in immigrant communities around the country, but it was not until November 17, 1978, that the practice, and the abuses inherent in it, were brought to the attention of official Washington. That was the day INS agents raided Blackie's House of Beef, a Washington, D.C., restaurant that is an expense account mecca for government executives, lobbyists, and journalists. The agents had with them a magistrate's warrant, obtained on the strength of affidavits stating that some of Blackie's employees had "foreign personal characteristics and attire that are native to Hispanics from Central and South America, including dark complexions and hair, foreign-style haircuts and grooming, ill-fitted and inexpensive clothing and foreign-style shoes." Moreover, some of the employees had actually been overheard speaking Spanish.

That description might as easily have applied to any number of legal resident aliens or even Hispanic-Americans, some of whom also wear cheap clothing and prefer speaking Spanish. Nevertheless, just before lunchtime a squad of ten INS agents stormed into Blackie's, sending busboys in white jackets sprinting out the doors, the agents hard on their heels. In the next twenty minutes the officers arrested 14 kitchen workers, 1 woman and 13 men, most of them from El Salvador. Blackie's sued, and a federal judge in Washington, declaring that the raid had been illegal, prohibited further raids without a full-fledged court order obtained on a showing of probable cause beyond the personal appearance of the suspected illegal aliens. But even after the ruling, INS area control teams in other cities continued to arrest as many as 600 suspected aliens in a single day, raiding not just restaurants and other work places but private homes as well, and without warrants of any kind.

The INS defends the "neighborhood raids" on the ground that the easiest place to arrest illegal aliens is in their homes. But for Hispanics such raids are a literal nightmare—they usually occur late at night or early in the morning, when residents are presumed to be asleep—of men with drawn guns knocking on bedroom windows, shining flashlights on couples in bed, climbing in windows and barging through doors without permission, and taking occupants away in various states of undress. Worst of all, perhaps, is the fact that the raiders are not very good at distinguishing between illegal aliens and citizens like Virginia Zepeda. It was about ten o'clock on the night of September 18, 1979, when Mrs. Zepeda, lying in bed with her husband, Domingo, thought she heard noises outside her suburban Los Angeles house. "My husband started to get out of bed to see who it was," she recalled in an affidavit. "He said he saw somebody at the bedroom window, and I heard someone trying to open the window screen." Thinking they were about to be attacked and robbed, the frightened couple fled to their living room, where Mr. Zepeda opened the front door to find the would-be intruders: a police officer and two INS agents. The three armed men barged into the house, Mrs. Zepeda said, "even though my husband did not give them permission to enter and they did not show us a warrant."

For Paz Flores, a Corcoran, California, resident who is also an American citizen, the knock on the door came at four in the morning. When he opened it, "four or five men" walked past him into his house. "They did not request permission to enter," Flores swore in his affidavit, "nor did they show me any papers allowing them to enter." The men, of course, were INS agents. But such encounters can take place anywhere, as Joe Paz knows. An American citizen and a senior at El Rancho High School in Pico Rivera, California, Paz was shipping some packages to relatives in Texas at the Greyhound bus depot in downtown Los Angeles when two INS agents walked up and asked him in Spanish if he had "immigration papers." Paz replied in English that he was a United States citizen and had his identification at home. The agents, he said, "responded by saying that if I did not have papers I was going to be arrested, and they proceeded to handcuff me. One of the agents called me a 'wetback.' I told him I was not, that he could just take me home and I would show him my identification, but he said that if he went to my house he would only end up arresting my family."

"INS harassment is a way of life for all Latinos, whether they are U.S. citizens, permanent resident aliens, or illegals," says Marc Van Der Hout, a San Francisco immigration lawyer. "We can't keep up with all the cases of INS harassment, false arrest, and illegal deportation." With the assistance of Peter Schey, a lawyer from the National Center for Immigrants' Rights, Virginia Zepeda sued the INS; and in November 1979 a federal judge in Los Angeles ordered an end to the warrantless neighborhood raids. The judge also ordered INS agents to refrain from stopping and questioning individuals like Joe Paz in public places unless they could demonstrate a "reasonable suspicion" that the person was in the country illegally. The person's appearance, the judge said, or the fact that he was speaking Spanish did not constitute a reasonable suspicion.

About the same time Attorney General Benjamin Civiletti, Griffin Bell's successor, issued an administrative order halting all area control raids "except in unusual circumstances." Civiletti was moved to act in part by the strong cries of protest from Hispanic rights groups and in part because it was thought that the raids would interfere with the counting of illegal aliens by the impending 1980 census. Whatever the reason, most Hispanics, perhaps savoring the prospect of an uninterrupted night's sleep, applauded Civiletti's action. For Leonel Castillo, who by then had left the INS, Civiletti's order meant that "the year of amnesty for aliens" had finally dawned. "The country has come to an accommodation with illegal aliens," Castillo declared. "It is willing to let the door be partway open. We need each other too much." But Castillo was too optimistic. Five days before leaving office, Civiletti lifted the suspension on warrantless workplace raids—though not on private homes—and under the Reagan administration the raids have been stepped up.

Those aliens who have to fear only INS raids, unethical immigration lawyers, gouging landlords, dishonest merchants, unscrupulous employers, *notarios publicos*, overzealous police officers, robbers, and murderers are the lucky ones. Negotiating such hazards is the price they pay for being in America, and they accept their lot with a certain fatalism. "Nothing happens before its time" is what they say. But for uncounted thousands of others who flee the crushing poverty of their homelands only to fall victim to this country's flourishing modern-day slave trade in illegal alien workers, the dream of *la vida americana* has an abrupt and cruel end.

On farms and ranches across the country, in the homes of the wealthy and middle class, the supremely luckless ones find themselves held in virtual bondage by employers who take advantage of the powerlessness their illegal status confers to force them to perform backbreaking labor for little money or none at all. The process of enslavement begins with the smugglers, who buy and sell the aliens for hundreds of dollars apiece on underground labor exchanges, then truck them to every corner of the country for delivery to farmers and other employers who shackle them with inflated debts they can never hope to repay, lock them up at night, threaten them with beatings or even death if they try to escape, perhaps even hold their children hostage to ensure their continued servitude.

Alien slavery is relatively uncommon in the American Southwest. Because of their proximity to the Mexican border, California, Arizona, and Texas are flooded with a surfeit of illegal alien workers, many more than are needed to fill available jobs. Rather, it is in the citrus and winter vegetable belts of Florida, the potato fields of Idaho, the apple orchards of Virginia, the tomato fields of Arkansas, and the tobacco farms of North Carolina that farmworkers are at a premium, and for those who venture far from the border, it is all too easy to fall into the abyss. Smugglers' fees to such distant points are substantial, and if the alien cannot pay for his passage out of his pocket, as many cannot, the smuggler will often bring him across the border "on consignment," then hold him captive until an employer is found who will pay the "transportation fee." Scarcely a month goes by that the INS does not come across a group of aliens being held prisoner in a ramshackle drop house somewhere, like the twenty-eight it found last year locked up in a house in Houston without mattresses, sanitary facilities, or food. How such things happen is not difficult to understand if one considers that from the moment the aliens cross the border they are under the nearly total control of the smuggler, penniless, far from home, marked by their appearance as immigrants, and with little choice but to work at whatever job is offered in order to survive, even if it pays them only room and board. A case in point is that of Durward Woosley, who pleaded guilty to alien-smuggling charges in San Antonio in 1978. According to court records, between January and August of that year, Woosley bought and sold more than 5,000 alien workers, paying recruiters $30 a head to bring them north from the Mexican border, then shipping them out to growers for up to $500 apiece. "Farmers in Arkansas were buying an alien from Woosley for four hundred dollars and withholding the guy's wages until the four hundred dollars was paid off," said Hugh Williams, the Border Patrol chief in Del Rio, Texas. "Then they would sell the alien to somebody else for four hundred dollars. The alien never saw any cash, and in effect each farmer was getting free labor. There were cases where we found Mexicans who were at their third or fourth farm and hadn't made a penny the whole time they were in the U.S."

"There's a significant amount of that going on," says Bert Moreno, the INS antismuggling chief, mentioning the recent case of a Colorado rancher who held a Mexican child hostage to ensure that his mother would return to her $40-a-week job tending his cows and pigs. "If I went on TV in Chicago and asked, 'How many of you have your children being held by someone? How many of you have to pay kickbacks to your smuggler?' the phones would never stop ringing. But articulating the facts to a United States attorney is another matter." The great majority of the victims are Hispanics, but they are not the only ones. In 1976 a Pakistani man, Syed Shah, a professor at Miami-Dade Community College, and his wife, Ishrat, a physician, were charged by a federal grand jury with bringing a ten-year-old girl from Sierra Leone into the United States illegally and forcing her into involuntary servitude in their home. The couple are still fugitives from justice.

A principal route on the alien-smuggling railway, investigators say, runs between the Arizona border and Florida. With the promise of $500 a week or more picking oranges or tomatoes, workers are easily lured there by coyotes who can sell them to citrus and winter vegetable growers for between $300 and $500 apiece. But it is only after the worker has arrived that he learns he is not free to leave until he has repaid that sum from his wages, and as he works, the debt grows larger still—charges are tacked on for room, board, clothing, cigarettes, and alcohol, all sold to him by the grower at inflated prices. The worker is given perhaps $5 a week for pocket money, with the rest of his earnings credited against what he owes. If he is lucky, when the harvest ends, he is set free with a few dollars to show for weeks of work. If he is not so lucky, he is "sold" by the farmer to another farmer, and the process begins again.

Under federal law, involuntary servitude exists wherever a worker is compelled by any means to work at a job he or she does not want. If a person is forced to work in order to pay off a debt, the crime becomes peonage. The size of the debt does not matter, and it makes no difference whether the peon initially agrees to take the job or whether he is paid for his work. According to recent court decisions, the law also takes no account of the means of compulsion; physically restraining a worker, harming him, and merely threatening harm are all sufficient grounds for involuntary servitude. So is withholding his pay or holding his relatives hostage. Even if a worker fails to take advantage of an opportunity to run away, servitude may still exist.

The Justice Department recorded its first peonage conviction involving illegal aliens from Mexico in November 1979, when Connie Ray Alford, a forty-one-year-old Truxno, Louisiana, chicken farmer, pleaded guilty to having kept four Mexican farmworkers chained in a chicken coop at his Welcome Home Ranch. According to court records, the workers had been brought to Alford's ranch by Francisco Cortez, an alien smuggler who picked them up in Kerrville, Texas. Alford paid Cortez $250 for each of the four workers, then forced them to work off the debt at the rate of $10 a week. The workers later testified that Alford held them captive for four months, menaced them with guns, and made them work twelve hours a day, seven days a week. Following the peonage convictions of Alford, his foreman, and another farmworker, federal agents in Louisiana were flooded with unsolicited tips about other aliens being held under similar circumstances, but because of the Mariel crisis, the INS did not have enough investigators to pursue them. Marty Stroud, the government lawyer in Shreveport who prosecuted Alford, said that while the case had "revolted" him, he understood the economics behind such situations. In Louisiana, Stroud asked, "Where else do you get farm labor" except from an alien smuggler? You take thirty workers at two hundred fifty dollars a head, that's an expensive proposition. The farmer's got to hold onto them to get his money back. What's he going to do if they start to run off—sue them?"

One man who shares that view is Benjamin Harrison Nelson, the forty-two-year-old owner of an oyster-processing plant at Smith Point, Texas, on Galveston Bay. His plant, Nelson said, was capable of processing 200,000 oysters a day, "but only if I got the help." Unfortunately, he said, it was becoming increasingly difficult to find workers willing to perform the difficult and tedious task of opening oysters. He had had seven families of Vietnamese working for him, Nelson said, "but when they got to the point where they had made enough money that they could go out and better their way of life, they went on. That's the American way, and I'm happy for them. But right now I could probably use twenty-five openers, and I got four." When the Vietnamese left, Nelson said, he "went all through Louisiana" looking for oyster openers, but to no avail, so when an alien smuggler came around one day and asked him whether he needed any help, he said he did.

Nelson paid the smuggler's $100 transportation fee for each of the fourteen Mexicans and Salvadorans delivered to him, and he had no complaints about their work. "These boys that come in here have got to work and want to work, if people would give them the right to work," he said. "If they took all the illegal aliens out of the United States right now, I believe our economy would go bankrupt." As Nelson saw it, he was simply lending each of the workers the $100 for their passage, and he expected the workers to repay him. "If I was to borrow $100 from you," he said, "you'd want your money back too. Wouldn't this be the legitimate and honest way of conducting business?" The only problem was that Nelson refused to let the workers leave until they had worked off their debts—at one point, according to court testimony, having forced two of the Mexicans to return to work at the point of a gun. In February 1981 Ben Nelson was found guilty of peonage.

The Nelson case was broken only because one of the Mexicans held captive, Francisco Avila, alerted his brother, Ramiro, the chauffeur for the Mexican consul in Brownsville. But because many illegal aliens are equally frightened of the authorities and the smugglers to whom they are chattel, most instances of slavery go largely unreported. "Usually the people are just so intimidated they don't do anything about it," says Vince Beckman, a lawyer with Michigan Migrant Legal Services. One of the few who did do something is José Corona, a young Mexican who worked until 1979 for a major citrus grower in La Belle, Florida. With the help of the Florida Rural Legal Assistance, Corona sued the man; in a sworn affidavit he declared that he received no wages at all for the first month he worked in the orange groves, all of his "salary" going for food and to repay the $200 transportation fee the grower paid the smuggler who had brought him to Florida. While he was there, Corona said, the grower and his sons "constantly warned and threatened me and the other members of the crew not to try to leave the camp. They threatened us with death or the possibility of being sent back to Mexico." On several occasions, he said, their captors "pointed guns at members of the crew, warning them not to try to escape," and one "beat up a crew member when it was learned that he was thinking of leaving." Corona was finally able to escape from the work camp just before Christmas 1978.

A similar experience was that of Mexican workers recruited the same year to pick tomatoes at a Florida labor camp operated by a farmer who, federal investigators say, was smuggling between 3,000 and 4,000 Mexicans a year across the border into Arizona, then shipping them in rented trucks to Florida. Seven of the workers subsequently filed a lawsuit against the grower, charging that it was not until they arrived in Florida that they learned they would have to work off the price of their transportation from Arizona—$450, more than the first-class air fare from Phoenix to Miami—and that, as one of them said, "until we paid the $450 we could not get out."

Fifty-five-year-old Maximiliano Aguilar was picking lemons in Arizona when a stranger approached him and offered better work in Florida. "Show me some work and take me there," Aguilar told the man. Only after he arrived at the camp, he said, did he learn "that we couldn't put a foot out of the place." Another of the workers, Esteban Guerrero, said he went to Florida "because I wanted to earn some pennies to send to my house" in Mexico. But when he arrived, he discovered that all his earnings except for $5 a week would go for food and to repay his $450 debt. Carmen Zuñiga said he was told before agreeing to come that "the least one would earn here was $70 a day." For his first six-day week Zuñiga was paid only $20, but that was more than Santos Martínez got—all his wages, he said, went "to the payment of the man who brought us to Florida."

When the workers complained, said Felipe Flores, the grower told them "that he was not interested in rules or laws, that what he said would go, that nobody could leave the field until they had paid everything they owed." A foreman there, Flores said, told him "that if he saw somebody try to take us out of the camp, he would kill that person." All the workers said they were forced to work very hard. "They treated us like dogs," said Remijo Saldana, who got $20 for four weeks' work. "They did not want us to rest while we were working," agreed Pedro de Santiago. "We had to work continuously or they would become upset. There was no rest there. One worked every day." Like the others, Arnulfo Ramírez had hoped to send money to his wife, Guadalupe, and their four children back in Mexico, but he could not manage that on only $5 a week. "It hurt me," he said. "I was eating, but I didn't know if my family could eat." Asked about the workers' allegations, an attorney for the grower dismissed them as the complaints of "ignorant Mexicans."

In November 1980 the grower was charged by the Justice Department with having operated what INS investigators described as one of the largest alien-smuggling rings ever uncovered in this country. Michael Hawkins, the U. S. attorney in Arizona who prosecuted the case, said it was characterized by "treatment of undocumented workers as bad as I have ever seen" in this country. In June 1981 a federal jury in Phoenix found the grower not guilty on two counts of transporting illegal aliens and was unable to reach any verdict on the other six counts. But Federico Villalón and Rafael Pedro González, two of the grower's drivers, were convicted. The Justice Department says it will try the grower again.

As the organized smuggling of illegal aliens increases, so does the possibility that an alien will find himself sold into slavery by his smuggler. As a result, the Justice Department's Civil Rights Division has now assigned a full-time lawyer, known as the peonage coordinator, to handle involuntary servitude cases, and the INS has begun instructing its antismuggling agents in the intricacies of the Reconstruction era slavery laws. But despite convincing evidence that foreign workers in this country are increasingly falling victim to slave traffickers who deal in brown bodies instead of black ones, federal prosecutors have had considerable difficulty in bringing to justice the smugglers, farmers, and other employers who are behind the trade.

The principal difficulty, one Justice Department lawyer says, "is in finding people who are willing to come forward. Most times the victims are very afraid." Such fears, prosecutors say, stem not only from the fact that the victims are usually in this country illegally but that many of them plan to return home, often to the same villages as the smugglers who hold them in thrall. Max Wolf, an official of the International Ladies Garment Workers Union in Los Angeles, tells of a young Mexican girl of perhaps fifteen who "was literally shoved into my office in a hammerlock by her father." The girl, Wolf said, had been working for four months for a garment contractor there without pay, and when she asked for her money, the employer told her, "I haven't paid off the coyote yet." Wolf said he "begged her to file a complaint. Her father screamed at her to file a complaint. She refused. She said she was in fear for her life, that she'd rather die."

Another problem, investigators say, is the reluctance of many Mexican men to admit that they have been held against their will. One investigator mentioned a case in which five Mexican workers found wandering the streets of Bossier City, Louisiana, told INS agents that they had escaped from a chicken farmer near Lufkin, Texas, who had kept them locked in his house at night and forced them to work at gunpoint during the day. But the men refused to testify against the farmer. "It was that macho image thing," the investigator said. In other instances, growers suspected of violating the peonage laws have taken advantage of their political connections to escape the consequences. Another INS agent told of developing evidence against a prominent Virginia apple grower, an important figure in that state's Democratic party and a deacon in his church, only to see the indictment dismissed by a local judge without explanation. Several Border Patrol agents mentioned a South Texas grower whom one described as "a big operator and a pretty rough customer" who was "shooting at aliens, holding their money, anything he could to keep them from running off.

We tried every way we could think of to get at him under the peonage statutes, but he was just too well connected."

The majority of aliens who unwittingly tumble into peonage are farmworkers, but they are by no means the only ones. Olivia Pérez had never set foot on a farm in her life, but she was enslaved as surely as any of the aliens who worked for Connie Alford or Ben Nelson. "They held her in the house," Hugh Williams said. "She worked from sunup to way after dark. She requested that her wages be sent to her father in Mexico, but no money was ever sent. This went on for about a year and a half; then she flipped—she became insane, broke out of the house, and ran down the street. That's when the Border Patrol got her." Williams, the longtime Border Patrol chief in Del Rio, Texas, was recalling the case of a twenty-two-year-old Mexican woman who came to the United States a few years ago to work as a live-in servant for a wealthy and prominent Nevada family, the owners of a large department store. But like too many young women who have made the same hope-filled journey, Olivia Pérez found for herself not a better life but a gilded prison controlled by her benefactors. "We tried to make a peonage case" against the family, Williams said. "The United States attorney told us we had a great case, but our only witness was insane."

Not very many years ago servants were a luxury only the well-to-do could afford. But the tremendous influx of illegal alien women—not just Mexicans but Central and South Americans, Asians, and Caribbean islanders—willing, even eager, to work as maids, cooks, and nannies—has created such a buyer's market that domestic workers are now a fixture of many middle-class households as well. In the American Southwest a live-in maid can be had for $40 a week plus room and board, and the growing availability of such jobs has itself proved a spur to illegal immigration. "If every housewife in Los Angeles didn't think she had a God-given right to a Mexican maid, we wouldn't have an illegal immigration problem," says an INS agent there. But federal investigators and prosecutors, migrant legal aid lawyers, and others say that all too often such young women end up as virtual captives of their employers, forced to work long hours as household drudges for little or no money and, sometimes, to endure sexual assaults by the male members of their households.

As with the male farmworkers, many of the young women who are abused are reluctant to report their employers, either out of shame or for fear of reprisals. Margo Cowan, a Tucson social worker, told of two young girls, fifteen-year-old Rosa and her sister Catalina, sixteen, who were smuggled to that Arizona city from Mexico to tend the household of an aerospace executive. At first, Cowan said, the girls were delighted with their situation—cooking, cleaning, and minding the family's two small children, not seeming to care that they were allowed outside the house only to attend church. To their family back in Mexico, their combined salary of $100 a month was a small fortune. Then, late one night, Rosa was raped by her employer. When she discovered she was pregnant, the man told her that he would pay for the delivery of her baby but that she and her sister could no longer leave the house at all. Moreover, he said, Rosa must put the baby up for adoption, and both she and Catalina would have to begin working for free to repay her medical expenses. Following the birth of the baby the girls got word to Margo Cowan, who went to the house and took them away. But they have rejected her pleas to file criminal charges against their employer. "They're in fear for their lives," Cowan said.

Two Mexican girls who did eventually complain about their treatment are Beatriz and Benita Orozco, ages twelve and fifteen, who were held prisoner by a Florida labor contractor known as "El Toro," who hired them out as field workers to neighboring farmers. The man, who smuggled them from their home in Tampisco, had promised their father that he would find the girls work and send their salaries to him. But in an affidavit Benita said her paychecks had been made out to El Toro's wife, who always cashed them. The money, she said, "was supposedly sent to my father," and during the girls' first year in Florida some money was sent home to Tampisco. But according to Juanita Sanchez, a legal services lawyer in Homestead, Florida, the next year the money stopped. The sisters told the INS that they had been given only $10 a week by El Toro—Benita for picking oranges, and Beatriz for doing housework and baby-sitting. El Toro, Benita said, refused to return her and Beatriz to their father as he had promised, hiring the two girls out to other growers instead. Benita was "rarely permitted" to see her younger sister, Beatriz, and never allowed to go outside alone.

Eventually the girls' father, concerned that he had not heard from his daughters for several months, asked their eldest sister, Maria, to try to locate the two. Maria contacted another legal services lawyer, Stuart Soff, who, accompanied by an FBI agent, drove to El Toro's house and knocked on the door. When there was no answer, the two men let themselves in. The man and his wife were nowhere to be found, but Benita and Beatriz were there, hiding in the bathroom and crying.

The enslavement of domestic workers appears to take place mostly on an individual basis. But just as some smugglers like Durward Woosley are now selling large numbers of farmworkers into slavery, there is some evidence that other organizations are importing domestic workers in quantity. One day early in 1981 the telephone rang on the desk of Ambrose Laverty, an INS antismuggling agent in Los Angeles. Laverty picked it up and, to his surprise, found himself listening to a well-to-do Los Angeles businessman complaining that his servant, an illegal alien from Indonesia, had "run away." The man wanted the INS to find the alien and bring him back, but Laverty had a couple of questions. Run away from what? he wanted to know.

Laverty began checking around. In the weeks that followed, the INS uncovered what it later described as the biggest organization of its kind ever to come to light: a smuggling ring that specialized in delivering maids, cooks, and gardeners from Indonesia to wealthy householders—not just in Los Angeles but also in Miami and New York. As Laverty and his fellow investigators pieced the details together, for more than two years the ring, headed by a Jakarta hotel owner, had been flying scores of Indonesians to Los Angeles on tourist visas, then selling them into domestic service for as much as $3,000 apiece. The workers had been recruited in Jakarta to fill orders from employers taken by the ring's Los Angeles operative. To induce them to make the trip, some of the workers were reportedly told that "high-paying jobs" had been arranged for them in Los Angeles. Others, who had worked for the hotelier in Jakarta, thought they were being given free vacations in the United States as a reward for faithful service. When they arrived in California, however, they discovered that they had been sold under two-year forced labor contracts that required them to work seven days a week for salaries of $100 a month.

Their return airline tickets and passports were confiscated; this to most of them meant that they had been enslaved as surely as if they had been shackled in chains. "In Indonesia," a Justice Department lawyer said, "if you're caught on the street without your papers, they put you in jail. They figured things were the same here." When some of the Indonesians suggested to their employers that these arrangements were not what they had had in mind, they were threatened—some with being turned in to the INS, others with beatings—to keep them from running away. Some who did try to escape were brought back at gunpoint.

One woman, a well-to-do Malibu resident, who had employed two of the Indonesians, failed to see what all the fuss was about. "All my neighbors have illegal aliens working for them," she said.

CHAPTER NINE

"We Could Go on Arresting Busboys Forever"

It was just after dawn on Monday, April 26, 1982. In New York, in Los Angeles, in Houston, in a half dozen other big cities around the country, 400 INS investigators and Border Patrol agents were preparing to set off through the still-sleepy streets in search of illegal aliens. Nothing unusual about that, except that this day the agents were going in search not of just any illegal aliens but of those the INS believed were working at jobs that paid good money, jobs that some among the 7.5 million unemployed Americans might be grateful to have.

The INS said that the week-long million-dollar operation, which somebody there had named Project Jobs, had been conceived after officials in Washington began raising questions about the value of the service's traditional area control operations, in which agents swept through a neighborhood or an industrial area, arresting anyone they came across who could not immediately establish that he or she was a citizen or a resident alien. Restaurants were a favorite target of such raids—the eating establishment, most agents were convinced, that did not employ at least a few, and sometimes many, undocumented workers to bus its tables, wash its dishes or cook its meals did not exist. Hotels were another rich lode of illegal workers, as were construction sites. The INS had never had trouble finding illegal aliens at work—in some years, it had apprehended

180,000 of them—but now it was wondering whether hunting down such lowly workers was the best use of its manpower.

"We could go on arresting three-dollar-an-hour busboys forever," one official said a few days before Project Jobs was scheduled to get under way. "But we know that those jobs are just going to be filled by other illegal aliens. What we're looking for now are aliens working in the higher-paying jobs." Said another: "We realize that if we arrest five hundred strawberry pickers, there simply won't be anyone to take their place."

It might have been a coincidence, but from the Reagan administration's standpoint the timing of Project Jobs could not have been better. That same Monday morning debate was scheduled to begin in the Senate on the administration-backed Immigration Reform and Control Act of 1982, also known as the Simpson-Mazzoli bill after two of its primary sponsors, Senator Alan Simpson of Wyoming and Representative Romano Mazzoli of Kentucky. The reform package, a controversial document from the moment it was introduced, contained one provision that had generated more emotion than the rest: a law that would for the first time make it a federal offense knowingly to employ an illegal alien. The proposal was not at all popular with corporations and businesses, many of which see illegal aliens as a needed source of cheap labor, or with those members of Congress sympathetic to business and its interests. But the INS, weary of arresting the same illegal workers again and again without being able to touch those who employed them, had wanted such a law for years. Hispanic rights groups like the Mexican-American Legal Defense Fund (MALDEF) worried that the raids might lead unemployed Americans to blame their plight on anybody with brown skin, and MALDEF also suggested that the INS might be using Project Jobs to press its case for an "employer sanctions" law by showing Congress that not all illegal aliens in this country were working for peanuts. Whatever the agency's motives, Project Jobs promised to be a test of the question that lay at the bottom of the increasingly acrimonious debate over immigration policy: Were illegal aliens, as the INS and groups like FAIR insisted, really making good salaries working at jobs Americans coveted? Or, as a growing number of economists and other researchers believed, were they benefiting the country by mainly doing jobs that Americans, for whatever reason, disdained? Most of the polls on the issue had shown that economic considerations more than cultural or linguistic differences had fueled America's growing concern about illegal immigration. The common fear seemed to be that the aliens were somehow draining the nation of its resources—as if, many Americans seemed to think, a stranger had walked into their house uninvited, cooked himself a nice dinner, and then retired to the bedroom for a nap.

Although word of the big raid had leaked out a few days in advance, many of those aliens who had heard the news either were not concerned enough to stay away from their jobs or needed the money badly enough to take a chance that their employer was not one of the 250 or so on the INS's hit list. As workers in the nine target cities began showing up for work on Monday morning, they were met by stern-faced immigration officers demanding, "¿*Tiene papeles?* ("Do you have papers?")" Many did not. In New York City and Newark, New Jersey, raids at eight businesses netted 175 illegal workers before noon, 22 of them at the G & T Fruit Company in the Bronx, where, according to Anthony Spinale, the owner, a dozen agents leaped from their cars and ran inside the firm's warehouse "like Jesse James, covering this door, covering that door," to prevent the escape of a work crew unloading a boxcar filled with potatoes. At Plated Plastic Industries in Brooklyn the INS got another 23 suspected illegals. In Houston, agents arrested 135 aliens at a tree-trimming firm called Trees, Inc., and picked up a few dozen more at several construction sites. The Melody Manufacturing Company in Fort Worth, a maker of mobile homes, lost 170 workers, nearly half its work force. The Caroline Shoe Company in Los Angeles lost 70, and the B. P. John Furniture Company nearby lost 50. Near Detroit 24 workers were taken from a Utica Packing Company plant, and 18 were arrested at a poultry company north of San Francisco. The raids, as dramatic as the INS could make them, attracted considerable public attention. Squads of agents with drawn guns were perfect fodder for local television newscasts, and as the week progressed, the three networks also made the story a regular feature of their evening news programs. Though newspapers in most of the target cities turned the daily tally of aliens arrested into front-page headlines, few of the stories pointed out that similar area control operations were conducted in the same cities every day or that the number of aliens arrested during Project Jobs was about the same as usual in those operations. Nor did the INS, which began the week basking in the unaccustomed glow of public approval for finally "doing something about the alien problem," take pains to point these things out.

Perhaps because of the concerns within the Mexican-American community that the raids threatened to generate a new wave of anti-Hispanic xenophobia, the INS did point out that three-quarters of the arrested aliens opted for voluntary departure, the implication being that the great majority of them had been caught without even an arguable case for remaining in the United States. In fact, the percentage of voluntary returnees was much lower than the usual 90 or 95 percent; that meant the INS was arresting more people than usual who thought they had a right to be here, not fewer. Newspapers in Mexico City compared the raids to "Gestapo actions during the times of Nazi Germany," and by Wednesday some of the complaints from Hispanic groups were beginning to filter into news accounts in this country—that families were being separated by the raids, husbands taken from their wives, children from their parents. Many of the arrested aliens, the group charged, were not even being advised by the INS agents of their right to a deportation hearing or a lawyer but were being summarily herded aboard buses bound for Mexico. "In the heat of the operation, people are not being asked gently about their citizenship," said José Medina, an attorney with La Raza Legal Alliance. "The raids themselves have been conducted without regard to property, constitutional and civil rights of citizens, permanent residents and undocumented workers alike." Some of those arrested swore out affidavits declaring that INS officers had told them that a lawyer would cost them $4,000 and that their fingers would be broken if they refused to provide their fingerprints.

The news media were also picking up scattered reports that legal resident aliens and even American citizens were being swept up in the raids. In Detroit, to the INS's acute embarrassment, none of the twenty-four workers arrested at the Utica Packing Company turned out to be illegal aliens, and one twelve-year-old boy arrested outside a Denver grocery store proved to be a U.S. citizen. In Los Angeles, Federal Judge William M. Byrne signed an order halting the return to Mexico of scores of aliens who the INS said had waived their right to a hearing and (the agency had not changed all that much since the Clean Sweep days) were already aboard a bus heading for the border. "To say the INS is really interested in the rights of these people is absurd," Byrne said. As the weeklong operation ended, the INS was calling it a success. But nearly all the evidence was to the contrary. A few highly paid aliens had been found—one worker for the Burlington Northern Railroad in Chicago was making $10 an hour, and a construction hand in Denver had been earning $400 a week; but they were the exceptions. The average salary of the 5,440 employed aliens arrested during Project Jobs was barely $190 a week, or less than $10,000 a year—a poverty-level income for an average urban family. The 356 alien workers arrested in New York—three-quarters of them from countries other than Mexico—earned an average of $174 a week in a city where, according to the Bureau of Labor Statistics, it took $251 a week to provide the most basic requirements for a family of four. The INS reported that some aliens arrested in Chicago had been earning "up to $9.00 an hour," as was true, but the average income of all those arrested there was less than half the city's average hourly manufacturing wage of $8.18. In fact, despite the preliminary fanfare by the INS about removing illegal aliens from high-paying jobs, the majority of the workers arrested appeared not to have been earning more than the minimum wage of $3.35 an hour and to have been working at essentially menial jobs.

The INS had said the real test would be whether the jobs vacated by the mass arrests were filled by American citizens. By that standard, the raids were a nearly total failure. "Very few of our applicants have expressed any interest in the jobs of the aliens that were arrested," admitted Joanne Palmieri of the New York State Department of Labor, and employment-office workers in other states were saying the same thing. The Texas Employment Commission found only forty-two unemployed citizens who wanted to apply for the 1,105 jobs in that state that had been opened up by the raids, and only 3 of the jobs were filled. One problem, an official there said, was that the wages being offered by raided employers were frequently $1 or $1.50

an hour less than the INS had said the arrested aliens were being paid. Nor did the employers find many citizens knocking at their doors. "I can't recall one American coming in here and asking me for a job," Tony Spinale of G & T Fruit, who had been paying his workers the minimum wage of $3.35 an hour, told *The New York Times*. "If they're trying to open up high-paying jobs to citizens," Spinale said, "this raid is a joke. Who else would do this work? You won't find any unemployed citizens standing in line for this kind of work."

"American citizens don't want to work for the minimum wage," said Nick Amish of Plated Plastic Industries in agreement. "There's no sense kidding ourselves—they simply can't get by on three dollars and thirty-five cents an hour. Aliens are the only people who will work for the minimum wage. It was true thirty or forty years ago for Italians and Greeks, and it's true today for Hispanics."

As if to confirm what Spinale and Amish were saying, a week after the raids 34 of the 45 aliens seized at G & T Fruit and PPI were back at their jobs. At a poultry processing plant in Petaluma, California, near San Francisco, 14 of the 18 citizens hired to replace the alien workers lost in the raids quit before the week was over, apparently deciding that not working at all was better than plucking chickens for a living. The arrest of 53 fish cleaners at a Northern California fishery brought a flock of job seekers to the factory's gates, but plant officials said they all had wanted jobs driving trucks, not cleaning fish. At B. P. John, several dozen citizens inquired about the fifty jobs left open by the raids, but only 20 of them actually went to work. The rest, the personnel manager said, had walked away after learning that the jobs paid minimum wage. He predicted that the 20 who stayed would quit "as soon as they find out how hard the work is." Rudy Reyes, a vice-president of Houston's Trees, Inc., said that as word of the raid on his business began to circulate, hundreds of unemployed Houstonians had picked up their telephones to inquire about work. But Reyes said that when the callers learned they would be making $4 an hour trimming and topping loblolly pines in the broiling Texas sun, "they told us to go to hell." Reyes added, "I could get workers, but I'd have to pay them a hundred dollars a day and tell them to sit on their cans and not do anything. I sure can't get Americans to trim

244

trees for four dollars an hour. If I could find them, I'd hire them. The problem is I can't, and nobody else can either." Paul Boyd, president of East-West Pipe Threaders, Inc., another Houston firm raided by the INS, said he had hired "one complete crew" of workers to replace the crew of aliens he lost and that the new crew lasted one day. "The next day they said, 'This is for the birds,' and walked off," Boyd said. In the end, Boyd was able to fill only sixteen of the seventy-one jobs vacated by the raid, and the situation was much the same everywhere in boomtown Houston, the self-proclaimed "golden buckle on the Sunbelt" to which out-of-work northerners were flocking by the thousands every week. The Midwest Steel Company, which had lost 114 workers to the INS, hired only 25 replacements; 68 of the 92 hired by another steel plant quit; the Vemar Corporation was unable to fill any of the thirty-eight jobs the INS had "made available to unemployed Americans."

As the weeklong Project Jobs came to an end, it became clear that if the INS was really looking for highly paid illegal aliens, it had been looking in all the wrong places. Raiding steel mills, light factories, shoemakers, fisheries, canners, poultry farms, and the like was bound to turn up relatively low-paid illegal Mexican workers. But despite the INS's insistence, the jobs such workers did were really not ones Americans wanted. The illegal aliens who were making good money were mainly well educated and spoke good English. They were working in office buildings and fancy shops and banks and brokerage houses and aerospace firms. They were not Hispanics but Asians, Europeans, or Middle Easterners. (The 5,440 aliens arrested during Project Jobs included 68 Poles and a worker each from Canada, Great Britain, and South Africa; none from Germany, France, Israel, Russia, Italy, Holland, Switzerland, Sweden, or Norway.) Most important, the well-paid illegals had come here not by crossing the border illegally but by using phony documents to get into the country or by overstaying legitimate visas. Had the INS illuminated this fact by arresting them in sizable numbers, however, there might have been questions about why it had deployed so much of its manpower and resources along the border to arrest unskilled Hispanic workers and so little at the airports, where the non-Hispanic aliens came into the country, or in the cities and towns where they lived and worked. The answer, of course, was that the concept of border enforcement to which the INS was overcommitted predated the jet age, that the INS was still doing its job in much the same way it had a half century before. But rather than acknowledge that the world had changed and that the United States had become home to a new kind of highly mobile, relatively well-educated, relatively affluent illegal alien who did present a threat to the job security of many Americans, the INS found it easier to run around arresting Mexican tree trimmers and shoemakers who really did not. Nor, in the end, was it clear that Project Jobs had engendered the kind of public support for which the INS had undoubtedly hoped. Only 25 percent of those questioned in a San Francisco poll thought the raids would free jobs for American workers, and a worker at the General Aluminum Corporation plant near Dallas, one of the factories on the INS hit list, spoke for many when he said, "I could see it if people would get out and take the damn jobs, but they won't do it. That's America for you. At least these aliens will work."

For all its shortcomings, Project Jobs did underscore the fact that growing numbers of illegal aliens are bypassing their traditional work as farmhands for jobs in the service, construction, and manufacturing industries of the nation's big cities; and despite their failure to put many unemployed Americans back to work, the raids intensified the debate over whether the United States should concede its lower-paid, less attractive jobs to immigrants who are eager for them. The question is a recurring one. When the economy is flush, nobody is overly concerned about alien workers. But as has been true since the days of the great transatlantic migration a century ago, when times are bad, the country begins to wonder how much of its troubles are caused by the uninvited newcomers.

No one doubts that the illegal aliens who still work in agriculture represent an economic benefit. Farm work, for the most part, is difficult, dirty, and dangerous, involving exposure to hazardous machinery and toxic chemicals. It is also a supremely low-status job, one that nearly all Americans, except for the poorest of blacks and Chicanos, consider beneath their dignity. A majority of the nation's farmworkers are Hispanics (official estimates of their numbers range from 900,000 to 1.5 million, but nobody knows for certain. "We keep better track of our migratory birds in this country than our migratory workers," says a rural legal services lawyer).

America has more and cheaper food than any country in the world—Americans typically spend about 15 percent of their income for food, compared to 50 percent in some other countries—but those who grow it have insisted for years that without the illegals to help them plant and harvest, that would no longer be the case. "There just aren't enough domestics that want to do the work," says Art Martori, a Phoenix citrus grower who for several seasons now has had to rely on illegal Mexican workers to pick his lemons, even though he pays $8 an hour—"a darn good wage in Phoenix, bank tellers don't make that kind of money"—and claims to serve "the best food in town." In 1979, Martori says, the U.S. Department of Labor sent him 800 citizen job applicants, "but 95 percent of them didn't last a week." Such, in fact, is the dearth of local workers willing to spend their days lugging a heavy canvas sack up and down the stepladders needed to reach the tops of the lemon trees and their nights sleeping on the bare ground that several Arizona lemon growers have received federal permission to import Mexican workers legally.

Under the H-2 program, named for the category of visa given to such workers, employers like Art Martori may bring foreign laborers into the country on a contract basis if, as the Immigration and Nationality Act of 1952 specifies, "unemployed persons capable of performing such service or labor cannot be found in this country," a proviso that has been applied not only to field hands but to Russian ballet dancers and English rock singers—anyone whom the Labor Department certifies can do a job for which no domestic worker can be found.

There are about 30,000 H-2 workers from Mexico and the Caribbean in the United States at any one time, not just picking citrus fruit in Arizona but cutting sugarcane in Florida (a particularly unattractive job because of the razor-sharp machetes the cutters swing as they move through the cane fields), picking apples in Virginia and New York, and harvesting tobacco in North Carolina—all tasks that no Americans will do at any reasonable wage. But the number of H-2 workers is not a reliable guide to American agriculture's dependence on foreign labor since most farmers and ranchers, knowing that the INS lacks the resources to come after their workers, prefer simply to hire illegal aliens rather than to wrestle with Labor Department bureaucracy for an H-2 certification.

Most farmers who employ alien workers, whether under the H-2 program or illegally, insist that raising wages and improving working conditions to the point where field work is attractive to citizen workers will increase the price of their produce to the point where many of those same citizens can no longer afford it. "You're talking about a five-dollar head of lettuce," said Bill Bishop, a grower in Texas's Presidio Valley, where for as long as anyone can remember the members of the local growers' association have hired workers from Ojinaga, Mexico, just across the Rio Grande, to help them get their onions, melons, and green peppers to market. That system had always worked to the advantage of everybody: The growers got their crops in on time, the Mexicans made money, and no one paid any attention until, one day in 1977, the immigration service announced that the practice would be stopped. "Some political reason, I guess," Bill Bishop muttered, tipping his broad-brimmed hat and mopping his brow as he looked out over 1,200 acres of honeydew and casaba melons threatening to overripen under the broiling Texas sun.

Bishop was right. Shortly after assuming the presidency, Jimmy Carter had declared, without any real evidence, that the influx of illegal aliens had "displaced many American citizens from jobs and placed an increased burden on many state and local governments." For reasons known only to itself, the Carter administration had chosen Presidio as the place to begin implementing the President's promise to begin reducing the number of foreign workers in the United States, and like most of Jimmy Carter's other attempts to make immigration policy, this one was ill-conceived. The Presidio Valley growers advertised in newspapers across the state for 1,800 field hands at a guaranteed minimum wage of $2.20 an hour plus a piece-rate bonus, but without much success. "Three hundred was all we could finally get," Bishop said, but he was not surprised. Presidio, a tiny, dusty town of 2,000 souls, is a long way from anywhere, and the only distinction it can point to is that several times each summer it records the highest daytime temperature in the

United States. "You can understand why people don't want to come down here," Bishop said. "I wouldn't want to do it."

A chagrined Carter administration was forced, "in the national interest," to approve the importation of 809 Mexican workers from Ojinaga after Richard White, the local congressman, pleaded with President Carter that the crop was rotting on the ground. In the end, the only difference from other years was that instead of slipping into Presidio under cover of darkness, the Mexicans walked into Presidio across the orange international bridge with the blessings of the American government. The Labor Department opposed the move, insisting that the only reason no American workers had turned up was that Bill Bishop and the other growers lacked proper housing for them, and it argued that bringing in the Mexicans served only to bail out the growers. But to Bishop, who estimated that to construct such housing would cost him "two or three million dollars," such an expense seemed the height of foolishness. The workers from Ojinaga, after all, were within walking distance of their homes and could actually commute across the border to harvest the crops. Charlie Perez, the INS chief in El Paso, agreed. "If the farmers built housing to federal standards," he said, "the farmhands would have better housing than the farmers."

As for the men and women of Ojinaga, the work they did was merciless, stooping for hours in noontime temperatures of 100 degrees or more to sack onions or plodding up and down the melon fields, dragging canvas bags filled with ripe fruit. But they were earning an average of $16 a day, easily four times what they could have made on the other side of the border, and it was not enough to say that they were willing to endure the hardships—for the Ojinagans the work and the money were a godsend. "We went over to Ojinaga to talk to a group of the workers," one Labor Department investigator said later, "just to ask them about their wages and a few other things. When we asked if they were getting the minimum wage, a bunch of the workers started screaming at us. 'We don't care about the minimum wage,' they said. 'We just want the work.' "

Agriculture is the most important American industry being kept afloat by illegal workers, but it is not the only one: Another is the equally labor-intensive garment industry. Sewing has been immigrants' work for nearly a century, ever since waves of newly arrived young Eastern European women found their way to the sweatshops of Manhattan's Lower East Side. Those who labor nowadays over the big single-needle sewing machines are still mostly women, but the majority of them are now illegal aliens. Of the 10,000 or so contract sewing factories in this country, about two-thirds are in New York City, a handful in Chicago and San Francisco, the rest in Los Angeles. In all they employ perhaps half a million workers, of whom 350,000 are thought to be illegal aliens—mostly Hispanics in Los Angeles and a combination of Hispanics and Chinese in New York. Because only half the New York workers, and only 1 in 5 in Los Angeles, are protected by the International Ladies Garment Workers Union, most of the garment workers are paid lower wages than their counterparts on the nation's farms and ranches.

The world of the garment worker is a shadowy one, and a rare inside glimpse was provided by Merle Wolin, a reporter for the Los Angeles *Herald-Examiner* who for several months in 1980 conducted an undercover investigation of what the Hispanics call La Costura. Posing as an illegal Brazilian immigrant with no husband and two children to feed, Wolin got jobs in several of the industry's sweatshops, and the working conditions she found there, she later wrote, were "worse than I ever imagined in this country." She also found employers who were quick to cheat those workers they presumed to be without rights or recourse to the law. No one, she said, cared that she seemed to be in the country illegally; when she pretended not to have a Social Security card, she was simply paid in cash. For her first nine-hour day, Wolin earned exactly $2.40. For nine days' work she was paid a total of $71.24 when, according to federal and California labor laws, she should have been paid $232.50. Many of her fellow workers, nearly all of them illegal aliens from Mexico ("Don't worry," one young man assured her, "nobody here has papers"), told her they earned $50 in an average week sewing skirts that might cost the manufacturer $10 apiece to make and retail for $120 at Saks Fifth Avenue. (About the same time federal agents conducting an investigation of the garment industry in New York City's Chinatown reported finding children as young as ten working twelve hours a day in rat- and roach-infested lofts for as little as $50 a week.)

The explanation from the garment manufacturers is uniformly the same: They cannot, they say, even hope to compete with the ready-to-wear industries in Taiwan, Hong Kong, and South Korea unless their labor costs can be kept to an absolute minimum, and for all but the finest *haute couture* shops that means using nonunion immigrant labor. The same competitive situation now exists in California's burgeoning electronics industry. In the so-called Silicon Valley south of San Francisco, microprocessors, the basic building blocks of everything from video games and home computers to pocket calculators and space age wristwatches, are increasingly being assembled by young Mexican women who are paid from $1 to $3 an hour to insert the tiny silicon chips into computer processor boards. (One San Francisco area maker of computer peripherals raided during Project Jobs was paying some illegal aliens up to $8 an hour.)

Like the garment manufacturers, the electronics companies say the alternative to using cheap illegal labor is either to close down their operations altogether or to move them to Third World countries with a supply of cheap labor, and many of the electronics firms have already moved to Mexico. Under that country's Maquiladora program, more than 600 U.S. companies, among them some of the biggest names in American industry, have closed their manufacturing and assembly plants in this country and reopened them in Mexican border cities like Tijuana and Juárez, where there is an oversupply of workers eager to work six days a week for $7 or $8 a day, not just assembling electronic components but producing everything from automobile taillights (for General Motors) to stuffed toys (Fisher-Price) to sunglasses (Foster Grant) to electric motors (General Electric) to tape cassettes (Ampex).

A third sector that has become the private preserve of the illegal alien is domestic labor, and even the INS, in tacit recognition that such workers are almost certainly not taking jobs from citizens, has made the apprehension of domestic workers its lowest priority, which is the same as saying that they are left alone. In the urban Northeast, domestic workers are both Hispanics and Caribbean islanders, principally Jamaicans and Haitians; in the West and Southwest they are mainly Mexicans. While illegal domestic workers are sometimes the victims of exploitative labor practices and even economic servitude, such conditions are by no means the rule; indeed, because these domestics are always in danger of being hired away by envious neighbors or friends, most employers make it a point to see that they are well treated.

For many of the young, single women who come north to work in the upper- and middle-class households of America, the experience can be a positive one. In most big cities the prevailing wage for a live-in maid is room, board, and $50 a week, more for those who will cook. Such young women are likely to be given a room that is larger than the one they shared with their brothers and sisters, a color television set, gifts of new clothes, and the use of the family car, all the while earning money to send back home. It is a chance to learn about America and Americans, to learn to drive and cook, to acquire sophistication. It is not, all in all, a bad way to spend a couple of years.

Were the undocumented labor force confined to those who pick our crops, sew our shirts and dresses, and clean our homes, the current debate over job displacement might never have arisen. The fact, however, is that in every year since 1972 arrests of aliens in the service, manufacturing, and construction industries have exceeded those of aliens on the farms, in the garment factories, and in household service. Of the 6,968 illegal aliens arrested on the job in August 1980—to take a month at random—only 2,970 were found during "farm and ranch checks." Of the others, 2,233 were working in light and heavy manufacturing, 1,212 in restaurants and hotels, and 553 at construction sites. Such figures are not a precise indicator of the shift in aliens' work habits because they reflect not only where aliens are working but also where the INS has chosen to look for aliens at work. Still, the pattern has been borne out consistently over the past decade as the number of aliens seized in the orchards and fields has continued to fall. In 1978 the percentage of aliens apprehended in the agricultural sector was 45.6; in 1980 it was 43.

The reasons for the shift are not hard to understand. Not only is farm work difficult and seasonal, but mechanization has steadily reduced the number of jobs available to field hands.

"We Could Go on Arresting Busboys Forever"

Washing dishes may not pay as well as picking Bill Bishop's melons, but it is both easier and steadier, and many of the factory jobs held by aliens pay better than picking crops. "Why work on a farm for two dollars or three dollars an hour," says Charlie Thompson, an INS antismuggling agent in Boise, "when you can take a job in a factory for five dollars or six dollars an hour?" Ted Giorgetti, the INS's chief investigator in Chicago, agrees. "Once the alien acquires a veneer of sophistication, once he learns his way around, once he learns the language, it's only human nature he'll seek a better job."

What jobs do the "sophisticated" illegals seek? One recent Los Angeles study found, to no one's surprise, that 86 percent of that city's dishwashers and busboys were illegal aliens, and the same is doubtless true in most other big cities. But the *indocumentados* are also our fast-food cooks, waiters, nursery and greenhouse workers, stable hands, parking lot attendants, janitors, trash collectors, cement finishers, street sweepers, construction site cleanup workers, roofers, bakers, shipyard workers, hod carriers, deliverymen, and security guards. They wash our windows, fix our cars, paint our houses, bag our groceries, drive our taxis, wash our hair, iron our shirts, empty our bedpans, polish our cars, clean our offices, and pump our gas. Look for a job that is physically demanding or dangerous, dirty, demeaning, or boring, offers little security or opportunity for advancement, and pays badly to boot, and the chances are excellent that it is being done by someone without permission to live and work in this country.

Illegal aliens also turn up in some unexpected places. In Maryland in 1981 INS agents arrested 2 state prison guards and 2 Prince Georges County social workers, all of them illegal aliens from Africa. In Fort Worth agents found illegal aliens working on the city's payroll at a bicentennial restoration site. In December 1981, 13 Mexican workers were arrested at the Palo Verde Nuclear Generating Station near Phoenix. In 1978 the Marine Corps found to its horror that it had signed up 243 illegal aliens from Panama, apparently with the help of recruiting sergeants concerned more with numbers than nationalities. They even work—yes, it's true—for the U.S. Immigration and Naturalization Service. In Tucson agents discovered that the night maintenance supervisor at the Border Patrol's big sector headquarters station there not only was an illegal alien but had been convicted of alien smuggling. "The man had the keys to the building," an embarrassed Border Patrolman admitted to the Tucson *Citizen.* "He had access to my office, to all our papers."

For the most part, however, the alien workers have become a mainstay of the nation's light industry. "If we were to pick up every illegal alien in this area," says Joe Howerton, the INS chief in Los Angeles, "we would close down not just 90 percent of the restaurants and car washes but many of the industries. There's not a business or industry of any type here that does not have undocumented workers. Years ago, we could walk into a factory and find maybe two or three illegal aliens. Now sixty or seventy percent of the workers in the place are illegal." A recent raid on a Los Angeles leather goods factory netted 487 illegal aliens out of 500 employees, but most of them were earning between $3 and $5 an hour. Not very many years ago $5 an hour was an enviable wage in this country but nowadays, Howerton asks, "who except illegal aliens can afford to live on those wages?"

As was inadvertently shown by Project Jobs, those illegal aliens who do work at jobs that pay good, and even excellent, salaries are usually the better-educated and relatively affluent visa overstayers, not the poorer and less-skilled Hispanic border crossers, who are the main target of the INS's enforcement efforts. In July 1980, to pick a month at random, the INS found an Iranian earning $19,000 a year as an electrical engineer for Pacific Gas & Electric in San Francisco, a Frenchwoman earning $470 a week as a musician with the San Francisco Symphony, a Hong Kong Chinese earning $13 an hour with a high-tech electronics company in La Jolla, California, and another Iranian earning $34,000 a year as a stockbroker in Los Angeles. But the agents assigned to Project Jobs did not raid the symphonies, the high-tech firms, and the brokerage houses, nor did they go after the tens of thousands of illegal aliens working as computer programmers, nurses, doctors, aerospace designers, laboratory technicians, and even journalists, many of whom came to this country as students, got their university degrees or dropped out of school, and then simply stayed on after their student visas expired. One reason might have been that, as several Hispanic rights groups charged in the wake of the raid, the Project Jobs agents were looking exclusively for Spanish-speaking workers, who tend to cluster at the bottom end of the pay scale. During the same month that the INS was arresting the engineer, the musician, and the stockbroker, for example, the list of Mexican nationals apprehended in Los Angeles included a mechanic ($205 a week), a cook ($116), a machinist ($280), a furniture factory supervisor ($300), a truck driver ($250), a painter ($280), a construction worker ($391), a fish cleaner ($280), a machine operator ($226), a butcher ($260), a custodian ($263), and a secretary with the Los Angeles County district attorney's office ($241). Some 350 Mexican nationals apprehended at businesses and factories in the suburbs south of Chicago were earning an average of $180 a week making plastic bottles, cheap alarm clocks, rubber stamps, and candy. Hispanic aliens arrested in New York City that month included a security guard at Roosevelt Hospital ($6.50 an hour), a doughnut maker ($5), an attendant at a Mobil gas station ($3.10), a dishwasher at the Hilltop Coach Diner ($3.10), and a gardener for a private home in Glen Cove, Long Island ($3).

Drawing firm conclusions from such data is risky since such samples are neither scientific nor statistically significant. (As Vernon Briggs, the Cornell University economist who has studied the displacement of American workers by illegal aliens puts it, "If good and reliable data exists about any major social problem, the problem must not really be important.") But the conclusion that suggests itself is that the illegal aliens who are taking better-paying jobs from Americans are more likely to be from Europe, the Middle East, or Asia than from Mexico or Latin America (87 percent of the aliens arrested during Project Jobs were from Mexico; 99 percent, from Latin America and the Caribbean). Some of Briggs's colleagues, among them Edwin Reubens of the City University of New York, go so far as to argue that the country is now faced with a "voluntary withdrawal" of American workers from jobs that offer low wages and difficult working conditions and that the resulting vacuum can be filled only by workers from Third World countries who are willing to endure a certain amount of personal privation, living a dozen to a room and sleeping in shifts on mattress-covered floors, in order to stretch the precious dollars they send home to relatives. ''There's a lot of things they have to undergo to live here,'' says one Chicago area employer, with more than a touch of admiration in his voice.

But there is also increasing evidence that foreign workers are actively sought after by employers not only because they will do unattractive jobs for less money but because they are among the most reliable and enthusiastic of employees. ''All the businessmen I talk to,'' said Leonel Castillo during his tenure as immigration commissioner, ''they say, 'Send us more,' not more whites, blacks, or even native-born Chicanos, but more immigrants.'' The personnel manager of one Chicago-area manufacturer says, ''They like to work. They work hard, and they show up on time. They work overtime, and they don't get into fights.'' An INS official agreed. ''The citizen will gripe about working conditions. The citizen will demand workmen's compensation, will demand retirement. The alien is tickled to death to go in there and work ten hours a day, and he knows if he doesn't show up, there's another alien standing in line to take his job. Many of the aliens are exceptional workers, and few of them complain about overtime hours, bad lighting, and nonunion shops.''

Charles Miller, the personnel manager at California's Strolee Corporation, a maker of children's car seats that lost seventy-five workers to the INS in a 1980 raid, adds that in his experience unskilled, labor-intensive jobs are simply not wanted by Americans. ''Chances are,'' Miller says, ''unless it's the guy's first job, you're getting somebody with a poor attitude. But if it's a Mexican worker, this is something beyond his wildest dreams.'' Other employers echo Miller's sentiments. ''The Mexican who is in the U.S.,'' says the owner of a Texas janitorial service company, ''has already shown by his presence that he has initiative and wants to work badly.'' The ironies of dragging such workers from their jobs and sending them out of the country are not entirely lost on some in the INS. ''You can't help think you're arresting the wrong people,'' one immigration agent told Robert Scheer of the *Los Angeles Times*. ''They're some of the best people you'll meet—hardworking, loyal to their families. Sometimes you think, why don't we arrest the bums that don't work and just steal? But these people have violated the immigration law and we have to arrest them." Like most employers, Miller says Strolee does not go out of its way to hire illegal aliens; it even asks each applicant whether he or she is living legally in the United States. "But once they say yes," he adds, "we're stuck," explaining that under the equal employment guidelines, to ask one worker for proof of legal status would require asking them all, "and anyway, eighty percent of the documents they have are forged."

"I'm sure some of the people working here are illegal," says Joe Moore, personnel director of Chicago's Weber-Stephen Products Company, which makes the popular Weber Kettle barbeque. "Everyone carries authorization cards, but if you ask INS, 'Is this person OK?' about fifty percent of these people turn out to be illegal." (The problem, INS officials say, is that counterfeiters often reproduce a valid green card issued to one person with the photograph of another; they also admit they have no way of guarding against the use of the same A [for alien registration] number for employment purposes by more than one person. On the other hand, as Joe Howerton says, "We don't get many calls," from employers who are eager to know whether their workers are illegal aliens.)

Ray Marshall, who was secretary of labor under Jimmy Carter, was quick to acknowledge that illegal aliens were hard workers. Before joining the Carter administration, Marshall had been a noted labor economist at the University of Texas, and he knew about the problem firsthand. "They make desirable employees," he said, "and normally have no difficulty in finding the work they seek. There is a vigorous market for, and in some instances active recruitment of, undocumented workers." But Marshall was convinced that the aliens, in his phrase, also worked "scared," their illegal status leaving them vulnerable to various forms of exploitation. "Undocumented workers are subject to blackmail of every conceivable sort," he pointed out. "If they complain to their employers about their paltry wages or their unsafe working conditions, they run the risk of having them contact the immigration service. As a result, they live a kind of half-life. They live among us, but they live in fear."

Marshall was speaking not just from personal conviction but

in his role as official defender of organized labor; indeed, big labor, with the notable exception of the garment workers' union, has called time and again for what Lane Kirkland, president of the AFL-CIO, calls "strong, determined and effective action to stop illegal immigration" and for criminal penalties for employers who hire illegal aliens. But the reality is that many unions are happy to sign up anybody, including illegal aliens. "They (the unions) are more concerned with membership than immigration status," says Ted Giorgetti, the chief INS investigator in Chicago, and James Caulfield, plant manager for the Wheaton Plastics Company in Chicago adds: "With the union, it doesn't make any difference." Aliens also make good union members; most of the seventy members of the United Auto Workers local in Los Angeles that struck a motor home builder, the Vogue Corporation, in May 1980 were illegal aliens.

To back up his fears about exploitation, Marshall could point to a two-year Labor Department investigation that had exposed thousands of employers who were taking advantage of their workers' illegal status and ignorance of American labor laws in various ways: by not paying them for all their hours, not paying time and a half for overtime, or paying less than the minimum wage. The investigators even found restaurateurs who had forced their waiters and waitresses to subsist entirely on their tips or even to share them with the management. When the investigation was finished, 8,224 places of business were found to owe more than $25 million in overtime wages alone to more than 161,000 illegal alien workers. One New York City painting contractor was ordered to pay six of his workers $125,000 in back wages.

In Houston alone, the investigators found that forty of the sixty-three employers it checked were cheating their workers in one way or another. Fred Worfe, who headed the Labor Department's strike force there, mentioned one company, a mail-order merchandise outfit, that had been paying its workers—all female illegal aliens who took orders and filled shipments—$1.25 an hour at a time when the minimum wage was $2.90. "These people were simply running a calculated risk that they wouldn't get caught," Worfe said. A painting contractor was found to owe seventy alien workers a total of $150,000 in back wages, and a construction firm with thirty undocumented employees owed them $60,000. Even when the workers suspected they were being cheated, Worfe said, "they were reluctant to report it because they don't know what the law is and they're afraid to expose themselves."

On its face, the investigation seemed to support Marshall's claim that illegal alien workers are generally taken advantage of. But as a careful analysis of the Labor Department's findings by David S. North of the New TransCentury Foundation showed, the bulk of the violations occurred not in large plants and factories but in smaller businesses—restaurants, nursing homes, hotels and motels, and laundries—located in smaller, poorer, or less-populated states with long histories of low pay and bad working conditions. Of the large industrial states, Michigan ranked twenty-second in the number of violations, Texas twenty-ninth, Ohio thirty-third, Pennsylvania thirty-sixth, Florida thirty-ninth, New York forty-third, California forty-fifth, and New Jersey forty-eighth.

What the North analysis suggests is that aliens are more likely to be underpaid or otherwise exploited in states that have traditionally underpaid and exploited all their workers, and less likely in states with solid histories of fair labor practices— where, not incidentally, most of this country's illegal alien workers happen to be employed. But the question also remains of whether the aliens see themselves as the victims of exploitation. In a single hour's work in an American factory, even an unskilled worker can earn the equivalent of half a day's pay in Mexico—if he could find a job there, something that is by no means certain in a country where half the adult labor force is either unemployed or severely underemployed.

Apart from his concern over their treatment at the hands of American employers, Marshall also worried that the illegal aliens flooding across the Mexican border were making an "important" contribution to the nation's rising level of unemployment. The degree to which the unemployment rate was a result of the Carter administration's economic policies is a subject for discussion elsewhere, but Marshall's position underlined the key question of whether Americans really wanted to—or could afford to—work for the wages being paid illegal aliens.

Marshall had at his disposal Labor Department studies showing that 75 percent of all illegal aliens working in this country hold unskilled or low-skilled jobs and that 25 percent earn below the minimum wage. In fact, there was no shortage of studies showing that illegal alien workers on the whole are not very well paid. One, by the U.S. Civil Rights Commission, found that the average hourly wage for aliens in Texas in 1980 was $2.75, 50 cents below what was then the minimum. Another study prepared for the San Diego Board of Supervisors, estimated that the 60,000 illegal aliens employed in that county were earning an average of $83 a week, or just over $2 an hour. And the INS itself had reported that 36 percent of the aliens it arrested around the country in 1980 were earning less than the minimum wage, while fewer than 5 percent were earning better than $7.25 an hour.

The fact that aliens are employed mostly in low-pay, low-status jobs, Marshall argued, was no evidence that they were not taking jobs from Americans. ''It is false to say American workers cannot be found for all of the jobs filled by undocumented workers,'' he said. ''The truth is that there are millions of American workers in all of these low-paying occupations already.'' This was indisputably true, but in its truth there lay a contradiction. There were also millions of unemployed Americans not working at those jobs, and one could reasonably assume that they had ''voluntarily withdrawn,'' in the words of Edwin Reubens, the City University of New York economist, from that sector of the labor market, leaving alien workers to take up the slack. Out-of-work Americans say they want such jobs; in a poll of unemployed citizens taken by the *Los Angeles Times* in 1982, 75 percent said they would apply for jobs paying between $3.35 and $4.50 an hour, 48 percent said they would seek work in a restaurant, and 40 percent said they were even willing to work in the garment industry.

There is, however, a discrepancy between what Americans say and what they do. To admit that they prefer collecting benefits to working at a difficult, low-paying job runs counter to the American work ethic, and while some citizens probably are willing to work for $4.50 an hour, the question is: Doing what? Cleaning fish? Emptying bedpans? Not likely. That is doubtless why, in study after study, efforts to replace illegal alien workers with American citizens have been singularly unsuccessful. As one labor expert explains the seeming contradiction, many Americans like the status and financial benefits conferred by *jobs*, but they do not like to *work*—the work ethic has been replaced by the job ethic. In an experiment in Los Angeles a couple of years ago the California State Human Resources Agency was unable to fill 2,154 jobs left vacant by INS raids, chiefly because most paid less than the minimum wage. Another study, this one in San Diego, failed to fill even one of 340 vacant jobs in that city's hotel and restaurant industries with an American citizen; the jobs were eventually filled by Mexican green card "commuters" from Tijuana.

Even when Americans do take jobs vacated by illegal aliens, they do not keep them for long. "Every time we get those vacancies, we fill them," says Walter Tupy, of the Illinois Department of Labor. "We've seen situations where Immigration is coming in one door and people are applying at the other." But in Chicago, as in every big city, the same factories and workplaces are raided by the INS year after year, suggesting that sooner or later the citizen workers depart, only to be replaced by aliens. Usually it is sooner. Within hours of an INS raid on the Woodruff-Edwards foundry in Chicago in 1980, for example, hundreds of applicants had lined up outside the plant gate. But Oluemi Folarin, the plant manager, said that "most of them left after finding out it was a foundry." Working at Woodruff-Edwards, Folarin admitted, was "dirty, noisy, hazardous work. This job is attractive only to the average white guy or black guy when there isn't any alternative. When an alternative opens up, the citizen moves on, while the alien will most likely stay and is glad to work."

Nearly a year after Project Jobs, Joe Reaves and Manuel Galvan of the *Chicago Tribune* sent a questionnaire to many of the businesses in that city that had been targets of the INS operation.

None of the companies queried admitted to knowingly hiring illegal aliens. But many employers suspected that they were often shown phony immigration documents and acknowledged that a number of their employees were probably living in the country illegally. Among the more interesting answers to the *Tribune*'s questionnaire were these:

THE TARNISHED DOOR

1. WHY DOES YOUR FIRM HIRE ILLEGAL ALIENS?
   —"They are good workers."
   —"They come to work every day."
   —"They are dependable. They work as many hours as they are needed and their productivity is much higher than the local help we have had."
   —"There is an unending stream. When nine are picked up there are 18 at the back door ready to take their place."
   —"They are trainable, respectful and good hard workers."
   —"Our business is a low-profit business using a lot of unskilled labor to hand-finish the product. The centers for our trade [the garment industry] are located in Texas and New Jersey and they use aliens and set the low prices, for they in turn must compete with products being brought in from everywhere there is cheap labor. Who made the shirt or blouse you are wearing today?"

2. IF THE SUPPLY OF ILLEGAL ALIENS SOMEHOW ENDED OR THE FEDERAL GOVERNMENT IMPOSED STIFF SANCTIONS AGAINST EMPLOYERS WHO HIRE ILLEGAL ALIENS, WHAT IMPACT WOULD IT HAVE ON YOUR FIRM?
   —"The importers would have no problem filling our void."
   —"It would cause many problems filling those positions."
   —"As we are a very large family and this is a family business we would all pitch in."
   —"We'll pay higher wages and can no longer compete with foreign companies."
   —"Only Mexicans are willing to work in a hot kitchen."
   —"The impact would be disastrous, like it was before they came around ten years ago. We will have no dependable help and the productivity will be lower."
   —"I would have a hard time trying to get employees to work here."

3. THE ARGUMENT HAS BEEN MADE THAT ILLEGAL ALIENS TAKE JOBS AWAY FROM AMERICANS. WHAT IS YOUR OPINION?
   —"From our experience this statement is false. The turnover rate is very low for our illegal aliens, but is high for some of our other employees. Many Americans are not interested in factory, blue collar jobs."
   —"We pay minimum & above. Who do you know who will work for this kind of money? Not many Americans. I am

sorry, but we cannot pay more. Our competition is in Taiwan, Korea. What do they pay?"

—"An American will accept these jobs, working for a minimum wage, until they [sic] are trained, and at that time they leave to find a better-paying job."

—"No! Not so! Very few legal persons come here looking for work . . . legal persons, altho [sic] out of work, look for higher-paying jobs (they usually have a set idea of what their work is worth)."

—"If illegal aliens can find jobs, why can't Americans? One of our employees tells of a friend who will not look for work and would not take work at McDonald's because he is doing much better on his unemployment check. Why go thru [sic] all the hassle and effort of going to work for only a few dollars a day more?"

—"Many Americans do not want to do the work or receive the lower pay these people do receive for this work."

—"We do not believe that a significant number of jobs are lost to willing-to-work Americans."

—"So-called illegal aliens take jobs away from Americans that don't want to work anyway."

—"Never. White collar workers would not do scrubbing and clean-up work."

—"Most Americans didn't want to fill the positions, the aliens do. In our case it is all kitchen help, and the ones that do it only work for a short time and they quit. Even students didn't want to work in the kitchen. Busing tables is about the only position they want to do."

And this, from a company manager who is himself an illegal alien:

—"Most American people do not want to work hard, get dirty, be hot, or be too cold. I do not think we are taking the jobs away from American people at all."

4. UNEMPLOYMENT IS HIGH IN CHICAGO'S BLACK COMMUNITY. DO YOU THINK HIRING ILLEGAL ALIENS CREATED THAT PROBLEM?

—"No. I don't think Black people want to work."

—"No. The black unemployment existed long before the illegal aliens came into the picture. With all the welfare programs that are in existence and for the taking, why would any minority want to work?"

—"Not at all. We had blacks working here before. They are the most unreliable help we have had."

—"Definitely not!"

—"Since there is work for illegals why then don't the legals or the blacks find these jobs?"

—"No. I believe that regardless of color there is some kind of work available if you are willing to accept any kind of work until something better has opened up."

—"The aliens moved into all the jobs no one really wanted—busboys, kitchen help, laundries, lawn care, farm labor. They took jobs you would not consider and in some cases jobs that had not been done for 20 years were done. Parking lots were raked, dead branches removed, old fences were painted, etc. Why was this not done before? Simple—it's not worth it at $8.00 per hour."

—"No! Without meaning to stereotype black workers, it has been our experience that many black workers have high absenteeism and poor work habits and are therefore not retained in their jobs. This has not been our experience with the majority of illegal aliens."

Some of the "other comments" at the end of the questionnaire were equally interesting:

—"I think it is very wrong and very unfair for immigration to enter a factory of any sort and pull these people (whose only crime is working) off their jobs. They suffer, and the production is wasted because all the machinery is abandoned. Also, immigration treats these good people like criminals. Is it a crime to earn a living and feed your family?"

—"We were the subject of a raid by the INS recently. All of those taken away that day have returned to work, most within 24 hours."

—"I believe Project Jobs with its fanfare and publicity was more political than anything else."

—"I think the people I have working for us deserve a chance or job as much as anyone else."

And finally:

"My father was an alien. He had 3 years of education. He spoke no English. He was a poor farmer boy with no parents. His uncle brought him to Chicago and got him a job. He learned to speak English at nights. He married at 22 and raised 4 children through the Depression. He never borrowed a cent, and he refused relief or aid of any kind. He was naturalized and never missed an election. He was very proud of America. I do not understand the difference between an alien that sneaks in and one we invite."

One variant of the Marshall argument is that while illegal aliens may not directly displace many American workers, the fact that they are willing to work so cheaply depresses wages to the point where most Americans cannot afford to even consider taking such jobs. Vernon Briggs, the Cornell economist, insists that an increase in the supply of labor, like an increase in the supply of anything else, serves to lower the price of that commodity, and he challenges those who disagree to explain why the laws of supply and demand work for all other commodities but do not apply to the increase in the size of the work force attributable to illegal immigrants.

One reason may be that aliens and citizens are not perfect substitutes for one another and that as a result, the demand for citizen workers is to some extent separate from that for aliens. As Wayne Cornelius, Briggs's colleague at the University of California, has pointed out, aliens tend to do jobs that require little or no ability to speak, read, or write English, leaving jobs that do require a knowledge of English, such as those that involve dealing with the public, for American workers. Moreover, the fact that alien workers tend to commute between this country and Mexico greatly reduces their chances of acquiring job seniority, perpetually relegating aliens to entry-level jobs and leaving the more senior positions to the citizen workers.

Another reason is that when wages drop below a certain level, citizens simply stop competing. Edwin Reubens, who thinks the competition between aliens and citizen workers is "rather limited" in any event because most of the aliens "have no skills other than peasant farming and simple crafts," a point well taken, notes that for Americans the alternatives to doing bottom-end work are many: "unemployment compensation, welfare and food stamps, support by relatives and friends and charitable agencies [and] earnings by hustling and by criminal activities not counted as 'work.'" Charles Miller, the Strolee executive, says there are "very, very few" citizens seeking jobs at his factory these days. "They've dwindled off over the years," he says. "I think there are too many incentives out there not to work for the minimum wage." According to Marvin Smith, a researcher at the Brookings Institution in Washington, welfare benefits available to some recipients in several of the larger states now add up to more money than a minimum wage salary. In New York, California, and Illinois, says Smith, "it doesn't pay to take a minimum wage job"— unless, of course, the worker is an illegal alien who cannot qualify for welfare. A third reason may be that as Wayne Cornelius has pointed out, many of the illegal aliens working in this country are not competing for places on business or corporate payrolls but are instead self-employed "entrepreneurs" who in effect determine their own wages—subcontractors, gardeners, repairmen, and the like.

The argument that illegal aliens drive down wages also ignores the reality that in those industries where alien workers are most heavily concentrated—agriculture, garments, hotels, restaurants, and construction—wages may already be about as high as they can realistically go. Were we to pay our field hands $10 an hour, our busboys and waiters $15 an hour, our seamstresses $15 an hour, and our hotel maids $20 an hour, the result might be not only Bill Bishop's $5 head of lettuce but also the $15 hamburger, the $50 necktie, and the $100-a-night motel room. Several leading economists, John Kenneth Galbraith among them, believe that never again will the least desirable jobs the American economy has to offer be filled by American workers at an "economical" wage—that is, a wage low enough to allow an employer to make a profit. Or, as Marvin Smith puts it, "If we want to have lower prices at all costs, then we should keep the system as it is."

As several studies have pointed out, when an employer is faced with the loss of a supply of cheap labor, he has several options besides raising wages, among them replacing his workers with machines, moving his operations overseas, or simply going out of business. A case in point is the agricultural industry in California. When the Bracero Program ended there in 1964, only the lettuce and citrus growers raised their wages in an attempt to attract domestic workers. The tomato growers began using mechanical harvesters, the asparagus growers moved to Mexico, and the marginal growers in every category sold their farms.

Those like Ted Giorgetti who believe that aliens are displacing American workers often point to the very high rate of unemployment among young blacks and Mexican-Americans. In Giorgetti's view, the aliens "are taking jobs from young people, those that are just starting out, from blacks and from other aliens who have gone through the proper immigration process in this country"—in other words, those Americans at the bottom end of the economic scale. George Montoya, Giorgetti's counterpart in New York City, agrees. "There are many black teenagers who would like to have some of the jobs these illegal aliens are taking," he says. But would they? The Select Commission on Immigration and Refugee Policy, after studying virtually all the available research on the question, reported finding "no strong evidence to support either hypothesis"—that illegal aliens take jobs from young and poor Americans or that Americans do not want the jobs that aliens take. Business executives are less uncertain. "Even high school kids don't want dishwashing jobs any more," an executive of the International House of Pancakes restaurant chain complained to *The Wall Street Journal*. "They want to be president of the company."

As for young Mexican-Americans, Wayne Cornelius notes that the menial, low-paying jobs traditionally filled by illegal aliens are so closely associated in the Hispanic community with "newcomers" that they are largely shunned by young Mexican-Americans as "wetback work." Whatever the reasons for black teenage unemployment—and they are still far from fully understood by American social planners—unemployment among young blacks has been on the rise in this country since 1954, long before alien workers entered the manufacturing, service, and construction industries in sizable numbers. There are, however, good reasons to believe that the raging unemployment among young blacks—by May 1982 it had reached 48 percent, compared to 20 percent for white teenagers and 9.5 percent for all Americans—is mainly a product of flawed educations, the lack of job training, racial prejudice, and what economists call structural factors, such as the fact that those jobs that do exist are usually not in the central cities, where most blacks live, but in the far-flung industrial suburbs. It may also be partly a product of "work disincentives" built into the welfare system, such as the law that requires the federal government, in calculating a family's total welfare eligibility, to take into account the earnings of a teenager not enrolled in school. According to the Social Security Administration, fewer than 5 percent of the teenage children in families that receive some form of welfare payment report that they are employed.

Those who argue strongly that alien workers are displacing Americans fail to recognize, moreover, that because the aliens are consumers as well as workers, they not only take a piece of the pie, but make the pie larger. In studying the 60,000 employed aliens in San Diego County, for example, researchers estimated that of the $260 million earned by aliens there each year, $115 million are spent in San Diego for rent, food, clothing, and other necessities. The reality, says Julian Simon of the University of Illinois, is that illegal aliens not only take jobs but make jobs, their expenditures creating a demand for goods and services that would not otherwise exist and that this in turn makes possible the employment of Americans. Aliens also create jobs directly since by filling the lowest-paid and least desirable jobs within a given business enterprise, they make possible the more highly paid jobs held by Americans. If it were not for the maids and restaurant workers in a hotel, there would be no need for the chefs, desk clerks, and assistant managers; for every brickmason there must be a hod carrier.

Because the principal purpose of most Mexican aliens in coming to this country is to earn money for the support of relatives back home (aliens from more distant countries tend to bring their families with them), every year hundreds of millions, perhaps billions, of dollars are sent back to Mexico to be spent. The 60,000 aliens studied in San Diego who spent $115 million of their earnings in this country also forwarded an estimated $97 million to their relatives in Mexico. According to Elwin Stoddard of the University of Texas, on the average 40 percent of the earnings of such aliens are spent in the United States, and another 40 percent taken or sent out of the country. (The remaining 20 percent goes for taxes of various kinds.) The preferred method of forwarding money is Western Union; the telegraph office in any big city is likely to have a long line of aliens in front of its money window at any hour of the day or night, and the forms for sending *giros,* as money orders are called in Latin America, are now printed in Spanish as well as English. Western Union estimates that half the money orders it sells in Texas alone are destined for Mexico.

There is a lot of money involved. In a 1976 study of 780 illegal aliens conducted for the Labor Department, David North and his colleague Marion Houstoun estimated that the average Mexican alien sent $100 a month to his family at home; the same year the INS estimated that some $16 billion a year was flowing out of the country unspent. (In typical INS fashion, the agency had asked six "experts" to estimate the number of illegals in the United States; the average estimate was 8 million, which the INS multiplied by $2,000 a year.) A better estimate, based on a more realistic assessment of the number of illegal aliens from Mexico and the Caribbean (the main receiving countries) would be about $2 billion a year—but even this sum is four times as much as American tourists spend in Mexico every year. "I used to travel around Mexican villages a lot," says Robert Kessler, a former Customs agent in El Paso. "In some villages you'd see TV antennas on the roofs and no adult males. You'd ask around and find out that all the males between, say, seventeen and fifty years old had gone to Chicago to work. They were sending money back and almost completely supporting the economy of the village."

Some economists contend that combined with American tourism, the resulting dollar drain has had a significant effect on America's balance of payments with Mexico. But the tourist flow is reversing; in 1981, for the first time, Mexican tourists spent more money in the United States than American tourists did in Mexico, and other analysts suggest that the outflow of dollars be viewed as foreign aid to Mexico (which, out of pride and principle, is one of the few countries that does not accept such aid from the United States). "If you view this money as foreign aid," says Leonel Castillo, "then Mexico is the only country which earns all of its foreign aid. Every busboy, bartender, yardman, and maid who sends money home earns it in the U.S. enterprise system. I don't know of any other country whose people are sweating for their millions of U.S. dollars like this.''

All in all, says Sidney Weintraub, a colleague of Ray Marshall's at the University of Texas, the illegal aliens ''aren't costing very much; they're contributing. In a way, they're subsidizing our standard of living. For a good many businesses, they provide the margin of survival. For the nation as a whole, I don't think this is a very serious economic issue.'' Julian Simon agrees. ''Theoretically,'' he says, ''there isn't the slightest doubt that some natives must be displaced.'' But Simon notes that native job seekers tend to move in response to worsened job conditions. ''The practical question,'' he says, ''is how many? It's not likely to be a very powerful effect or people would have found some existence of it.''

Quite apart from whether aliens take jobs from Americans is the question of whether they take undue advantage of publicly funded social services during their time in this country. The question is not a new one. As Carey McWilliams, the former editor of *The Nation* wrote in 1945:

> From 1907 to 1940, the ''Mexican problem'' was a hardy perennial in Southern California. Every winter the business interests of the region worked themselves into a lather of excitement over the cost of Mexican relief, hospitalization and medical care. With the return of the crop cycle in the Spring, however, the ''Mexican problem'' always somehow vanished or was succeeded by the problem of ''an acute labor shortage.''

The ''Mexican problem'' was given new life in 1975 when Leonard Chapman, at the time INS commissioner, declared that undocumented aliens were taking $16 billion a year more out of the American economy in public services than they put in by paying taxes. Since then, however, researchers like Wayne Cornelius, Julian Simon, and David North have addressed that question, and their findings suggest the opposite: Illegal aliens actually pay more in taxes than they use in social services.

That illegal aliens do pay taxes is beyond dispute: They pay income taxes, Social Security taxes, sales taxes, gasoline taxes, excise taxes, property taxes—the full range of taxes that are paid by any American citizen. Sales, gasoline, and excise taxes are, after all, difficult to avoid for anyone who spends money in this country (a study for the San Diego County Board of Supervisors estimated that illegal aliens were paying $7 million in sales taxes alone there every year), and though relatively few illegal aliens own property in this country, as renters they pay property taxes as surely as any homeowner (in California an average of 17 percent of all rental payments goes to property taxes). And as aliens forsake the nation's farms to labor in its businesses and factories, they increasingly find that federal and state taxes are being deducted from their paychecks (the Labor Department study by North and Houstoun found that 73 percent had had federal income taxes withheld from their salaries and that 77 percent had had Social Security payments withheld).

Similar findings have resulted from more than a dozen other studies, several of them carried out in Southern California, where the concentration of illegal aliens is the heaviest in the nation. One, in Orange County, California, estimated that illegal aliens there were paying as much as $145 million a year in taxes of all kinds, and the study of 60,000 aliens in neighboring San Diego County estimated that they were paying $49 million a year to the federal government alone. Aliens in Los Angeles are thought to account for $120 million in property taxes a year, all of which led to the Select Commission on Immigration and Refugee Policy to conclude in its 1981 final report that "illegal migrants pay taxes consistent with their earnings levels."

This is not as surprising upon reflection as it might seem at first. No one suggests that alien workers enjoy paying taxes any more than Americans do or that if given the choice, they would rather not pay them. That they do pay, and in such large numbers, is largely because they have no other choice, even where income taxes are concerned. Unless they are paid in cash, and sometimes even when they are, employers make payroll deductions on their behalf. Because business firms are not breaking any law by employing an illegal alien, they fail to see why they should do so by failing to withhold income and Social Security taxes from those people's paychecks. And contrary to what one might expect, tax withholding seems to be as prevalent among small businesses as large ones; a 1980 study by Sheldon Maram of the California State University at Fullerton found that 92 percent of illegal garment workers and 87 percent of illegal restaurant workers in Los Angeles had had taxes deducted from their wages.

Illegal alien workers, on the other hand, rarely collect the tax refunds that are due them. Only 32 percent of the aliens studied by North and Houstoun, and only 22 percent of the Mexican aliens, had ever filed federal income tax returns; the percentage among the garment and restaurant workers studied by Maram was about the same. Again, this should come as no surprise. Filling out a tax return is no easy task for most Americans; for an alien with little or no English and a marginal ability to read and write, completing even the 1040-A "short form" is a near impossibility. Moreover, any alien who files a return runs the risk of bringing himself to official attention.

For all the same reasons, few alien workers ever apply for Social Security benefits. "Mexican migrants," Wayne Cornelius asserts, "are clearly subsidizing the U.S. Social Security system to the tune of hundreds of millions of dollars per year, since those who work in the United States for only brief periods [will] never draw benefits unless they somehow legalize their status." The Social Security system is in serious straits. Not very many years ago there were sixteen workers paying into the system for every retiree receiving benefits. Today there are only four payers for every recipient. Without the several million aliens who pay in but will never collect their benefits, Cornelius declares, "the Social Security trust fund would be depleted even earlier than current financing schedules indicate." Or as Princeton's Douglas Massey puts it, "Far from ripping off the system, illegal aliens are more likely to be subsidizing it."

What do the alien taxpayers get in return for their tax dollars? Despite Commissioner Chapman's assertion that "We often find illegal aliens receiving welfare or food stamps," only 1 percent of the aliens studied by North and Houstoun had ever received food stamps (compared with about 10 percent of the U.S. population as a whole), and only half of 1 percent had collected some sort of direct welfare payment. Moreover, only 4 percent had ever received unemployment compensation, and only 1.4 percent had participated in federally funded job-training programs.

"We Could Go on Arresting Busboys Forever"

The two states with the largest population of illegal aliens are Texas and California, and in Texas welfare is almost non-existent for those who are not over sixty-five or children without the support of one or both parents. Public assistance is easier to obtain in California, but several studies there have shown a pronounced reluctance by aliens there to take advantage of such benefits. One study found that only 726 of an estimated 90,000 illegal aliens living in San Diego were found to be receiving direct welfare payments and that only 99 out of 285,000 food stamp recipients there were illegal aliens. In neighboring Orange County the numbers of illegal aliens collecting welfare payments (2.8 percent) or food stamps (1.6 percent) were equally minuscule. In a third study only 17,000 of Los Angeles County's estimated 1 million illegal aliens were found to be receiving welfare. The Social Security Administration has estimated that "an insignificant fraction of one percent" of all persons receiving federal welfare payments in 1977—about 2,000 people—were illegal aliens.

Illegal aliens, it seems, use social services far less than do native Americans. But then it is to work, not to go on welfare, that they come here in the first place. (Sixty-two percent of the aliens interviewed by Cornelius had jobs within ten days of their arrival, and INS apprehension statistics indicate that aliens who do not find work within a relatively short time are likely to return home.) The welfare ethic has not yet become a fixture of most Third World countries, where the rule of thumb remains "work or starve." Mexico, for example, has no national welfare system, and a Mexican working in this country may not have the least idea what benefits are available to him or how to go about applying for them. Even if he does, his continuing fear of attracting the attention of the authorities may well dissuade him. As one immigration lawyer puts it, "The last thing an illegal wants to do is call attention to himself by going to some government agency." To anyone who has studied the problem, the notion of hordes of aliens crossing our borders to collect welfare is absurd.

There is one exception to the aliens' general reluctance to take advantage of public services, and that is emergency health care. It is an exception born of necessity, for how else are they to cope with an acute illness or injury or the impending birth of a baby? Twenty-seven percent of the aliens studied by North and Houstoun had visited clinics and hospital emergency rooms, but four out of five had paid for such services in cash or through a health insurance program to which the alien or a working member of his family subscribed. (By one estimate, aliens paid $247 million in health insurance premiums in California alone during 1977.) One San Diego clinic administrator told Wayne Cornelius, "People who pay their hospital bill in cash, who have a large wad of money—my experience tells me they are illegal." Said another, "They usually come in with cash, so they don't get involved with billing."

In fact, the reluctance of most aliens to seek medical treatment they cannot pay for directly is a source of growing concern within the public health community, particularly since many aliens work in places, such as restaurants and hotels, where they come into contact with the general public. Unlike legal immigrants, illegal aliens are not examined for communicable diseases before entering the United States, and several studies have shown that illegal aliens tend to carry and communicate infectious diseases to a greater extent than the general population. Illegal immigrants from Asia and Latin America are believed responsible for the 30 percent increase in tuberculosis cases in Southern California, at a time when the incidence of that disease is declining nationwide, and the steady increase in reported cases of leprosy in recent years—300 new cases were discovered in 1980 compared to half that many in 1979—has been traced to immigrants from Mexico and the Philippines. Some public health officials suspect that the aliens are not bringing such diseases with them but that they contract them after arriving here and then fail to seek treatment.

Even those few aliens whose medical care is financed with public funds are not receiving a due return for their taxes. In Orange County, where illegal aliens paid $83 million in local taxes in 1978, their use of medical services that year cost the county only $2.7 million. Yet, the provision of health services to illegal aliens has become an emotional issue in several cities. Typical are the sentiments expressed by Mike Antonovich, a member of the Los Angeles County Board of Supervisors, which last year cut off medical care at county hospitals for illegal aliens. "They are here illegally," Antonovich told those who opposed the move, "yet you want us to take funds away from programs for citizens who are here legally . . . and spend them [on illegals]." He did not mention that illegal aliens had paid an estimated $120 million in Los Angeles County taxes that same year.

Such feelings are fueled by the handful of seemingly sensational cases that catch the attention of the news media, like that of forty-five-year-old Candalario Pérez, who spent half of 1980 in Dallas's Parkland Memorial Hospital after he was injured when the truck in which he was riding to his job as a bricklayer was hit from behind. Pérez, who suffered a broken jaw and damage to his spinal cord, had no money to pay his $30,000 hospital bill and no family in the United States to pay it for him, nor would his injuries permit his transfer to a Mexican hospital. For Pérez, this was perhaps just as well. A few months before, two Mexicans who had been critically injured in another accident had been sent back to Mexico by Austin's Brackenridge Hospital because they, like Pérez, could not pay their bills. Both men later died. As a result of the furor, Brackenridge simply stopped admitting aliens who had no money, including a nine-year-old Mexican boy. "We treat a dog better than that," said Travis County Commissioner Richard Moya in anger, "because if a dog gets sick we take him to the Humane Society and they don't ask him where he came from."

An equally emotional issue in Texas has been whether the children of illegal aliens should be admitted to public schools; a 1975 amendment to the Texas Education Code gave local school districts the right either to turn such children away or to charge them tuition. By contrast, other states do not even attempt to determine the immigration status of their students; in California, where large numbers of alien children are enrolled in public schools (they are believed to make up a fifth of the 550,000 children enrolled in Los Angeles County schools alone), the state law requires only that students reside in the school district in question. Following the passage of the amendment some cities, like Dallas, barred alien children altogether, while others began charging tuition—which, considering the steepness of the fees, was the same as turning the children away. In Houston the tuition was $135 per child per month, an impossible sum for most alien families, but the move was politically popular. Portraying the aliens as freeloaders, Governor William Clements declared that it was neither "fair" nor "equitable" to educate the children of illegal aliens at the taxpayers' expense. The governor did not mention that public education in Texas is financed primarily by local property taxes and state sales taxes, both of which are contributed to by illegal aliens. In 1977 the San Francisco-based Mexican-American Legal Defense and Education Fund, which had been watching the Texas school situation with growing alarm, filed suit against James Plyler, the school superintendent in the East Texas town of Tyler, which had decided to impose a tuition of $1,000 a year on the children of three dozen families of illegal aliens there, some of whom had lived in Tyler for more than a decade.

MALDEF argued that the law was unconstitutional; and when the case reached federal court, the Carter administration sided with the children. In a friend of the court brief, the Justice Department argued that the tuition law deprived the young aliens "of a critically important social benefit" because of their parents' illegal status, "over which the penalized children have neither control nor responsibility." Lawyers for MALDEF noted that while the state of Texas had passed a law denying the alien children a free education, it had not prevented their parents from working and paying the taxes that financed that education. The state of Texas maintained that if the tuition law were repealed, as many as 120,000 alien children would flood the state's schools, at a cost of some $120 million a year. A key witness for the plaintiffs was Meliton Lopez, the assistant superintendent of the Chula Vista, California, school system, who had entered Texas schools as an illegal alien at the age of thirteen, graduated from his Rio Grande Valley high school as valedictorian, and later earned a doctorate in education.

In September 1978 Federal Judge William W. Justice of Tyler ruled that the tuition law violated the Fourteenth Amendment, which holds that no state may "deny to any person within its jurisdiction the equal protection of the laws" and which Judge Justice maintained—for the first time—applied to illegal aliens as well as citizens. Judge Justice added for the record that all the alien families in Tyler on whose behalf the case had been brought were productive members of society (several were homeowners), not a social burden. In upholding the decision,

Federal Appeals Judge Frank Johnson acknowledged that to include illegal aliens under the umbrella of the equal protection clause might make them eligible for a whole range of public benefits. But Johnson thought the alternative was unwise. "If illegal aliens were not afforded equal protection of the laws," he asked, "what would invalidate a state statute that established the maximum penalty for theft of ten years if committed by a citizen, but fifty years if committed by an illegal alien?"

The question posed by the Texas law was resolved in June 1982, when the Supreme Court, in the closing days of its term, ruled 5-4 that to deny free public education to alien children was both an unconstitutional and shortsighted practice that could lead only to the creation of "a sub-class of illiterates within our boundaries." The decision permanently reopened the schools of Texas to all illegal alien children; it also left open the question, to be decided by other courts, of whether the Fourteenth Amendment's equal protection clause could be extended to cover the provision of free medical care and other social services to illegal aliens. The reaction to the Court's decision was not uniformly approving. "Once again," grumbled Texas Governor Clements, "we have created a situation that makes illegal immigration attractive."

The only problem was that the state's predictions that free schooling would attract a flood of alien students did not come true. Instead of 120,000 alien children, by the fall of 1982 fewer than 30,000 of the state's 2.2 million schoolchildren were illegal aliens, most of them sixth graders or younger. A dozen of them were assigned to Doug Hall's fifth-grade class at the David Crockett Elementary School in East Dallas, and Hall was happy to have them. "They're much more motivated than my regular students," he said. "If I don't give them homework, they ask for it. They always want to be working ahead. Most of them can run circles around our students in math [and] they're very knowledgeable in history and science."

CHAPTER TEN

"You Won't Become Pregnant Asking Questions"

During the last decade the number of Spanish-speaking students in the Seattle school system increased by 700 percent. In Detroit, Hispanics now have their own television program, *Para Mi Pueblo*. Cleveland publishes a Spanish-language newspaper, *Ecos de Cleveland*. In Philadelphia the city fire department has hired Spanish-speaking dispatchers, and school report cards are being printed in Spanish as well as English. The Mexican government has opened a consulate in Salt Lake City.

The Latinization of America is under way, and there is no big city that has not been touched by it, and in some cases transformed. Though the impact of the new immigrants is being felt most sharply across the Sunbelt, where more than three-fifths of the nation's Hispanics reside, two of the five cities with the largest Hispanic populations—Chicago with half a million and New York with three times that many —are in the very heart of the Snowbelt. So are five of the ten states with the most Hispanic residents—New York, Illinois, New Jersey, Colorado, and Michigan. Not all of the new immigrants are Hispanics by any means. There are also Asians, Caribbean islanders, Middle Easterners, and Europeans, and they, too, are spreading out across the country—Armenians to Boston, Iraqis to Detroit, Taiwanese to San Francisco (which is now one-fifth Asian), Indians to the Midwest, Koreans and Maltese to Maryland, Filipinos to New Jersey, Albanians to Ohio, Afghans to Massachusetts, Kuwaitis to Michigan, Saudis to Virginia. There is even a single Romanian living somewhere in Hawaii.

But the majority of the new immigrants are clearly Hispanic, and while no big city is now without at least some Latin ambience, the phenomenon is no longer exclusively urban. Half the nation's Hispanics do live in central cities, but 5 million have moved to the suburbs of those cities, and another 2 million live in rural counties. Many of the nation's Hispanics are native-born Americans, but according to census studies, the majority are immigrants—47 percent of all Mexicans currently living in the United States came here from Mexico, 82 percent of all Puerto Ricans from Puerto Rico, 87 percent of all Dominicans from the Dominican Republic, 93 percent of all Cubans from Cuba. While the Cubans and Puerto Ricans are here with permission, most of the others are not; according to the Census Bureau, "a sizeable but unknown" proportion of the increase in the country's Hispanic population between 1970 and 1980 was due to the counting of illegal aliens by the 1980 census. The Hispanic population is the fastest-growing in the country.

"Persons of Hispanic origin," as they are known to the census, now account for 14.6 million of the nation's 226 million residents, compared with just 9 million a decade ago, an increase of 61 percent. By contrast, the number of Anglo-Americans, while far larger, grew by only 1 percent, the number of blacks by only 1.5 percent. At that rate, demographers say, by 1990 one-fifth of all U.S. residents will be either black or Hispanic, and they predict that sometime before the end of this century Hispanics will have replaced blacks as the largest, youngest, and most fertile American minority.

Chicago, a city with a strong immigrant heritage, is now home to nearly half a million Hispanics, roughly a third of them Mexicans, and some blocks of the former Czechoslovak neighborhood of Pilsen look as though they had been moved there brick by brick from Mexico. Chicago's Mexicans have also settled in the industrial suburbs to the south, where immigration raids on apartment complexes and factories have become an almost daily occurrence. One of the main alien-smuggling routes runs directly from El Paso to Chicago, the fee for the three-day trip averaging $500. There is also a steady stream of buses going the other way, filled with aliens seized in raids who are being taken to the INS detention center in El Paso.

Southern California and South Florida are the most heavily Latinized regions of the country, but New York is still the city with the nation's largest Latino population, and it is likely to remain so for some time to come. For while the city's population as a whole declined by 10 percent over the last decade, its Hispanic population increased by 16 percent, to the point where today Hispanics, blacks, and Asians make up nearly half the 6.7 million residents of Manhattan, Brooklyn, Queens, and the Bronx. The first Hispanic immigrants began trickling into New York from Puerto Rico during the Depression, but it was not until the end of the Second World War that the Puerto Ricans, who as American citizens require no permission to emigrate to the mainland, began arriving there in large numbers. With the fall of the Batista government in 1959, they were followed by waves of Cubans and, after the death of Rafael Trujillo in the early 1960's, by Dominicans, many of whom emigrated illegally by entering Puerto Rico with "annotated visas"—essentially shopping passes issued by the State Department in furtherance of the interisland economy—then flying to New York from San Juan as Puerto Ricans.

The Dominicans have come in such numbers that after the Puerto Ricans, they make up the largest Hispanic community in New York City. The Catholic Archdiocese there estimates that as many as 400,000 Dominicans were living in New York in 1979, along with 500,000 Colombians, Ecuadorians, and Peruvians, many of them settling in the same neighborhoods settled by Germans, Irish, Eastern Europeans, and Italians during the great transatlantic migration. The Dominicans have adopted the once-Jewish neighborhood of Washington Heights on the city's Upper West Side, while the Lower East Side, for decades an enclave of the Eastern Europeans, is now largely Filipino.

In Brooklyn, Panamanians have settled in Crown Heights, Brazilians in Williamsburg. There are Trinidadians in Cambria Heights, Azoreans and Cape Verdeans in Jamaica, Argentinians, Peruvians, and Colombians in Jackson Heights, and West Indians in East Tremont.

Estimates are that perhaps half a million illegal aliens (but who knows?) are now living in the New York metropolitan area, where the attraction, apart from the ethnic diversity, is that menial jobs are easy to find—so easy that a few years ago six illegal Colombians were found working in the cafeteria of the Federal Plaza office building that houses the New York office of the Immigration and Naturalization Service. One of the barmen at Sardi's, the famed theater-district restaurant, is a twenty-seven-year-old illegal alien from Chihuahua.

New York City may have more Latinos than any city in the country, but it is still only 20 percent Hispanic, and for raw numbers even the greater New York region, with 1.5 million Hispanics, cannot compare with Southern California's 4.5 million, as many as New York and Texas together. Nearly half the Hispanics, the majority of whom are immigrants, live and work in Los Angeles County alone, and in the city of Los Angeles, where Hispanics, Asians, and blacks now account for just over half the total population of 3 million, the minorities have become the majority. Forty years ago a quarter of the nation's immigrants lived in New York; most of the rest, in Pennsylvania, Massachusetts, and Illinois. But like the millions of Americans who have since moved south and west in search of clean air and snow-free winters, the new immigrants are discovering the Sunbelt.

Forty percent of the 5 million legal resident aliens in the United States now reside in California, Florida, and Texas, and Texas and Florida alone have more immigrant residents than all of New York State. Los Angeles, with a quarter of the 5 million legal immigrants and perhaps another million illegal ones, has replaced New York City as the most favored destination of the immigrant. Not since the turn of the century, in fact, have so many immigrants from so many different countries gathered together in a single metropolitan area—a million Mexicans, Central and South Americans living side by side with hundreds of thousands of Iranians, Vietnamese, Thais, Taiwanese, Fijians, Koreans, Filipinos, and Samoans.

Los Angeles is now the most cosmopolitan city in the nation and, with the possible exception of London, the world. More than eighty different languages and dialects, from Farsi to Tagalog, are spoken in the city's public schools, sixty of them in the hallways of Hollywood High alone, and the Los Angeles schools are a polylingual, polycultural testament to the fact that with some persistence and very little luck, nearly any foreigner who wishes to live and work in the United States and who can afford the passage can probably do so. Apart from its temperate climate, Los Angeles is the closest American port of entry to both Asia and Latin America, the most potent sources of the new immigrants, and many of those who come there are in search of the idealized portrait of palm trees, swimming pools, and big cars that has been purveyed to much of the postwar world by movies and television programs exported from Hollywood. For most of the new immigrants, of course, that California does not exist. In Los Angeles they find not a palm-fringed paradise but vastly overcrowded housing, fierce competition for jobs that pay subsistence wages, predatory merchants, racial discrimination, and, increasingly, racial conflict.

While Los Angeles has now achieved an ethnic diversity surpassing even that of New York at the turn of the century, it is still an overwhelmingly Hispanic city. After Mexico City, Los Angeles has more Mexican residents than any city in the world, residents it has acquired in fewer than three decades. In 1950, just as the city embarked on its era of booming growth, its population was only 7 percent Hispanic. The city has grown enormously since then, and Hispanics now account for 3 Los Angelenos in every 10. Legal immigration to Los Angeles is huge; according to INS records, another 16,000 legal resident aliens arrive there every month. But the flow of illegal immigrants into the area is just as great as and probably greater than that; INS officials estimate 1 Southern Californian in 10, more than 1 million people altogether, is an illegal alien.

The ethnic influences the new immigrants bring with them to Los Angeles are visible everywhere. Just a few years ago the city's Mexican residents were confined to the traditional east side barrio known as East Los, but now downtown Los Angeles has been thoroughly Latinized as well. The Koreans have settled in the neighborhood around Olympic Boulevard that is now called Little Seoul. More than a third of the residents of Monterey Park are Chinese, and Samoans and other Pacific islanders have settled in Carson. More than a third of the 250,000 Vietnamese refugees who have fled to the United States since 1975 have settled in Southern California, 20,000 of them in the tiny community of Westminster, now Little Saigon.

But as in New York and Miami, as the immigrants have arrived in Los Angeles, the natives have left. According to the 1980 census, more than a million non-Hispanic whites have fled Los Angeles County in the last decade for Orange County and points south, and now many blacks are following them. Watts, once a black stronghold, is now a largely Latino neighborhood; and as Hispanics move into other formerly black communities like Downey and Compton, pushing their residents west toward the Pacific, the ethnic topography of the city is being altered radically. Landlords admit that they prefer to rent to immigrants, particularly to illegal aliens, who, in their desperation to avoid attracting official attention, are willing to pay high rents without demanding much in the way of services. The resentment blacks feel at being dislocated by the newcomers is making itself felt. INS officials in Los Angeles say that most of the tips they receive about where illegal aliens are living and working come from blacks.

The western end of the Sunbelt is struggling mightily under the impact of the new immigrants, but no place has been more affected than the eastern end. Los Angeles may be the nation's first big minority city, but Miami is its first big Latino city. Both have grown with remarkable speed, but the tall bank and office towers that have redrawn the Miami skyline over the past decade face south, not west or north. The city has become the hub of the trans-Caribbean banking trade, its once-seedy downtown rejuvenated by expensive shops and restaurants that cater mainly to wealthy Latin Americans flocking to what Jaime Roldos, the president of Ecuador, calls the capital of Latin America. Not all the Latinos are visitors. The population of surrounding Dade County grew by nearly a third during the last decade, and much of that growth was Hispanic. Twenty years ago Miami's Latinos numbered only 50,000. Today there are ten times that many; some 36 percent of Dade County's 1.6 million residents are Hispanics, and in the city of Miami itself they make up the majority, 56 percent.

Four out of every five are Cuban—for good reason Miami is known as the seventh province of Cuba. The first Cubans, many of them middle-class entrepreneurs and upper-class professionals, began arriving there twenty years ago aboard the "freedom flights" authorized by Fidel Castro as an escape route for those who did not want to participate in his socialist experiment, and most of them have prospered. More than a third of Cuban heads of households in Miami have attended college, a far higher percentage than for any of the nation's other Hispanic groups. About the same number have monthly incomes of more than $1,200, and the total annual income of Miami's Latin community is now $2 billion, as much as all of Trenton, New Jersey. As the city's attraction as a mecca for American tourists has waned in recent years, it has been the Latinos who have kept Miami's economy afloat. They also run the city politically. Hispanics are now the largest single group among the city's voters, with a participation rate twice that of whites; for nearly a decade the city's mayor has been Maurice Ferre, a Puerto Rican, and three members of its five-member city commission are Latinos.

As the Latinos have become an economic force in Miami, however, they have also grown to dominate the city's labor market to the point where the prime requisite for many jobs is now the ability to speak Spanish, not English. "I don't care if my people can speak English," says one shopkeeper there, himself an Anglo. "But they have to speak Spanish because most of my customers don't speak English." The Cubans have displaced large numbers of black workers in Miami, and the riot in 1980 that left block after block of the city's northwest side a smoking, burned-out shell undoubtedly had its roots in the 20 percent unemployment rates among black Miamians. The fifteen people killed by the rioters and most of the hundreds injured were either Anglo or Cuban. According to a study by the Ford Foundation, not since the antebellum slave uprisings have blacks rioted with the primary objective of beating or killing whites.

Not very many years ago, or so our cultural history tells us, the singular dream of the American immigrant was to eradicate every trace of dress, speech, and custom that might identify him as a "foreigner" from the old country. Whether one's last name ended in a vowel or a consonant, whether one's skin was swarthy or fair, the common ideal seemed to be to dive head-long into the melting pot and emerge speaking and acting like that homogeneous species known as an American. Immigrants worked as hard at night as they did during the day, studying the English language and the laws and Constitution of their new homeland in preparation for becoming a citizen, and the contest for their proudest moment was a contest between raising their hands to swear their allegiance to the United States of America and casting their first vote.

That, at least, is the popular impression left to us by the books and movies of a less complicated era. The reality, not quite so tidy, is that many ethnic groups, particularly those from Southern and Eastern Europe, managed to assimilate on the most obvious level while also ensuring the preservation of important elements of their heritage, among them religion, cuisine, music, literature, and national holidays. In 1920, just as the great transatlantic migration was nearing its end, a record 13.5 million of the nation's residents told the Census Bureau that they had been born abroad. But as generation gave way to generation, and immigrant to native-born, the ethnic distinctions inevitably blurred. The nation's homogeneity reached its all-time high in 1970, when the census reported finding only 8 million foreign-born residents, about 4 in every 100. But after a decade of heavy immigration the proportion is once again on the rise. According to the 1980 census, some 14 million U.S. residents, *half a million more than in 1920*, were born abroad, the preponderance of them in Asia and Latin America, and the true number of foreign-born is almost certainly higher, given the disinclination of aliens in general, and illegal aliens in particular, to answer the census truthfully about such matters.

America is once again becoming a nation of immigrants, but the difference this time is that the new immigrants, whether they have come here legally as resident aliens or refugees or as illegal aliens, are not nearly as inclined as their predecessors of a century ago to embrace without reservation the fundamentals of American society—its culture, values, and language. Quite apart from concerns about the economic impact of the new immigrants, many Americans are now beginning to wonder what their ultimate effect will be on the cohesion of our society, to wonder if the United States is on its way to becoming a nation permanently divided by language and culture—a giant twenty-first century Quebec.

Of all the possible reasons for the reluctance of the new immigrants to assimilate, several stand out. One may well be that as the nation's image abroad has grown increasingly tarnished in the years since World War II, being an American no longer carries the cachet it did in a less-sophisticated world. The Bay of Pigs, Vietnam, Watergate, the civil rights movement, and other national traumas have certainly diminished America's reputation, however well deserved it might once have been, as the land of freedom, truth, and justice for all. Another reason may be that many of the new immigrants, even those admitted as permanent residents, have no intention of staying here for good and therefore no wish to put down very deep roots, expecting to return to their native lands after a few years of making and saving money or, in the case of political refugees, when the government changes at home.

Even Puerto Ricans, who are U.S. citizens by birth, like to describe themselves as having "one foot on the mainland, the other foot on the island." Many of the Vietnamese refugees who have come here since the fall of Saigon still pray for a non-Communist Vietnam. For hundreds of thousand of Cubans in Miami, even those who were born in this country, the dream of Cuba without Castro is very much alive. Haitians in New York and Miami await the overthrow of the Duvalier regime, and the Salvadorans flooding across the Mexican border look upon the United States as a temporary refuge from their country's civil war. Such a sense of impermanence is equally characteristic of economic refugees, particularly of Mexicans, who tend to view themselves much like the laid-off auto worker who goes off to seek his fortune in Houston, always believing that he will someday return to Hamtramck. This attitude manifests itself in a variety of ways; a surprising number of the Mexican aliens interviewed by Wayne Cornelius in this country had retained their ownership of property in Mexico, and INS statistics show that only one Mexican in ten admitted as a permanent resident alien ever takes advantage of the opportunity to become a citizen.

Many Mexicans also retain strong familial ties to their homeland that reinforce their view of themselves as temporary visitors, making frequent, in many cases yearly, visits to relatives back in Mexico. Those Mexicans who have settled in California and the Southwest, moreover, find it particularly difficult to see themselves as "foreigners" or "newcomers" surrounded by a strange culture to be studied and absorbed, in the way European immigrants did a century ago. The Southwest, after all, was once part of Mexico. Not only does it resemble that country physically, but many of its place-names and much of its food, architecture, music, and dress are possessed of a strong Mexican influence. The Mexican immigrant who settles in the Southwest, as a third of the nation's 15 million Hispanics have done, finds himself or herself with two cultures, one of them very much his own, to choose from. It should come as no surprise that so many make the most comfortable choice, and as the Hispanic communities in the nation's big cities grow ever larger, the same familiar ambience is being exported to the north and east.

Yet another reason for the high degree of cultural alienation these immigrants experience must surely be the racism with which Hispanics, especially Mexicans, are still afflicted in this country. We enjoy their food and music, wear their fine embroidered shirts and guyaberas, steal words from their language (the Spanglais dictionary begins with "armadillo" and "arroyo" and ends with "zinc" and "zorro"), and vacation at their seaside resorts while reviling them as "greasers," "beaners," and worse.

Though it defies apology, such racism has probably been fostered in part by the physical isolation into which Mexicans have been thrust in this country since the turn of the century, when the first of them, called Cholos, were imported by the Southern Pacific Railroad to lay track when the flow of coolie labor was cut off by the Chinese Exclusion Act. Since then new arrivals from Mexico have tended to cluster together in monocultural urban and semirural enclaves—partly by choice, partly because they were forcibly excluded from the mainstream culture and consigned to "beantowns" in the same way the Chinese were pushed together into Chinatowns. But the Mexican culture is a rich one, and in concentrated form it has not only survived but flourished. As a result, the barrio of any big or even medium-sized city today is a world apart, a cultural stronghold where the Anglo visitor never suspects that the old lady who cooks his enchiladas or sells him a silver necklace may also be the local *curandera*, a folk healer who cures disease by rubbing raw eggs on the stomach or using herbal remedies, many of them quite effective, invented by the Aztecs and Mayans.

Whether the acculturation of our Mexican residents would have been greater without the racism and exclusionary practices to which they have been subjected in this country can never be known; having separated them from our culture so effectively, we can hardly expect them to try very hard to gain entry to it. Wayne Cornelius argues, on the other hand, that cultural maintenance cannot be equated with cultural separatism, which "implies an active rejection of, or hostility toward, the host society." Cornelius points to a Ford Foundation study asserting that Hispanic immigrants, by and large, have not evidenced un-American behavior "except in their rejection of English mono-lingualism." But it can also be argued that by far the most important mode of assimilation is language and that as Hispanic immigrants increase in number, perhaps surpassing blacks as the nation's largest minority group sometime before the end of this decade, America will become home, however temporarily, to ever more millions of residents who speak and understand little or none of our language.

That the widening linguistic gulf is a direct product of immigration seems clear from the latest census data, which show that though first-generation Hispanic immigrants, like Chinese and Greeks, tend to retain their native language for longer periods than did the European migrants of a century ago, most of whom had abandoned it entirely by the second generation, three-quarters of third-generation Hispanics speak English most or all of the time. If immigration were halted today, by the middle of the next century the number of Spanish-speaking residents would be minuscule, equal to the number of Americans—about 2 percent—who now speak predominantly German or Italian.

But immigration continues to accelerate, and according to the 1980 census, 1 U.S. resident in every 10, some 22 million individuals, now speaks a language other than English in his or her home, more than half of them Spanish. (A decade ago only 5.6 million U.S. residents acknowledged speaking Spanish "usually or often.") A separate study by Alejandro Portes, a Johns Hopkins sociologist, of 1,400 Cuban and Mexican immigrants who had lived in the United States for at least six years found that a third of the Mexicans and half the Cubans knew almost no English, that a quarter of each group had ''some command'' of English, and that only 1 in 10 was ''fluent.'' A third study, by the opinion polling firm of Yankelovich, Skelley and White, found that 23 percent of Hispanics interviewed knew no English at all and that another 20 percent knew only ''enough English to get by.''

If there is a growing cultural schism in this country, the rift is mostly likely to be along linguistic lines. Rejection of other elements of one's culture is somehow easier to abide than a rejection, apparent or otherwise, of one's language. Strange as it may be for a country with a polyglot heritage, there is still a pervasive sense here that to be an American one must above all speak English and that the growing number of new arrivals who do not are somehow failing the foremost obligation of the immigrant to his new country. Apart from the personal frustration experienced by non-Hispanics in their dealings with Spanish-speaking immigrants, the rising public anger seems to stem from a vaguely unfocused feeling that newcomers who fail to assimilate are diluting or weakening—stealing—the mainstream culture and that those immigrants who do not take the trouble to learn English are rude, contemptuous, and ungrateful. ''For years people have viewed language as transmitting culture and cultural loyalty,'' says Samuel Betances, a Puerto Rican sociologist at Northeastern Illinois University. ''It was the single most important label that said you accepted the new land with its new conditions.'' Already there is a linguistic backlash that seems to be gaining in intensity. In 1980 residents of Dade County, Florida, which is nearly half Cuban, passed an antibilingualism law forbidding the spending of public funds ''for the purpose of utilizing any other language than English, or promoting any other culture than that of the United States.'' Similar measures are currently on ballots in other cities.

The speed with which the United States is moving closer to true bilingualism is largely due to the fact that for newcomers to America, there is far less incentive to learn to speak English than there was a century, or even a decade, ago. As recently as the 1950's, those who spoke little or no English were effectively prevented from participating in the public life of the nation or, in many cases, any life beyond the confines of an ethnic neighborhood. For news of the world outside they might have had access to a newspaper published in Yiddish, say, or German or Italian and, if they lived in a large city, perhaps a single radio station. They could have read and listened, but if they spoke no English, their voices went unheard. Dealing with any kind of bureaucracy presented immense difficulties. Not speaking English at work could cost them their jobs. In all likelihood their children were confounded by school, perhaps even beaten with rulers, as were Hispanic children for speaking their native language in class in Texas until twenty years ago. Practically nothing was done by government to ease the burden of those imprisoned in another language; the theory was that to survive in an English-speaking society, one must learn English, and of course, the theory was self-fulfilling. Since the passage of the civil rights laws in the mid-1960's, however, it has become increasingly less necessary to speak English to survive, and even prosper, in America. Despite the efforts of California's Senator S. I. Hayakawa, a semanticist who is himself a naturalized American citizen, to enshrine English as the country's official tongue in hopes of forestalling the rise of "another Quebec," the United States has no constitutional language, and among the panoply of civil rights established by the courts in the last dozen years is the right to speak the language of one's choice.

The choices are many, and so are the accommodations being made for those whose primary language is not English. Public school instruction is now offered in more than eighty languages around the country, seventeen of them in Chicago alone. The Los Angeles public school system includes students who speak Khmer, Albanian, Norwegian, and even the African tongue of Ibo. The state of Louisiana administers drivers' license examinations in Vietnamese. Voters in San Francisco can ask for a ballot printed in Mandarin Chinese. A radio station in Flagstaff, Arizona, broadcasts all its programs and messages, even the ads for weekly specials at the local Safeway, in Navajo. But as both government and the private sector have now recognized, America's unofficial second language is Spanish. Since the Census Bureau first reported in 1970 that chiefly because of immigration from Mexico and Latin America, the Spanish-speaking population had displaced the country's 3 million speakers of Italian as the nation's largest linguistic minority, there have been a host of efforts by governmental and private institutions, some of them voluntary, others mandated by lawsuits brought by minority rights advocates, on behalf of Spanish-speaking residents. It is a trend that seems irreversible. As Vernon Briggs warns, while there "is a tendency for most people to believe that the gradual encroachment of Spanish is but a fleeting development, nothing could be further from the truth."

In nearly every large American city and in many smaller ones, bilingual notices and advertisements are now commonplace. In El Paso, Texas, and Fresno, California, the WALK/DON'T WALK signs at downtown corners have been replaced with the pictographic figures of a walking man and an upraised palm. In New York, Citibank has put instructions in Spanish on its cash-dispensing machines, and New York Telephone includes Spanish notes in its customer newsletters. Public telephones in Chicago carry dialing information in Spanish. The Philadelphia Fire Department has Spanish-speaking dispatchers, and the Cleveland Public Library has assembled an impressive collection of more than 20,000 Spanish-language books and periodicals. Twenty-three states currently have special agencies to assist the Spanish-speaking residents, and in California, which held its 1870 constitutional convention in both Spanish and English and which is on the verge of becoming the nation's first truly bilingual state, all state agencies must provide services in both languages. Pacific Telephone, which has employed bilingual operators to handle emergency calls since 1972, now publishes a Spanish-language supplement to its telephone directories. San Francisco General Hospital employs thirty Spanish-language translators. The list seems endless.

In state and federal offices across the country, brochures and forms are increasingly available in Spanish, as are bilingual personnel to help visitors with their questions. In 1980 the Census Bureau for the first time made its questionnaires available in Spanish, and federal law now requires that Spanish-language ballots and election materials be available in hundreds of communities around the country, among them Bridgeport, Connecticut, Scotts Bluff, Nebraska, and Malheur, Oregon. The Supreme Court has held that except when dealing with the public or when the safety of co-workers is involved, no employee can be fired for speaking a language other than English on the job. The U.S. Department of Health and Human Services has translated into Spanish pamphlets on such topics as Medicare, Social Security, and civil rights, though some of its efforts are unintentional illustrations of the difficulty of bridging the linguistic gulf. ''Don't worry,'' one HHS publication promises in attempting to allay one of the main fears of many Hispanics in confronting official agencies. ''You won't become pregnant asking questions.'' (One Spanish word for ''pregnant'' is *embarazado*. ''To be embarrassed'' is *desconcertar*.)

One of the principal ways that immigrants of an earlier era learned English was through their exposure to the popular culture, through the media and advertising. But now, hoping to cultivate the rich and largely untapped Spanish-speaking market, newspapers, broadcasters, and advertisers are increasingly talking to Hispanics in their own language. Most big cities now have at least one Spanish-language newspaper—*El Mañana* in Chicago, *El Sol* in Dallas, *La Opinión* in Los Angeles, *El Diario* in New York and San Francisco, even *La Verdad* in Las Vegas—and several have more than one. English-language newspapers like the Miami *Herald* and the Chicago *Sun-Times* now publish Spanish editions, and the Gannett Company, which owns *El Diario* in New York City, says it plans a national edition of the paper. The Associated Press has more than sixty domestic subscribers to its Spanish-language news service. Whereas a decade ago there was scarcely a Spanish-language radio station outside New York, Miami, or Los Angeles, there are now 120 of them around the country, and 17 Spanish-language television stations as well, most of which are affiliated with SIN, America's national Spanish television network. Like its three English-language counterparts, SIN has a nightly network newscast, *Noticiero Nacional*, which is produced in Washington, and it also links Hispanics in the United States with their home countries via satellite, beaming programs such as *24 Horas*, the nightly newscast from Mexico City, into millions of American homes along with live soccer matches and florid Mexican soap operas.

Ten years ago the little Spanish-language advertising there was in this country was for pesticides, used cars, and easy loans, but that too has changed with market studies showing that Hispanics buy and use a number of products more often than the general population, among them baby food, white bread, coffee, fruit juices, soft drinks, and rice. Billboards, radio and television commercials, and magazine and newspaper advertisements now extol the virtues of Aspirina Bayer ("*Tenga siempre a mano,*") and the high *calidad* of Sunkist oranges. Budweiser "*es para Usted.*" The Kraft cheese company urges the purchase of *los Singles de Kraft*. Coca-Cola and Pepsi both are courting Hispanic consumers ardently, as is McDonald's with its *hamburguesas*. Royal now markets its custard pudding as *flan*.

"Our ads used to be all local used car dealers," says Don Balsamo, sales manager for KEMO-TV, San Francisco's predominant Spanish-language station. "Now our ad base is almost entirely big corporate advertisers: Bank of America, Chevron Oil, Ford, and Datsun." Moreover, such advertisers are getting their messages across to the desirable younger segment of the Hispanic population, the eighteen- to thirty-year-olds, who seem happy to hold on to their primary language. "Second- and third-generation Asians tune into Anglo radio and TV," Balsamo says, "but second- and third-generation Hispanics continue to relate to us."

Even those Hispanics who speak English well often prefer Spanish—which they see, not without some justification, as a warmer, more expressive, and more intimate language—and for them the issue of language rights can be as important as for the non-English speakers. As Eziquiel Quintana, a Lubbock, Texas, cosmetologist, told Allen Pusey of the Dallas *Morning News*, "I got blown up in Vietnam. I got three purple hearts just to come back and be told where I can speak my own language?" It is because of such attitudes that the speaking of Spanish by bilingual workers on the job, something that makes English-speaking supervisors and co-workers uncomfortable, has become a potentially incendiary issue. The problem first gained national attention in 1975 after Hector García, a lumber salesman in Brownsville, Texas, was fired for answering a customer's question in Spanish. The Supreme Court upheld García's firing, agreeing that English-on-the-job rules do not contravene federal antidiscrimination guidelines only (1) if they require that English be spoken in public areas, (2) when the clerk is dealing with English-speaking customers, or (3) in situations where the safety of English-speaking co-workers might be endangered.

It was the safety issue that the Champlin Petroleum Company cited last year when it posted a notice at its refinery in Corpus Christi, Texas, that prohibited the speaking of "languages other than English." Chicano workers at the refinery were outraged, insisting that safety had nothing to do with the rule, since they could switch to English whenever an emergency arose, and one worker called the refinery officials who issued the dictum "a bunch of narrow-minded red-necks." Whatever the motive behind it, the action was applauded by local Anglos, like the woman who wrote to a Corpus Christi newspaper: "If the Mexican language and the Mexican customs are so important to these people, perhaps if they lived in Mexico they would be happier."

So far, however, the brunt of the linguistic backlash has been reserved for bilingual education—the process of teaching children whose primary language is not English in their native language, while helping them learn English at the same time. Those who oppose bilingual education, and they are many, see nothing wrong with—indeed, see much virtue in—the sink-or-swim approach to linguistic assimilation of a century ago. Among the more thoughtful critics is Richard Rodríguez who entered the first grade in Sacramento, California, knowing fewer than 100 words of English and who later received degrees in Renaissance literature from Stanford and Columbia. Like most other Hispanics who have conquered the system against such enormous odds, Rodríguez opposes compensatory bilingual education on the ground that it keeps children "poised at the edge of language too long," delaying or even preventing eventual assimilation. "What I needed to learn in school," he writes in his controversial book, *Hunger of Memory*, published in 1981, "was that I had the right—and the obligation—to speak the public language of *los gringos*. Only when I was able to think of myself as an American, no longer an alien in gringo society, could I seek the rights and opportunities necessary for full public individuality."

Another who wrestled the system and won is Hector Nava, who recalls that when he arrived in New York City from his native Argentina at the age of sixteen, he hadn't the faintest idea "of how to ask to go to the bathroom" in English. Nava found his way into the city's labyrinthine public school system, where he was promptly given a standard placement test—in English. Thoroughly adrift, the young man picked answers at random. "It was a guessing game," he says now, and he did not guess very well. Despite his age, Nava was put in the eighth grade at a junior high school on Manhattan's West Side. Oddly, or so he thought at the time, all his classmates were immigrants: a few Greek boys, a French girl, some Eastern Europeans, and many Cubans. "Some of the students were very intelligent," Nava recalls, but they shared a common failing: None of them spoke English.

At the end of the eighth grade Hector Nava did not receive an application for high school. In fact, he did not know that high school existed and was planning to look for a job until his brother-in-law told him he had an opportunity to continue his education. With much difficulty he found a Queens high school willing to admit him, but it offered no bilingual education, so Hector Nava taught himself English by plodding through *A Tale of Two Cities* with an English-Spanish dictionary at his side. Apart from the help of a couple of sympathetic teachers, he said, "I really don't think I received a great deal of guidance." Finally, at the age of twenty, Nava graduated from high school. He won a scholarship to Harvard, where he majored in government and was graduated with honors. He went on to the Georgetown University Law School and is now a trial specialist for the National Labor Relations Board in Phoenix.

Hector Nava is far from bitter, but he is also less sanguine than Richard Rodríguez about the ability of others like him to succeed. "I hope my kids have the same advantages I had," he says now, "without the disadvantages, of course." Rodríguez's book has attracted much attention among opponents of bilingual education, but many Hispanics argue that his "you can too" approach does not take account of how much more difficult learning in a foreign language can be for those with less natural equipment than he or Hector Nava. One who does is Rodríguez's fellow Stanford alumnus Oscar Martinez, now the director of the Institute of Oral History at the University of Texas's El Paso campus. "Those of us who have professional positions," says Martinez, "are often singled out as evidence that ample opportunity is available if we only apply ourselves and work hard. My own situation fits within this perception. I am an immigrant and former illegal alien. My father was an undocumented field worker for over a decade; my family suffered from deportations several times. Now, after attending schools like Stanford University, Berkeley, and UCLA (where he received his Ph.D. in 1975), I have achieved middle-class respectability as a professor and published author. Yet I am very uncomfortable with the notion that 'If I made it, others can too.'

"On the way upward a minority person of limited means faces an infinite number of obstacles not encountered by the members of the mainstream society. Guts, wits, ingenuity, assertiveness, hard work, sacrifice, delayed gratification, good advice, financial assistance, luck, and 'being at the right place at the right time' are among the variables that comprise the formula for 'success.' If these things fall into place correctly, the chances for upward mobility are enhanced. Unfortunately only a few from the ranks of the Hispano working class have been lucky enough to experience the right combination of these critical factors in their lives. The vast majority have not made it, and that is powerful evidence that the system is a tough one to penetrate without extraordinary effort and the 'right circumstances' being present."

It is curious that so many of those who resent the inability of the new immigrants to speak English should be so fierce in their opposition to bilingual education, which is, after all, an attempt to provide the 5 to 10 percent of public school students who speak little or no English with the circumstances they need to "penetrate the system." And in truth, the need for some sort of compensatory instruction is difficult to ignore; as study after study has shown, Hispanic children thrust into the schoolrooms of America without the language ability to learn at the same pace as their classmates almost never catch up.

One result is that Hispanics are less well educated than Anglos. According to the Yankelovich study, 32 percent of Mexican-Americans in this country have not gone beyond the eighth grade, compared with 8 percent of the population as a whole. Only 20 percent have graduated from high school, compared with 35 percent of the entire population. A Carnegie Corporation study found that fewer than 7 Hispanic students in every

100 had graduated from college, and those who had received fewer than 3 percent of the advanced degrees awarded.

Another result is that Hispanic children are far more likely to fall behind in school. A report by the U.S. Department of Health and Human Services reported that children whose native language is Spanish are more than twice as likely as native English speakers to be one or two grades below the normal level for their age, sometimes through no fault of their own. Large numbers of Hispanic children, in some cities as many as 1 in 5, have been wrongly classified as educationally impaired or mentally retarded because of their subnormal scores on placement and intelligence tests administered in English, a language they cannot understand.

A third result is that Hispanics do not stay in school as long as Anglos. Like other children with foreign-language backgrounds, slightly less than half drop out of high school before graduation, compared with only 10 percent of native English-speaking children. In some school districts around the country, the attrition rate for Hispanic students is as high as 85 percent.

Perhaps most important, since it is probably the main cause of the other failings, Hispanic children do not read as well as Anglos. In Texas, which has one of the least adequate bilingual education programs of any state, 64 percent of those Hispanics who remained in school through graduation left reading below twelfth-grade level, compared with 32 percent of all students. In 1977 the Education Commission of the States, a Denver-based organization, found that on the average thirteen-year-old Hispanic children scored eleven percentage points below the national mean in reading scores.

All this is hardly surprising when one considers that an average child from an English-speaking family enters the first grade with a vocabulary of between 4,000 and 5,000 words of English; a Hispanic first grader may know as many words of Spanish or more but, like Richard Rodríguez and Hector Nava, only a handful of English words or none at all. Quite apart from the educational disability involved, the psychic damage to a child who cannot understand his teacher, his lessons, or his English-speaking classmates can be grave. At best, he is made to feel an outcast whose culture and language are second-rate and that the responsibility both for his handicap and for overcoming it is his alone—like a deaf child thrust among children who can hear and told somehow to keep up.

At worst such children are made to feel un-American or, most traumatic of all, mentally defective. "I felt lost in a jungle," recalls Arcadia López, a Texas elementary school teacher who came to the United States from Mexico as a young girl. "My teacher couldn't understand me and I couldn't understand her. My teacher considered me a mental retardee. I hate to tell you how many times I repeated the first grade." López survived, but her experience is far from uncommon. A few years ago Olivia Martínez, then a guidance counselor with the San Francisco public school system, was asked to have a look at a ten-year-old Hispanic girl in a class for mentally retarded children. "Her name is Elena," the class's puzzled teacher told Martínez, "and I know she's higher than a forty-five," an IQ score indicating severe retardation. "So I went into this classroom," Martínez recalled, "and here were all these kids quietly doing arts and crafts. I went over to Elena and asked her in Spanish where she was from, and her whole demeanor changed. She sat up very straight and her eyes sparkled. She told me she'd been in the country six months from Nicaragua." Like uncounted thousands of Hispanic children before her, Elena had been placed in a class for the mentally handicapped because of her performance on a standarized English-language test. After studying Elena's case, Martínez examined the histories of the other Hispanic children in the class and found that all of them had been given the same test with approximately the same results. She arranged for the group to be tested again, this time in Spanish.

Elena's IQ was measured at a nearly average ninety-four, a score that was probably still too low because of the cultural bias of the few intelligence tests for children that have been translated directly into Spanish. According to Roger Shuy of the Center for Applied Linguistic Studies in Washington, when a Hispanic child is instructed to draw an object "on the lines" he will place the object beneath the line as often as on top of it. "The saddest thing," says Olivia Martínez, "is that despite all of what we know about how easy it is to misplace children, there still has not been any concerted effort, even here in California, to develop more appropriate instruments of assessment. And California is ahead of the rest of the country.''

Luís Jaramillo, a California lawyer deeply involved with the issue of Hispanic children's rights, tells of another such case, a Salinas, California, fifth grader named Raúl, who was labeled retarded after he scored below sixty on an English-language intelligence test he could not understand. ''With that score he shouldn't have even been able to tie his shoes,'' Jaramillo says. ''And the only reason it happened is that the psychologist didn't have an adequate interpreter, was in a hurry, and decided not to wait for one.'' Elena, Raúl, and others like them are what have come to be called six-hour retardants, normal children who because of linguistic problems are treated during the school day as if they were mentally disabled—in many instances without the parents' ever having been told their children have been diagnosed as retarded, and sometimes having been assured that the ''special class'' is one for ''gifted'' children.

One Mexican-American woman, a doctoral candidate at Stanford, recalled that when she was in high school a few years ago, she happened to glance at a school picture and noticed that her two younger brothers, though different ages, were in the same class. Their sister investigated, found that the class was one for retarded children, and asked for an explanation. ''The teacher wasn't very cooperative,'' the woman said. ''She just told me that not everyone was made to go to college.'' The woman had her brothers' intelligence tested again, in Spanish, and their scores won them admission to one of the school's regular classes. But by then the boys were fourteen and sixteen, and ''so far behind in school that it was a losing battle,'' the woman said. ''It's tragic what could have been done with them if this kind of stuff had not gone on.''

No one can say how many such children have been misclassified, but most experts are sure it is not a small number. ''Throughout the Southwest, where you've got a substantial number of Hispanic children, this is one of the main problems,'' says Richard Figueroa, an instructor in the education department at the University of California at Davis. But the problem also exists around the country. Michael Dale, a lawyer who helped prepare a challenge to such practices in New York City, put the proportion of misclassified Hispanic children there at between 15 and 20 percent, most of them Puerto Ricans. In Detroit, a court-ordered survey found that a quarter of the Hispanic children labeled "retarded" because of low test scores were of normal or above-average intelligence. Even in California, which has gone further than most states in searching out remedies, nearly one of every ten school districts reported three years ago that the percentage of Hispanic children in classes for the "educable mentally retarded" exceeded the percentage of Hispanic children in the district, in some cases by as much as 40 percent.

For reasons that are not fully understood by linguistics experts, Hispanics tend to have more difficulty learning English than do natives of some non-Spanish-speaking countries. Part of the difficulty may have to do with the character of Spanish grammar, in which personal pronouns, compound verbs, and even direct objects are optional or nonexistent. In Spanish the phrase "No, I don't have it" comes out *No, no tengo.* The Hispanic who applies the rules of Spanish grammar to English is therefore likely to say, when asked whether he has something, "No, no have," which sounds crude and uneducated to the English speaker. For many Hispanics, mastering the more elaborate rules of English grammar can prove vexing, but much more so for adults. Because young children are less "locked in" to their primary language and its peculiarities, they have a far greater facility for learning a second language. As Wayne Cornelius notes, Hispanic children "who are born or raised from infancy in the U.S. seem to have little difficulty acquiring English-speaking ability," while "children who have spent much of their childhood in Mexico and began their schooling in Mexico tend to have greater difficulty."

If there is reason to be concerned about the social stresses that threaten to develop when the majority of a nation's citizens cannot communicate with many members of its largest ethnic minority, one place to begin improving communications is with the nation's 3.5 million schoolchildren, three-quarters of them Hispanics, who speak little or no English. The opposition to bilingual education is considerable, but it does not come from the parents of those children who can benefit from it. Numerous surveys have shown that while many immigrants want their children to retain their linguistic heritage, they recognize that

English will remain this country's "power language" and that a knowledge of it is absolutely crucial for educational and social advancement. Among Anglos, however, bilingual education is surely the nation's least understood social program, and no one has displayed greater misunderstanding of its aims and methods than President Reagan, who declared shortly after taking office that it was "absolutely wrong and against American concepts to have a bilingual education program that is now openly, admittedly, dedicated to preserving their (students') native language and never getting them adequate in English so they can go out into the job market and participate."

The President's assertion notwithstanding, bilingual education is precisely what the name implies—education in two languages at once. In some programs, instruction in academic subjects such as arithmetic, history, and geography is given in the student's native language in the morning, with English lessons in the afternoon. In other programs, some subjects are taught in English and others in the native language. A third variation involves using both languages interchangeably throughout the day. There are also two basic formats. Most of the bilingual programs funded by the states are "maintenance" programs, which seek to teach a child English while maintaining, and even improving, his competence in his primary language until he is equally fluent in both. Most programs funded by the federal government, on the other hand, are "transitional," in which the aim is gradually to wean the student away from his primary language until he is receiving instruction entirely in English. Transitional instruction for Hispanic children, for example, might be 80 percent in Spanish and 20 percent in English in the first grade, the proportions gradually changing until by the fourth grade they are reversed. But whatever the format, the main goal of every bilingual education program is to develop fluency in English.

Despite the intensity of the debate it has aroused, there is nothing new about bilingual education in this country. In the last century the New York City schools provided instruction in Yiddish and Italian. Schools in some parts of Texas settled by German immigrants taught elementary students in German, and so did those in Cincinnati and St. Louis. Children in Albany, Louisiana, a tiny Hungarian community, are still taught

Hungarian through the fourth grade. But it was the Bilingual Education Act of 1968, passed in response to growing concern among educators over the poor performance of schoolchildren whose first language was not English, that fostered the modern rebirth of bilingual education in America by making federal funds available to set up such programs.

The real impetus came six years later, with a landmark Supreme Court decision in the case of *Lau* v. *Nichols*, brought on behalf of 2,423 Chinese-speaking students in San Francisco who were receiving instruction only in English. In its opinion, the Court decreed that teaching children in a language they did not understand denied them the "equal educational opportunity" to which they were entitled by the Fourteenth Amendment. The U.S. Department of Health, Education and Welfare issued informal guidelines, known as Lau remedies, to help the nation's 16,000 school districts with non-English-speaking students comply with the Supreme Court's ruling. The response was the creation of thousands of bilingual programs in scores of languages in cities and towns across the country.

Hispanics account for a third of the public school students in New York City and Miami, half in Los Angeles and San Antonio, a fifth in Chicago, and bilingual education, for better or worse, has now become irretrievably identified as a Hispanic issue. A good deal of the debate that surrounds it has focused on whether Hispanic children should be encouraged to retain their use of Spanish, with Hispanic rights groups generally supporting maintenance types of programs, arguing that the Spanish language is an inseparable part of every Hispanic's heritage. Many linguists agree. Dr. Barbara Burns, who was chairwoman of President Carter's Commission on Foreign Language and International Studies, notes that the number of Americans who can speak a language other than English has been declining steadily since the 1950's. She observes, "It does seem absolutely ridiculous not to encourage the retention of a foreign language by those Hispanics." Other experts point out that it makes no sense to discourage elementary school pupils from speaking a second language only to encourage them to learn one in high school and college. Not surprisingly, it is the maintenance programs that have generated the most resistance among taxpayers, many of whom resent spending public money to preserve a minority culture, resentment that has only intensified in recent years as school districts from Colorado to Suffolk, Long Island, have combined their bilingual programs with bicultural education in Hispanic history, literature, art, and music.

To be fair to its critics, bilingual education is not without its problems, some of which stem from the haste with which many of the programs were put into effect following the *Lau* decision and from the broad lack of agreement about which methods and techniques to use. Educators have also had difficulty in identifying which children are eligible for, and can benefit from, bilingual classes—whether they are "English-dominant" or more fluent in their primary language—something difficult to measure in young children but crucial nonetheless because of evidence that the progress of children even slightly stronger in English is actually retarded by bilingual instruction. Yet another point of disagreement is when to take a child out of a transitional bilingual program and immerse him entirely in English instruction. In Texas, children are "exited" after the third grade or after they rise above the twenty-third percentile in an English achievement test, which some experts say is far too soon.

By far the greatest obstacle, however, is the lack of teachers certified to teach bilingual classes, a skill that requires not only total fluency in two languages but training in specialized teaching techniques. Though the shortage is acute—in Los Angeles, which needs 3,000 fully accredited bilingual teachers, there are fewer than 1,000—the reasons for it are in dispute. Among the problems cited by educators are the lack of adequate teacher-training programs and of enough interested candidates and the failure of many school districts to pay bilingual teachers enough of a salary differential to make the added training worthwhile. All too often the result is that many bilingual teachers are less than qualified. According to Henry Pascual, the director of bilingual education for the New Mexico Department of Education, none of that state's 136 bilingual teachers and teacher's aides could pass a fourth-grade Spanish examination, and only 1 percent could pass a third-grade exam. The problem, Pascual says, appears to be that even in university programs set up to train bilingual teachers, "a great number of professors also lack the necessary skills. The result has been a terrible disregard for academic standards when dealing with the Spanish language and most aspects of the culture.''

Nor has the progress of bilingual education been helped by the outright hostility of some state officials to the requirements imposed on them by the federal government. Among the most outspoken is Alton O. Bowen, who as Texas education commissioner created a furor among Hispanics by declaring that the responsibility for bilingual education lay in the home, not the schoolroom. "For two hundred years," declared Bowen, who opposed expanding bilingual education beyond the third grade in Texas schools, "this country has been well served by the melting-pot concept of one nation." The school day, he added, contained only seven hours, and the schools "simply don't have time to be all things to all people. We cannot solve all of society's social problems."

Despite such opposition, in August 1980, the Carter administration, recognizing that only about 60 percent of those students who needed bilingual education were enrolled in such classes, moved to strengthen the informal Lau remedies with tougher regulations *requiring* for the first time that two-language instruction be made available to every child in the nation who was not "English-dominant" and also mandating that Spanish-speaking children be given some instruction in Hispanic culture. School districts with more than twenty-five foreign-language students that did not comply with the regulations risked losing all their federal grants. Despite assurances from Shirley Hufstedler, Carter's secretary of education, that such programs would emphasize two principles—that "students must be taught English as quickly as possible" and that they "should not be permitted to fall behind their English-speaking classmates while they are learning English"—the reaction was furious. The House of Representatives quickly responded by adopting an amendment forbidding the withholding of federal funds to school districts that did not comply with the new guidelines.

Less than a month after President Reagan took office, Terrel Bell, Hufstedler's successor, announced that the new guidelines were being thrown out. It would have cost school districts a billion dollars, Bell estimated, to implement the new regulations, which he—and presumably the President—saw as "intrusive" and "symbolic of many of the ills that have plagued the Federal Government." The reversal did not threaten many of the big-city bilingual programs, which are too well entrenched to be disbanded. But officials in many smaller school districts, for whom the search for bilingual teachers and the disputes about which methods to use had been an unwanted headache, were delighted. The Reagan administration, Bell said, would go back to using the Lau remedies, which never had the force of law or even the authority of a federal regulation. School districts that did not follow the guidelines would be out of compliance with the Supreme Court decision, but since the decision was not to be enforced, what motive did they have to comply?

The Reagan administration's first budget contained an allocation for bilingual education funds that was 20 percent less than the $163 million proposed by the Carter administration, requiring a reduction in the number of pupils enrolled in such programs from 334,000 to 222,000. Then, in the spring of 1982, Bell announced that even the Lau remedies were being abandoned. A month earlier the Reagan administration had released its proposed budget, in which bilingual funds were reduced still further, to $92 million. The administration even introduced legislation that would no longer require school districts receiving those funds to provide any instruction in a child's native language, suggesting as one alternative "immersion" courses in which non-English-speaking children were taught entirely in English—the old sink-or-swim approach.

The future of bilingual education is not bright. According to MALDEF, which monitors bilingual programs around the country, the general reaction to the retrenchment in Washington has been not the elimination of existing programs but rather a refusal to begin the new ones needed by the four non-English-speaking children in every ten for whom such classes are not available—a number that, considering current levels of legal and illegal immigration, grows larger by several thousand every day. The result, most experts outside Washington agree, can be only to heighten the linguistic divisions that already exist in this country and to slow further the assimilation of Hispanic immigrants. As Josue González, director of the federal Office of Bilingual Education under President Carter, put it, "Hispanics haven't gotten even close to the fireplace, let alone the melting pot."

CHAPTER ELEVEN

"Somewhere Along the Line We're Going to Have to Say No"

Concern over the immigration issue had been slow to build, but by the late 1970's, partly because of the highly publicized warning from Leonard Chapman of a "silent invasion" by 12 million Mexicans aliens and partly because of the worsening economy, it had moved very near the top of the public agenda.

A few months after taking office in January 1977, Jimmy Carter made what, considering the willingness of his predecessors to ignore the immigration perplex in hopes that it would somehow go away, had to be counted as the first bold attempt to resolve the growing dilemma. Carter, who had offered amnesty to most of the young Americans who had fled to Canada and Sweden to escape the Vietnam draft, proposed a similar amnesty for most of the millions of foreigners then living in the country illegally. The idea was no more popular than amnesty for draft evaders had been: A Gallup poll found that only 37 percent of Americans favored it. But Labor Secretary Ray Marshall calmly explained that the alternatives—closing off the Mexican border with armed troopers and ordering mass round-ups of suspected illegal aliens—were simply "not our style."

The Carter Plan, as it became known, also called for penalizing employers who hired illegal aliens and for replacing the Border Patrol with a new Border Management Agency within the Treasury Department that would enforce both the immigration and customs laws. The plan made sense. But Carter and his aides were new to Washington, where no issue is ever decided entirely on its merits, and they had failed to gauge the degree to which their proposals threatened some solidly entrenched interests. The plan met with instant opposition from within the Justice Department, which did not wish to surrender any of its enforcement functions, even those it admitted it could not adequately perform, to another Cabinet department. Partly because of determined opposition from Senator James O. Eastland, the crusty Mississippi cotton planter who was not unsympathetic to the use of illegal Mexican labor by farmers in the South and West, and partly because of a prevailing attitude in Congress typified by the congressman who wondered if "our immigration problems are soluble anyway," the Carter Plan died a quiet death somewhere deep in the recesses of the Senate Judiciary Committee.

The reluctance of Congress to confront the immigration issue squarely had been a source of exasperation for years to the few in the executive branch who had some idea of the acute need for a workable immigration policy. One was Leonel Castillo, Carter's immigration commissioner, who said that during his tenure with the INS he had "realized that Congress likes what we have now. Clearly, some people there derive great benefit from the present situation." Though Castillo did not name them, the main beneficiaries of the country's muddled and unenforceable immigration policies had been the agricultural and business interests that employ illegal aliens at low wages and that, not coincidentally, exerted disproportionate influence on important members of Congress. It was, in fact, at the behest of big business lobbyists that the Senate, in 1972 and 1973, had refused to act on legislation passed by the House of Representatives forbidding the employment of illegal aliens, calling after each refusal for "further study."

But all that was before the Cuban boatlift, before the public opinion polls, before the angry letters from out-of-work constituents began arriving by the truckload on Capitol Hill. Now there seemed to be a new mood in Congress, best expressed by Alan K. Simpson, the first-term Wyoming Republican picked to spearhead immigration reform in the Senate, who believed that the nation was suffering from what he called compassion fatigue. "At the risk of sounding nationalistic," Simpson said bluntly, "the real issue is what is best for the existing human beings who are U.S. citizens. I don't hear anybody saying wait a minute, what about those of us who are already here? Somewhere along the line we're going to have to say 'no.' "

The further study Congress so often called for was to have been provided by the blue-ribbon Select Commission on Immigration and Refugee Policy, set up after the demise of the Carter Plan to conduct for the first time a comprehensive investigation of immigration policy and practice that would clear away all the mythology and misinformation surrounding the issue and come up with some hard answers to the multitude of questions about what should be done. The panel, an impressive group, included senators, representatives, and Cabinet members; its chairman was the Reverend Theodore M. Hesburgh, the distinguished president of Notre Dame University, and its staff director was Lawrence Fuchs, a highly respected Brandeis University historian. The immigration policies ultimately laid down by the Congress and the Reagan administration, Fuchs predicted, would "shape the future character of our country" for decades to come. Nor was the select commission to be just another of the inconsequential executive study groups for which Washington is famous; it actually had been given a couple of million dollars to spend. In its statement of purpose the commission declared that it would do no less than produce "an immigration and refugee policy to serve the nation's interests in the decades ahead."

The commission took over most of a whole floor of offices in the Federal Building in downtown Washington; hired dozens of investigators, researchers, and consultants; held public hearings in a dozen cities around the country; and sifted seemingly every shred of data that bore on the immigration problem. But when the commission's work, slowed by internal disputes and external politics, was finally finished, nothing resembling a clear mandate for reform had emerged from its two-inch-thick final report.

Almost none of the commission's votes on key immigration issues was unanimous, and on some crucial matters the panel was split down the middle. So divided, in fact, were the commission's sixteen members on the basic questions confronting them that a dozen of the commissioners filed opinions dissenting from the conclusions of the final report. Some of the recommendations were relatively matter-of-fact, such as the suggestion for a marginal increase in legal immigration from the current ceiling of 270,000 a year to 350,000, with an extra half million visas to be made available over five years to help clear up the backlog in some of the visa preference categories for relatives of U.S. citizens and resident aliens. At the same time the panel recommended allocating more money for Border Patrol operations and upgrading the INS, which it said had become ''an inbred, mismanaged and, at times, corrupt agency.''

But on the increasingly crucial question of visa abusers, whose numbers were now approaching those of illegal border crossers and who appear to represent a far greater threat to the job security of Americans, the commission's only suggestion was to establish a system of computerized ''non-immigrant document control'' that would permit the INS to keep track of foreign visitors and verify their departure—a task easier said than done with or without computers. As for refugee policy, the commission agreed that the Refugee Act of 1980, which had been so thoroughly mauled by the Mariel crisis, was fundamentally sound. To deal with future seaborne invasions, the commission recommended the establishment of a new federal agency.

The two proposals that caught the public's attention, however, were borrowed from the Carter immigration plan: the commission's call for an amnesty for illegal aliens already in the country and for a new federal law prohibiting the employment of future arrivals. But both recommendations contained huge holes. By failing to endorse any sort of program under which foreign workers could legally be imported to fill jobs not wanted by American citizens, the commission ignored the reality that certain segments of the American economy, such as agriculture and the garment industry, had become almost entirely dependent on cheap foreign labor and that not to provide them with a continuing supply would mean that many of the firms in those sectors would close down or move their operations abroad or would stay in business in this country and go on acting as a magnet for illegal immigration.

The second, and most important, of the commission's oversights was its inability to agree on any system for assisting the millions of employers who were now to be subject to civil and criminal penalties for hiring illegal aliens to determine whether workers applying for jobs were in the country legally—a flaw, said the Reverend Hesburgh, that made the proposed employer sanctions law "about as meaningful as kissing your sister." Those commissioners who feared that the creation of any sort of government-issued "identity card" might pose a threat to civil liberties argued that it would be enough to require a job applicant to show an employer his birth certificate or Social Security card. Other commissioners, noting that both documents were easily counterfeited, recommended the creation of a more secure form of Social Security card that would be harder to counterfeit. Yet a third group, less devoted to the protection of individual privacy, suggested establishing some kind of central computer data bank in Washington that would contain the names of all American citizens and legal resident aliens against which job applicants could be checked.

The commission's report was published in March 1981, barely six weeks after Ronald Reagan assumed the presidency. Reagan had made an issue of immigration policy during his campaign, at one point having told a rally in Corpus Christi, Texas, that Mexican workers should be given visas that would admit them to the United States for as long as they wanted to stay. "Hispanics," Reagan said, "have a deep and abiding belief in the value of work. There is a great attachment to the great human right of property ownership . . . we both have always believed that in this land of freedom men and women could create wealth and prosperity."

Several of those present for Reagan's remarks that day, including some news reporters who recorded them on tape, were not sure of what they had heard: Was the candidate saying that the Mexican border ought simply to be opened to all comers? No one on either side of the immigration issue had ever made a suggestion quite as radical as that. The astonishment passed the next day, when Reagan insisted, tape recordings or no, that he had been misquoted, that what he had actually proposed was that a limited number of Mexican workers be allowed into the United States for a few months at a time. Still, coming from the same man who as governor of California a decade before had signed the first state law in the country making it illegal to hire illegal aliens, the statement seemed to presage Reagan's willingness to search for new answers to some old questions.

To close observers of his campaign, then, it was no surprise that among Reagan's highest priorities upon becoming President was seeking some resolution to what he had taken to calling the immigration mess. Like Congress, the Reagan White House had hoped that the select commission's report would provide clear guidelines for reform. But Reagan's disappointed aides quietly put the ambiguous document in a drawer and appointed their own presidential task force to hammer out a new set of recommendations. Unfortunately the task force had no better success at achieving a clear consensus than had the select commission; the immigration policy dilemma, the Reagan administration was quickly learning, did not lend itself to unambiguous solutions. When the task force finally submitted its recommendations, two months behind schedule, they were nearly as confused and divided as the select commission's report had been. As a result, the President's eagerly awaited proposals for immigration reform were a mélange, some of them taken from the Carter Plan, some from the select commission report, some from the task force's proposals.

After assuring the nation that he wished to "preserve our tradition of accepting foreigners to our shores, but to accept them in a controlled, orderly fashion," Reagan called for a limited amnesty that, he said, would transform between 3 and 5 million illegal aliens into legal resident aliens and, eventually, American citizens—many such people, he said, came to this country "a long time ago and literally think of themselves as belonging in this country." He also wanted an employer sanctions law, and he proposed a 20 percent increase in the INS's inadequate and inflation-ravaged budget to help the agency enforce it. In keeping with his earlier call for a "special relationship" with Canada and Mexico, Reagan proposed increasing from 20,000 to 40,000 the number of immigrant visas available each year to Canadians and Mexicans. (He also suggested that any unused Canadian visas be made available to citizens of Mexico. Since Canadians typically use only about half of their 20,000 visas, in practice the proposal would mean an annual total of some 70,000 visas for Mexico, or about three and a half times the existing limit.) Finally, the President called for a two-year pilot guest worker program, in which 50,000 Mexicans each year would be permitted to enter the United States to work at jobs that would otherwise go unfilled.

Both the proposed increase in the number of Mexican visas and the guest worker program, along with Reagan's campaign talk about a special relationship and a "North American alliance" were not-so-subtle signals that the balance of power between the United States and Mexico, traditionally tilted toward the north, was shifting in favor of Mexico. The reason, of course, was Mexico's oil—proved reserves of 72 billion barrels, possible reserves of another 163 billion barrels—nearly as much oil as Saudi Arabia, enough to power every automobile in the petroleum-hungry United States for the next forty-two years.

Mexico had a lot of oil, it was true, but it also had a lot of people—so many that at current growth rates Mexico's population could double by the middle of the next century—and half of them were either out of work or working at marginal and unproductive jobs. The United States, on the other hand, had a lot of low-level jobs that were going unfilled by American citizens, and according to Reagan's aides, the President was prepared to trade some of those jobs for oil. "He thinks," one aide said, "that the folks coming from Mexico for the most part are doing work that's necessary, that they're not replacing U.S. citizens, and that Mexico needs this kind of assistance. He's in favor of doing away with the abuses of the undocumented worker, where people don't pay their wages and these kinds of things."

It did seem somewhat incongruous that a President so firmly committed to reducing the size and cost of government in other areas and its control over the lives of its citizens was calling for measures like employer sanctions that would cost billions and could lead only to more government intrusiveness and bigger bureaucracies, but the broad reasoning behind some elements of the Reagan plan was hard to fault. Most laudable was the President's acknowledgment that most of those illegal aliens already here could not be deported without the government's resorting to the police state tactics of the Palmer Raids and Operation Wetback. The best way to remove such people from the exploited underclass, after all, was to permit them to rise to the

313

surface of society, to take advantage of the same protections against abuse that are enjoyed by any citizen.

Nor was a serious issue of equity involved. Since the vast majority of the illegals were productive members of society who worked hard and paid their share of taxes, it was not difficult to argue that they had earned the right to remain here. In explaining the amnesty proposal to the Senate Judiciary Committee, Doris Meissner, an extremely able assistant attorney general who had taken over from Dave Crosland as the latest acting INS commissioner, acknowledged that "the United States had neither the resources, the capability nor the desire to uproot and deport millions of illegal aliens, many of whom have become integral members of their communities." Displaying a degree of sensitivity not commonly found within the INS, whose officials had for years bitterly opposed the mere suggestion of amnesty as a reward for lawbreakers, Meissner insisted: "The costs to society of permitting a large group of persons to live in an illegal status are enormous. Society is harmed every time an undocumented alien is afraid to testify as a witness in a legal proceeding, to report an illness that may constitute a public health hazard or to disclose a violation of U.S. labor laws."

Reagan's appeal for the legal importation of 50,000 Mexican guest workers a year to plug the holes in those sectors of the labor market that had been abandoned by domestic workers, while much too cautious in its scope to make much of a difference in practice, could in theory only be described as enlightened. It was also immediately controversial. Among Hispanic rights groups the proposal inevitably evoked memories of the World War II era Bracero Program, now widely criticized as a form of legalized slavery. The braceros (the word is Spanish for "strong-armed ones") had been brought into the country under a temporary contract that bound them to a particular employer, who in turn was personally responsible for seeing that each of his workers returned to Mexico at the appropriate time. The system led to serious human rights abuse. In their efforts to maintain control over their workers, employers often held the braceros under armed guard during the day and locked them up at night; some took advantage of their employees' serflike status to pay them subminimum wages and work them long hours, with the understanding that any bracero who complained about his treatment would be returned to Mexico.

Reagan's guest worker plan included some measures designed to guard against the kinds of abuses the braceros endured. The guest workers would be free to change jobs during the twelve months they were in the country, they would be protected by federal minimum wage and fair labor standards laws, and they would be eligible for health care benefits and union membership. The plan had a couple of potentially serious flaws. The Mexicans would be allowed to work only at jobs for which American workers could not be found at any reasonable wage. But the necessary job certifications would be provided not by the U.S. Labor Department, which performed that function in connection with the existing H-2 program, but rather by the governors of those states that agreed to accept the guest workers, raising the possibility that the employers who ended up with approval to use the guest workers would not be those who had a genuine need for them but those who had made the largest contributions to the governor's last campaign.

There was also a question of whether employers who might legitimately be entitled to employ the guest workers would bother to seek such certifications. There was, after all, an existing imported labor program, the so-called H-2 program, under which some 30,000 foreign workers were allowed into the United States each year: Jamaicans who cut sugarcane in Florida and picked apples in Virginia, Canadians who worked as lumberjacks in Maine, and even Basques who herded sheep in Idaho. But most employers who could have obtained such workers simply found it easier to hire illegal aliens than to go through the cumbersome process of seeking a Labor Department certification, which involved such requirements as placing a series of newspaper advertisements asking for American workers. It was difficult to see why they should not do so, given the inadequacies of the proposed employer sanctions legislation.

There were other problems with the Reagan guest worker proposal, among them the undeniable fact that turning 50,000 illegal Mexican workers a year into legal guest workers would not make even a dent in the cross-border flow of illegal aliens, which was perhaps fifty times that large. It was foolish to assume that those Mexicans who were not given guest worker visas would simply stay home and equally foolish to believe that those who did get to come would leave their families in Mexico, as the proposal required. As Representative Pat Schroeder of Colorado put it, "I know if my spouse were going north I'd find a way to get up here." Yet another question was whether the guest workers would leave when their visas had expired. How could the same agency that could not keep track of 100,000 Iranian students possibly administer a new program in which it would have to keep track of 100,000 Mexican workers? The acknowledgment by INS officials that there was bound to "be some slippage" in the record-keeping system was not encouraging.

Neither was the experience of several European nations that had imported temporary workers in the recent past. In an effort to rebuild their shattered economies and to find replacements for the young men killed in World War II, France and Germany (the term "guest worker" is from the German *Gastarbeiter*) had begun in the 1950's to admit unskilled laborers from the poorer countries of Southern Europe. For several years such programs were a huge success; the postwar German "economic miracle" was accomplished largely with the assistance of workers from Italy and Spain. Most of the other Common Market countries adopted similar programs, and some 30 million European guest workers eventually found employment in neighboring countries. The only trouble was that many of them found that they liked their host countries better than their homelands, and something like 5 million workers from Greece, Italy, Spain, Turkey, and Yugoslavia, along with another 7 million of their dependents, have refused to return home, even though some of the host countries offered to pay them substantial sums of money to do so.

The most disturbing of the proposed immigration reforms was the Reagan administration's request for broad emergency powers to help it deal with any future crisis like the Mariel boatlift. The Cuban influx was over, but INS intelligence continued to pick up rumors that the Cuban government had cleared another 250,000 "undesirables" for emigration to the United States and that Fidel Castro was simply waiting for the most opportune time to reopen the port of Mariel. The new law the administration sought would have authorized the use of the American military to seal any of this country's ports or harbors and also to seize any vessel *on the high seas* believed to be bringing illegal immigrants to this country. The proposal, of highly dubious legality, would have permitted exclusion and asylum hearings for such aliens to be held on board ship, after which, said Attorney General Smith, "the examining officer would make an immediate decision to exclude the alien." In such cases the aliens would be returned to wherever they had come from without ever setting foot on American soil.

These procedures would do serious harm to the reputation of America as refuge for those yearning to breathe free, and the administration actually acknowledged that they might be "inconsistent with international law," though it promised, if the authority were granted by Congress, not to invoke them "except in the most compelling of circumstances." Then, in September 1981, without waiting for congressional approval, President Reagan ordered the use of the intercept procedure to halt the flow of Haitian refugees, who were arriving in Miami at the rate of about 1,000 a month. The Coast Guard's involvement with the Haitians until then had been limited to fishing them out of the water when their sailboats capsized and ferrying them to Miami. But following the President's order, a big Hamilton-class cutter was assigned to patrol the northwestern coast of Haiti for refugee boats. The cutter carried a Haitian naval officer and a contingent of Creole-speaking INS agents who could conduct asylum hearings for any Haitians who were intercepted.

The intercept program seemed to contravene the United Nations convention on refugees, ratified by the United States in 1978, which declared that no signatory "shall expel or return a refugee in any manner to the frontiers of territories where his life or freedom would be threatened." Noting this fact, the American Civil Liberties Union suggested that decisions on whether political asylum was warranted ought not to be made on the basis of brief interviews on Coast Guard boats on the high seas in the middle of the night, in the presence of Haitian military personnel, and without access to legal counsel. *The New York Times* went further, calling the seagoing hearings nautical kangaroo courts and adding, "What a stirring portrait of

317

American democracy they summon up for the world to see." Others pointed to the sharp criticism leveled at the Soviet Union by the United States for the USSR's failure as far as emigration of Soviet Jews was concerned to live up to the provision of the Helsinki Accords, which declared that "everyone has a right to leave any country, including his own."

As is so often the case, however, the best protection against bad policy proved to be the difficulty of implementing it. By December 1981, four months after the patrols began, the Coast Guard had intercepted only one thirty-foot boat with fifty-seven Haitians aboard. The INS was talking about a "tremendous drop-off" in the number of refugees leaving Haiti because of the "deterrent effect" of the patrols, but when Gérard Jean-Juste, the unofficial mayor of Little Haiti, heard that, he just laughed. "They're still coming," he said. "They're just not caught. They drift in, and I meet them every day myself."

Not long after these reform proposals were announced by the President, the White House sent them to Congress. But many members of Congress found themselves troubled by some aspects of the Reagan plan, particularly the guest worker program and the absence of any provision for a worker identity card to assist in enforcing employer sanctions. After months of hearings Congress countered with a reform package of its own—Senate Bill 2222 and its counterpart, House Bill 6514, the Immigration Reform and Control Act of 1982, whose primary sponsors were Senator Alan Simpson of Wyoming and Representative Romano Mazzoli of Kentucky, the respective chairmen of the Senate and House immigration subcommittees. "If there is one significant thing that we send throughout the world through the aegis of this legislation," Senator Simpson declared with a grand flourish on the day the bill was introduced, "it would be that the United States is determined to control legal and illegal immigration. We have to live within limits. The nation wants to be compassionate but we have been compassionate beyond our ability to respond."

At first glance, a freshman senator from Wyoming and a Roman Catholic congressman from the South, both of them relative unknowns, might have seemed unlikely choices for the difficult task of shepherding the complicated and controversial immigration reform bill through Congress. But Ron Mazzoli, a twelve-year veteran of the House, was greatly admired by his colleagues, respected as much for his ability to grasp and translate into legislation highly technical subjects as for his personal probity and high ethical standards.

As for Alan Simpson, the tall, balding senator, known for his strong streak of Western-style individualism, was nothing if not determined—he had taken the time to brief personally every interested senator on the details of his bill—and immigration was an issue about which he had been concerned ever since, as a teenager in Cody, Wyoming, he had grown up next to a wartime internment camp for Japanese-Americans. Wyoming, Simpson was quick to tell reporters, had a surprisingly large Hispanic population, and among his clients during his days as a small-town lawyer had been more than a few illegal Mexican aliens who had come to Wyoming in search of work in the sugar beet fields and had run afoul of predatory merchants or the immigration authorities. More than most senators, Simpson knew from experience about the shortcomings of the immigration process.

The Simpson-Mazzoli bill, which differed from the Reagan immigration proposals in several crucial respects, was truly a landmark event, the first real attempt by Congress to overhaul the immigration system since it passed the McCarran-Walter Act in 1952. Getting his bill through both the Senate and the House in the few remaining months of the Ninety-seventh Congress, Simpson conceded, was "going to be a tough, hard road." But he had hopes of succeeding, the senator said, "because the alternative is to do nothing."

Unlike the President's proposals, the Simpson-Mazzoli bill included no provision for a guest worker program of any size, substituting instead an "expanded" and "streamlined" version of the existing H-2 program that theoretically would make it easier for employers to import temporary agricultural and other workers from Mexico. The bill also eliminated the President's request for emergency powers to deal with a future Mariel crisis. It included an employer sanctions statute that differed from the Reagan proposals in one important way—it would not apply to any illegal alien employed before the bill was enacted—and it also called upon the administration to produce, within three years of the bill's passage, some form of "secure'' worker identification card to assist employers in determining who was in the country illegally and who was not. Moreover, the penalties for violating the employer sanctions law would be more severe: A first offense would bring a fine of $1,000 for each alien employed, a second offense, a fine of $2,000, and those employers who persisted in hiring illegal aliens would also be liable for six months in jail.

In keeping with Senator Simpson's ''carrot-and-stick'' approach to immigration policy, the Simpson-Mazzoli bill also proposed a more generous amnesty for those already here. Instead of requiring every alien living in the United States before 1980 to wait an interminable ten years before obtaining permanent resident status, the Simpson-Mazzoli bill would enable those who had lived in the country continuously since January 1, 1978, to apply immediately for permanent residence. (Aliens who had arrived in 1978 or 1979 would have to wait two years to apply; those who had arrived after 1979 would be eligible for nothing and, if apprehended, could be deported summarily.) During the waiting periods the aliens would pay taxes but would not be eligible to collect public welfare services funded by those taxes, such as food stamps or unemployment benefits; nor could they bring their families into the country, although they would be able to leave the United States to visit relatives abroad.

The Simpson-Mazzoli proposals were for the most part well received. *The New York Times*, plucking a phrase from Senator Simpson's introductory remarks, declared in an editorial that the bill was ''Not nativist, not racist, not mean,'' that it was, in fact, ''a rare piece of legislation: a responsible immigration bill'' that was at once ''tough, fair and humane.'' But after something of a splashy start in March, the progress of the immigration reform bill through Congress seemed to hit a snag. By late July 1982 the bill had cleared both the Senate Judiciary Committee and Ron Mazzoli's immigration subcommittee in the House, but not the full House Judiciary Committee, whose chairman, Peter W. Rodino, said his panel would not even consider the bill unless it first passed the full Senate, something that was beginning to seem less and less likely as opposition to one or another of the bill's proposals began to develop among various interest groups.

One of the most powerful of these, the AFL-CIO, which considered illegal alien workers to be a threat to the job security of its members, was all in favor of an employer sanctions law. But the U.S. Chamber of Commerce, many of whose members were among the most enthusiastic employers of those same illegal workers, was devoutly opposed to such a law—a "selfish perception of employers' short-term, purely economic interest," Senator Simpson called it. Equally opposed were most Hispanic rights groups, which feared that the law would give employers a basis for further discrimination against Hispanic Americans, that employers might refuse to hire anyone who even looked Hispanic. Civil libertarians worried that the new procedures for seeking political asylum might deny some political refugees the due process to which they were entitled. Organized labor and Hispanic Americans both were opposed to the idea of an amnesty, because of either the principle involved or the cost of implementing such a program.

But with unemployment now topping 10 percent, the highest level since the Great Depression, the public pressure for some kind of immigration reform was increasing, and it was coming from some unexpected quarters. An open letter to Congress, demanding that it "not let the number of immigrants grow so large as to threaten the jobs of poor Americans," included some surprising signatories, among them Edward Asner, the ultraliberal president of the Screen Actors Guild; Sam Ervin, the former chairman of the Senate Watergate Committee; B. F. Skinner, the Harvard psychologist; Stewart Udall, the secretary of the interior under President Kennedy; and Barbara Jordan, the black former congresswoman from Houston.

Despite signs that the increasingly heated debate and the impending election might require work on the immigration reform bill to be put off until the next Congress, shortly after ten o'clock on the morning of August 11, 1982, Howard Baker, the Senate majority leader, put before the Senate the Simpson-Mazzoli bill, the text of which occupied nearly eleven pages of tiny type in that day's *Congressional Record*. When Senator Simpson opened the debate the next morning, he began by asserting that the country's existing immigration policy was "hopelessly inadequate to deal with modern conditions, including the growing immigration pressure yet to come in this country.''

As Simpson spoke, he displayed an unmistakable sense of conviction that what he was doing was of vital importance. ''Immigration to the United States,'' he told his colleagues, ''is out of control, and it is so perceived at all levels of government by the American people—indeed, by people all over the world. I deeply feel that uncontrolled immigration is one of the greatest threats to the future of this Nation, to American values, traditions, institutions, to our public culture, and to our way of life.'' The number of legal immigrants, Simpson went on, had increased from 450,000 in 1976 to nearly 800,000 in 1980. On top of that, an estimated 500,000 illegal immigrants were now entering the United States every year. Taken together, the two now accounted for half the country's annual population increase. If something were not done to reduce the flow, Simpson said, the population of the United States would reach 30 million within a century.

The immigration issue, Simpson conceded, was ''a very, very, tough one,'' a subject that evoked in many ''feelings and accusations of guilt, emotionalism, and racism.'' But he insisted, nonetheless, ''Now is the time to act. Every poll taken in the Nation shows that over 90 percent of the American people believe our immigration laws and policies are out of control and must be reformed. Pressures to migrate are increasing worldwide and some of the greatest pressure is on this country. As long as people around the world know that once they arrive in the U.S. illegally they will be able to obtain jobs, they will obviously continue to come in increasing numbers.''

His bill, Simpson said, was ''not an end-all, all-seeing piece of legislation. But it is the first step toward doing two things: the first and most important duty of a sovereign nation is to get control over its borders, and we [must] start. The second message sent throughout the entire world will be, 'Hey, to work in the United States of America, you have to have some kind of documentation,' which every other developed country on Earth has.'' Immigration reform, he warned, was critical for the future of American society. If, he said, the new immigrants ''do not follow the historical patterns of earlier immigrant groups in becoming full participants in American society . . . then they have the potential to create here a measure of the same social, political and economic anguish which exist in the countries from which they have voluntarily chosen to depart. This," he said, "is reality."

As Simpson took his seat, several other senators rose to offer their views on immigration reform, among them Ted Kennedy, the ranking Democratic member of the Senate's immigration subcommittee. Kennedy agreed that immigration reform was a most important subject—"I can't think of another issue," he said, "that affects so many people's lives so directly"—but he objected to the reform bill's hard-line approach. "What started out to be immigration reform," he said, "has become, in too many provisions, immigration restriction," and he was especially concerned "that this bill must not become a vehicle for discriminatory action against Hispanic Americans and other minority groups."

Earlier, in the immigration subcommittee, the Massachusetts Democrat had attempted unsuccessfully to water down some provisions of the Simpson-Mazzoli bill. Then SIN, the national Spanish-language television network, had broadcast an editorial blasting the proposed legislation as "the most blatantly anti-Hispanic bill ever" and urging its viewers to "show the racial bigots in Washington that when pushed too far, Hispanics will react and defend their rights." The editorial described Kennedy as "an old friend of the Hispanic community who is being pressured into turning his back on our people" and asked Hispanics to tell the senator "to stand up for our civil rights and our dignity." The response was impressive: More than 8,000 letters and mailgrams from outraged Hispanics were delivered to Kennedy's Capitol Hill office in less than a week, and his telephones were constantly jammed by those who preferred to express their outrage more directly.

On the Senate floor, Kennedy again offered several amendments that would have deleted those provisions of the Simpson-Mazzoli bill that were of most concern to Hispanic Americans. One would have made it easier for American citizens and legal resident aliens to be reunited with relatives from Mexico and elsewhere abroad. Another would have done away with the proposed expansion of the H-2 temporary worker program, which many Hispanics feared would only intensify competition for their jobs. The third and most important—a so-called sunset provision—would have eliminated employer sanctions after only three years unless the President could certify to Congress that they had not resulted in ethnic discrimination against American citizens.

The whole question of sanctions, in fact, was of concern to Kennedy. "How in the world," he asked his colleagues, "do we think we will ever be able to enforce employer sanctions when we cannot enforce existing laws?" Similar concerns were voiced by other senators, one of them Alan Cranston of California, the respected minority whip. There was much, Cranston began, that was right about the Simpson-Mazzoli bill. By increasing the immigration quotas for Canada and Mexico, it finally recognized the special relationship that had always existed between those countries and the United States. Moreover, he said, the bill's amnesty provisions recognized "the existence of a valued population of undocumented workers who have contributed substantially to our national productivity, to our culture, and who have become welcome members of many communities."

But Cranston, like Kennedy, found the employer sanctions provisions, which in effect would require all American citizens to establish their legal right to work when applying for a job, "offensive and repugnant to the concept of individual dignity and liberty. What more is there," he asked, "that a 'Big Brother' government can do to obtain control over every citizen and resident of the United States?" But concerns for humanitarianism and civil liberties were clearly running counter to the strong reformist sentiments in the Senate. All of Kennedy's amendments were defeated.

Far more controversial than employer sanctions was the "legalization" proposal in the Simpson-Mazzoli bill, which amounted to a general amnesty for most of the illegal aliens already living in the United States. Simpson had defended the amnesty provision earlier by pointing out that there was no practical way to find and deport the millions of illegal residents. "If they could not be located when they were coming in," he asked the Senate, "how can we find them to get them out?" But Jesse Helms of North Carolina, the congressional standard-bearer for the Moral Majority, was offended by the very notion of an amnesty. "It is wrong to reward lawbreakers," he said, "to set in motion a program which will encourage further law-breaking and which will polarize our society. Citizenship in our great Republic is too precious to grant in a vast blanket program to millions of foreign nationals who have flagrantly violated our laws."

Helms offered an amendment that would have done away with the amnesty altogether. The Helms amendment was defeated handily, 82–17, but there was more support for tightening the conditions under which amnesty could be made available. Senator Charles E. Grassley, a slow-talking Iowa farmer who had been in the Senate less than two years, saw the wisdom of a general amnesty clearly enough. "I suppose," Grassley said, "if any of us stood up and said that all these people should be rounded up and shipped home, there would be much agreement with our position. But when you look at the practical aspect, it just is not an answer. We do not have the resources to put forth." Grassley nevertheless felt that as drafted, the bill made amnesty available to too many aliens, and he introduced an amendment to make permanent resident status available only to those illegal aliens who had entered the United States before January 1, 1977, rather than the cutoff date of January 1, 1978, contained in the original bill. Those aliens who had entered the country between 1977 and 1979 would be given temporary resident status and would be eligible for permanent residence after three years; those who had arrived after January 1980 would be deportable, as always. Though they would still be required to pay taxes, temporary residents would be ineligible for all federal assistance programs, and permanent residents would be ineligible for the first three years of residency. The Grassley amendment passed as easily as the Helms amendment had been defeated, 84–16.

Next up was Walter D. Huddleston of Kentucky, a Democrat who, with Simpson and Grassley, was one of the reform bill's primary sponsors. Huddleston offered an amendment that would include all refugees and people seeking political asylum within the 425,000 annual limit for total legal immigration proposed by the Simpson-Mazzoli bill. Never again, if the amendment were adopted, would the White House be able to make room on the spur of the moment for another Mariel type of refugee invasion, as the provisions of the 1980 Refugee Act had allowed Jimmy Carter to do. The amendment would also have tied the President's hands in admitting far more deserving refugees, like Vietnamese boat people or Hungarian freedom fighters, but Huddleston still thought that the existing power of the President to let in an undetermined number of refugees over and above the limit for legal immigration was "a glaring flaw" in U.S. immigration policy.

"Refugees," he told the Senate, "must also be recognized as the immigrants that they are. By failing to establish an all-inclusive ceiling, we are admitting that a substantial portion of our refugee policy will not be based on a rational and logical determination of what is in the best interest of our Nation. Instead, we will continue to permit special interest groups, outside pressures, the political process itself, to dictate our immigration policy." But despite Huddleston's arguments, the prevailing mood seemed to be that any such restriction would seriously diminish the historical role of the United States as a last refuge for the oppressed, and Huddleston's amendment was defeated, 63–35.

When debate resumed on Friday, August 13, however, the prevailing mood had shifted. Employer sanctions and amnesty, the most controversial provisions, had survived intact. Now some of the more liberal senators were expressing concern over the ways in which the new law they were attempting to fashion would be enforced by the INS. One of those most worried was William Armstrong of Colorado, a first-term Republican and former radio announcer. Armstrong told the Senate that he was troubled by reports of abuses that had accompanied the INS's recently completed Project Jobs, the nine-city roundup of illegal alien workers carried out in a way that "suggested a publicity stunt" on the part of the immigration agency.

"I note with dismay," Armstrong said, "that two U.S. citizens were, in fact, included in this roundup and were detained for several hours under circumstances which do not suggest the most scrupulous regard for their constitutional rights," and he offered an amendment expressing the sense of Congress that the immigration laws "should be enforced vigorously and uniformly" but also "with due caution toward safeguarding the constitutional rights and human dignity of citizens and aliens alike." Armstrong's amendment gained some unexpected support when Senator Peter Domenici of New Mexico, not widely regarded as a member of the Senate's liberal wing, rose to speak. Both his parents, Domenici began, were Italian immigrants, and his mother had been "an illegal alien for a long time and did not even know that she was." When he was a young boy, Domenici said, some INS agents "visited my home, and the experience was one of the most frightening memories of my childhood. I think sometimes the Immigration officials act as if they are hysterical."

Perhaps because of Domenici's dramatic speech, the Armstrong amendment was agreed to, and now, with passage of the Simpson-Mazzoli bill all but assured, a few senators began trying to tack onto the bill some not particularly germane amendments that concerned their personal *bêtes noires*. First up was S. I. Hayakawa, the eccentric Japanese-American semanticist who was Cranston's fellow senator from California and who, during the Iranian hostage crisis, had actually suggested rounding up and interning all Iranians living in the United States "the way we did the Japanese in World War Two." Given his curmudgeonly spirit, it came as no surprise when Hayakawa, a language purist and himself a naturalized American citizen, introduced a resolution declaring English to be "the official language of the United States."

The former university professor lectured his colleagues. "Language is the unifying instrument which binds people together. When people speak one language they become as one, they become a society." To support his argument he quoted the Book of Genesis: "They are one people, and they all have the same language . . . and nothing which they propose to do will be impossible for them." Hayakawa pointed to Belgium, where "half the population speaks French and the other half speaks Flemish. Those who speak Flemish do not like the people who speak French and those who speak French do not want to speak Flemish." He even made an example of Congress itself, a body in which, he said, "we have the descendents [sic] of speakers of at least 250 to 300 languages but we meet as speakers of one language. We may disagree when we argue, but at least we understand each other when we argue." Hayakawa's resolution, a "sense of the Senate motion" that did not have the force of law, was agreed to, 78–21. Not to be outdone, Jesse Helms introduced yet another amendment, inspired by the Supreme Court's recent decision in the Texas school case, giving states the right not to provide free public schooling and other benefits to illegal aliens. The Helms amendment failed, as did one by John Tower of Texas, to provide $68 million to school districts with large numbers of illegal alien students.

When the final vote came on the Simpson-Mazzoli bill on the morning of Tuesday, August 17, the Senate approved it overwhelmingly, 80–19. The eight Democrats and eleven Republicans who voted against the bill included those on the far right, like Helms, who opposed the amnesty program; those from the left, like Kennedy, who were equally offended by the employer sanctions provisions; and Senators Hayakawa, Domenici, and Harrison Schmitt, the former astronaut and Domenici's Republican colleague from New Mexico, whose farmer constituents had wanted a broad-based guest worker program.

In a stroke, the Senate had approved the most sweeping changes in the nation's immigration laws in three decades. After the dust stirred up by the surprisingly impassioned four-day debate had settled, it was clear that the final version was not so unlike the original bill introduced by Senator Simpson the week before. In addition to the original employer sanctions provisions, the Senate had included the requirement that the President come up with some kind of system—whether a universal identity card, a nationwide computer bank, or just what was not specified—that would enable employers to tell whether or not job applicants were legal U.S. residents. It retained the new, tougher limitations on the reunification of families and the expanded version of the H-2 temporary worker program. Despite the stricter time limitations set by the Grassley amendment, the bill still provided amnesty for the great majority of the illegal aliens living in the United States. It had made political asylum harder to come by, but it had also refused to reduce the existing annual limit of 425,000 legal immigrants or to include unanticipated refugees within that ceiling.

No one was happier than Roger Conner, the executive director of FAIR, the Federation for American Immigration Reform, which of all the special interest groups had lobbied hardest for passage. The bill did not contain everything FAIR had wanted, but Conner treated his staff to champagne anyway. Indeed, the bill's passage was something of a historic moment. So often before it had been the Senate, with its strong ties to the powerful special interests of business, labor, and agriculture, that had proved the insurmountable obstacle to immigration reform. The battle in the Senate had been won, but the war was only half fought. The Simpson-Mazzoli bill still had to pass the House of Representatives, and the November election, in which most of the 435 House members would have to stand for reelection, was drawing perilously close. If the immigration bill failed to clear both houses of the Ninety-seventh Congress, it would die on the spot, and there was no assurance that the sentiment for reform would be anywhere near as compelling after the Ninety-eighth Congress, whose political makeup was of course still unknown, was sworn in the following January.

But it began to look as though the House was going to try for passage at the last minute. True to his word, Peter Rodino, the chairman of the House Judiciary Committee, took up the immigration reform bill within days of the vote in the Senate. After four days of contentious debate, and only after several motions that would have effectively killed it were narrowly defeated, on September 22 the Judiciary Committee approved the bill and sent it to the floor of the House. There were a few minor differences between the version of the bill passed by the Senate and the one approved by the House committee, but nothing that could not easily be worked out in a House-Senate conference, and Rodino urged the full House to act on the legislation as soon as possible.

President Reagan had asked the Congress to meet in a special session following the November elections to take up a number of pressing financial matters—more than nineteen crucial appropriations bills were still pending and more than a few government programs and agencies were in danger of running out of money by the end of the year. Shortly before Congress reconvened, however, the U.S. Embassy in Mexico City sent an unusual dispatch to the State Department in Washington, the gist of which was promptly reported by Robert Pear of *The New York Times*.

The Mexican government had been officially silent on the subject of the Simpson-Mazzoli bill, but the seventeen-page dispatch, signed by John Gavin, the American ambassador, noted that many Mexican officials had privately expressed great concern about the effect the bill would have on U.S.-Mexico relations were it to pass. At least a couple of million Mexicans found ineligible for amnesty, maybe more, would be forced to return home at a time when the shaky Mexican economy could least absorb them.

The consequences for Mexico, the embassy suggested ominously, might include "political unrest"—a most fearful spectre for the U.S. government, which lived in dread of the possibility that the political convulsions that had ripped apart El Salvador and Guatemala and now threatened Honduras might spread northward to the U.S.-Mexico border. True, the Simpson-Mazzoli bill also called for enhanced enforcement of the immigration laws, particularly along that vital border, but the embassy warned that "effective enforcement of this measure is seen [here] to require authoritarian measures amounting to a militarization of the border zone." Moreover, the embassy reported, many Mexican leaders disliked the amnesty plan on the grounds that those Mexicans who qualified for amnesty would be required to pay taxes but would be ineligible for most forms of public assistance, a kind of "second-class citizenship" they found offensive.

When the House began its special session in late November, it found more pressing matters awaiting its attention, among them a basing plan for the controversial MX missile and the President's proposal to increase the federal gasoline tax by five cents a gallon. But the substantial Democratic gains in the November elections were being interpreted by Democrats and Republicans alike as an expression of anger and frustration in a country where unemployment was now verging on 11 percent, and some congressmen were now talking about passing the Simpson-Mazzoli bill *without* the amnesty provision and calling it a *jobs* bill.

By retaining employer sanctions and getting rid of amnesty, such a measure would presumably make available to unemployed Americans hundreds of thousands, maybe millions, of jobs now held by illegal aliens. Never mind the plethora of surveys and studies showing that most of the 5,400 jobs "opened up" by the INS during Project Jobs had ultimately been filled again by illegal aliens, the American workers who took them initially quitting in disgust after a few weeks or even days.

A few days before, *The Wall Street Journal* reported that most of the citizen workers who had "benefitted" from Project Jobs by replacing illegal alien workers had found the jobs "dead-end, demeaning or underpaying." One, Fred Luttjohann, a thirty-five-year-old California carpenter who had been unemployed for several months before the raids, told the *Journal's* Merle Linda Wolin that he had left his $3.50-an-hour job at Santa Ana's B. P. John Furniture Co., one of the factories raided by the INS, after only two and a half weeks because the work—putting drawers in cabinets as they moved along an assembly line—was simply too exhausting. "I told the foreman, 'I can't do this anymore,' " Luttjohann said. " 'My arms are tired, my back is tired. For what you're paying me, and for what I'm doing, I just can't do it.' " He added, "I wouldn't think Americans would want to do the work. I wouldn't recommend it for anybody, that's for sure. It's too much work for one person."

Nonetheless, with so many millions of Americans out of work the idea of transforming the immigration reform bill into an employment bill was politically difficult to resist, and on Saturday, December 18, the Simpson-Mazzoli bill finally reached the floor of the House. But congressional critics of the bill, knowing that the special session was soon to expire and that time was on their side, set out to kill the bill on the floor by amending it to death.

Some of the amendments were little more than delaying tactics, but others reflected a genuine concern in the House over the potential for discrimination against Hispanic Americans contained in the employer sanctions provision. "Anyone who looks like me," said Kika de la Garza, the longtime Texas congressman whose family has resided in the southwestern United States for 250 years, "is going to have to identify himself every time he asks for a job. People have trouble pronouncing my name in the realms of Capitol Hill. Can you imagine what happens if I show up looking for a job in Alabama or west Texas or Kentucky, maybe?"

As the floor debate wore on, more than 300 separate amendments were offered to the Simpson-Mazzoli bill, far too many to dispose of in time to adjourn for Christmas. "We could beat any of those amendments," sighed a weary Ron Mazzoli, "but I don't know if we could beat them all."

Mazzoli couldn't, and late Sunday afternoon he threw in the towel. Whether the publicity given the embassy's dispatch had had a significant effect on the House was never clear. But the bill had, after all, come out of the Senate very late in the year, and to debate and decide such a thorny issue in the space of a few hours had seemed to many members, whatever their political orientation, ill-advised. As one congressional aide said later, "No one wanted to be the person who stopped it, but no one really wanted to see it pass."

And so it was over. After the Iranian student debacle, after the spectacle of Mariel, after the tragedy of the Haitians; after all the commissions and hearings and investigations and reports and proposals and debates; after the thousands of hours of agonizing effort that had gone into fashioning the Simpson-Mazzoli bill and shepherding it through a seemingly endless succession of committees and subcommittees; after the impassioned debate on the Senate floor and the frantic lobbying by dozens of special interest groups, there would be no immigration reform in 1982, and maybe never. The moment, it seemed, had been allowed to slip away.

When the Simpson-Mazzoli bill was reintroduced early in 1983, neither the bill's sponsors nor the new Congress displayed much enthusiasm. Some congressmen pointed out that every conceivable argument against and defense of the bill had already been raised, and it was unclear to them how simply restaging the wrenching debate would lead to the bill's passage.

In the end it was just as well. As with price controls, gasoline rationing, and other public policy concepts that work better on paper than in practice, the immigration reform proposals were bound to prove unworkable. Nearly every aspect of the Simpson-Mazzoli bill, it seemed, called for more of the very things— more regulation, more laws, more enforcement, more bureaucracy, more computers, more hardware, and more money— that, as should have been clear by now to the White House and Congress, were incapable of significantly reducing illegal immigration. Implementing the reform proposals would have cost an enormous amount of money, more than $2 billion a year according to an estimate by the Congressional Budget Office, most of it to finance the amnesty program and the enforcement of employer sanctions. But it is doubtful that any amount of money could have made the reforms effective. If the unhappy experience of the INS had any lesson to offer, it was that in a fundamentally free society, it is impossible to keep precise track of the comings and goings of individual human beings, of where they live and where they work and how long they have been here, and it is on such precise knowledge that the effective control of immigration depends. The KGB, the intelligence service that also functions as the Soviet Union's immigration agency, knows with great precision who visits the country, where they are while they are there, and when they leave. But who wants an American KGB?

The problem with the amnesty plan lay not in its general conception, which was certainly humanitarian, but in its implementation. As Congress had outlined the idea, the plan would create three classes of illegal aliens: those who had entered the country before January 1, 1977, those who had arrived between then and January 1, 1980, and those who had come after that. The INS estimated (but who really knew?) that some 60 percent of the 3 million to 6 million illegal aliens it said were living in the country would be eligible for either temporary or permanent residence under the amnesty program—somewhere between 1 million and 3.5 million people altogether. But that meant that there were also several million illegal aliens who were not eligible for amnesty, and sorting the eligibles out from the ineligibles would have presented the fragile immigration bureaucracy—or, indeed, any bureaucracy—with an insurmountable problem.

No matter how many aliens the INS believed were eligible (and the true number might as easily be twice its upper limit of 3.5 million), it was not at all certain that they would be the only ones to apply. Why, after all, should those who had *not* lived here continuously since the dates in question or who had arrived here *after* the beginning of 1980 not try their luck? Somehow they might slip through the bureaucratic net. How could the immigration bureaucracy, which was already running two years behind in adjudicating naturalization petitions, was nearly paralyzed by a mere 130,000 asylum petitions from Cubans and Haitians, and could not find the majority of the erst-while Iranian students, be expected to handle the painstaking and laborious job of determining which aliens fitted into which categories? Suppose the offer of an amnesty brought something like 5 million applications that had to be adjudicated; if the INS hired 10,000 claims examiners and each examiner decided ten claims a day, the job would take nearly fourteen years. Even John Kratzke, a government management expert who was try-ing to drag the INS into the computer age, admitted that am-nesty was a disaster waiting to happen. If the INS were pre-sented with millions of amnesty claims, said Kratzke, "We might as well just close the service right now."

And this was assuming that amnesty was something most of the eligible aliens wanted. Another possibility, as one worried Justice Department official put it, was: "What if we gave a party and nobody came?" Other countries—among them Canada (for American draft evaders) and Great Britain (for Pakistanis and other Commonwealth citizens who had overstayed their visas)—had offered amnesty to illegal residents in recent years, and none of the programs had been very successful; in Britain, astonishingly, fewer than 2,000 illegal residents had come for-ward to accept the amnesty. Under the rather harsh terms of the Simpson-Mazzoli amnesty—the five- to eight-year waiting period for citizenship, the ineligibility for public services, the lack of any provision for family reunification—millions of illegal aliens might decide that given the slim chance of being caught, they were not much worse off as things stood now. And why present a claim for amnesty when if, for some unforeseen rea-son, it were denied, the result would be a deportation hearing?

Perhaps the most serious shortcoming of the amnesty pro-posal was the method by which aliens would be required to es-tablish that they had lived in this country continuously since one of the two cutoff dates, an extraordinarily difficult thing to prove in a society that prizes freedom of movement. According to the Reagan administration, virtually any document attesting to an individual's presence in the United States during the peri-ods in question would suffice: a bankbook showing an unbro-ken string of deposits, for example, rent or tax receipts, birth records of children born in the United States, employment rec-ords, utility receipts showing dates of service, affidavits from "credible witnesses" attesting to the continued presence of a friend or neighbor, even postmarked mail addressed to the individual in question. But many of those documents would be easy to fabricate. When the FBI arrested Oscar the forger, the man who specialized in turning Mexicans into instant Americans, they found most of the "documents" waiting to be filled in, lying in the trunk of his car.

There have been federal laws controlling immigration for more than a century, but never a federal statute prohibiting the employment of illegal aliens—something many policymakers have long considered a serious oversight in view of the fact that most illegal immigrants come here seeking employment. In its efforts to rectify that oversight, the Simpson-Mazzoli bill would have subjected any employer who had more than four workers on his payroll and had *knowingly* hired an illegal alien to civil fines ranging from $500 to $2,000 for each alien hired. There were several things wrong with the concept, among them one that citizens who could not convince an employer of their citizenship would have nowhere to go to appeal their case. But the real question was the extent to which such a law could possibly be enforced. The beleaguered INS, which in addition to administering the amnesty program would have had that responsibility, could barely scrape together 400 agents during its highly advertised and largely unsuccessful Project Jobs, and during the course of an entire week those agents managed to raid only 250 businesses and arrest 5,440 workers, about the same as in an average week of area control operations.

But there are millions of individual businesses in this country that employ illegal aliens, and even if the investigative manpower of the INS had been increased by ten times, the odds against any one of those businesses' ever being raided would have still been minuscule. "Do we really believe," *The Wall Street Journal* asked in a particularly enlightened editorial, "that the I.N.S. is going to barge in on every Chinese restaurant or Texas garage or San Diego building contractor or Chicago apartment with a maid?" The INS would have been far more likely to concentrate its meager resources on raiding a few large businesses, and for such employers the fines levied under the law would not have been much of a deterrent, considering the money they would be saving by paying their undocumented workers substantially lower salaries. Even small employers might not have been dissuaded by the few thousand dollars in fines that would result from what, for them, would be a once-in-a-lifetime raid.

The whole notion of employer sanctions, moreover, was cast in doubt by the experience of several foreign countries that already have such laws, among them Canada, France, Switzerland, and West Germany. According to a Senate study that for some reason was not made public until after the Simpson-Mazzoli bill had been passed, employers in most of the twenty countries surveyed, "either were able to evade responsibility for illegal employment or, once apprehended, were penalized too little to deter such acts." Moreover, the study found that "the laws generally were not being effectively enforced because of strict legal constraints on investigations, noncommunication between government agencies, lack of enforcement resolve, and lack of personnel."

The Justice Department readily admitted that like immigration agencies elsewhere in the world, the INS did not have anything like the resources needed to enforce effectively an employer sanctions law. But the department said it hoped that most employers would comply with such a law anyway. The Reagan administration, maintained Alan C. Nelson, a former executive of Pacific Telephone who in 1981 became the first permanent commissioner of immigration since the resignation of Leonel Castillo, believed that "many employers presently hire illegal aliens because they are aware that there is no law that makes this practice illegal. With the passage of an employer sanctions law, we are confident that most employers will uphold the law."

Whether or not most employers were prepared to put their respect for the law above their economic self-interest, there remained the question of how an employer was expected to know if a person applying for a job was living in the country with or without permission. It would have been up to the employer to decide whether or not a prospective employee's documents were genuine. But the reason that state laws forbidding the employment of illegal aliens have rarely been enforced is that all an employer has to do to excuse himself is to maintain that he had no way of knowing for sure that his employee was an illegal alien—that the employee's documents *looked* genuine to him. Several countries issue some form of national identity card that can be used to establish work eligibility—in France citizens and legal resident aliens carry the *carte d'identité nationale,* Germans the *Personalausweis.* But under the Simpson-Mazzoli plan, a U.S. passport alone would have been considered proof of employability. If the prospective employee had no passport, he would have to produce either a Social Security card or a birth certificate as well as a driver's license or other state-issued identity card—no difficult task with people like Newton Van Drunen around.

Van Drunen, a fifty-four-year-old alien smuggler and master forger, recently told the Senate permanent investigations subcommittee how he had obtained Social Security cards for countless Mexican illegals in the Chicago area, first by simply filling out the application forms on their behalf, later by printing up his own phony cards. "I began producing my own Texas birth records, Selective Service cards, and Social Security cards," he said. "All of the Mexicans I sold to, through a network of vendors, knew the documents and the Social Security numbers were phony. I was selling identification packets consisting of the Social Security card, Texas birth certificate, baptismal certificate, and the Selective Service card for $75 per package. On a scale of one to 10, the Social Security card is a 'one.' It's just extremely simple to reproduce. As far as I was concerned, phony Social Security numbers were undetectable by employers."

The President's immigration task force had suggested that to solve the documentation problem, all working Americans be issued a new, "counterfeit-resistant" Social Security card containing not only the individual's name and Social Security number but his or her photograph and, possibly, a fingerprint or thumbprint. But that proposal was abandoned after administration cost cutters estimated that it would cost more than $2 billion, and it was still far from certain that the cards could have foiled the master counterfeiters of Tijuana and Juárez. The same day the Reagan plan was announced, said a senior Border Patrol agent in Laredo, "we arrested a guy coming across the bridge with nine hundred phony Social Security cards. In Chula Vista it's driver's licenses. They're all geared up for it."

337

* * *

In putting together its proposals for immigration reform, Congress seemed not to have thought much about how any of them would work in practice, perhaps because the appearance of having acted to halt illegal immigration was more important than whether or not the measures adopted could ever be enforced. Still, it was more than ironic that the one area in which the government might easily have made a significant difference in the flow of illegal aliens and in their impact on the American economy was ignored by the reform bill altogether.

By most estimates, somewhere between 250,000 and 500,000 foreigners—perhaps as many as the number of illegal border crossers—enter the United States every year with valid tourist or student visas and then take up illegal residence here when their visas expire. Even more important than their numbers, however, is the fact that the visa abusers are, for the most part, different from the illegal border crossers, who tend to be poor and badly educated, many of them illiterate and not able to speak English. The visa abusers come mostly from the middle or even the upper middle classes of their native societies. Rather than walk across the border in the middle of the night, they have the wherewithal to buy a round-trip airplane ticket and to convince an American consul somewhere in the world that they are coming to the United States for a vacation or to study. Most of the visa abusers, particularly those who come here as students, are reasonably well educated and speak passable English, so it is not surprising that when they set out to look for work, the jobs they take are likely to be those that require English or other skills and that, not coincidentally, also pay better—in short, jobs that many out-of-work Americans would be glad to have. For the same reasons, it is also much easier for them to blend into the background once they are here.

If illegal aliens are displacing American workers to any significant degree, it is far more likely to be the visa abusers than the menial workers who cross the border to take bottom-end jobs. But it somehow never occurred to any of those involved in reforming the immigration laws to try to limit the increasing incidence of visa abuse by improving the haphazard screening process to which most visa applicants are currently subjected by understaffed and overworked American embassies and consulates abroad. How much easier it would be to exert control over those intending immigrants who arrive in an orderly fashion at airports with their passports in hand than over the nameless, faceless ones who slip across thousands of miles of rugged border in the middle of the night. But the Simpson-Mazzoli bill missed that chance. Incredibly, when it addressed the subject of visa abusers at all, what it did do was to propose *waiving* the visa requirement altogether for citizens who come from countries that did not require visas of American visitors and were considered good risks to return home. But then, as the consul general in one of the largest U.S. embassies frankly pointed out, "Part of our job is to promote tourism."

By the time the Simpson-Mazzoli bill was laid to rest, I had been reporting and writing about immigration in America for nearly three years. I had watched the Cubans land at Key West and visited Miami's Haitians in their decrepit houses. I had traversed the border from San Ysidro to Brownsville and back, spent days and nights with the Border Patrol, drunk tequila with alien smugglers, walked through the desert with illegal aliens and visited the villages in Mexico they had left behind, sat through interminable congressional hearings, and pored over thousands of pages of government documents, court records, and official reports. I still had questions for which there were no answers, but some things were becoming clear.

Given the determination of those from the south to find their way across the rugged Mexican border, any attempt to seal it off physically seemed bound to fail. Hiring more border guards, for example, was likely to mean only that the same border crossers would be arrested more often before finally making a successful entry. With each passing day it is less and less clear how the influx of aliens can be halted or even slowed without posting Border Patrol agents shoulder to shoulder from the Pacific Ocean to the Gulf of Mexico, and according to my calculations, that would require about 2.5 million of them for every eight-hour shift.

Such an effort also seemed to me supremely misguided. Nothing I had seen had convinced me that Bernabe Garay and the millions like him who walk or swim across that border to pick lemons, wash dishes, or something of the sort were harming America. To the contrary, many of the immigrants were doing work that Americans will not do, were making jobs as well as taking them, and were paying more than their share of taxes in return for less than their share of public benefits. The visa abusers presented more of a problem, and they would continue to do so until Washington became more concerned about them than about the balance of payments.

It also became clear that the new immigrants were changing America. Miami and New York scarcely resembled those cities as I first knew them a decade ago, and Los Angeles was not at all like the place I remembered from my California boyhood. Even Houston had been changed in the six years since I had lived there, not least by the substantial Vietnamese community it had acquired. Whether such changes are ultimately good or bad is open to question, but I thought that in many cases the new immigrants were making our cities livelier, more diverse, more complex, and more interesting; they were rejuvenating decaying downtown areas and adding bright cosmopolitan touches to suburbs that had assumed a depressing fast-food and shopping-mall homogeneity. But many Americans clearly did not share my view, and the potential for new antagonisms along racial and ethnic lines was a very real one.

There were some things I found deeply distressing: the abuse of aliens by the INS, and the discovery that a form of slavery still existed in America. But neither of those was beyond remedying. The INS could be taken apart and put back together again—it would not be the first federal agency to undergo a wholesale housecleaning—and some of the Border Patrol agents who were not having much effect along the Mexican border could be detailed to enforce the peonage laws instead. All that was necessary was the determination to do something.

Most distressing of all, however, were the efforts of Congress and the Reagan administration to take back control of the borders with more laws, more money, and the other traditional tools of government. In addition to missing the point that the border crossers are, by and large, not the problem, such efforts seemed to ignore entirely a reality of the late twentieth century: Whether or not it relishes such a role, the United States, with its strong democratic traditions and unrivaled affluence, is destined to become an increasingly attractive sanctuary for those fleeing political or economic oppression.

That idea is profoundly disturbing to many since it is another way of saying that unless it turns itself into a Bulgarian-style police state, the United States must surrender the most elemental component of its sovereignty: the ability to decide who can cross its borders and who cannot. Yet no practical alternative presents itself. Nothing in the Simpson-Mazzoli bill or in any of the immigration reform bills that might follow its tortuous path through future Congresses can possibly address the root causes of immigration: the press of poverty and population around the world or the stark inevitability of famine, political oppression, and civil war. Handing over the entire federal budget to poorer countries in the form of foreign aid would scarcely raise the world's standard of living. Nor would withdrawing this country's support for repressive governments like those in Haiti and El Salvador diminish by much the flow of political refugees, for there are refugees from leftist governments like Nicaragua as well as from those of the right.

Even a more expansive economic policy toward Mexico, from which we can expect ever more uninvited visitors in the years ahead, is not likely to make much difference. Mexico refuses out of nationalism to accept development assistance from the United States, and while the United States might agree to buy more Mexican oil or lower the protectionist trade barriers that separate the two countries, such measures would be far too little and too late. With the value of its peso having plummeted in less than a year from 4 cents to 1 cent and its income from petroleum exports having been sliced in half by the world oil glut, Mexico is experiencing its worst economic crisis in modern memory, head over heels in debt to the world's banks and facing several bleak years of economic austerity.

So severe is the crisis, in fact, that the already staggering number of unemployed Mexicans is on the increase. In the first eight months of 1982 more than half a million Mexican workers lost their jobs, and many of them are now joining their country-men heading north in search of work. Within days after the peso had been devalued in August 1982, Border Patrol stations from San Ysidro to Brownsville were reporting record apprehensions of illegal border crossers—El Paso alone chalked up nearly 1,500 arrests in a single day, an all-time record. "You're going to have more people out of work here, and you're going to have all sorts of other pressures," a worried John Gavin, the American ambassador in Mexico City, told me a month later. "That means we're going to have an increased flow of people across the border into the U.S."

Gavin was sounding an alarm. But there have been altogether too many alarms sounded in recent years whenever the subject of immigration has been raised and far too little attention paid to the fact that America has not only survived but has been strengthened by the great waves of immigrants that have come before, that many of the same concerns and fears now being raised were first heard upon the arrival of the Irish 100 years ago. Looking through the prism of history, one might as well conclude that just as the late nineteenth century belonged to the Germans and the early twentieth century to the Eastern Europeans and the Italians, the late twentieth century is the era of the Hispanic immigrant.

It is also useful to remember that the three principal kinds of resources—natural, human, and industrial—have always been unevenly distributed among the nations of the world, that no country has ever had each of them in the precise proportions necessary for maximum development and growth. But just as the inequities of natural and capital resources have historically been rectified by trade and foreign investment, the imbalance in human resources has traditionally been adjusted by migration. During the last century millions of transatlantic immigrants gave the United States the human capital that, in the decades that followed, enabled it to become the richest nation on earth. Now that the United States has established a society in which, unlike Mexico, it is no longer necessary either to work or to starve, the country is faced with an increasing shortage of unskilled workers willing to perform the millions of menial and low-paying jobs that are still necessary for the continued expansion of our advanced postindustrial economy.

The American work force is not only getting older but getting smaller—so much smaller that economists are now suggesting that because of the slowdown in U.S. population growth, the United States is no longer able to produce enough workers to fill the available jobs. Some researchers predict a net shortage of as many as 27 million workers by the year 2000. This being the case, is it not fortunate that the United States is so near a country like Mexico, which for the foreseeable future will have many more human resources than its struggling economy can absorb? And is it not equally fortunate for Mexico and its impoverished millions that they are so near the United States? Poverty, after all, is a waster of human resources. The Mexican farmer struggling to grow enough food on arid and depleted soil to feed his family is not working to anyone's best advantage. With a job in an American restaurant or factory, he can earn far more money with the same amount of work. In doing so, he helps himself, his family, and because he is more productive, the economies of both countries.

There is yet another dimension to the alien perplex, one not to be found in any federal statute or econometric equation but which is well understood by thirteen-year-old Fidel Orozco, the Los Angeles sixth grader who submitted a classroom essay on the subject.

> People from Mexico come to the United States to make some money because there is no opportunity to work in Mexico and people are very poor there. It is hard for them to be in and work in the United States, because they never know if the immigration would get them or not.
>
> If they do catch the illegals the law sends them right back to Mexico. I and my family are not afraid of the immigration because we have our papers. I feel very sorry for those people that always have to watch out for who is coming. But why can't all people enjoy this earth and work where they want as long as they earn it all in an honest way?

INDEX

Index

Index

Index

Index